ORACLE® *Oracle Press™*

# Oracle Troubleshooting

Rama Velpuri &
Anand Adkoli

Osborne **McGraw-Hill**

Berkeley  New York  St. Louis
San Francisco  Auckland  Bogotá  Hamburg  London  Madrid
Mexico City  Milan  Montreal  New Delhy  Panama City
Paris  São Paulo  Singapore  Sydney  Tokyo  Toronto

Osborne **McGraw-Hill**
2600 Tenth Street
Berkeley, California 94710
U.S.A.

For information on translations or book distributors outside the U.S.A., or to arrange bulk purchase discounts for sales promotions, premiums, or fundraisers, please contact Osborne/**McGraw-Hill** at the above address.

**Oracle Troubleshooting**

234567890 DOC 998

ISBN 0-07-882388-9

**Publisher**
Brandon A. Nordin

**Editor In-Chief**
Scott Rogers

**Project Editor**
Mark Karmendy

**Indexer**
Rebecca Plunkett

**Computer Designer**
Peter Hancik

**Illustrator**
Peter Hancik

**Series Design**
Jani Beckwith

For our parents

## About the Authors

Rama Velpuri and Anand Adkoli are respected names in the Oracle community and have over 12 years of Oracle tech support experience between them. Velpuri is the Director of the Oracle India Product Engineering Center. He has previously been a Senior Manager of the Mission Critical Support Center and has worked with Oracle Worldwide Customer Support for over seven years. He has presented more than 15 technical papers at various IOUW and other Oracle user conferences on disaster recovery, and has trained Oracle support personnel in 15 countries in problem-solving techniques. Velpuri is the author of *Oracle Backup & Recovery Handbook* and *Oracle Backup & Recovery Handbook Edition 7.3*.

Adkoli is the manager of the Electronic Services Group at Oracle India Product Engineering Center. Prior to this position, Anand was the Technical Lead for the Desktop group in Oracle Worldwide Customer Support. He trained the support personnel during the setup of the Global Support Center in Melbourne, Australia. Adkoli has published over 40 technical bulletins for Oracle Worldwide Customer Support and has presented seminars on Performance Tuning at various IOUW and Oracle User Conferences.

# Contents At A Glance

# Contents

# Foreword

n today's ever-changing technological world, due to globalization, competitive pressure, and cost of downtime, businesses are demanding more from their information systems, expecting higher availability, while at the same time pushing the outer limits of technology. This poses a great challenge on the service delivery organizations. A reactive service paradigm alone no longer provides adequate solutions. A proactive approach, on the other hand, is required to meet the demands of running any business operation.

In a survey done by Oracle Worldwide Customer Support, we realized that operations-related outages are caused mainly by improper setup of networks and systems, as well as by a lack of DBA skills required to install and manage databases. Most of the problems encountered by DBAs occur when they least expect them. Given the time constraints under which a DBA has to resolve problems and the nature of the problems themselves, problem solving can become a challenging, arduous, and frustrating task. Although the problems themselves are of various kinds, the causes can be easily tracked by adopting a scientific approach.

Almost every DBA would like to have easy access to a solution to the problem at hand, especially a solution that would need the least amount time to implement. With a combined experience of twelve years in Oracle Worldwide Support, Rama Velpuri and Anand Adkoli have embarked on sharing with users their extensive knowledge of troubleshooting and problem solving. *Oracle Troubleshooting* provides installation tips and proper setup of various Oracle products on enterprise and desktop platforms to avoid problems proactively. In addition, if you do run into a problem, this guide tells you the best and fastest way to diagnose and resolve it, thereby reducing the Mean Time To Recover (MTTR).

*Oracle Troubleshooting*, therefore, is an indispensable companion to application developers, database administrators, system administrators, network administrators, Oracle Worldwide Customer Support analysts, or any Oracle user who has a need to solve problems.

Randy Baker
Senior Vice President
Oracle Worldwide Customer Support

# Introduction

oday, Oracle customers are pushing the outer limits of technology while trying to strive for higher availability. This is further complicated by the diversity in heterogeneous networks and the increasing trend towards client/server architecture. To meet the customer's demands, Oracle Corporation is expanding its product range in markets around the world. This puts pressure on service delivery organizations, such as Oracle Worldwide Customer Support, to provide quality support for its customer base around the world. Oracle Worldwide Customer Support receives thousands of inquiries from customers every week. Our experience tells us that 80 percent of the technical issues being reported to Oracle Worldwide Customer Support (WWCS) can be resolved with 20 percent knowledge of Oracle products. This book is an attempt to bring that 20 percent knowledge to Oracle users around the world. We decided to organize this book in a manner that would benefit a large number of customers by providing information that will aid them in solving their problems in a methodical way. This saves you time—whether you are installing Oracle products for the first time or you are encountering a failure. We also emphasize the proactive measures that you need to take to avoid problems. This book will also help Oracle WWCS analysts in providing quality support, consistently, around the world.

# Audience and Scope

This book focuses on practical information that will aid application developers, database administrators, network administrators, system administrators, and any individuals working with Oracle software in resolving problems at their site. It is a one-stop source for useful information spanning many Oracle manuals, technical bulletins, and many years of experience. The book is targeted for all Oracle Worldwide Customer Support analysts (within Oracle) and individuals or companies that are using any product of Oracle or are gearing up to use Oracle software (outside of Oracle). It assumes that you possess basic concepts of networking and are sufficiently proficient in the use of your operating system. Since basic installation problems are discussed in this book, it is useful for all Oracle users regardless of the level of proficiency.

# How to Use this Book

The information in this book is organized in three parts. In the first part (Chapters 1-6), we provide installation tips and troubleshooting techniques on operating systems ranging from the desktop to large systems. Some good proactive tips, while you set up the Oracle system, are discussed in this part. In the second part (Chapters 7-10), we deal with popular Oracle products such as Precompilers, Developer/2000, SQL*Net, and of course the RDBMS. In this section, we give practical information on diagnosing and/or solving Oracle problems. The third part of the book (Chapter 11) provides information about the internal processes and various offerings provided by Oracle Worldwide Customer Support. Reading this section should help you utilize the services of WWCS optimally, to get better support.

We have included references to many sources of information, available in print and in electronic form, that should help you shorten your development cycles and also maintain high availability of production applications. After reviewing hundreds of TARs (Technical Assistance Requests made by customers to WWCS) in the customer support database, we present a section on *Frequently Asked Questions (FAQ)* at the end of each chapter. You can access most of this information in the CD-ROM that is included with this book. In addition, all of the information on the CD-ROM is available on the Worldwide Web.

While reading this book, you need not necessarily follow the order of the chapters. You can move directly to a chapter that refers to the platform on which you have installed Oracle products, or the chapter concerning the product you are using. One exception, however, is if you are using Oracle products on Windows NT; you need to read Chapter 2 on Windows 95 before reading Chapter 3 on Windows NT.

When you have a problem, you can refer directly to the chapter concerning your platform or product. You might want to check the Frequently Asked Questions section of the chapter first before reading the chapter itself. The recommended method is to first read through the chapters specific to your platform and product, and later use them as references to solve problems. There are a total of 11 chapters in this book.

Chapter 1, *Preventive Maintenance on MS-Windows 3.1*, delineates the important installation files, the environment variables to be set, and the types of installation. This chapter also provides proactive tips to prevent problems while installing Oracle products on MS-Windows 3.1 platform. Some pre-installation and post-installation checks are given along with information on tuning MS-Windows 3.1 to run Oracle products.

Chapter 2, *Preventive Maintenance on MS-Windows 95*, describes the important installation files, the environment variables to be set, and installation techniques. This chapter also provides proactive tips to prevent problems while installing Oracle products on MS-Windows 95 platform. Pre-installation and post-installation checks are given.

Chapter 3, *Preventive Maintenance on MS-Windows NT*, is an extension of Chapter 2. It shows how to avoid problems usually faced by users while installing Oracle products on MS-Windows NT platform. You need to refer to Chapter 2 before you proceed with this chapter, as information provided there is a prerequisite to information found in Chapter 3. We also present a section on tuning Windows NT to run Oracle.

Chapter 4, *Preventive Maintenance on Solaris*, explains the important installation files, configuring the Sun SPARC Solaris 2.x server, the environment variables to be set, the types of installation (stand-alone as well as client/server), and the various problems usually faced by users while installing Oracle products on Solaris.

Chapter 5, *Preventive Maintenance on UNIX*, provides information to configure your UNIX system. Some of the generic UNIX issues such as semaphores, shared memory, and core dumps are discussed. If you have installed Oracle Products on a UNIX platform other than Solaris, you need to refer to this chapter. We suggest that you browse Chapter 4 even if you have a UNIX server not running Sun Solaris 2.5.

Chapter 6, *Preventive Maintenance on OpenVMS*, deals with the installation of Oracle7 Server on OpenVMS and the various problems usually faced by users while installing Oracle products on OpenVMS. Pre-installation checks and post-installation tests have been provided.

Chapter 7, *Problem Solving RDBMS*, provides information on creating and maintaining an Oracle database. Issues related to user management, space management,   and performance tuning, as well as backup and recovery are covered. Separate sections on common Oracle errors and diagnostic features of Oracle are designed to aid any Oracle DBA resolve issues safely and quickly.

Chapter 8, *Problem Solving Connectivity Issues*, explains the major components of SQL*Net and installation and configuration of SQL*Net on Server and Client ends. We also explain the SQL*Net architecture, Multi-Threaded Server, and Oracle Names. Techniques to create SQL*Net trace files and interpret their content is provided. We have also included connectivity issues related to ODBC in this chapter. Common errors and fixes for these errors are provided for your reference.

Chapter 9, *Problem Solving Developer/2000*, presents tips on installation and porting issues. Also discussed here are common issues such as printing- and font-related problems that are specific to Developer/2000. We have also included a comprehensive discussion on upgrade techniques.

Chapter 10, *Problem Solving Oracle Precompilers*, discusses developing programs with Precompilers and supported compilers. Common "gotchas" with CHAR and VARCHAR datatypes, along with treatment of floating-point numbers, are discussed. We have also presented information on the handling of large amounts (greater than 64KB) of data.

Chapter 11, *Interacting with Oracle Worldwide Customer Support*, provides excellent information on optimizing your interaction with WWCS. We provide information on recording configuration information relevant to your installation and also an insight into the nature of information you must have ready with you, before contacting Oracle WWCS.

# Acknowledgements

hen we first presented the idea of writing a book on troubleshooting, Carolyn Gannon, Vice President of Product Division Operations, strongly encouraged us. Randy Baker, Senior Vice President of Oracle Worldwide Support, immediately acknowledged that this book would be very useful not only to the customer base but also to WWCS analysts. Without Carolyn Gannon's and Randy Baker's help, support, and encourgement, we couldn't have done this book.

While writing the book, we relied on the help of a lot of WWCS analysts and developers at Oracle Corporation. We specifically would like to thank the developers of product division, Norman Woo, Scott McKinley, Steven Breyer, Rita Morin, Steve Bower, David Wong, Daniel Ryan, Marcus MacNeill, Paul Turner, Darek Kozlowski, Gael Turk, Amrish Srivastava, Dattatri Ramanna, and Shivkumar Narasaih for reviewing various chapters of the book and giving us their valuable input.

Thanks to Zeke Duge, Ming-Bong Lee, Christian Shay, Preeti Somal, Lisa Giambruno, Bimal Patel, Poonam Gupta, Lawrence To, Roderick Manalac, and Ranu Sharma of WWCS for their input and direction.

Several other people have directly or indirectly contributed to this book. We would like to acknowledge Sharon Castledine, Simon Slack, Per Brondum, Greg Lawson, Steve Essery, Richard Powell, Andrew Beecroft, Lalji Varsani, Adam Fleet, Philip Heagney, Russell Hodgson, Martin Hall, Jose Aphang-Lam, Probal Shome, Raghu Viswanathan, Robert Pearson, and Michael Hussey.

Thanks to the crew at Osborne/McGraw-Hill—Scott Rogers, Ann Sellers, Mark Karmendy, Erik Van Eaton, Peter Hancik, and their entire production staff.

Thanks to Anu Velpuri and Deepak Aatresh for their input and support. Last but not least, we would like to thank Jayashree Rangaswamy for helping us with the technical review.

# CHAPTER 1

## Preventive Maintenance on MS-Windows 3.1

racle Worldwide Customer Support (WWCS) finds that most problems users have can be attributed to the installation process—either their systems weren't properly set up or an important step was missed. In this chapter, we will first provide pre- and post-installation tips, as well as installation routines for the server and top products. Then we will cover important tuning tips. Finally, we close the chapter with a series of tips and tricks that will help you avoid many of the most common troubles that users experience when running Oracle on Windows 3.1.

Oracle Corporation makes several products for Windows 3.1. These products generally fit into two categories: Oracle7 RDBMS and Tools. The Oracle7 RDBMS for Windows 3.1 is distributed with the product set *Personal Oracle7 for Windows* along with a few utilities to manage your database. *Developer/2000 for Windows, Designer/2000 for Windows,* and *Oracle Power Objects for Windows* are examples of application development tools made by Oracle. Other products, such as *SQL\*Net for Windows* and the *Oracle ODBC Driver,* might be required for purposes of connectivity between the application and the Oracle7 RDBMS. Many combinations for the use of this range of products exist. Some of the common combinations are dealt with later in this chapter. General tasks and tips for a successful installation are provided below.

# Pre-Installation Tasks

A few simple tasks will ease the installation process considerably. We recommend that you take a few moments to complete these tasks.

## 1. Verify Availability of Resources

Determine the hardware and software requirements of the products you wish to install. Every Oracle product set is distributed with an installation guide. Most of the product CDs also have installation instructions in the CD-ROM insert. In the first few pages of the installation guide, you should find a table that lists the hardware and software requirements of that product. We have some general recommendations that are listed here for your reference:

- Use an IBM, Compaq, or 100 percent compatible PC with an 80486 66 MHz or better CPU. We suggest a Pentium-based 90 MHz or better PC.

- We suggest 32MB RAM if you are using Personal Oracle7 and any of the smaller Oracle tools such as Oracle Power Objects. We suggest 32MB RAM if you are using Developer/2000 Designer tools against a remote database, and 64MB for optimal performance if you are using Developer/2000 with Personal Oracle7.

- Access to a CD-ROM drive, local or on the network, to perform the installation as Oracle software is not distributed on floppy disk media.

- MS-DOS 5.0 or 6.x, PC-DOS 6.0, or Dr. DOS 6.0

- Windows 3.1 or Windows for Workgroups 3.11

- Appropriate networking software, such as TCP/IP, SPX, or Microsoft. We recommend Winsock-compliant TCP/IP software.

**NOTE**

*Oracle Developer/2000 and Personal Oracle7 represent high-end products on Windows 3.1. Less complex products like Oracle Power Objects will function optimally with lesser hardware resources. Consult the installation guide included with your product for requirements suggested by Oracle Corporation.*

# 2. Backup Configuration Files

The installation process of Oracle products on Windows 3.1 modifies a few configuration files on your PC. While the changes should have no impact on your existing applications under normal circumstances, it is best that you have a backup copy of these files for future reference. You can use the standard COPY command provided by DOS or use the File Manager to create copies of the files listed below. We recommend that you create a directory such as C:\ORAWIN\BACKUP, and copy the appropriate files, shown below, into this directory. Information obtained from these files can be very useful to Oracle Worldwide Customer Support in resolving future issues.

Throughout this chapter we will assume that C:\ is your boot drive, Windows is installed in C:\WINDOWS and other Oracle products are installed in C:\ORAWIN.

| | |
|---|---|
| **CONFIG.SYS** | Resides in the boot drive of your PC, C:\. |
| **AUTOEXEC.BAT** | Resides in the boot drive of your PC, C:\. |
| **WIN.INI** | Resides in the Windows 3.1 home, C:\WINDOWS. |
| **SYSTEM.INI** | Resides in the Windows 3.1 home, C:\WINDOWS. |
| **ORACLE.INI** | If you already have other Windows 3.1 products from Oracle installed, you will have this file in C:\WINDOWS. This file contains a variety of parameter settings that are used by Oracle products on Windows 3.1. |
| **ODBC.INI** | Only for ODBC installations; located in C:\WINDOWS. All ODBC database definitions are stored in this file. |
| **WINDOWS.RGS** | If you already have other Windows 3.1 products from Oracle installed, you will have this file in C:\ORAWIN\ORAINST. This file contains a listing of all products installed on your PC and is used by the Oracle Installer to determine installed components at any time. |
| **TNSNAMES.ORA** | If you have Oracle SQL*Net Version 2 installed, you will have this file in C:\ORAWIN\NETWORK\ADMIN. |
| **SQLNET.ORA** | If you have Oracle SQL*Net Version 2 installed, you will have this file in C:\ORAWIN\NETWORK\ADMIN. |

# 3. Other Tasks

As part of the pre-installation process, there are some miscellaneous tasks that you need to do, such as verifying your file system and environment variables. These important tasks are described below.

## Verify the Integrity of Your File System

PCs frequently have minor problems with the File Allocation Table (FAT). We recommend that you run Microsoft ScanDisk, or use a utility such as Norton Disk Doctor to verify the integrity of your file system before you begin the installation.

## Check Your Disk Compression Utility

If you are planning to install Personal Oracle7 for Windows, you must install it on a partition that is not being compressed. Ensure that disk compression utilities are not in use on the partition where Oracle7 RDBMS is being installed.

## Check DOS Environment Variables

Ensure that the following variables are set in DOS:

- ■ TEMP   must be pointing to a valid directory.

- ■ TMP    must be pointing to a valid directory.

We suggest that you add something similar to the lines shown below to your **AUTOEXEC.BAT**. Do ensure that the directory C:\TEMP exists.

```
SET TEMP=C:\TEMP
SET TMP=C:\TEMP
```

Ensure that the following variables are not set in DOS:

- ■ CONFIG         is an obsolete variable for DOS products.

- ■ ORA_CONFIG   is an obsolete variable for DOS products.

To verify this, type **SET** and press ENTER at the DOS prompt. If you see the CONFIG or the ORA_CONFIG parameter set, then you must unset it as follows:

**SET CONFIG=**(press ENTER)
**SET ORA_CONFIG=**(press ENTER)

# 4. Special Tasks for File Server Installations

If you are installing Oracle products on a file server (i.e. the ORAWIN directory is on a network drive), then the following additional information is useful.

### Assign a Permanent Drive Letter for Your Network Drive

Oracle products on Windows 3.1 read settings from a configuration file called **ORACLE.INI**. Most of the parameters in this file will use a DOS path with a DOS drive letter. It is therefore necessary that you assign a permanent drive letter for the network directory where Oracle products are to be installed.

On Novell Netware, you can use the **MAP ROOT** command to accomplish this as shown below:

```
MAP ROOT G:= ORACLE:TOOLS\
```

In this example, ORACLE: is the volume name and Oracle products would be installed in ORACLE:TOOLS\ORAWIN. Please look at the Novell Netware documentation for further information on mapping drives.

On Windows NT and Windows 95 you can use Map Network Drive in the Explorer to accomplish this. You must ensure that the mapped drive letter is not changed. You must provide appropriate sharing rights to this location. Oracle products will not function if you change the mapping.

More details on file server installations are usually provided in an appendix in the installation guide for your product.

# Understanding the Oracle Installation Process on Windows 3.1

We will now take a look at the Oracle Installer and the installation process on Windows 3.1. Some minor errors during installation can be resolved with a better understanding of the files used by the installer during the installation process.

## I. Preview

The Oracle Installer on Windows 3.1 performs three primary tasks:

- ■ It checks dependencies.
- ■ It copies necessary product files.
- ■ It configures the system environment.

First, the Oracle Installer verifies that sufficient disk space is available to install the desired products. It then verifies that other Oracle dependencies are satisfied. Oracle products on Windows 3.1 share a substantial portion of code that is made available under components like Required Support Files and GUI Common Files. If you already have an Oracle product installed, the installer will verify that dependencies related to this shared code are satisfied for the new product. The installer will upgrade the common software components only if required. Since most of these components are implemented as *Dynamic Link Libraries* (DLLs) on Windows 3.1, the Oracle Installer ensures that multiple copies of the same DLL are not available to a product at run time. You will see warnings during installation if there are multiple copies of a DLL, and corrective action will be suggested automatically.

Next, the Oracle Installer copies the required files for every product. The files are placed in appropriate directories automatically. The Oracle Installer will allow the user to choose the directory in which a product is installed. However, all the executables and DLLs are usually placed in a directory labeled C:\ORAWIN\BIN.

Finally, the Oracle Installer creates the program groups and icons required for the products installed. The installer adds a record of the product versions installed to a registration file, the **WINDOWS.RGS**, for future reference. The configuration file **ORACLE.INI** is also completed at this time.

# 2. Important Installation Files

The Oracle Installer for Windows 3.1 uses some key files. A brief description of these files is provided for your reference and understanding of the installation process. Even though all the files below are plain text files, *do not manually modify or delete these files at any time.* You are free to view them at any time to understand the installation process used by Oracle. If you are unable to find any of these files, try searching the contents of your install media using the File Manager's search function.

## WINDOWS.PRD

This file contains a listing of all products and their components available on the install media. The installer reads this file to get a listing of available products on the media. This file typically resides in a directory called

INSTALL on the install media. If you want to quickly determine the products available on any Oracle media for Windows 3.1 without invoking the installer, you can look at this file in any text editor.

## WINDOWS.INS

This file contains the Oracle installation script used by the installer. It is typically located in the INSTALL directory on the install media. In addition to this file, every product typically has an installation script in its product directory on the media.

## WINDOWS.DEI

This file contains the Oracle de-install script used by the installer. It is also located in the INSTALL directory on the media. It gets copied to C:\ORAWIN\ORAINST during installation. In addition to this file, every product typically has a de-install script in its product directory on the media.

## WINDOWS.STP

This file contains the script that initializes the environment variables for Oracle products on Windows 3.1. It is read by the Oracle Installer at start up.

## PRODINFO.ORA

This file contains complete information on the product, such as the part number, version, and operating system requirement. It is usually located in the root directory on the product media. Some older Oracle products might not have this file on the install media.

### Files with an Extension .VRF

These files contain scripts that the installer uses for verification of some settings and dependencies. For example, the file **PATH.VRF** is used to verify that the path being added to the **AUTOEXEC.BAT** file does not exceed DOS limitations.

### Files with an Extension .MAP

These files contain a listing of all the physical files for each product component, their source directories on the install media, and their target directories. The size of the individual files are also documented here. The installer uses **.MAP** files to determine whether the available disk space is sufficient.

### RELNOTES.WRI and README.TXT

These files will contain any last minute changes and alerts for the user. It is recommended that you view these files before beginning any installation. These files are typically located in the root directory of the install media.

# 3. Products/Components Available for Installation

When you start the Oracle Installer, you get a complete listing of Oracle products available on the product media. It is best that you select the high-level product (such as Developer/2000 Forms and SQL*Net) from the list of products to install. The installer will ensure that all dependent files such as Required Support Files are copied over to your installation. While Oracle provides many different products on Windows 3.1, some of the common components that you will see during an installation are described in Table 1-1.

### NOTE
*The components described in Table 1-1 are used by most Oracle products. As a rule of thumb, it is sufficient to install the latest version of any of these components. Generally speaking, they are all backward compatible. An exception to this rule is the Required Support Files (RSF) component. The version of the RSF usually corresponds with the version of the database. For example, Oracle7 Version 7.2 will use RSF 7.2 (only the first two digits are significant) and not RSF 7.3. Similarly SQL*Net Version 2.3 will use RSF 7.3 and not RSF 7.2. If you have both Oracle7 Version 7.2 and SQL*Net 2.3 installed, you should see both RSF 7.2 and 7.3 installed. This is perfectly normal.*

| Product to Be Installed | Description |
| --- | --- |
| Developer/2000 Forms | Complete Developer/2000 Forms Designer and run-time installation |
| Developer/2000 Reports | Complete Developer/2000 Reports Designer and run-time installation |
| Developer/2000 Graphics | Complete Oracle*Graphics Designer and run-time installation |
| Forms Runtime | Run-time files required to run Developer/2000 Forms applications |
| Reports Runtime | Run-time files required to run Developer/2000 Reports applications |
| Graphics Runtime | Run-time files required to run Oracle*Graphics applications |
| Developer/2000 Procedure Builder | Oracle Procedure Builder |
| Oracle Translation Manager | Tool to translate Developer/2000 applications into other languages |
| Developer/2000 Open Interfaces | PVCS Interface, Tuxedo and Clearcase Interfaces for Developer/2000 |
| Oracle Open Client Adapter | Adapter that allows Oracle tools to talk to other non-Oracle ODBC compliant databases |
| SQL*Net V2 | Oracle's network interface software |
| Oracle Protocol Adapters | Provide communication protocol for the network such as TCP/IP, SPX and Named Pipes |
| Intersolv Datadirect Drivers | Drivers that allow Developer/2000 applications to connect to non-Oracle databases such as SQL Server, Informix (4 & 5), and Sybase System10 |
| GUI Common Files | Common files that provide user interface to run Oracle products under Windows 3.1 |
| Required Support Files | Shared libraries needed for all Oracle applications |
| Tools Utilities | Libraries and tool kit for Oracle products |
| System Support Files | Files that provide OLE2 and VBX support |
| Oracle Installer | The Oracle Installer Executable |
| Oracle7 RDBMS | The Oracle7 Database |

**TABLE 1-1.** *Common Oracle Product Components on Windows 3.1*

## 4. The Installation Process

Precise instructions to perform the installation are always listed in the installation guide that is provided with the product. This section provides some additional information that should be useful.

- Install all Oracle products for Windows 3.1 in one directory path such as C:\ORAWIN. It is necessary for all 16-bit products from Oracle to be in one directory structure. However, *do not* install Oracle 32-bit products (Windows 95 or Windows NT) to C:\ORAWIN. It is best to install these to their own directory structures such as C:\ORAWIN95 or C:\ORANT. The best approach is to accept the default target directories suggested by the Oracle Installer. Feel free to change the drive letter to ensure that the product is installed on the intended target drive.

- Shut down all Oracle applications before starting any installation. The exception to this is a component called *database tables*. This component requires access to the database to create system tables for some products. More details on this are available in later sections of this chapter and also in the installation guide of the product.

- Remember to back up your configuration files, especially **ORACLE.INI**, if one is available from a previous installation.

- Select only the high-level products that you are interested in installing. Do not concern yourself with sub-components such as Required Support Files or GUI Common Files. For example, if you are interested in Developer/2000 Forms, choose Developer/2000 Forms from the list of products available for installation. The Oracle Installer is intelligent enough to ensure that all dependencies are satisfied.

# Post-Installation Tasks

When your installation is complete, you should take a few moments to complete a few more tasks that will ensure that you can start your application design with no worries.

## 1. Backup Configuration Files

Make a copy of **ORACLE.INI**, **ODBC.INI** (for ODBC installations only), and C:\ORAWIN\NETWORK\ADMIN\**\*.ORA** files (for SQL\*Net installations only). These files can be of tremendous assistance to Oracle Worldwide Customer Support in case any diagnosis or recovery is required in the future.

## 2. Scripts for Tables Required by Tools

Some of the tools from Oracle store information (such as security details) in tables. Oracle provides scripts to create such system tables (also called database tables). Follow the instructions in the installation guide under the section "Creating Database Tables" to create the system tables required by your product. If you are having trouble connecting to the Oracle7 database, refer to the section on SQL\*Net connectivity in this chapter before completing this task.

## 3. Additional Environment Variables

It is convenient to add some environment variables of your own to the **ORACLE.INI** file. Some common variables are provided in Table 1-2 for your reference.

# Four Types of Installation

There are four typical types of installation:

- **A stand-alone installation**  Applications built with Oracle's client tools being used with Personal Oracle7 for Windows.

- **A client-server installation**  Applications built with Oracle's client tools being used with a remote (residing on a separate machine) Oracle7 server.

- **Third-party products**  An application built with a third-party tool such as Microsoft Visual Basic being used with Oracle7.

- **Non-Oracle RDBMS**  An application built with Oracle's client tools being used with a non-Oracle ODBC-compliant database such as Microsoft Access.

| Environment Variable | Description | Example |
|---|---|---|
| FORMS45_PATH | Path information for Developer/2000 Forms application files (**.FMX**, **.MMX**, **.PLL**, etc.) | FORMS45_PATH=C:\MYAPP;C:\ OTHERAPP |
| REPORTS25_PATH | Path information for Developer/2000 Reports application files | REPORTS25_PATH=C:\MYAPP;C:\ OTHERAPP |
| REPORTS25_TMP | Directory for temporary files for Developer/2000 Reports | REPORTS25_TMP=C:\TEMP |
| TK21_ICON | Location of **.ICO** files | TK21_ICON=C:\MYICONS |
| FORMS45_EDITOR | Editor invoked for multi-line items in Developer/2000 Forms | FORMS45_EDITOR=C:\WINDOWS\ **NOTEPAD.EXE** |
| FORMS45_ DEFAULT FONT | Font used for boilerplate text in the Developer/2000 Forms layout editor | FORMS45_DEFAULTFONT="Arial.8" |
| LOCAL | Provides default connect string information for your database location (see Chapter 8 for further information). If you do not specify an explicit connect string when you connect to Oracle, this string will be used as the connect string. | LOCAL=mydb where "mydb" is a SQL*Net V2 alias defined in **TNSNAMES.ORA** |

**TABLE 1-2.** *User-defined Parameters in ORACLE.INI*

We will give an example for each of the installation types to illustrate the installation process. The examples can easily be extended to cover every installation need of Oracle products on Windows 3.1.

# An Oracle Stand-alone Installation

A stand-alone installation is one in which an Oracle tool is used to build an application by connecting to an Oracle7 database that is running on the same machine. We will illustrate a stand-alone installation by using Developer/2000 Forms 4.5 to create an application that will connect to Personal Oracle7 for Windows. Here are the necessary steps:

1. Install Personal Oracle7 for Windows 3.1.

2. Verify installation of Personal Oracle7.

3. Install Developer/2000 Forms Designer 4.5 for Windows 3.1 .

4. Verify connectivity to Personal Oracle7.

5. Install database tables for Developer/2000 Forms.

6. Create a sample application using Developer/2000 Forms.

7. Run sample application.

8. Ensure that database tables are properly installed.

## Step 1: Install Personal Oracle7 for Windows 3.1

Install Personal Oracle7 for Windows 3.1 per instructions in the installation guide and following the guidelines provided earlier in this chapter. Install the seed (also called the *starter database*) by choosing "Typical Install". This should use about 60MB of space on the hard disk. About 40MB of space is used by the software and utilities to maintain the database. The remaining space of about 20MB is used by the database and is distributed approximately as shown in Table 1-3.

| Tablespace Name | Files | Space (Kilobytes) |
|---|---|---|
| SYSTEM | **WDBSYS.ORA** | 10,486 |
| RBS | **WDBRBS.ORA** | 3,146 |
| TEMP | **WDBTEMP.ORA** | 2,097 |
| USER | **WDBUSER.ORA** | 3,146 |

**TABLE 1-3.** *Personal Oracle7 Database Files in a Starter Database*

In addition to the database files described in Table 1-3, Oracle creates a control file that uses about 160KB and two log files that use 512KB each.

## Step 2: Verify Installation of Personal Oracle7

Once Personal Oracle7 for Windows 3.1 is installed, it is best to reboot the PC to ensure that changes made to the **AUTOEXEC.BAT** take effect. After restarting Windows 3.1, you can now ensure that the Oracle7 database was installed properly.

Start the Database Manager (may be called Instance Manager in your installation) and start the database by clicking on the Start button. You should see a green light after the database starts up. At this time, you can run Oracle's SQL*DBA tool. An executable called **SQLDBA71.EXE** (your executable might have a slightly different name depending on your version of Personal Oracle7) should be available in C:\ORAWIN\BIN. You should see a prompt for SQL*DBA. Perform the steps shown in the code below. The user input is given in bold letters.

```
SQL*DBA: Release 7.1.3.2.1 - Production on Thu Jan 23 19:10:11 1997

Copyright (c) Oracle Corporation 1979, 1994.  All rights reserved.
Personal Oracle7 Release 7.1.3.2.1 - Production
With the distributed and replication options
PL/SQL Release 2.2.2.3.1 - Production

SQLDBA> connect internal
Connected.
SQLDBA> show sga
Total System Global Area        4303420 bytes
              Fixed Size          38296 bytes
           Variable Size        3847332 bytes
        Database Buffers         409600 bytes
            Redo Buffers           8192 bytes
SQLDBA> exit
SQL*DBA complete.
```

When you connect to the database you may be asked for a password. Type the password that you selected during the installation. The default password is *oracle*. Be sure to leave the Oracle database running before proceeding to the next step.

## Step 3: Install Developer/2000 Forms Designer 4.5 for Windows 3.1

At this time, you are ready to install an Oracle application development tool of your choice. We will install the Developer/2000 Forms 4.5 (from Developer/2000) product.

Start the Oracle Installer again and select Developer/2000 Forms 4.5. The installer will copy all the files related to Developer/2000 Forms 4.5.

## Step 4: Verify Connectivity to Personal Oracle7

Start Developer/2000 Forms Designer and ensure that you can connect to the database. Choose the File|Connect option to view the login screen. Type a username and password for a valid Oracle user. If you are unsure, you can use an account created by Oracle. You can use the username SCOTT and the password *tiger*. Leave the field for the *connect string* blank.

You should see the status *<Con>* in the status bar at the bottom of the Developer/2000 Forms Designer screen as seen in Figure 1-1. The item Disconnect should also now be available under the File menu.

Exit from the Developer/2000 Forms Designer at this time.

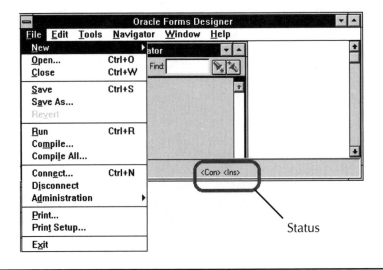

**FIGURE 1-1.** *Developer/2000 Forms Designer screen after connection to Oracle*

## Step 5: Install Database Tables for Developer/2000 Forms

We are now ready to create the database tables required by Developer/2000 Forms. Revert to the Oracle Installer and choose to install the component Developer/2000 Forms Database Tables (you might need to expand the component Developer/2000 Database Tables). You should be prompted for a password for the database user SYSTEM. The default password is *manager*. At this time, you can quit the installer. We are ready to verify that the Developer/2000 Forms product is installed properly by creating a small sample application.

## Step 6: Create a Sample Application Using Developer/2000 Forms

Start the Developer/2000 Forms Designer again and connect to the database as in Step 4. We will create a small sample application to ensure that the product is installed correctly. Double-click Blocks in the Object Navigator of the Forms Designer. You should see a screen similar to the one shown in Figure 1-2. Next, click the Select button next to the Base Table field. You will see a screen similar to the one shown here:

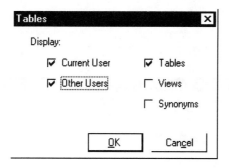

Select the Current User, Other Users, and Tables check boxes, and click the OK button. Now, pick any table from Tables list you see and you will then see a screen similar to the one shown in Figure 1-3. We have selected a table called EMPLOYEE owned by a user called DEMO in our example. You can type any name for the Block Name field or accept the default and click the OK button. Your sample application is ready.

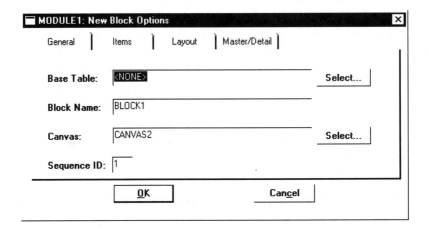

**FIGURE 1-2.** *New Block window in Developer/2000 Forms Designer*

## Step 7: Run Sample Application
Run the sample application by choosing File|Run.

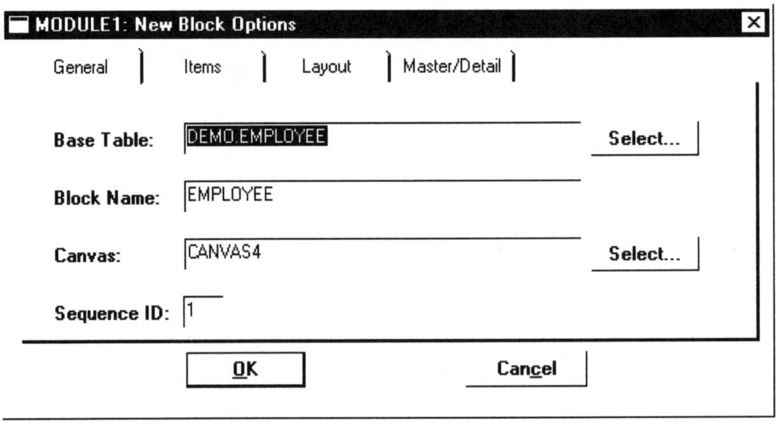

**FIGURE 1-3.** *Base Table and Block Name selection*

## Step 8: Ensure That Database Tables Are Properly Installed

Now that we have managed to run a small application, we can try saving this to the database. First, ensure that you have selected the option to save to the database. Select Options in the Tools menu and choose the Designer options as shown in Figure 1-4. Now select the option File|Save and choose the options shown here:

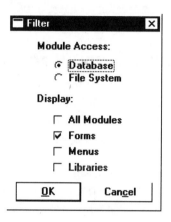

**FIGURE 1-4.**   *Designer options in Developer/2000 Forms*

Click the OK button to save the application to the database. If you do not get any errors, you have confirmed that Developer/2000 Forms and Personal Oracle7 are installed properly. Note that while it is easy to save an application to the file system, in a multi-user environment you typically will have to save applications to the database so that they can be shared by many users. If you are not concerned about saving applications to the database, you can ignore the step to create the database tables (Step 5). However, if you are planning to save applications to the database, this is a useful exercise.

## An Oracle Client-Server Installation

A client-server installation is one in which an Oracle tool is used to build an application by connecting to an Oracle7 database that is running on a separate machine. The connectivity is obtained by using Oracle's SQL*Net software. For more information on SQL*Net, please refer to Chapter 8 in this book.

We will illustrate a client-server installation using Developer/2000 Forms 4.5 connecting to an Oracle7 database running on a Sun Solaris 2.5 machine across TCP/IP. The salient steps are listed below:

1. Verify network connectivity between the PC and the Solaris machine.

2. Verify that SQL*Net is installed correctly on the Solaris machine.

3. Install Developer/2000 Forms 4.5 for Windows 3.1.

4. Install SQL*Net V2 for Windows 3.1.

5. Verify connectivity to the Oracle7 Server on the Solaris from the PC.

6. Install database tables for Developer/2000 Forms.

7. Create a sample application using Developer/2000 Forms.

8. Run the sample application and save it to the database.

## Step 1: Verify Network Connectivity Between the PC and the Solaris Machine

Oracle's SQL*Net relies on the underlying network layer to provide for connectivity between the client and server. The first step in a client-server application must be to verify this network connectivity.

Install TCP/IP on the Sun Solaris Machine and the PC. There are several vendors of TCP/IP for Windows 3.1. In general, it is best to choose a vendor that is Windows Socket Library (Winsock) compliant. A list of vendors is available in the SQL*Net Installation Guide for Windows 3.1. Once TCP/IP software is installed on the PC and the Solaris machine, we can verify connectivity.

From the PC, use a Ping or Telnet utility to ensure that the Solaris machine is visible on the network. Be sure to note the server name and/or IP address of the Solaris machine. Now, from the Solaris machine, Ping the PC. Both of these checks must be successful. As an additional precaution to ensure that there are no duplicate IP addresses in your network, switch off the PC, then Ping the PC from the Solaris machine. This Ping must now fail. If it doesn't, you have a duplicate IP address on the network.

## Step 2: Verify That SQL*Net Is Installed Correctly on the Solaris Machine

Install SQL*Net V2 and the SQL*Net TCP/IP adapter on the Solaris machine per the installation guide. Create the **TNSNAMES.ORA**, **LISTENER.ORA**, and **SQLNET.ORA** files per instructions. In the **TNSNAMES.ORA** file, create a SQL*Net V2 alias definition for Oracle7 on the Solaris machine called "mydb".

**NOTE**
*Sample SQL*Net configuration files are
provided in the media supplied with this book.*

Start the listener and ensure that it is running properly:

```
% lsnrctl start          /* Start the listener */
% lsnrctl stat           /* Status of the listener */
```

Now, attempt a loop-back test, i.e. use a tool such as SQL*DBA on the server and connect back to the same server using SQL*Net:

```
% sqldba
 sqldba> connect scott/tiger
```

If the above command lets you connect successfully, it shows that Oracle7 is running on the Solaris machine.

```
sqldba> connect scott/tiger@mydb
```

If the above command lets you connect successfully, it shows that SQL*Net is installed properly on the Solaris machine.

## Step 3: Install Developer/2000 Forms 4.5 for Windows 3.1

At this time, you are ready to install an Oracle application development tool of your choice on the PC. We will illustrate proper installation technique using Developer/2000 Forms 4.5 (from Developer/2000).

Start the Oracle Installer on the PC, and choose to install Developer/2000 Forms 4.5. The installer will copy all the files related to Developer/2000 Forms 4.5.

## Step 4: Install SQL*Net V2 for Windows 3.1

Since we are using TCP/IP, we now have to install SQL*Net V2 TCP/IP for Windows 3.1 on the PC. In the Oracle Installer, choose to install the components SQL*Net V2 (sometimes called SQL*Net V2 client) and the SQL*Net V2 TCP/IP Protocol Adapter.

Now, we need to create the SQL*Net configuration files **TNSNAMES.ORA** and **SQLNET.ORA** on the PC. If you do not already have these files from a previous installation, it is best to copy these files from the Solaris machine using the FTP utility. The **TNSNAMES.ORA** and **SQLNET.ORA** files on the Solaris machine are usually located in the $ORACLE_HOME/network/admin directory. FTP these files to the C:\ORAWIN\NETWORK\ADMIN directory on the PC. The **TNSNAMES.ORA** file should contain the SQL*Net V2 alias mydb that we created earlier.

## Step 5: Verify Connectivity to the Oracle7 Server on the Solaris from the PC

Start Developer/2000 Forms designer and ensure that you can connect to the database. Choose the Connect option from the File menu, or press CTRL-N for the login screen. Type a user name and password for a valid Oracle user. If you are unsure, you may use an account created by Oracle. The user name is SCOTT and the password is *tiger*. Type **mydb** in the field for the Connect String. You should see the status *<Con>* in the status bar at the bottom of the Developer/2000 Forms Designer screen. The item Disconnect should also now be available in the File menu.

Be sure to exit from the Developer/2000 Forms Designer at this time.

## Step 6: Install Database Tables for Developer/2000 Forms

We are now ready to create the database tables required by Developer/2000 Forms. Revert to the Oracle Installer and choose to install the component Developer/2000 Forms Database Tables (you might need to expand the component Developer/2000 Database Tables). You should be prompted for a password for the database user SYSTEM. The default password is *manager*. Provide the string **mydb** for the connect string.

At this time, you can quit the installer. We are ready to verify that the Developer/2000 Forms product is installed properly by creating a small sample application.

## Step 7: Create a Sample Application Using Developer/2000 Forms

Start the Developer/2000 Forms Designer again and connect to the database as in Step 5.

Create a sample application per instructions given in the previous section "An Oracle Stand-alone Installation."

## Step 8: Run the Sample Application and Save It to the Database

Run the sample application and try saving it to the database per the instructions in the stand-alone installation section earlier in this chapter.

# Third-party Products

Sometimes it is necessary to use an application built with a third-party tool, such as Microsoft Visual Basic, and connect to an Oracle7 database. This can be accomplished rather easily using the ODBC standard. More information on ODBC is available in Chapter 8 on connectivity, later in this book.

We will use a sample Microsoft Visual Basic application and a Personal Oracle7 database. Note that you can just as easily connect to a remote Oracle7 database using a combination of ODBC on Windows 3.1 and SQL*Net. The only piece of information that changes is the SQL*Net connect string. The steps are listed below:

1. Install and verify Personal Oracle7 for Windows 3.1.

2. Install and configure Oracle7 ODBC driver for Windows 3.1.

3. Test ODBC installation using the Oracle ODBC sample program.

4. Install Microsoft Visual Basic.

5. Verify connectivity using the VISDATA application.

## Step 1: Install and Verify Personal Oracle7 for Windows 3.1

Install and verify the installation of Personal Oracle7 for Windows 3.1 per instructions in the installation guide and following the guidelines provided earlier in this chapter.

## Step 2: Install and Configure Oracle7 ODBC Driver for Windows 3.1

Create a backup of C:\WINDOWS\**ODBC.INI** and C:\WINDOWS\**ODBCINST.INI** if they are already present. Now, install the Oracle7 ODBC driver using the Oracle Installer per the installation guide. Create a ODBC database definition per instructions in the installation guide. For the Database name, provide the text string **2:** if you are using Personal Oracle7. If you are connecting to a remote Oracle7 server, provide the SQL*Net V2 alias name here. Ensure that C:\ORAWIN\BIN is in your DOS path.

## Step 3: Test ODBC Installation Using the Oracle ODBC Sample Program

Oracle Corporation provides an ODBC sample program with its installation. Your Oracle ODBC driver documentation should have details on using this. A similar sample application is also provided with this book. Run the ODBC sample application and you should see a screen similar to the one shown in Figure 1-5. Now, connect to the Oracle7 database and execute the sample query as shown in Figure 1-6. If you can successfully retrieve data, the Oracle7 ODBC driver is installed correctly.

## Step 4: Install Microsoft Visual Basic

We will also take a quick look at a sample application using Microsoft Visual Basic. Install Microsoft Visual Basic for Windows including the sample applications. A directory called SAMPLES will contain all the sample applications. In the release of Microsoft Visual Basic we used, a sample application called VISDATA was available. You can use this or other sample applications available to test the connectivity to Oracle7 through ODBC.

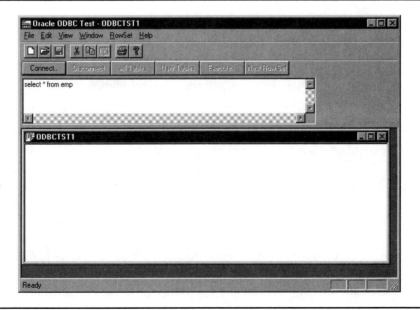

**FIGURE 1-5.**   *Oracle ODBC Test program before connecting to Oracle*

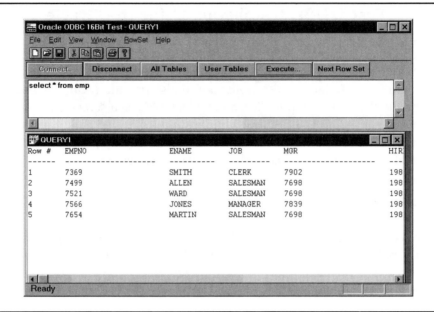

**FIGURE 1-6.** *Query results from Oracle ODBC driver*

### Step 5: Verify Connectivity Using the VISDATA Application

Run the VISDATA application and open the Oracle7 database using File|Open. Run a few queries on any of the available tables.

## Non-Oracle RDBMS

The final combination is one in which you want to use an application built using Oracle's client tools and connect to a non-Oracle ODBC-compliant database. We will create a sample report on a table named "Customer" in a Microsoft Access database using Developer/2000 Reports. The following steps are required:

1. Install Developer/2000 Reports Designer along with Oracle Open Client Adapter and Microsoft Access for Windows. Ensure that you install the ODBC component using the custom installation process.

**2.** Start Microsoft Access and create a table called "Customer" with some definition and save it to a database called "Test".

**3.** Create an ODBC database definition called "acctest" for the database Test. You can use the Oracle ODBC administration utility for this purpose.

**4.** Start Developer/2000 Reports and connect using the definition "acctest" as shown here:

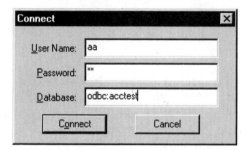

**5.** You need to provide **odbc:<name of ODBC database definition>** for the connect string. You can also bring up a list of all available databases by using the connect string **ODBC:*** as shown here:

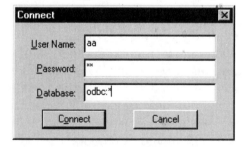

**6.** At this point, once you click the Connect button, you should see a listing similar to the one shown below. Notice the definition called "acctest" in the listing.

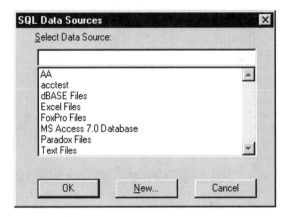

**7.** Create a sample report based on the table Customer in the database defined by the definition "acctest" and run it. One point to note here is that Developer/2000 Reports will not be able to provide a listing of all the tables in the database Test since Microsoft Access does not have the necessary data dictionary tables to provide such functionality. While designing the report, you can enter a SQL string similar to **select * from customer** and this should provide the expected results.

# Tuning

Applications written for the Windows 3.1 Operating System have grown considerably over the last few years. Many applications now have rather large requirements for resources on the PC to perform in a satisfactory manner. All products distributed by Oracle have recommended hardware and software requirements which are documented in the installation guide. We provide a few simple tips which should help you improve the performance of some of the complex products such as Developer/2000. Most of these tips are applicable to all Windows 3.1 applications, but a few of them are specific to Developer/2000. We encourage you to make backup copies of your configuration files before taking any suggestions in this document. Some of these changes might have adverse effects on other Windows 3.1 applications.

The suggestions included here should assist you in maximizing the performance of your Windows 386 Enhanced mode installation (Windows is capable of using virtual memory in 386 Enhanced mode). Many of these suggestions apply to standard and real modes as well. Of course, running Windows 3.1 in Standard mode is much faster than 386 Enhanced mode, but many applications, including Oracle's SQL*Net for Windows require Windows in 386 Enhanced mode.

# SMARTDrive

The Microsoft SMARTDrive disk caching driver can produce the largest single Windows 3.1 performance improvement. Use SMARTDrive whenever possible. You can enable SMARTDrive by loading the **SMARTDRV.SYS** driver in your **CONFIG.SYS** or by loading **SMARTDRV.EXE** in your **AUTOEXEC.BAT**. There are a variety of options available on these drivers. We recommend turning off write caching if you are using Personal Oracle7 on your PC. For basic information on SMARTDrive installation and operation, refer to the *Microsoft Windows Users Guide version 3.1*, or type **SMARTDRV /?** or **HELP SMARTDRV** at the DOS prompt.

# Hard Disk Optimization

A fragmented hard disk greatly impacts Windows performance, especially when a temporary swap file and/or SMARTDrive is installed. Use a hard disk optimizer program on a regular basis to keep your disk contiguous. It is also a good habit to run a utility like Microsoft ScanDisk on a regular basis. One word of caution if you are using Personal Oracle7: always shut down the database and back up all your database files (see Chapter 7 on Oracle7 RDBMS later if you need help with this) before running any such utilities. Such utilities have been known to corrupt database files occasionally.

# Permanent Swap File

Use of a permanent swap file improves performance over using a temporary file. Under Windows 3.1, if supported by your hardware, also choose the Use 32-Bit Disk Access. You can do this by selecting the 386 Enhanced icon in the Control Panel, choosing the Virtual Memory button, then the Change button.

# FILESYSCHANGE

Turn off the FILESYSCHANGE= setting. Windows 3.1 386 Enhanced mode can monitor disk access by DOS applications and send directory update messages to the File Manager. This allows the File Manager to be automatically updated by changes that DOS applications have made to files or directories. To disable this feature, set FILESYSCHANGE=OFF in the [386Enh] section of the **SYSTEM.INI** file.

# Graphics Port

Turn off graphics port trapping. The speed of DOS applications running under 386 Enhanced mode can be noticeably improved by not selecting any of the Monitor Ports options in the Advanced section of the PIF Editor. The High Graphics option provides the widest range of DOS application compatibility but is not required for most Windows applications.

# DOS Buffers

Use the right number of DOS buffers. If you are using SMARTDrive, set the number of DOS disk access buffers in your **CONFIG.SYS** file to 15 (BUFFERS=15). Using a greater number of buffers with SMARTDrive will actually decrease efficiency. If you are not using SMARTDrive, use BUFFERS=30.

# Display Driver

Use the lowest common display driver. Using a display driver with a high resolution or large number of colors results in slower display performance. If you do not require the extra features of the display driver, use a driver with less capability. Usually this suggestion applies to display systems that are VGA compatible but offer an extended mode driver, such as the Video Seven or 8514. Using the standard VGA driver instead offers faster display performance but less resolution and/or color support.

# RESERVEPAGEFRAME

Turn off the RESERVEPAGEFRAME= setting. Turn this setting off if you do not require expanded memory support for DOS applications. Turning this option off ensures that you're getting the most possible memory in virtual

DOS machines. To disable this feature, set RESERVEPAGEFRAME=OFF in the [386Enh] section of the **SYSTEM.INI** file.

# D2KINIT.EXE (Developer/2000 Only)

A large percentage of the code behind Oracle Developer/2000 is implemented in Dynamic Link Libraries (DLLs). You can pre-load this code while Windows 3.1 is starting up, by placing C:\ORAWIN\BIN\**D2KINIT.EXE** in your Windows StartUp group. On the older installations this executable may be called **CDEINIT.EXE.**

# Reports Server (Developer/2000 Reports Only)

Execution of Developer/2000 Reports can be enhanced considerably by adding the Oracle Reports Server executable C:\ORAWIN\BIN\**R25SRV.EXE** to your Windows StartUp group.

# Extended Memory

Windows 3.1 is only capable of using extended memory. If you are using external memory managers, be sure to configure these to provide extended memory. Refer to the documentation provided with your memory manager for additional information. For example, for the Emm386 memory manager, the syntax would be something like:

```
DEVICE=C:\WINDOWS\EMM386.EXE NOEMS
```

# Font Aliasing (Developer/2000 Only)

If you are not using the Font Aliasing features of Developer/2000, rename or delete the file **UIFONT.ALI**.

# Some Miscellaneous Tips

The previous section provided some useful tips that should improve the performance of Oracle applications on Windows 3.1. In this section we provide a few tips that should save the average user some precious time.

# Define a Default Connection

If you are using a client-server configuration and you always connect to the same remote Oracle7 server, i.e. use the same SQL*Net connect string, then it is better to define a default connection in the **ORACLE.INI** file. Edit the **ORACLE.INI** file and add the following parameter:

```
LOCAL=<SQL*Net V2 alias name>
```

(Example: LOCAL=mydb)

Ensure that there are no spaces anywhere in the line. Now, when you want to connect to the database, you can leave the connect string field blank in the login window and the Oracle tool will automatically use the connect string defined by the LOCAL parameter.

# Provide Command Line Arguments for Program Items

It is best to edit the program items for the various Oracle products and provide command line arguments that ensure minimal typing. For example, if you want to start Developer/2000 Forms and connect as the user SCOTT with password *tiger* and use the connect string *mydb*, edit the Program Item for the Forms Designer and change the command line to: **F45DES.EXE USERID=SCOTT/TIGER@MYDB**. Now, when you start the Developer/2000 Forms Designer, you will be connected to the database on start up.

# Provide Login Parameters in the User Name Field

For example, if you want to connect as user SCOTT with password *tiger* to the database using the connect string *mydb*, type **scott/tiger@mydb** in the Username field as shown here:

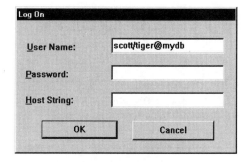

# Override Parameters in the ORACLE.INI in WIN.INI

Sometimes it is required to override some parameter settings in the **ORACLE.INI** file. You can do so, by adding the parameter to the **WIN.INI** file. For example, if you want to override the setting LOCAL=mydb in **ORACLE.INI**, add the following to the **WIN.INI** file under the section labeled [Oracle]:

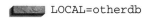 `LOCAL=otherdb`

The setting *otherdb* will override mydb. You can add as many parameters as you wish anywhere in **WIN.INI**. We recommend that you add them to the section labeled [Oracle] so they will be self-documenting.

# Discarding Parameters from the ORACLE.INI

We do not recommend that you edit any parameters in the **ORACLE.INI** file. Occasionally it is necessary to remove some settings or add some comment lines in **ORACLE.INI** file. You can do so by adding the string REM at the beginning of the line as given in the following example:

```
REM The following line defines a default connect string
REM It was added by AA with Shay's permission on 1/23/97
REM LOCAL=mydb
```

# Frequently Asked Questions (FAQ)

We round off this chapter by presenting some frequently asked questions (FAQs) to Oracle Worldwide Customer Support. The FAQ is presented in a question-answer format for easy reading.

**Q.** How much memory and hard disk space do I need to run Personal Oracle7?
**A.** The default installation of Personal Oracle7 uses about 60MB of disk space in total. Of this, the default database files use about 20MB of disk. If you are building your own custom database, you should plan on using 40MB plus the size of your database. We recommend using at least 32MB of RAM.

**Q.** Why is Oracle so intense on resources?
**A.** Oracle products are more complex and have more features than some of the other vendor's products. Even though the products will run in 16MB of RAM, it is better to provide sufficient physical memory and avoid swapping. Windows 3.1 applications can get very slow if physical memory is limited.

**Q.** Why do I have to install the Oracle tools and database separately?
**A.** Unlike other products, such as Microsoft Access, Oracle products are built to facilitate a client-server architecture. Therefore, tools to build front-end applications are made separately from the RDBMS. This also facilitates application development. You can design and build an application in a stand-alone environment and then deploy it in a client-server environment readily.

**Q.** Can I use Oracle Windows 3.1 tools like Developer/2000 on Windows 95 and Windows NT?
**A.** You can use Oracle Windows 3.1 tools (16 bit) on Windows 95 or Windows NT 3.51. Windows NT 4.x is not supported. Table 1-4 provides the compatibility matrix.

**Q.** I have just received an Oracle install CD for Windows 3.1. How do I find out its contents without installing it?
**A.** View a file called **PRODINFO.ORA**, if present on the CD, in a text editor. This will give you the part number, product name, version and

|  | Win 3.1 | Win 3.11 (32-bit client) | Win 95 (16-bit client) | Win 95 (32-bit client) | Win NT 3.51 | Win NT 4.0 |
|---|---|---|---|---|---|---|
| Oracle 16-bit tools | Yes | Yes | Yes | Yes | Yes | No |
| Oracle 16-bit tools with 16-bit SQL*Net V2 | Yes | Yes | Yes | Yes | Yes | No |

**TABLE I-4.**    *Oracle 16-bit Windows 3.1 Software Compatibility Matrix*

operating system requirements. In addition, you can view a file called **WINDOWS.PRD** on the CD (usually under a directory named INSTALL) to get a listing of all the software products on the CD.

**Q.** How do I know which products are installed on my machine?
**A.** You can start the Oracle Installer for Windows 3.1 and view a list of all the products installed on your machine. An alternative would be to view the file C:\ORAWIN\ORAINST\**WINDOWS.RGS** in a text editor. Take precautions to *not* modify the **WINDOWS.RGS** file manually.

**Q.** I get an error when I run the installer. The error is something about a **.VRF** failure. What do I do?
**A.** Oracle install media has many verification scripts in **.VRF** files. Sometimes when you attempt to install a product with a copy of the Oracle Installer that was provided with another Oracle product, one of the environment variables in a **.VRF** file might not be defined. If you do get an error message with mention about a **.VRF** file, try using a copy of the Oracle Installer that is available on the product media itself. The Oracle Installer on the media can be invoked by running **SETUP.EXE** or **ORAINST.EXE**

**Q.** I have an Oracle product CD. Do I run **SETUP.EXE** or **ORAINST.EXE**?
**A.** You can typically run either of the executables. The Windows 3.1 standard suggests that the installation program for a product be called **SETUP.EXE**. In the case of Oracle's Windows 3.1 products, **SETUP.EXE** just invokes **ORAINST.EXE**, the Oracle Installer executable.

**Q.** How do I know whether I am using a 16-bit or 32-bit Oracle application tool?
**A.** If a product is labeled for Windows 3.1, it is a 16-bit tool. 32-bit tools are labeled for Windows 95 or Windows NT. The name of the product executable usually provides information on the type of tool. For example, the 16-bit Developer/2000 Forms Designer executable is called **F45DES.EXE** and the 32-bit executable is called **F45DES32.EXE**.

**Q.** I am using a third-party application that was written by somebody else. How do I find out whether this is a 16-bit or 32-bit application?
**A.** The brute force method is to rename some required files and determine the kind of application you are using. Go to the C:\ORAWIN\BIN directory and identify all the files that have a name similar to **ORA7x.DLL** or **ORA7xWIN.DLL**. The DLLs having **WIN** in their name are for 16-bit applications. Rename them by changing the extension to something other than DLL, say **.BAK**. For example:

```
REN ORA73.DLL ORA73.BAK
REN ORA72WIN.DLL ORA72WIN.BAK
```

Now, try to use the application again. You should see an error which warns you about a missing file. This should indicate whether your application is 16 bit or 32 bit. You should see an error similar to the one shown here:

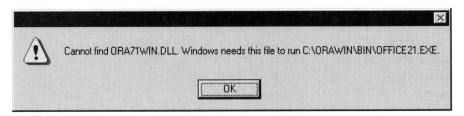

In this example, since the application **OFFICE21.EXE** is looking for **ORA71WIN.DLL**, it is a 16-bit Windows application. Do remember to rename the files back to the original name.

**Q.** I get an error on start up when I try to start Developer/2000 Forms Designer. What is wrong?
**A.** Most Oracle tools including Developer/2000 Forms look for certain message files and terminal resource files during start up. These files are located using a product parameter in the **ORACLE.INI** file. For example,

Developer/2000 Forms looks at the parameter FORMS45 to find the directory which designates the location of the message files and resource files. If this parameter is missing, then you would get an error on start up.

**Q.**  But I haven't changed anything, why do I get an error on start up?
**A.**  The **ORACLE.INI** file is located by looking up a parameter called ORA_CONFIG in the **WIN.INI** file. If you have reinstalled Windows or somehow created a new **WIN.INI** file, your **ORACLE.INI** will not be located by the Oracle tool. Another common problem is that in file server installations, you have re-mapped a DOS drive letter. For example, you had mapped the drive G:\ to the path on the file server containing the ORAWIN directory. If you lose this mapping the drive G:\ will not point to the same physical location on the file server and the start-up files will not be found.

**Q.**  I created the database tables for Developer/2000 Forms as described but I still get an error "ORA-942 Table or View Does Not Exist". What is the issue?
**A.**  Sometimes when you use the Oracle Installer to create the database tables, and the SQL scripts to create these tables fail, the error is not readily noticed. All the system tables required might not have been created properly. A common problem is that there is insufficient room in the SYSTEM tablespace to hold all the objects that need to be created. You need to ensure that there is about 15MB of free space in the SYSTEM tablespace and then install the database tables again. (If you need help on this, refer to Chapter 7 on RDBMS.) Take a close look at the log file created to spot any errors.

**Q.**  I get an error "Insufficient Memory to Run this Application. Close one or more applications and try again" when I try to start my application. I have plenty of physical RAM available. What is the problem?
**A.**  When Windows 3.1 starts an application it tries to make an entry in a Windows Task Database that is actually in conventional memory (below the DOS 640K line). If you are low on conventional memory, you get such an error. Quit Windows and try to free up more conventional memory by removing unwanted DOS drivers or run MemMaker and try again. Alternatively, you can use a utility called Fix1MB which is available on the Internet and also on CompuServe under the Microsoft Forum.

**Q.**  I get an error "Call to Undefined Dynalink" when I run my application. What is this?

**A.**  This error is actually from Windows 3.1. It generally means that a program or DLL is calling for another DLL which is not found. Occasionally, if a function call in a DLL is wrongly invoked, you get a similar error. If you get this error while running an Oracle application, ensure that C:\ORAWIN\BIN is in your DOS path. Also ensure that you do not have multiple copies of Oracle DLLs (old and newer versions) in your DOS path. The best way to resolve such an issue is to search all the directories in your DOS path for files matching **ORA\*.DLL**. If you get multiple hits then you want to ensure that the latest copy is the only one in the path.

**Q.**  I get a General Protection Fault while running an application. What is it?

**A.**  Occasionally, when developing applications on Windows, you might encounter problems that can lead to a crash of the application with a *General Protection Fault* (GPF). A GPF is a direct result of a misbehaving Windows application. It can be caused by a memory leak, or as a result of an application trying to access an area of memory beyond bounds, or sometimes even as a result of running out of some kind of resource under Windows.

**Q.**  What do I do when I get a GPF?

**A.**  When a GPF is encountered you should try to shut down the application as cleanly as possible and at the very least restart Windows at the earliest opportunity. Even better, reboot your PC altogether to ensure that memory is cleaned up entirely. Remember that the GPF has resulted in Windows becoming unstable and a failure to restart Windows could result in more serious problems such as file corruption.

While a product crash due to a GPF is not desirable for anyone, a GPF being caused consistently can definitely be considered a bug and should be reported as such to Oracle Worldwide Customer Support. Be sure to note down the exact steps that caused the GPF before you call Oracle Worldwide Customer Support.

**Q.**  What are the common causes of a GPF? How do I avoid them?

**A.**  The more common causes of a GPF are listed below:

■ Using incompatible versions of dependencies (see explanation below)

■ Poor Windows configuration or running low on resources

All Oracle tools are dependent on certain other files that are installed as one or more of the following products:

- Required Support Files (RSF)

- Tools Utilities (TU)

- GUI Common Files (GCF)

By far the most common cause for a GPF is the fact that proper versions of one of the above is not being used with the tool. Please look at the release notes or installation guide for the tool you are using and verify that you have the right version of the RSF, TU, and GCF installed. You can start the Oracle Installer under Windows and look at the listing of installed products and compare these with the requirements for your tool. If you have installed a later version of RSF, TU, or GCF, you should not have problems as these are backward compatible.

Another common problem is having multiple copies of run-time DLLs (Dynamic Link Libraries) on your installation. Always ensure that you have only one copy of each DLL required by the Oracle product. When Windows loads a DLL, it loads the first DLL in the search path that matches the name. This can very easily result in a bad mix of old and new DLLs, which will almost certainly lead to problems. Run a file search on your system and ensure that you do not have duplicate copies of Oracle DLLs. You can search for files **ORA\*.DLL** and if you see multiple copies of DLLs in different locations, ensure that you only have the latest version in the path.

**Q.**  What if I continue to encounter GPFs?
**A.**  If you have satisfied yourself about your installation and you still see GPFs, you must call your local Oracle Support organization and log a bug report. The development team for the product in question will determine the problem and help you resolve the issue. There is some information about filing bug reports in Chapter 11 under the FAQ section.

**Q.**  What are Required Support Files? Why are they needed?
**A.**  All Oracle applications are developed using APIs that allow for embedded SQL and *Oracle Call Interface* (OCI) calls. The Required Support Files (RSF) contain libraries that define the API. On Windows 3.1 they are implemented as DLLs. The first two digits of the RSF version match the

version of the RDBMS. For example, RSF 7.2.3.x contain libraries for Oracle 7.2 RDBMS. It is perfectly normal for tools to be linked with different versions of Oracle libraries. Therefore, if you have installed many Oracle tools on your PC, it is normal to see many versions of RSF installed, i.e. RSF 7.1, 7.2 and 7.3 might be installed on your PC. This is all right since the DLLs have different names based on the version. For example, you might see **ORA72.DLL** and **ORA73.DLL** on your PC.

**Q.** I want to deploy my Windows 3.1 application across many PCs. How do I avoid going through the entire installation procedure each time?
**A.** You can use the Oracle Installer to install just the run-time components for all the tools that you need to run your application. For example, if you need Developer/2000 Forms and Developer/2000 Reports to run your application, then you must install only the run-time component of Developer/2000 Forms and Developer/2000 Reports. If you do not want to install the run-time components on several PCs, here is a step-by-step approach that could work with the right care:

**CAUTION**
*Use this approach only if you do not have any Oracle products for Windows 3.1 installed on the PC already.*

### Step 1: Install the Run-time Components Required on a PC with No Oracle Products Installed:

Use the Oracle Installer to install Developer/2000 Forms Runtime into C:\ORAWIN. You might have to double-click the item to get an expanded listing. For example:

```
+ Developer/2000     -     Forms 4.5.x.x.x
```

If you double-click you should see something similar to the following:

```
-- Developer/2000     -     Forms 4.5.x.x.x
        Forms Demos 4.5.x.x.x
        Forms Designer 4.5.x.x.x
        Forms Online Documentation 4.5.x.x.x
        Forms Runtime 4.5.x.x.x
```

Select Forms Runtime and install it.

## Step 2: Install SQL*Net for Windows 3.1 and Verify Installation

If required, install SQL*Net for Windows at this point and all required adapters. Make sure that you can connect to the database using either the Ora*Ping or NetTest utility provided with SQL*Net, or even use your Forms application.

## Step 3: Review Changes to .INI Files and Windows Directories

At this point the following changes should have been made:

■ In the **WIN.INI** file, you should have an entry similar to

```
[Oracle]
ORA_CONFIG=C:\WINDOWS\ORACLE.INI
```

■ You should have two new files C:\WINDOWS\**ORACLE.INI** and C:\WINDOWS\**VSL.INI** (this is only present if you have installed SQL*Net). You should also see the following files in the C:\WINDOWS\SYSTEM directory:

| | | |
|---|---|---|
| CTL3D.DL | CTL3DV2.DLL | COMPOBJ.DLL |
| OLE2.DLL | OLE2CONV.DLL | OLE2DISP.DLL |
| OLE2NLS.DLL | OLE2PROX.DLL | TYPELIB.DLL |
| STORAGE.DLL | VSHARE.386 | STDOLE.TLB |
| MFC250.DLL | MFCD250.DLL | MFCO250.DLL |
| MFCOLEUI.DLL | COMMDLG.DLL | MSOLEVBX.DLL |
| VBOA300.DLL | | |

Several Program Groups should have been added to the Program Manager at this time. You can view C:\WINDOWS\**PROGMAN.INI** and the last few lines should indicate Oracle added groups. Note the **.GRP** files associated with Oracle products from the **PROGMAN.INI**.

## Step 4: Duplicate Environment on Other PCs

At this point, you can duplicate the environment on other PCs by transferring files over a network. We are going to illustrate this process by recreating the environment in D:\ORAWIN on the second PC. Remember that the first installation was on C:\ORAWIN.

1. Create a directory D:\ORAWIN on the second PC.

2. Copy all files in C:\ORAWIN on the first PC to D:\ORAWIN on the second PC. Ensure that all recursive directory paths are maintained.

3. Copy **ORACLE.INI** and **VSL.INI** (if present) from first PC to C:\WINDOWS of the second PC.

4. Edit **WIN.INI** on the second PC and add the following two lines at the bottom of the file:

   ```
   [Oracle]
   ORA_CONFIG=C:\WINDOWS\ORACLE.INI
   ```

5. Edit **ORACLE.INI** on the second PC and change all references to C:\ORAWIN to D:\ORAWIN.

6. Copy all **.GRP** files in C:\WINDOWS of first PC to C:\WINDOWS on the second PC. Start Windows on the second PC and add all the groups by using the File|New menu option. You can provide the names of the **.GRP** files directly. Alternatively, edit **PROGMAN.INI** and add the group files directly.

7. Copy all the files (listed above) from C:\WINDOWS\SYSTEM of the first PC to C:\WINDOWS\SYSTEM on the second PC.

**Q.** I have purchased SQL*Net. I want to use this to connect a third-party application to a remote Oracle7 server. I am unable to connect. What is the problem?
**A.** Issues that encompass products from different vendors can sometimes be hard to resolve. You must first determine if the third-party application is capable of using Oracle SQL*Net directly, or whether it requires an additional layer such as ODBC. Oracle does provide a sample program that can be used to test connectivity. This will help isolate the problem to either the SQL*Net layer or the application layer. Search in your C:\ORAWIN\BIN directory for an executable with a name similar to Ora*Ping or NetTest. This is the sample connect program. On executing this, you should see a window similar to the one shown here:

```
┌─────────────────────────────────────────────────┐
│          Oracle Database Ping Utility             │
│                                                   │
│    User ID  ┌──────────────────────────────┐      │
│             └──────────────────────────────┘      │
│                                                   │
│   Password  ┌──────────────────────────────┐      │
│             └──────────────────────────────┘      │
│                                                   │
│ Connect String ┌───────────────────────────┐     │
│                └───────────────────────────┘      │
│                                                   │
│              ┌──────────┐     ┌──────────┐        │
│              │    OK    │     │  CANCEL  │        │
│              └──────────┘     └──────────┘        │
└─────────────────────────────────────────────────┘
```

If you are able to connect to the Oracle server using this program, then SQL*Net is installed properly and you need to determine the cause at the application layer. In any case, if you do get a connect error, this sample utility should provide a better response by way of an Oracle error that should help determine the cause of the problem.

**Q.**  I have a file called **NETINIT.EXE** (or **NETINIT7.EXE**) on my installation, what does this do?
**A.**  This executable was specially created to pre-allocate DOS memory for users of Windows 3.1 applications and SQL*Net for DOS. If you are using SQL*Net for DOS (a terminate-stay-resident program) and a Windows 3.1 application, then it is recommended that you run **NETINIT.EXE**. This has no benefit if you are not using SQL*Net or if you are using SQL*Net for Windows 3.1.

**Q.**  I want to install Personal Oracle7. It says something about installing Win32s. What is this all about?
**A.**  Personal Oracle7 for Windows 3.1 is a 32-bit database. It therefore requires Microsoft's 32-bit extension to Windows 3.1 called Win32s. Please install this from the Personal Oracle7 media before installing Personal Oracle7.

**Q.**  I have installed Personal Oracle7. It keeps asking me for a password when I try to start it. What do I do?
**A.**  Personal Oracle7 uses a password to provide some protection on privileged operations like start up and shut down. The default password for this is *oracle*. If you have changed it during installation, be sure to use the

password you provided at that time. You can disable this feature entirely by adding the following line to the **ORACLE.INI** file:

 `DBA_AUTHORIZATION=BYPASS`

Be sure to restart Windows 3.1. Changes in **ORACLE.INI** take effect only during start up.

# CHAPTER
# 2

## Preventive Maintenance on MS-Windows 95

icrosoft's Windows 95 is fast replacing Windows 3.1 on the desktop. Being a 32-bit operating system, it has generally allowed for more complex applications. The new look and feel of Windows 95 has given users an interface that is quick and easy to use. In addition, Windows 95 has immensely improved networking. Oracle has a range of products, from client-tools to the RDBMS, that take advantage of the features of Windows 95. In this chapter we will take a look at some of the more common issues with Oracle products on Windows 95. We present some general installation guidelines to start with and then present some common install scenarios.

# Pre-Installation Tasks

We present some important pre-installation tasks that will help a great deal towards an easy installation.

## 1. Verify Availability of Resources

Determine the hardware and software requirements of the products you wish to install. Every Oracle product set is distributed with an installation guide. Most of the product CDs also have installation instructions on the inside cover. In the first few pages of the installation guide, you should find a table that lists the hardware and software requirements of that product. We have listed some general recommendations here for your reference:

■ Use an IBM, Compaq, or 100 percent compatible PC. We suggest a Pentium-based 90 MHz or better PC.

■ We suggest 32MB of RAM if you are using Personal Oracle7 by itself. We suggest 32MB of RAM if you are using Developer/2000 Designer tools against a remote database, and 64MB for optimal performance if you are using Developer/2000 with Personal Oracle7.

■ Access to a CD-ROM drive, local or on the network, to perform the installation as Oracle software is not distributed on floppy disk media.

■ We also recommend about 20MB of free disk space after you have installed Personal Oracle7. This may be used by Windows 95 for expanding a swap file. Unpredictable behavior will result if

Windows 95 runs out of disk space while expanding the swap file. Refer to the installation guide distributed with your product set for hard disk requirements. A typical install of Personal Oracle7 for Windows 95 Release 7.2 and Developer/2000 1.3 consumes about 70MB of disk space of which about 20MB is the seed (or starter) database.

**NOTE**
*Oracle Developer/2000 and Personal Oracle7 represent high-end products on Windows 95. Less complex products will function optimally with lesser hardware resources.*

# 2. Backup Configuration Information

The installation process of Oracle products on Windows 95 modifies (or even adds) a few configuration files on your PC. While the changes should have no impact on your existing applications under normal circumstances, it is best that you have a backup copy of these files for future reference. You can use the standard copy command provided by DOS or use the Windows Explorer to create copies of the files shown below. We will assume that C:\ is your boot drive, Windows is installed in C:\WINDOWS, Oracle 16-bit Windows 3.1 products are installed in C:\ORAWIN and Oracle 32-bit Windows 95 products are installed in C:\ORAWIN95 throughout this chapter.

| | |
|---|---|
| **AUTOEXEC.BAT** | Resides in the boot drive of your PC, C:\. |
| **WIN.INI** | Resides in the Windows home, C:\WINDOWS. |
| **ODBC.INI** | Only for ODBC installs; located in C:\WINDOWS. All ODBC database definitions are stored in this file. |
| **PO7.INI** | If you already have Personal Oracle7 installed, then you may have this file in C:\WINDOWS. This file is created with some versions of Personal Oracle7. |
| **WIN95.RGS** | If you already have Windows 95 products from Oracle installed, you will have this file in C:\ORAWIN95\ORAINST. This file contains a listing of all Oracle Windows 95 products installed on your PC and is used by the Oracle Installer for Windows 95 to determine installed components at any time. |

| | |
|---|---|
| **TNSNAMES.ORA** | If you have Oracle SQL*Net Version 2 installed, you will have this file in C:\ORAWIN95\NETWORK\ADMIN. |
| **SQLNET.ORA** | If you have Oracle SQL*Net Version 2 installed, you will have this file in C:\ORAWIN95\NETWORK\ADMIN. |
| **TOPOLOGY.ORA** | This file is located in C:\ORAWIN95\NETWORK\ADMIN, if present from a previous installation. |

We recommend that you create a folder such as C:\ORAWIN95\BACKUP and copy the above files into this folder. Information obtained from these files can be very useful to Oracle Worldwide Customer Support in resolving your issues.

In addition, it is a good habit to make a copy of your Windows registry. To accomplish this, run **regedit** on Windows 95, expand HKEY_LOCAL_MACHINE, then SOFTWARE, and then ORACLE. Now select Export Registry File from the File menu and provide an appropriate name for the file in which to store your registry. If you ever want to import this registry file, you can just double-click the file in the Windows Explorer.

# 3. Other Tasks

As part of the pre-installation procedures, there are some miscellaneous tasks that you need to perform such as verifying your file system. These important tasks are listed below.

## Verify the Integrity of Your File-system

PCs frequently have minor problems with the File Allocation Table (FAT). We recommend that you verify the integrity of your hard disk before you begin the installation. For example, if you are installing Oracle software in C:\ORAWIN95, do the following:

1. Start Windows Explorer.

2. Select C: in the left section of the Explorer.

3. Select File|Properties.

4. Select the Tools tab, and you should see something similar to Figure 2-1.

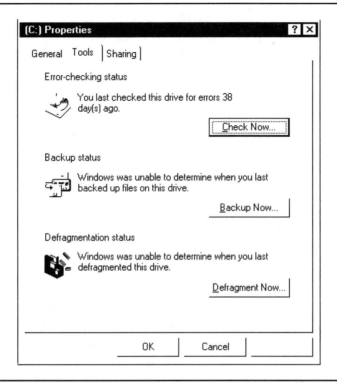

**FIGURE 2-1.**   *File properties in the Windows Explorer*

Click the Check Now button and you should see a window as shown in Figure 2-2. Select the options as shown, and click Start.

## Disk Compression Utility

If you are planning to install Personal Oracle7 for Windows 95, you must install the database files on a partition that is not being compressed. You can install the Personal Oracle7 software itself on a compressed partition, but the database that you create must be in an uncompressed partition. You can do this by manually creating your database in an uncompressed partition. For more information, look at the **README** file provided with Personal Oracle7 for Windows 95. The **README** file can be viewed by selecting Start|Programs|Personal Oracle7 for Windows 95.

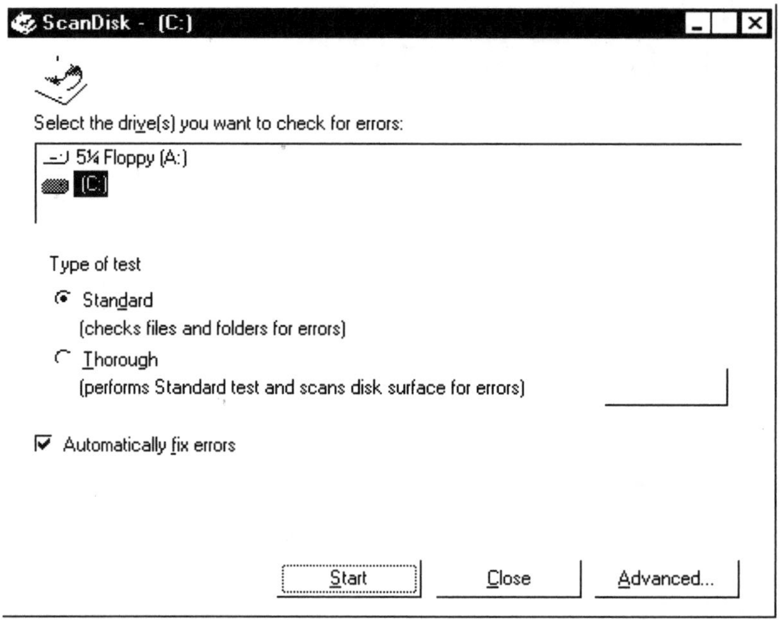

**FIGURE 2-2.** *ScanDisk dialog box in Windows 95*

### Language Selection

Install the required language on Windows 95 before installing Personal Oracle7. The language chosen for Personal Oracle7 must be the same as the language on Windows 95. Note that multi-byte Oracle languages will not work on single-byte editions of Windows 95.

## 4. Special Tasks for File Server Installations

If you are installing Oracle products on a file server (i.e., the ORAWIN95 folder is on a network drive), then the following additional information is useful:

### Assign a Permanent Drive Letter for Your Network Drive

Oracle products on Windows 95 read settings from the Windows registry. For example, if you install Oracle Windows 95 products in a folder G:\ORAWIN95, some of the entries in the registry will refer to G:\ORAWIN95. It is therefore necessary that you always assign the drive letter G: to the same location.

More details on file server installations are usually provided in an appendix in the installation guide for your product. In the FAQ section of this chapter, we provide details on deploying multiple clients for a server installation.

# Understanding the Oracle Installer and the Installation Process on Windows 95

In order to better understand the Oracle Installer and the installation process on Windows 95, follow the outline explained below.

## 1. Preview

The Oracle Installer on Windows 95 performs three primary tasks:

- It checks dependencies.
- It copies necessary product files.
- It configures the system environment.

First, the Oracle Installer verifies that sufficient disk space is available to install the desired products. It then verifies that other Oracle dependencies are satisfied. Oracle products on Windows 95 share a substantial portion of code that is made available under components like Required Support Files and GUI Common Files. If you already have an Oracle product installed, the installer will verify that dependencies related to this shared code are satisfied for the new product. The installer will upgrade the common software components only if required. Since most of these components are implemented as DLLs on Windows, the Oracle Installer ensures that multiple copies of the same DLL are not available to a product at run time. You will see warnings during installation if there are multiple copies of a DLL, and corrective action will be suggested automatically.

Next, the Oracle Installer copies the required files for a product to function normally. The files are placed in appropriate folders automatically. The Oracle Installer will allow the user to choose the folder into which a product is installed. However, all the executables and DLLs are usually placed in a folder called C:\ORAWIN95\BIN.

Finally, the Oracle Installer creates the program groups and icons required for the products installed. The installer adds a record of the product versions installed into a registration file, the **WIN95.RGS**, for future reference. Necessary entries for a product in the Windows registry are also completed at this time.

# 2. Important Installation Files

The Oracle Installer for Windows 95 uses some key files. A brief description of these files is provided for your reference and understanding of the installation process. Even though all the files below are plain text files, *do not manually modify or delete these files at any time.* You are free to view them at any time to understand the installation process used by Oracle. If you are unable to find any of these files, try searching the contents of your install media using the Windows Explorer's find function.

## WIN95.PRD

This file contains a listing of all products and their components available on the install media. The installer reads this file to get a listing of available products on the media. This file typically resides in a folder called INSTALL on the install media. If you want to quickly determine the products available on any Oracle media for Windows 95 without invoking the installer, you can look at this file in any text editor.

## WIN95.INS

This file contains the Oracle installation script used by the installer. It is typically located in the INSTALL folder on the install media. In addition to this file, every product typically has an installation script in its product folder on the media. It is therefore normal to have many files with the extension **.INS** on the install media.

## WIN95.DEI

This file contains the Oracle de-install script used by the installer. It is also located in the INSTALL folder on the media. It gets copied into C:\ORAWIN95\ORAINST during installation. In addition to this file, every product typically has a de-install script in its product folder on the media. You should have many files with the extension **.DEI** in the C:\ORAWIN95 folder.

## WIN95.STP

This file contains the script that initializes the environment variables for Oracle products on Windows 95. It is read by the Oracle Installer at start up.

## PRODINFO.ORA

This file contains complete information on the product, such as the part number, version, and operating system requirement. It is usually located in the root folder on the product media. Some older Oracle products may not have this file on the install media.

### Files with an Extension .VRF

These files contain scripts that the installer uses for verification of some settings and dependencies. For example, the file **PATH.VRF** is used to verify that the path being added to the **AUTOEXEC.BAT** file does not exceed DOS limitations.

### Files with an Extension .MAP

These files contain a listing of all the physical files for each product component, their source folders on the install media, and their target folders. The size of the individual files are also documented here. The installer uses the information in **.MAP** files to determine if the available disk space is sufficient.

## RELNOTES.WRI and README.TXT

These files will contain any changes or instructions that were put in place after the product media was created. It is recommended that you view these files before beginning any installation. These files are typically located in the root folder of the install media.

# 3. Brief Description of Products/Components Available for Installation

When you start the Oracle Installer, you get a complete listing of Oracle products available on the product media. It is best that you select the high-level product (such as Developer/2000 Forms and SQL*Net) from the list of products to install. The installer will ensure that all dependent files such as Required Support Files are copied over during installation. While Oracle provides many different products on Windows 95, some of the common components that you will see during an installation are described in Table 2-1.

**NOTE**
*Some of the components shown in Table 2-1 are used by most Oracle products. As a rule of thumb, it is sufficient to install the latest version of any of these components. Generally speaking, they are all backward compatible. An exception to this rule are the Required Support Files (RSF). The version of the RSF usually corresponds with the version of the database. For example, Oracle7 Version 7.2 will use RSF 7.2 (only the first two digits are significant) and not RSF 7.3. Similarly SQL*Net Version 2.3 will use RSF 7.3 and not RSF 7.2. If you have both Oracle7 Version 7.2 and SQL*Net 2.3 installed, you should see both RSF 7.2 and 7.3 installed. This is perfectly normal.*

| Product to Be Installed | Description |
| --- | --- |
| Developer/2000 Forms | Complete Developer/2000 Forms Designer and run time installation |
| Developer/2000 Reports | Complete Developer/2000 Reports Designer and run time installation |
| Developer/2000 Graphics | Complete Oracle*Graphics Designer and run time installation |
| Forms Runtime | Run-time files required to run Developer/2000 Forms applications |
| Reports Runtime | Run-time files required to run Developer/2000 Reports applications |
| Graphics Runtime | Run-time files required to run Oracle*Graphics applications |
| Developer/2000 Procedure Builder | Oracle Procedure Builder |
| Oracle Translation Manager | Tool to translate Developer/2000 applications into other languages |
| Developer/2000 Open Interfaces | PVCS Interface, Tuxedo and ClearCase Interfaces for Developer/2000 |
| Oracle Open Client Adapter | Adapter that allows Oracle tools to talk to other non-Oracle ODBC-compliant databases |
| SQL*Net V2 | Oracle's network interface software |
| Oracle Protocol Adapters | Provide communication protocols for the network, such as TCP/IP, SPX, and Named Pipes |
| Intersolv Datadirect Drivers | Drivers that allow Developer/2000 applications to connect to non-Oracle databases such as SQL Server, Informix (4 and 5), and Sybase System10 |
| GUI Common Files | Common files that provide user interface to run Oracle products under Windows 95 |
| Required Support Files | Shared libraries needed for all Oracle applications |
| Tools Utilities | Libraries and tool kit for Oracle products |
| System Support Files | Files that provide OLE2 and VBX support |
| Oracle Installer | The Oracle Installer executable |
| Oracle7 RDBMS | The Oracle7 database |

**TABLE 2-1.**   *Common Oracle Product Components on Windows 95*

# 4. The Installation Process

Precise instructions to perform the installation are always listed in the installation guide for Windows 95 that was provided with the product. This section provides some additional information that should be useful.

- Install all Oracle products for Windows 95 in one path such as C:\ORAWIN95. It is necessary for all 32-bit products from Oracle to be in one folder structure. Do not install Oracle 32-bit products (Windows 95 or Windows NT) into C:\ORAWIN, which is used by 16-bit products from Oracle. At all times, install Oracle 16-bit products for Windows 3.1 and Oracle 32-bit products for Windows 95 into separate directories. The best approach is to accept the default target directories suggested by the Oracle Installer. Feel free to change the drive letter to ensure that the product is installed on the intended target drive.

- Shut down all Oracle applications before starting any installation. The exception to this is a component called Database Tables. This component requires access to the database to create system tables for some products. More details on this are available in later sections of this chapter and also the installation guide of the product.

- Remember to back up your configuration information, especially the Windows registry. Information in the registry is always useful to troubleshoot installation issues.

- Select only the high-level products that you are interested in installing. Do not concern yourself with sub-components such as Required Support Files or GUI Common Files. For example, if you are interested in Developer/2000 Forms, choose Developer/2000 Forms from the list of products available for installation. The Oracle Installer is intelligent enough to ensure that all dependencies are satisfied.

# Post-Installation Tasks

As part of the post-installation procedures, there are some miscellaneous tasks that you need to perform such as backing up files. These important tasks are listed below.

# 1. Backup Configuration Information

Make a copy of **ORACLE.INI**, **ODBC.INI** (for ODBC installs only), and C:\ORAWIN95\NETWORK\ADMIN\*.ORA files (for SQL*Net installs only).

# 2. Scripts for Tables Required by Tools

Some of the tools from Oracle store information (such as security details) in tables. Oracle provides scripts to create such system tables (also called database tables). Follow the instructions in the installation guide under the section "Creating Database Tables" to create the system tables required by your product. If you are having trouble connecting to the Oracle7 database, refer to the section on SQL*Net connectivity in this chapter before completing this task.

# 3. Adding Environment Variables to Ease Use of Oracle Products

It is convenient to add some environment variables of your own to the Windows registry, or to edit some existing variables. Some common entries are provided in Table 2-2 for your reference.

| Environment Variable | Description | Example |
|---|---|---|
| FORMS45_PATH | Path information for Developer/2000 Forms application files (.FMX, .MMX, .PLL, etc.) | FORMS45_PATH= C:\MYAPP;C:\OTHERAPP |
| REPORTS25_PATH | Path information for Developer/2000 Reports application files | REPORTS25_PATH= C:\MYAPP;C:\OTHERAPP |
| ORACLE_TEMP | Folder for temporary files | ORACLE_TEMP=C:\TEMP |
| TK23_ICON | Location of .ICO files | TK23_ICON=C:\MYICONS |
| DEV2000_SCVIEWER | Editor invoked to view the output generated by an archive difference report | DEV2000_SCVIEWER= NOTEPAD.EXE |

**TABLE 2-2.**    *User-defined Parameters in the Windows Registry*

# Four Types of Installation

There are four typical installation scenarios:

- **A stand-alone installation** This installation would enable applications built with Oracle's client tools to be used with Personal Oracle7 for Windows 95.

- **A client-server installation** This installation would allow applications built with Oracle's client tools to be used with a remote (residing on a separate machine) Oracle7 server.

- **Third-party products** This installation would enable an application built with a third-party tool, such as Microsoft Visual Basic, to be used with Oracle7.

- **Non-Oracle RDBMS** This installation would allow an application built with Oracle's client tools to be used with a non-Oracle ODBC-compliant database, such as Microsoft Access.

An example of each type will illustrate the installation process. The examples may easily be extended to cover every installation need of Oracle products on Windows 95. Some special issues for Windows 3.1 tools under Windows 95 are also addressed.

## A Stand-alone Installation

A stand-alone installation is one in which an Oracle tool is used to build an application by connecting to an Oracle7 database that is running under Windows 95 on the same machine. We will illustrate a stand-alone installation by using Developer/2000 Forms 4.5 to create an application with Personal Oracle7 for Windows. Here are the necessary steps:

1. Install Personal Oracle7 for Windows 95.

2. Verify installation of Personal Oracle7.

3. Install Developer/2000 Forms Designer 4.5 for Windows 95.

4. Verify connectivity to Personal Oracle7.

5. Install database tables for Developer/2000 Forms.

6. Create a sample application using Developer/2000 Forms.

7. Run sample application.

8. Ensure that database tables are properly installed.

9. Run 16-bit Windows 3.1 applications in this configuration.

## Step 1: Install Personal Oracle7 for Windows 95

Install Personal Oracle7 for Windows 95 per instructions in the installation guide and following the guidelines provided earlier in this chapter. Install the seed database by choosing "Typical Install". This should use about 60MB of space on the hard disk. About 40MB of space is used by the software and utilities to maintain the database. The remaining space of about 20MB is used by the database and is distributed approximately as shown in Table 2-3 (we installed Personal Oracle7 for Windows 95 version 7.2).

In addition to these database files, Oracle creates a control file that uses about 160KB and two log files that use 200KB each.

## Step 2: Verify Installation of Personal Oracle7

Once Personal Oracle7 for Windows 95 is installed, it is best to reboot the PC to ensure that changes made during installation take effect. After restarting, you can now ensure that the Oracle7 database was installed properly.

Start the database by clicking on Start|Programs|Personal Oracle7 for Windows95|Start Database. You should see a series of messages with an

| Tablespace Name | Files | Space (Kilobytes) |
|---|---|---|
| SYSTEM | **SYS1ORCL.ORA** | 10,486 |
| ROLLBACK_DATA | **RBS1ORCL.ORA** | 3,146 |
| TEMPORARY_DATA | **TMP1ORCL.ORA** | 2,097 |
| USER_DATA | **USR1ORCL.ORA** | 3,146 |

**TABLE 2-3.**   *Personal Oracle7 Database Files in a Starter Database*

ending message of "Oracle7 Database Started Successfully". You should also see the Oracle symbol in the Taskbar at the bottom right of your screen as shown here:

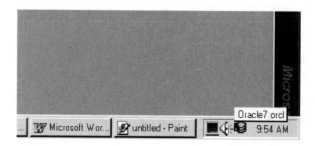

On Windows 95, the above step is actually unnecessary. When you attempt the first connection to Personal Oracle7, the database should start automatically. However, we recommend this step.

At this time, start the Personal Oracle7 Navigator (again under the group Personal Oracle7 for Windows 95). Expand the item Local Database and look at a few objects. If you are asked for a user name and password, we suggest you login as a DBA. You can use the default Oracle user name *system* with a password of *manager*. In any case, you should be able to view a few objects once you are connected to the database as any Oracle user. Be sure to leave the Oracle database running.

## Step 3: Install Developer/2000 Forms Designer 4.5 for Windows 95

At this time, you are ready to install an Oracle application development tool of your choice. We will illustrate proper installation technique using Developer/2000 Forms 4.5 (from Developer/2000).

Start the Oracle Installer again and select Developer/2000 Forms 4.5. The installer will copy all the files related to Developer/2000 Forms 4.5.

## Step 4: Verify Connectivity to Personal Oracle7

Start Developer/2000 Forms Designer and ensure that you can connect to the database. Choose the File|Connect menu item to view the login screen. Type a user name and password for a valid Oracle user. If you are unsure, you may use an account created by Oracle; the user name is *scott* and the password is *tiger*. Leave the field for the connect string blank.

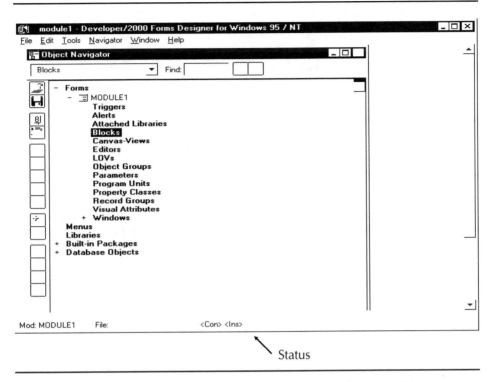

Status

**FIGURE 2-3.** *Developer/2000 Forms Designer screen after connecting to Oracle*

You should see the status *<Con>* (shown in Figure 2-3) in the status bar at the bottom of the Developer/2000 Forms designer screen. The item Disconnect should also now be available under the File menu.

Exit from the Developer/2000 Forms Designer.

## Step 5: Install Database Tables for Developer/2000 Forms

We are now ready to create the database tables required by Developer/2000 Forms. Revert to the Oracle Installer and choose to install the component Developer/2000 Forms Database Tables (you may need to expand the component Developer/2000 Database Tables). At this point, you should see a program item called Developer 2000 Admin for Win95.

You must have SQL*Plus for Windows 95 installed in order to run the scripts that create the necessary database tables. If you do not have

SQL*Plus installed, use the Oracle Installer to do so before attempting the next step.

1. Click Start and then Programs|Developer 2000 Admin for Win95|Common Build.

2. Run Programs|Developer 2000 Admin for Win95|Common Grant.

3. Run Programs|Developer 2000 Admin for Win95|Forms Build.

4. Run Programs|Developer 2000 Admin for Win95|Forms Grant.

Each of the steps above invoke SQL*Plus and run SQL scripts. You should get a log file from these SQL scripts. Pay close attention for any errors in running these scripts. We are ready to verify that the Developer/2000 Forms product installed properly by creating a small sample application.

## Step 6: Create a Sample Application Using Developer/2000 Forms

Start the Developer/2000 Forms Designer again and connect to the database as in Step 4. We will create a small sample application to ensure that the product is installed correctly.

Double-click Blocks in the Object Navigator of the Forms Designer. You should see a screen similar to Figure 2-4. Now click the Select button next to the Base Table field. You will then see a screen similar to this:

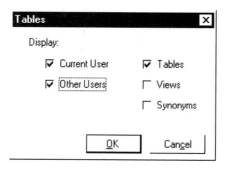

Select the Current User, Other Users, and Tables check boxes, and click the OK button. Pick any table from the list of tables you see and you will see a screen similar to the one in Figure 2-5. We have selected a table

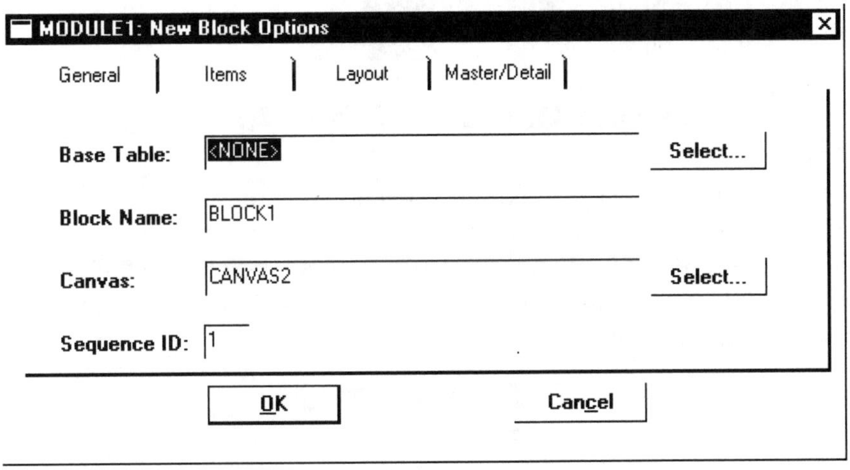

**FIGURE 2-4.**  *New Block window in Developer/2000 Forms Designer*

called EMPLOYEE owned by a user called DEMO in our example. You can type any name in the Block Name field or take the default and click the OK button. Your sample application is now ready.

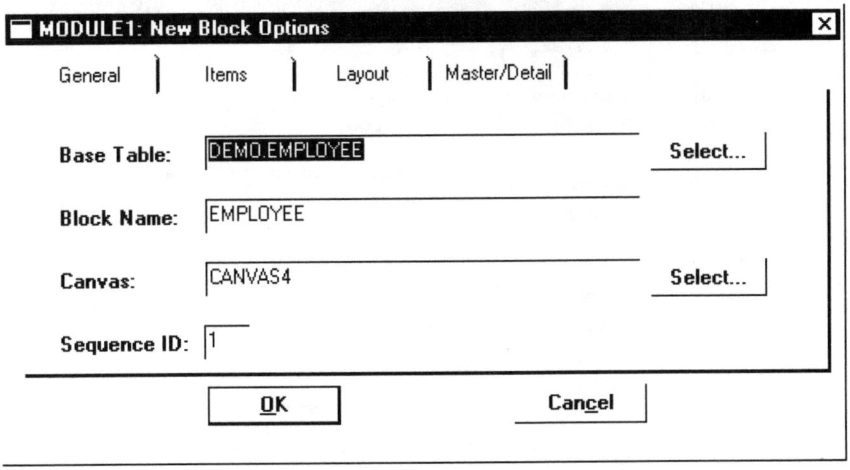

**FIGURE 2-5.**  *Base Table and Block Name selection*

## Step 7: Run Sample Application

Run the sample application by choosing File|Run.

## Step 8: Ensure that Database Tables Are Properly Installed

Now that we have managed to run a small application, we can try saving this to the database. First, ensure that you have selected the option to save to the database. Select Options in the Tools menu and choose the Designer options as shown in Figure 2-6. Then select the option File|Save and choose the options as shown here:

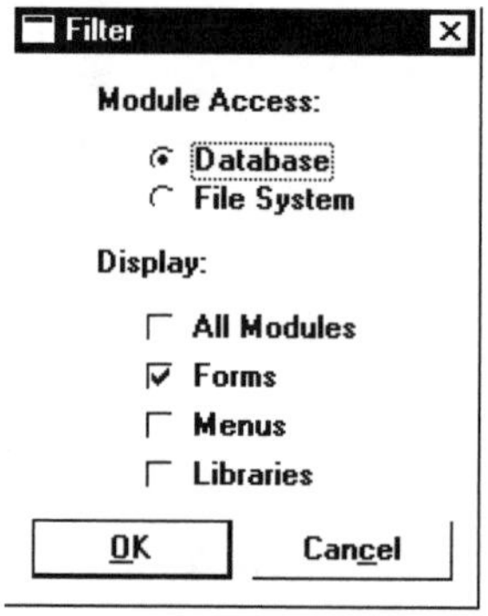

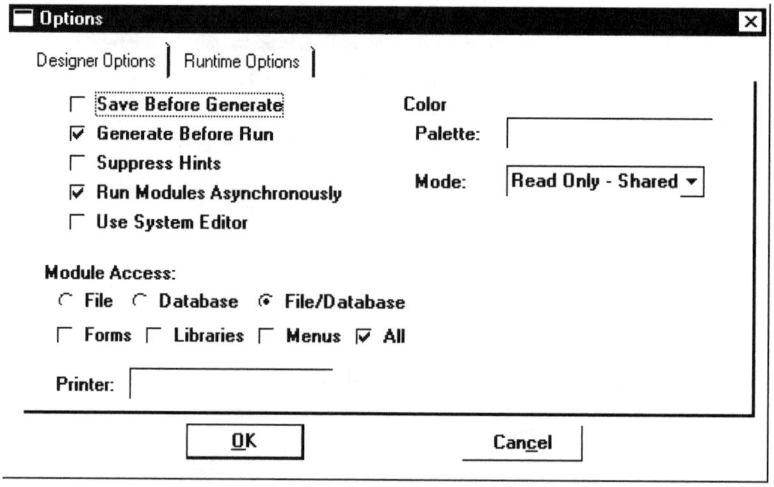

**FIGURE 2-6.** *Designer options in Developer/2000 Forms*

Click the OK button to save the application to the database. If you do not get any errors, you have confirmed that Developer/2000 Forms and Personal Oracle7 are installed properly. Note that while it is easy to save an application to the file system, in a multi-user environment you typically will have to save applications to the database so that they can be shared by many users. If you are not concerned about saving applications to the database, you can ignore the step to create the database tables (Step 5). However, if you are planning to save applications to the database, this is a useful exercise.

### Step 9: Running 16-bit Windows 3.1 Applications in this Configuration

If you are planning to run a 16-bit Windows 3.1 Oracle application with Personal Oracle7 on Windows 95 (both on the same PC), most of the information in Steps 1 through 8 still applies to you. You can use these applications in the same manner as 32-bit applications. However, you must ensure that the 16-bit applications are installed in a different folder structure on the PC, such as C:\ORAWIN, and not in the same C:\ORAWIN95. You can leave the connect string field blank or type **2:**.

# A Client-Server Installation

A client-server installation is one in which an Oracle tool is used to build an application by connecting to an Oracle7 database that is running on a separate machine. The connectivity is obtained by using Oracle's SQL*Net software. For more information on SQL*Net, please refer to Chapter 8 of this book. We will illustrate a client-server installation with an application using Developer/2000 Forms 4.5 with Oracle7 running on a Sun Solaris 2.5 machine across TCP/IP. The salient steps are listed below:

1. Verify network connectivity between the PC and the Solaris machine.

2. Verify that SQL*Net is installed correctly on the Solaris machine.

3. Install Developer/2000 Forms 4.5 for Windows 95.

4. Install SQL*Net V2 for Windows 95.

5. Verify connectivity to Oracle7 on the Solaris machine via SQL*Net from the PC.

6. Install database tables for Developer/2000 Forms.

7. Create a sample application using Developer/2000 Forms.

8. Run the sample application and save it to the database.

9. Run 16-bit Windows 3.1 applications in this configuration.

## Step 1: Verify Network Connectivity Between the PC and the Solaris Machine

Oracle's SQL*Net relies on the underlying network layer to provide connectivity between the client and server. The first step in a client-server application must be to verify this network connectivity.

Install TCP/IP on the Solaris machine. Configure TCP/IP on your PC by using the program labeled Network in the Control Panel. Once TCP/IP software is installed and configured on the PC and the Solaris machine, we can verify connectivity.

From the PC, use a Ping or Telnet utility to ensure that the Solaris machine is visible on the network. Be sure to note the server name and/or IP address of the Solaris machine. Now, from the Solaris machine, Ping the PC. Both of these checks must be successful.

## Step 2: Verify that SQL*Net is Installed Correctly on the Solaris Machine

Install SQL*Net V2 and SQL*Net TCP/IP adapter on the Solaris machine per the installation guide. Create the **TNSNAMES.ORA**, **LISTENER.ORA**, and **SQLNET.ORA** files per instructions. In the **TNSNAMES.ORA** file, create a SQL*Net V2 alias definition for Oracle7 on the Solaris machine called *mydb*.

**NOTE**
*Sample SQL*Net configuration files are
provided in the media supplied with this book.*

Start the listener and ensure that it is running properly:

```
% lsnrctl start          /* Start the listener */
% lsnrctl stat           /* Status of the listener */
```

Now, attempt a loop-back test, i.e. use a tool such as SQL*DBA or Server Manager on the server and connect back to the same server using SQL*Net:

```
% sqldba
sqldba> connect scott/tiger
```

If the above command lets you connect successfully, it shows that
Oracle7 is running on the Solaris machine.

```
sqldba> connect scott/tiger@mydb
```

If the above command lets you connect successfully, it shows that
SQL*Net is installed properly on the Solaris machine.

## Step 3: Install Developer/2000 Forms 4.5 for Windows 95

At this time, you are ready to install an Oracle application development
tool of your choice on the PC. We will use Developer/2000 Forms 4.5
(from Developer/2000) in our example. Start the Oracle Installer on the PC,
and choose to install Developer/2000 Forms 4.5. The installer will copy all
the files related to Developer/2000 Forms 4.5.

## Step 4: Install SQL*Net V2 for Windows 95

Since we are using TCP/IP, we now have to install SQL*Net V2 TCP/IP for
Windows 95 on the PC. In the Oracle Installer, choose to install the
components SQL*Net V2 (sometimes called SQL*Net V2 client) and the
SQL*Net V2 TCP/IP Protocol Adapter.

Now, create the SQL*Net configuration files **TNSNAMES.ORA** and
**SQLNET.ORA** on the PC. If you do not already have these files from a
previous installation, it is best to copy these files from the Solaris machine
using the FTP utility. The **TNSNAMES.ORA** and **SQLNET.ORA** on the
Solaris machine are usually located in the $ORACLE_HOME/network
/admin directory. FTP these files to the C:\ORAWIN95\NETWORK
\ADMIN folder on the PC. The **TNSNAMES.ORA** file should now contain
the SQL*Net V2 alias mydb that we created earlier.

## Step 5: Verify Connectivity to Oracle7 on the Solaris Machine via SQL*Net from the PC

Start Developer/2000 Forms Designer and ensure that you can connect to
the database. Choose the Connect option from the File menu, or press
CTRL-N for the login screen. Type a user name and password for a valid

Oracle user. If you are unsure, you may use an account created by Oracle. The user name is *scott* and the password is *tiger*. Type **mydb** in the field for the connect string. You should see the status *<Con>* in the status bar at the bottom of the Developer/2000 Forms Designer screen. The item Disconnect should also now be available in the File menu. Be sure to Exit from the Developer/2000 Forms Designer at this time.

## Step 6: Install Database Tables for Developer/2000 Forms

We are now ready to create the database tables required by Developer/2000 Forms. Revert to the Oracle Installer and choose to install the component Developer/2000 Forms Database Tables (you may need to expand the component Developer/2000 Database Tables).

You must have SQL*Plus for Windows 95 installed in order to run the scripts that create the necessary database tables. If you do not have SQL*Plus installed, use the Oracle Installer to do so before attempting the next step.

1. Click Start and then Programs|Developer 2000 Admin for Win95|Common Build.

2. Run Programs|Developer 2000 Admin for Win95|Common Grant.

3. Run Programs|Developer 2000 Admin for Win95|Forms Build.

4. Run Programs|Developer 2000 Admin for Win95|Forms Grant.

Each of the steps above invoke SQL*Plus and run SQL scripts. You should get a log file from these SQL scripts. Pay close attention for any errors in running these scripts. You are now ready to verify that the Developer/2000 Forms product is installed properly by creating a small sample application.

## Step 7: Create a Sample Application Using Developer/2000 Forms

Start the Developer/2000 Forms Designer again and connect to the database as in Step 5.

Create a sample application per instructions given in the section on stand-alone applications.

### Step 8: Run the Sample Application and Save it to the Database

Run the sample application and try saving the application to the database per the instructions in the section on stand-alone applications earlier in this chapter.

### Step 9: Running 16-bit Windows 3.1 Applications in this Configuration

It is possible to use Oracle 16-bit Windows 3.1 applications on Windows 95 and connect to a remote Oracle7 server. You must install your application and SQL*Net V2 for Windows 3.1 into a separate folder, such as C:\ORAWIN. You can now connect to the remote Oracle7 server using the instructions in Chapter 1 for a client-server application. You must place the **TNSNAMES.ORA** and **SQLNET.ORA** files in the C:\ORAWIN \NETWORK\ADMIN folder. Note that 32-bit SQL*Net for Windows 95 will not work with 16-bit Windows 3.1 applications.

# Third-Party Products

Sometimes it is necessary to use an application built with a third-party tool, such as Microsoft Visual Basic, with Oracle7. This can be accomplished rather easily using the ODBC standard. More information on ODBC is available in the "An Overview of ODBC" section of Chapter 8 in this book.

We will use a sample Microsoft Visual Basic application with a Personal Oracle7 database. Note that you can just as easily connect to a remote Oracle7 database using a combination of ODBC on Windows 95 and SQL*Net. The only piece of information that changes is the SQL*Net connect string. The steps are listed below:

1. Install and verify Personal Oracle7 for Windows 95.

2. Install and configure Oracle7 ODBC driver for Windows 95.

3. Test ODBC installation using the Oracle ODBC sample executable.

4. Install Microsoft Visual Basic per instructions in Microsoft documentation.

5. Verify connectivity using a sample application with Oracle7.

### Step 1: Install and Verify Personal Oracle7 for Windows 95

Install and verify the installation of Personal Oracle7 for Windows 95 per instructions in the installation guide and by following the guidelines provided earlier in this chapter.

### Step 2: Install and Configure Oracle7 ODBC Driver for Windows 95

Create a backup of C:\WINDOWS\**ODBC.INI** and C:\WINDOWS\**ODBCINST.INI** if present. Now, install the Oracle7 ODBC driver using the Oracle Installer per the installation guide. Create a ODBC database definition per instructions in the installation guide. You can use the 32-bit ODBC icon in the Control Panel of Windows 95. For the database name, type the text string **2:** if you are using Personal Oracle7. If you are connecting to a remote Oracle7 server, provide the SQL*Net V2 alias name here. Ensure that C:\ORAWIN95\BIN is in your path.

### Step 3: Test ODBC Installation Using the Oracle ODBC Sample Executable

Oracle Corporation provides an ODBC sample program with its installation. Your Oracle ODBC driver documentation should have details on using this. A similar sample application is also provided with this book. Run the ODBC sample application and you should see a screen similar to that shown in Figure 2-7. Connect to the Oracle7 database and execute the sample query as shown in Figure 2-8. If you can successfully retrieve data, the Oracle7 ODBC driver is installed correctly. If you get an error similar to the one shown here,

ensure that C:\ORAWIN95\BIN is in your path.

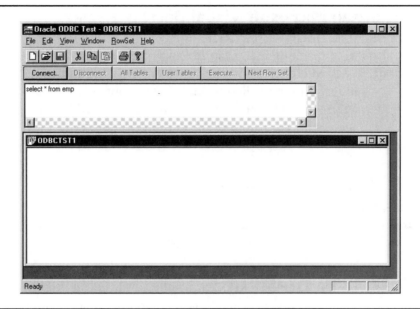

**FIGURE 2-7.** *Oracle's ODBC sample under Windows 95*

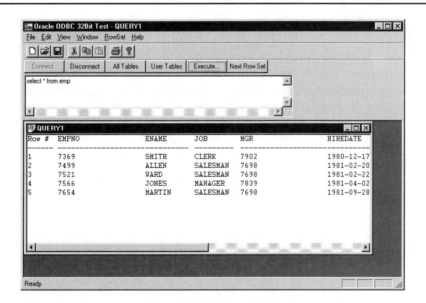

**FIGURE 2-8.** *Query results from Oracle ODBC driver*

### Step 4: Install Microsoft Visual Basic per Instructions in Microsoft Documentation

We will also take a quick look at a sample application using Microsoft Visual Basic. Install Microsoft Visual Basic for Windows 95 including the sample applications. A folder called SAMPLES will contain all the sample applications. At the time of writing this book, a sample application called **VISDATA** was available. You can use this to test connectivity to Oracle7 via ODBC.

### Step 5: Verify Connectivity Using a Sample Application with Oracle7

Run the **VISDATA** application and open the Oracle7 database using File|Open. Run a few queries on any of the available tables.

## Non-Oracle RDBMS

The final combination is one in which you want to use an application built with Oracle's client tools with a non-Oracle ODBC-compliant database. We will create a sample report on a table named Customer in a Microsoft Access database using Developer/2000 Reports.

1. Install Developer/2000 Reports Designer and Microsoft Access for Windows 95. Ensure that you install the ODBC component by using the custom installation process. A component called *Oracle Open Client Adapter for ODBC* should now be showing in the list of installed products.

2. Start Microsoft Access and create a table called Customer with some definition and save it to a database called Test.

3. Create an ODBC database definition called **acctest** for the database Test. You can use the 32-bit ODBC icon in the Control Panel to do this.

4. Start Developer/2000 Reports and connect using the definition acctest as shown here:

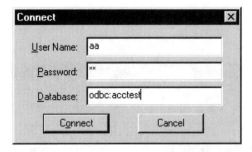

**5.** You need to provide **odbc:<name of ODBC database definition>** for the connect string. You can also bring up a list of all available databases by using the connect string **ODBC:*** as shown here:

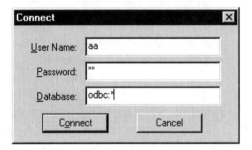

**6.** Now you should see a listing similar to the one shown here if you click the Connect button:

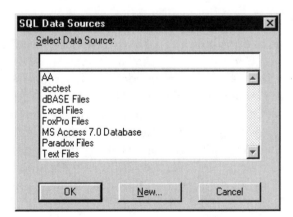

**7.** Notice the definition called acctest in the listing. You might see an error similar to this one:

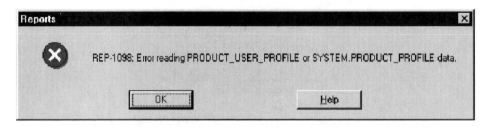

**8.** This is because the Access database does not have some system tables used by Developer/2000 Reports at start up. Click the OK button if you get this error—it is fairly harmless.

**9.** Create a sample report based on the table Customer in the database defined by the definition acctest and run it. One point to note here is that Developer/2000 Reports will not be able to provide a listing of all the tables in the database Test since Microsoft Access does not have the necessary data dictionary tables to provide such functionality. While designing the report, you can enter a SQL string similar to **select * from customer** and this should provide the expected results.

# Tuning

Many applications on Windows 95 have rather large requirements for resources on the PC to perform in a satisfactory manner. All products distributed by Oracle have recommended hardware and software requirements which are documented in the installation guide. We provide a few simple tips that should help you improve the performance of some of the complex products such as Developer/2000. Some of these tips have been compiled from a variety of sources at Microsoft Corporation. We also present few tips specific to Developer/2000. We encourage you to make backup copies of your configuration files before taking any suggestions in this document. Some of these changes may have adverse effects on other Windows applications.

## Hard Disk Optimization

Keep your hard disk optimized. A fragmented hard disk greatly impacts Windows performance, especially when a swap file is necessary. Use a hard disk optimizer program on a regular basis to keep your disk contiguous. It is also a good habit to run a utility like Microsoft ScanDisk on a regular basis. This is available standard with the Windows 95 Explorer. One word of caution if you are using Personal Oracle7: Always shut down the database and back-up all your database files (see Chapter 7 on the Oracle7 RDBMS if you need help with this) before running any such utilities. Such utilities have been known to corrupt database files occasionally.

## Virtual Memory

We suggest that you provide your own virtual memory settings versus letting Windows 95 manage it automatically. However, if you are allowing Windows 95 to manage virtual memory, ensure sufficient free disk space for a swap file. We suggest that you ensure 15 to 20MB of free disk space at all times for the Windows 95 swap file. Unpredictable behavior can result if Windows 95 is unable to create a swap file as needed. Use the System icon in the Control Panel to set virtual memory (under the Performance tab). Also ensure that virtual memory is not disabled.

## Reports Server (Developer/2000 Reports Only)

Execution of Developer/2000 Reports can be enhanced considerably by adding the Oracle Reports Server executable C:\ORAWIN95\BIN \**R25SRV32.EXE** to your Windows StartUp group. Note that this will increase the start-up time for Windows 95, but will definitely improve the performance of Developer/2000.

# Frequently Asked Questions (FAQ)

**Q.** I have a whole bunch of applications that were written for Windows 3.1. Can I use these with Windows 95?

**A.** Generally, all 16-bit Windows 3.1 applications will work with no changes on Windows 95. You must, however, be careful to ensure that Oracle Windows 3.1 and Oracle Windows 95 products are installed in separate folder structures. For example, if you have installed all Windows 3.1 products in C:\ORAWIN, install all Windows 95 products in C:\ORAWIN95. Table 2-4 should clarify the compatibility issues.

| | Win 3.1 | Win 3.11 (32-bit client) | Win 95 (16-bit client) | Win 95 (32-bit client) | Win NT 3.51 | Win NT 4.0 |
|---|---|---|---|---|---|---|
| Oracle 16-bit tools | Yes | Yes | Yes | Yes | Yes | No |
| Oracle 16-bit tools with 16-bit SQL*Net | Yes | Yes | Yes | Yes | Yes | No |
| SQL*Net 16-bit version 2.0 or higher | Yes | Yes | Yes | Yes | Yes | No |
| SQL*Net 32-bit version 2.2 | No | No | No | Yes | Yes | No |
| SQL*Net 32-bit version 2.3.2 or higher | No | No | No | Yes | Yes | Yes |
| Oracle 32-bit tools | No | No | Yes | Yes | Yes | Yes[1] |
| Oracle 32-bit tools with 16-bit SQL*Net | No | No | No | No | No | No |
| Oracle 32-bit tools with 32-bit SQL*Net | No | No | Yes | Yes | Yes | Yes[1] |

[1]Products shipped with Oracle7 Server for NT 7.3.2.2.0 and above only.

**TABLE 2-4.** *Oracle 16-bit and 32-bit Compatibility Matrix*

**Q.**  I have the option to use both Developer/2000 for Windows 3.1 and Developer/2000 for Windows 95. Which one should I use?
**A.**  In general, it is better to use 16-bit Windows applications on Windows 3.1 and 32-bit applications on Windows 95 (or Windows NT). Avoid using 16-bit applications on Windows 95, if possible. If you have both options, we suggest that you choose 32-bit applications on Windows 95.

**Q.**  During installation, I saw a message that said something about copying files to my WINDOWS\SYSTEM folder. What was that?
**A.**  Oracle Developer/2000 needs some files that provide support for OLE, ODBC, and Visual Basic. These files are provided by Microsoft but are copied into the WINDOWS\SYSTEM folder. The files that are copied are:

| | |
|---|---|
| **MSVCRT2X.DLL** | **COMDLG32.OCX** |
| **OC30.DLL** | **MFCANS32.DLL** |
| **ODBC32.DLL** | **ODBCINT.DLL** |
| **CTL3D32.DLL** | |

Normally, this should not impact existing applications.

**Q.**  I want to make a copy of Oracle settings in the Windows registry. What do I need to do?
**A.**  You can use **regedit** to make a file with Oracle settings in the Windows registry. Run **regedit** and select the key HKEY_LOCAL_MACHINE \SOFTWARE\ORACLE. Choose Registry|Export Registry File. You can later use Registry|Import Registry File to recover any lost settings.

**Q.**  I want to install Oracle products for Windows 95 on a file server and then share these across many clients. What do I have to do?
**A.**  Follow these steps:

  **1.** Install the necessary products to the network drive using the Oracle Installer from one of the clients.

  **2.** Run **regedit**, expand HKEY_LOCAL_MACHINE, then SOFTWARE and highlight Oracle. Export the registry by choosing Registry|Export Registry File.

  **3.** Copy this file to all necessary clients.

  **4.** From these clients, run Windows Explorer and double-click the registry file (**.REG**) that you have just copied.

5. Include C:\ORAWIN95\BIN in the path.

6. Run the Oracle Installer and choose to install the component System Support Files if your product needs them (such as Developer/2000 or ODBC). You must do a selective product install.

7. Using the installer, click the Restore Icons button to create items for all the products.

8. If you are using ODBC, run the 32-bit ODBC utility in the Control Panel and create data sources as needed.

**Q.** I have Oracle 32-bit software. Should I use Windows 95 or Windows NT?
**A.** You can use Windows 95 or Windows NT (Some Oracle products are only supported on Windows NT 3.51. Refer to the Table 2-4 earlier in this chapter to verify whether your version of Windows NT is supported). Generally speaking, Windows 95 is better for a stand-alone environment since it is easier to use.

**Q.** I have installed Oracle software on Windows 95. I am running low on disk space. Can I delete something safely and still use the Oracle software?
**A.** Most of Oracle tools come with demos and a quick tour. You can use the Oracle software to de-install these safely. You can recover about 20 to 80MB of disk space depending on the products you have installed. Also, remember to empty your recycle bin. In most cases, Windows 95 will prompt you if you are low on available disk space.

**Q.** Can I use the Windows Universal Naming Convention (UNC) with Oracle products?
**A** Until recently, Oracle only supported the standard DOS 8.3 naming conventions. Some of the newer products, such as Oracle Developer/2000 for Windows 95 Release 1.3, do support UNC. Consult your installation guide for details on this issue. However, we recommend that you use the DOS 8.3 file naming convention as far as possible because this works in all versions of all Windows products. You should also not use the '\\' notation for directory paths.

**Q.** How do I connect to Personal Oracle7 for Windows 95 from other machines?

**A**   You cannot. Personal Oracle7 for Windows 95 is for stand-alone machines only. You may use Oracle Workgroup Server for Windows NT as an alternative.

**Q.**   I want to verify the ODBC driver that I have installed. How do I go about doing this?
**A**   You can run the 32-bit ODBC executable in the Windows Control Panel. Click the Drivers button and then select the Oracle7x driver and click About to obtain complete information about the ODBC driver.

**Q.**   What is Oracle's Open Client Adapter (OCA). How is this related to ODBC?
**A**   The OCA allows Oracle tools to connect to non-Oracle RDBMS. It makes Oracle tools ODBC-compliant. The Oracle7 ODBC driver on the other hand, allows non-Oracle ODBC-compliant tools to connect to an Oracle7 database. In some sense, the Oracle7 ODBC driver makes Oracle RDBMS ODBC-compliant.

**Q.**   Can I use Oracle7 ODBC driver with SQL*Net?
**A**   Absolutely! You can use a non-Oracle application on Windows 95 with a remote Oracle7 database. In such a case, you would need the ODBC driver as well as SQL*Net. You need to specify SQL*Net connect information in the ODBC database definition.

# CHAPTER
## 3

# Preventive Maintenance
# on MS-Windows NT

icrosoft's Windows NT has become a popular operating system on the desktop for advanced users. Windows NT provides more protection for applications and security to the users. Its popularity is only rising with the new look and feel of Windows 95 given to Windows NT 4.0. Oracle has a range of products from client-tools to the RDBMS that have taken advantage of the features of Windows NT. For the most part, the concepts detailed in Chapter 2 on Windows 95 also apply to Windows NT. The installation procedures are almost identical to Windows 95 and will not be repeated here. We will only provide information on aspects of Windows NT that are different from Windows 95.

**NOTE**
*The screens and commands on Windows NT might differ slightly from Windows 95, but we decided not to repeat information unnecessarily since Windows NT 4.0 has almost an identical look to Windows 95.*

# Pre-Installation Tasks

As with Chapters 1 and 2, we begin with information that will help you complete a smooth installation. We recommend that you take a few moments to complete these pre-installation tasks.

## Verify Availability of Resources

As always, the first step should be to verify that you have sufficient resources to run the product(s) of your choice. We have some general recommendations that are listed here for your reference:

- Use an IBM, Compaq or 100 percent compatible PC. We suggest a Pentium-based 90 MHz or better PC.

- We suggest 32 MB of RAM if you are using Oracle Workgroup Server for Windows NT by itself. We suggest 32 MB RAM if you are using Developer/2000 Designer tools with a remote database, and 64 MB for optimal performance if you are using Developer/2000 with a local Oracle database.

■ Access to a CD-ROM drive, local or on the network, to perform the installation as Oracle software is not distributed on floppy disk media.

■ We also recommend that you assign at least 20 MB for virtual memory.

**NOTE**
*Oracle Developer/2000 and Oracle Workgroup Server for Windows NT represent high-end products on Windows NT. Less complex products will function optimally with lesser hardware resources.*

## Backup Configuration Information

The installation process of Oracle products on Windows NT does modify (or even add) a few configuration files on your PC. You can use the standard COPY command provided by DOS or use the Windows Explorer to create copies of the files shown below. We will assume that C:\ is your boot drive, Windows NT is installed in C:\WINNT, Oracle 16-bit Windows 3.1 products are installed in C:\ORAWIN, and Oracle 32-bit Windows NT products are installed in C:\ORANT throughout this chapter.

| | |
|---|---|
| **AUTOEXEC.BAT** | Resides in the boot drive of your PC, C:\. |
| **WIN.INI** | Resides in the Windows home, C:\WINNT. |
| **ODBC.INI** | Only for ODBC installations; located in C:\WINNT. All ODBC database definitions are stored in this file. |
| **NT.RGS** | If you already have Windows NT products from Oracle installed, you will have this file in C:\WINNT\ORAINST. This file contains a listing of all Oracle Windows NT products installed on your PC and is used by the Oracle Installer for Windows NT to determine installed components at any time. |
| **TNSNAMES.ORA** | If you have Oracle SQL*Net V2 installed, you will have this file in C:\ORANT\NETWORK\ADMIN. |
| **SQLNET.ORA** | If you have Oracle SQL*Net V2 installed, you will have this file in C:\ORANT\NETWORK\ADMIN. |
| **TOPOLOGY.ORA** | This file is located in C:\ORANT\NETWORK\ADMIN, if present from a previous installation. |

We recommend that you create a folder such as C:\ORANT\BACKUP and copy the above files into this folder. Information obtained from these files can be very useful to Oracle Worldwide Customer Support in resolving your issues.

In addition, it is also a good habit to make a copy of your Windows Registry. To accomplish this, run **regedit** on Windows NT, expand *HKEY_LOCAL_MACHINE -> SOFTWARE -> ORACLE*. Now select *File->Export Registry File* and provide an appropriate name for the file to store your registry. If you ever want to import this registry file, you can just double-click on the file in the Windows Explorer.

## Other Tasks

It is important to ensure the integrity of your hard disk before starting your installation. Refer to the section titled "3. Other Tasks" in Chapter 2 for Windows 95. All those tasks apply equally for Windows NT.

## Special Tasks for File Server Installations

Be sure to assign a permanent drive letter to the folder containing Oracle products if you are installing these on a file server. Once you have used *Map Network Drive* in the Windows Explorer, do not modify the drive letter after installing Oracle products.

# Understanding the Oracle Installation Process on Windows NT

The installation process for Oracle products on Windows NT is identical to Windows 95. Refer to Chapter 2 for details. The only differences are that the Oracle default folder is WINNT and the installation files are named NT rather than WIN95. For example, the product listing file would be **NT.PRD** instead of **WIN95.PRD.**

The post-installation tasks and the types of installations are also identical to Windows 95 and we will not repeat those sections here.

# Tuning Windows NT

In this section we present some ideas that should help the NT administrator tune the Windows NT server for the Oracle RDBMS. A lot of improvement in performance can be obtained by tuning I/O (Input/Output). In addition, there are a few tasks to ensure that users see the best response time possible. We also recommend that you read the "Performance Tuning" section in Chapter 7.

It is important to ensure that there is little or no waiting on I/O. This indicates that the system processors always have some work to do while there are outstanding I/Os. You can verify this by running the Windows NT Performance Monitor and observing the processor utilization, the disk utilization, the length of the processor queue, and the threads performing I/O operations. You should also observe disk activity by using the Performance Monitor. You might need to run the **diskperf** utility (with the *-y* option) that comes with Windows NT to activate your system's disk-performance measurement. If you run **diskperf** you will need to shut down and restart your system.

Most of the system-processor utilization is allocated to the shadow threads for Oracle and *not* the background threads. Use the Performance Monitor to verify the system-processor utilization at the Oracle thread level. Make sure that the users' shadow threads are getting the majority of the system processor. Also, ensure that a large percentage of processor time is spent on user tasks (user time) and not on privileged tasks. You can view such information using the Windows NT Performance Monitor.

An extra tip that we would like to bring to your attention (in addition to those mentioned for Windows 95) is that you should make your foreground and background applications equally responsive. You can use the System icon in the Control Panel and select the Tasking button to set this option.

# Backing Up the Oracle7 Workgroup Server on Windows NT

GUI utilities on Windows NT make it a popular server platform for the Oracle7 RDBMS. The administration tasks are fairly simple and intuitive for most users. We will now present information that will help Windows NT administrators back up the Oracle7 Server. We would like to caution you that it is *not* sufficient to copy all the Oracle files to a secondary location while the database is in use. We have often seen users copying the entire ORANT directory to tape and assuming that it is a valid backup!

Many users of Oracle on Windows NT are unsure about a proper strategy for a database backup. We suggest that you take a *cold database backup* if you can afford to shut down the database completely at some fixed time during the 24 hour day. If you cannot afford to shut down the database, then you must take an *online backup.* We will provide examples of both strategies that can be used on your Windows NT machine.

# Cold Backup

A cold backup is only feasible if you can shut down your database completely. It is also possible to automate this task if you have a fixed time for a shutdown using the **at** command of Windows NT. Alternatively, you can use the GUI version of the Scheduler that is shipped with the Windows Resource Kit.

The overall procedure consists of three steps:

**1.** Shut down the database.

**2.** Back up all the files using a COPY facility.

**3.** Restart the database.

We will now illustrate the process with both the GUI version of the Scheduler and by using the **at** command in Windows NT.

First, ensure that the service for Scheduler has already been started. You can verify this by using the Services applet in the Control Panel. Ensure that the Scheduler is started.

Next, create a batch file, say, **orabak.bat**, and add the following statements to this file (we are assuming that you have Oracle RDBMS version 7.2 and all the database-related files are located in the *rdbms72* folder. You must provide appropriate directory paths for your installation):

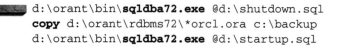

```
d:\orant\bin\sqldba72.exe @d:\shutdown.sql
copy d:\orant\rdbms72\*orcl.ora c:\backup
d:\orant\bin\sqldba72.exe @d:\startup.sql
```

Next, create a **shutdown.sql** file that contains the following:

```
set instance P:<NT Server Name:>ORCL
connect internal/<password>
shutdown immediate
exit
```

**NOTE**
*In the above script, we are doing a Shutdown
Immediate to ensure that the database shuts
down even if there are users connected to the
database.*

Now create a file called **startup.sql** that contains the following:

```
set instance P:<NT Server Name>:ORCL
connect internal/<password>
startup
exit
```

If you have several databases, then you need to modify your **startup.sql**
and **shutdown.sql** files to include all of them. In the above example, we
have used the default Oracle database with an SID of "ORCL".

Now you can schedule your backup job in Windows NT. Start the NT
Scheduler and click on Add. In the command line, enter the full path of the
**orabak.bat** file that we created and enter the time to run the batch file.
Alternatively, you can issue the following command from the NT DOS
command prompt:

```
d:> at <time> <command>
```

For example, to run our **orabak.bat** file at 2:00 A.M., you could use the
command

```
d:> at 02:00 "d:\orabak.bat"
```

# Online Backup

It is not always possible to shut down a database completely in order to
perform a cold backup. In this case, it is necessary to perform the backup

while users are connected to the database, i.e., the database is in use. We will illustrate this process here.

**NOTE**
*Throughout this section we will assume that Windows NT is installed in C:\WINNT and Oracle7 (Version 7.3) for NT is installed in D:\ORANT. We are also using the default installation of Oracle on NT with a default SID of "ORCL".*

The first task is to ensure that Oracle7 runs in *archivelog mode*. This is necessary in order to perform an online backup. Edit C:\WINNT \DATABASE\INITORCL.ORA and add the following lines:

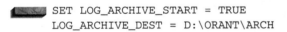
```
SET LOG_ARCHIVE_START = TRUE
LOG_ARCHIVE_DEST = D:\ORANT\ARCH
```

Do not use a drive that is configured for RAID for the destination of archive log files. Next, issue the following commands from Server Manager or SQLDBA to start the database in archive log mode.

```
SVRMGR23> CONNECT INTERNAL/<Password>
SVRMGR23> STARTUP MOUNT
SVRMGR23> ALTER DATABASE ARCHIVELOG;
SVRMGR23> ALTER DATABASE OPEN;
SVRMGR23> ALTER SYSTEM SWITCH LOGFILE;
```

The last command is to ensure that an archive log file is created by forcing a log file switch. You now need to obtain the *oldest log sequence number*. In order to do this, issue the following command:

```
SVRMGR23> ARCHIVE LOG LIST
Database log mode            ARCHIVELOG
Automatic archival           ENABLED
Archive destination          d:\orant\arch
Oldest online log sequence    59
Next log sequence to archive  61
Current log sequence          61
```

In the example above, the oldest online log sequence is 59. This means that you need to retain all archive log files starting with sequence number

59 (the name of the log file itself depends on the *log_archive_format* setting in your **initorcl.ora** file. Nevertheless, it will have 59 in it) as part of your online backup.

You are now ready to run scripts that set your tablespaces for backup. The idea is to mark a tablespace ready for backup and then copy all datafiles associated with that tablespace to create a backup of that tablespace (if you are not sure what datafiles belong to a tablespace, you can query *DBA_TABLESPACES* and *DBA_DATA_FILES*). Once the copy operation is complete, you need to issue a command to mark the end of the backup. We will illustrate the backup of a tablespace called *user_data* in this example:

```
svrmgr23> @d:\temp\begin_user_backup.sql
```

The begin_user_backup.sql file contains:

```
connect system/manager
alter tablespace user_data begin backup;
exit;
```

Next, use the Oracle **ocopy** or Windows NT **copy** to copy all the files associated with the tablespace *user_data*.

```
d:\orant\bin\ocopy73 d:\orant\database\usr1orcl.ora
      d:\temp\usr1orcl.bak
```

Once you are finished copying all files associated with the tablespace being backed up, you need to issue a command to mark the end of backup.

```
svrmgr23> @d:\temp\end_user_backup.sql
```

The end_user_backup.sql file contains the following:

```
connect system/manager
alter tablespace user_data end backup;
exit;
```

You can also include the **copy** or **ocopy73** command in the script itself. If you wish to do this, you can use the **host** command in the SQL script. In our example above, you could combine all the commands into one SQL script similar to the following:

```
connect system/manager
alter tablespace user_data begin backup;
host d:\orant\bin\ocopy73 d:\orant\database\usr1orcl.ora d:\temp\usr1orcl.bak
alter tablespace user_data end backup;
exit;
```

Now, issue the **archive log list** command again to determine the *current log sequence number*. You need to retain all archive log files starting from the oldest log sequence number until the current log sequence number (63 in our example). These archive log files, along with the file d:\temp\usr1orcl.bak, provide a backup of the tablespace *user_data*. Again, you must force a log file switch by issuing an **alter system switch logfile**.

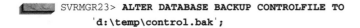
```
SVRMGR23> alter system switch logfile;
SVRMGR23> archive log list
Database log mode            ARCHIVELOG
Automatic archival           ENABLED
Archive destination          d:\orant\arch
Oldest online log sequence   61
Next log sequence to archive 63
Current log sequence         63
```

You can back up your control file using the command:

```
SVRMGR23> ALTER DATABASE BACKUP CONTROLFILE TO
     'd:\temp\control.bak';
```

### NOTE

*If you want to make a backup of Oracle files on tape, the* **ocopy73** *executable cannot be used. You must depend on Windows NT administrator utilities.*

# Frequently Asked Questions (FAQ)

We suggest that you also take a look at the FAQ section in Chapter 2. Most of that information does apply to Windows NT.

**Q.**  I have a whole bunch of applications that were written for Windows 3.1 and Windows 95. Can I use these with Windows NT?
**A.**  Generally, all 16-bit Windows 3.1 applications should work with no changes on Windows NT. You must, however, be careful to ensure that Oracle Windows 3.1 and Windows NT products are installed in separate folder structures. For example, if you have installed all Windows 3.1 products in C:\ORAWIN, install all Windows NT products in C:\ORANT. You will have to re-generate your Windows 3.1 and Windows 95 applications before using them on Windows NT. For example, if you have a Developer/2000 Forms 4.5 application of Windows 95, you can re-generate the **.FMX** files on Windows NT and use the application. Table 3-1 should clarify the compatibility issues.

**Q.**  I was told I cannot run Developer/2000 on Windows NT 4.0. Is that true?
**A.**  You can run Developer/2000 version 1.3.2 on Windows NT 4.0. This has been certified by Oracle Corporation in January 1997.

| Tools | Win NT 3.51 | Win NT 4.0 |
|---|---|---|
| Oracle 16-bit tools | Yes | No |
| Oracle 16-bit tools with 16-bit SQL*Net | Yes | No |
| SQL*Net 16-bit version 2.0 or higher | Yes | No |
| SQL*Net 32-bit version 2.2 | Yes | No |
| SQL*Net 32-bit version 2.3.2 or higher | Yes | Yes |
| Oracle 32-bit tools | Yes | Yes[1] |
| Oracle 32-bit tools with 16-bit SQL*Net | No | No |
| Oracle 32-bit tools with 32-bit SQL*Net | Yes | Yes[1] |

[1]Products shipped with Oracle7 Server for NT Version 7.3.2.2.0 and above only.

**TABLE 3-1.**  *Oracle 16-bit and 32-bit Compatibility Matrix on Windows NT*

**Q.** Can I use Oracle Workgroup Server for Windows NT as a true server? How do other clients connect to it?

**A.** Absolutely! Oracle Workgroup Server is meant for multiple clients. You can run SQL*Net Server on your Windows NT server and connect Oracle clients to this server. Refer to Chapter 8 in this book. We have included a description of setting up SQL*Net server on Windows NT.

**Q.** Can I use Windows NT authentication for Oracle? Why do I have to create a separate user account for Oracle?

**A.** Oracle allows for operating system authentication using what are termed OPS$ accounts. Refer to your Oracle7 Server documentation for more information on these accounts. We will show you how to create a simple OPS$ account on Windows NT.

First create a user account, say ABC, on the Windows NT Server using the User Manager program under the Administrative Tools group. Now connect to the Oracle database as a *DBA* user using SQL*DBA or SQL*PLUS and issue the SQL command:

```
SQL > CREATE USER OPS$ABC IDENTIFIED EXTERNALLY;
SQL > GRANT CONNECT TO OPS$ABC;
```

You can modify this account and define a default and temporary tablespace. We will assign a default tablespace of *USERS* and a temporary tablespace of *TEMP.*

```
SQL > ALTER USER OPS$ABC DEFAULT TABLESPACE USERS TEMPORARY
          TABLESPACE TEMP;
```

In order to connect to Oracle7, login as the *user* to the Windows NT server and then provide a '/' in the user name field on the login screen. This should connect you to Oracle.

**Q.** What about Windows 95 and Windows NT clients? Will the above solution work for them also?

**A.** You can use a Windows 95 or Windows NT client with an Oracle7 server running on Windows NT server and still use operating system authentication. If you are using SQL*Net Named Pipes (the default network protocol on Windows NT), no additional steps are required.

For other protocols, you will need to physically connect to the Windows NT Server as the defined *user* before OPS$ authentication will work. Here are the steps to accomplish this:

1. Go to the File Manager or Explorer on the server and *share* a directory using some name (*share as*).

2. Select the *Permissions* button and assign appropriate permissions to access the shared directory created in Step 1.

On the Windows 95 or Windows NT client login as the defined *user*, run File Manager or Explorer and select *Disk -> Connect Network Drive* to connect yourself to the directory shared on the server in Steps 1 and 2. You should be able to connect to the Oracle7 server using Windows NT authentication.

For the Oracle login information use '/@<*SQL\*Net alias*>'. The '/' substitutes the Oracle user name and password and the *SQL\*Net alias* is the alias defined in the **tnsnames.ora** on the client.

**Q.**  How do I ensure that the Oracle7 Server starts up automatically when I boot Windows NT?

**A.**  Some of the newer releases of Oracle7 Server on Windows NT do start up automatically when you boot Windows NT. Look for the Oracle services *OracleServiceORCL* and *OracleStartORCL* (Click on the icon labeled *Services* in the Control Panel), and ensure that these are set to *Automatic*.

If you do not have the services mentioned above, here is a workaround: First, create a Windows NT command file (a **.CMD** file). We will create a command file called C:\ORANT\**MYDB.CMD**. Place the following information in this command file:

```
C:\ORANT\BIN\ORADIM72 -startup -sid orcl -usrpwd oracle
     -starttype srvc, inst
```

In our example, we have an executable called **oradim72** (for Oracle 7.2) and we are starting up an Oracle instance with name *orcl*. The password for starting Oracle is *oracle*. We are specifying that we want to start the Oracle services using *srvc* and that we will also start the Oracle database instance with *inst*. Replace your instance and password information as required. You can also place commands to start more than one Oracle instance on your server. If you are using a different version of Oracle, you might have an **oradimXX** that is named slightly different. You can refer to Appendix I of the *Oracle7 Server User's Guide for Windows NT* for more information.

Run **regedit** and expand the tree in the registry HKEY_LOCAL_MACHINE -> SOFTWARE -> MICROSOFT ->

WINDOWSNT -> CURRENT VERSION -> WINLOGON. Edit the
WINLOGON entry and put an entry c:\orant\**mydb.cmd.**
    Reboot the Windows NT server and verify that the database does start.

**Q.** I have the choice of using either TCP/IP or Named Pipes for my
connectivity to Windows NT. Which is better for Oracle?
**A.** Oracle really has no preference. You need to consider a few things
before you make the decision. If you have a network that consists only of
Windows (3.1, 95 and NT) -based machines, you should probably stay with
Named Pipes since it is the native protocol. If you have a heterogeneous
network consisting of, say, UNIX machines that use TCP/IP, you should
probably configure both TCP/IP and Named Pipes. You can always
manipulate the protocol that you use to connect to Oracle by changing the
SQL*Net alias.

**Q.** I am using Oracle clients from Windows 95 to connect to an Oracle7
Server on a Windows NT server. Do I need to give the Windows 95 users
any kind of file permissions to the Oracle database files on the Windows
NT server?
**A.** No, you do not need to give any permissions for clients. The SQL*Net
listener on the Windows NT server takes care of all your connections to the
Oracle database. The permissions for database objects are taken care of at
the Oracle RDBMS level.

**Q.** Do I need to use the Windows NT Server in order to install an Oracle7
server or can I get by with Windows NT Workstation?
**A.** It is sufficient to use Windows NT Workstation for Oracle. In any case,
SQL*Net will take care of your connection requests to Oracle. However,
there might be licensing issues with Microsoft Windows NT itself. We
recommend that you consult with your Microsoft Windows NT vendor for
Microsoft licensing issues.

**Q.** How do I remove an Oracle installation from my Windows NT box?
**A.** You can use the Oracle Installer to remove the required products from
your Windows NT box. However, this can be slightly tedious. If you do not
want to retain *any* Oracle products for NT, you can follow these
instructions to get rid of all the Oracle products:

    **I.** First, stop all Oracle Services by using the Services applet in the
        Control Panel. All the Oracle services should have a name

containing 'ORCL' or 'Oracle' or 'TNS'. Highlight these one at a time and click the Stop button.

2. Next, run **regedit**, the Windows NT Registry Editor, and select *HKEY_LOCAL_MACHINE/SOFTWARE/ORACLE*. Delete this entry by using the DEL key.

3. Now, select *HKEY_LOCAL_MACHINE->SYSTEM/CurrentControlSet /Services*. Scroll down this list and delete all Oracle entries.

4. You can now delete the Oracle Program groups from the Desktop and the Oracle Toolbar icon from the Startup group.

5. Delete all the files associated with Oracle. Using NT Explorer, select the Oracle home directory, *C:\ORANT*, by default. Delete this entire directory and all its subdirectories. Also, delete the following files from the Windows NT home directory (normally, *C:\WINNT*):

```
ORACLE.INI        ORADIM.INI        OTOOLBAR.INI*
OTEMP.INI         VS10.INI*
```

6. If you have Oracle 16-bit Windows 3.1 applications (normally in the *C:\ORAWIN* folder), you can delete this folder also.

7. Finally, if you have a section labeled *[Oracle]* in your **WIN.INI** file, delete it.

# CHAPTER
## 4

# Preventive Maintenance
# on Solaris

racle Corporation makes products for many variants of UNIX. We will discuss issues related to Sun SPARC Solaris 2.x (2.3, 2.4, and 2.5) in this chapter. Oracle products fit into two categories: Oracle7 RDBMS and Tools. In addition, you might need connectivity software, such as SQL*Net. Almost all Oracle products for Sun SPARC Solaris 2.x are distributed on CD-ROM media. General tasks and tips for a successful installation are provided in this chapter. We also provide some information on the operating system aspects and utilities that should help the beginner system administrator.

**NOTE**
*Throughout this chapter, a reference to Solaris or Sun Solaris indicates Sun SPARC Solaris 2.x, a registered trademark owned by Sun Microsystems, Inc.*

# Pre-Installation Tasks

A few simple tasks will ease the installation process considerably. We recommend that you take a few moments to complete the following tasks:

## Verify Availability of Resources

Determine the hardware and software requirements of the products you wish to install. Every Oracle product set is distributed with an installation guide. Most of the product CDs also have installation instructions in the CD-ROM insert or include a **README** file. In the first few pages of the installation guide, you should find a table that lists the hardware and software requirements of that product. We will provide information on some utilities and commands that should help you verify if the necessary resources are available on your Solaris server.

We suggest that you check the disk space available on your machine by using the **df** command. On our test server, the output of **df -k** looked like this:

```
Filesystem         kbytes     used     avail   capacity  Mounted on
/dev/dsk/c0t3d0s0  96455      24285    62530   28%       /
/dev/dsk/c0t3d0s6  288391     194320   65241   75%       /usr
/proc              0          0        0       0%        /proc
fd                 0          0        0       0%        /dev/fd
/dev/dsk/c0t3d0s5  38383      17561    16992   51%       /var
/dev/dsk/c0t3d0s7  424239     360324   21495   95%       /home1
swap               118296     1132     117164  1%        /tmp
```

You can now take a look at the memory resources on your machine.
You will need to consider both physical memory and swap space. You can
use the **vmstat** command to view memory resources and **sar -r** to get free
memory and free swap space information. You can also use the **swap**
command if you can become root on your machine. We advise you to look
at the man pages for these commands for detailed information.

Next, we will look at the resources allocated to shared memory and
semaphores on your machine. On Solaris, these resources are specified in
/etc/system. Sample settings for these parameters on our test server are
shown below:

```
shmsys:shminfo_shmmax = 31457280
shmsys:shminfo_shmmin = 1
shmsys:shminfo_shmmni = 200
shmsys:shminfo_shmseg = 50
shmsys:seminfo_semmns = 200
shmsys:seminfo_semmni = 70
shmsys:seminfo_semmsl = 100
```

You can use the **ipcs - a** command to view the available resources for
shared memory, semaphores, and message queues on your machine. We
advise you to view the man pages for **ipcs** and **ipcrm.** There are several
helpful options to these commands.

You are now ready to check the operating system dependencies. Review
Chapter 1 of the installation guide and also any **README** that came with
your Oracle media. The required patches for the operating system,
compiler dependencies, and such information will be documented. We will
present a few more UNIX commands that will help you in this task.

To get a listing of the operating system version and patches, you can use
the **showrev** command. Alternatively, you could try using the **pkginfo**
command. An excerpt of the output from the **showrev** command on our
server is shown below:

```
% showrev -p
Patch : 101416-02  Obsoletes: Packages: SUNWcsu.2
     11.5.0,REV=2.0.18, PATCH=61
Patch : 101378-08  Obsoletes: Packages: SUNWcsr.2
     11.5.0,REV=2.0.19, PATCH=103
Patch : 101318-54  Obsoletes:
     101294-02,101267-01,101326-01,101349-01,101319-02
```

# Configure UNIX Environment

The last few tasks before starting the installation process are to configure and verify your environment settings. Many installation failures are caused by improper settings of some necessary environment variables.

First, ensure that you are logged in to your UNIX system as the right user. You need to log into your server as the UNIX user who is going to "own" the installation. Typically, this is a user called *oracle* who is a part of the *dba* group.

Next, ensure that the directories /bin, /usr/bin and /usr/ccs/bin are available in your path. You can use the **echo** command to complete this task.:

 `% echo $PATH`

You might have some additional directories in your path. If you have /usr/ucb in your path, make sure it is at the end of the list.

Next, set the required Oracle environment variables to appropriate values. Provide appropriate values in the angle brackets for your installation.

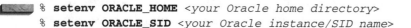 `% setenv ORACLE_HOME <your Oracle home directory>`
`% setenv ORACLE_SID <your Oracle instance/SID name>`

If you are using the character mode Oracle Installer, you need to set the ORACLE_TERM variable.

`% setenv ORACLE_TERM <value>`

Some common values for ORACLE_TERM are shown in Table 4-1.

We recommend that you use the Motif (GUI) version of the Oracle Installer, if it is available. It is much more user-friendly than the character

| ORACLE_TERM Setting | Type of Window | Keyboard Type |
|---|---|---|
| sun | **shelltool** or **cmdtool** | Type 4 |
| xsun | **xterm** -sf | Type 4 |
| sun5 | **shelltool** or **cmdtool** | Type 5 |
| xsun5 | **xterm** -sf | Type 5 |

**TABLE 4-1.**   *Settings for ORACLE_TERM on Sun SPARC Machines*

mode version. Ensure that the environment variable DISPLAY is set properly if you are using the Motif installer.

 `% setenv DISPLAY ourhost:0.0`

You can use the host name or the IP address of the UNIX host from which you are running the Oracle Installer.

Finally, use the **env** command to ensure that all the variables discussed here are set properly.

# The Oracle Installation Process on Sun Solaris 2.x

We will now take a look at the Oracle Installer and the installation process on Sun Solaris. Some minor errors during installation can be resolved with a better understanding of the files used by the installer during the installation process.

**NOTE**
*The concepts discussed in this section are very much applicable to other implementations of UNIX.*

## Preview of the Oracle Installer

The Oracle Installer on Sun Solaris performs three primary tasks:

- It checks dependencies.
- It copies the necessary product files.
- It configures the system environment.

First, the Oracle Installer verifies that sufficient disk space is available to install the desired products. It then verifies that other Oracle dependencies are satisfied. Oracle products on Solaris share a substantial portion of code that is made available under components like Required Support Files. If you already have an Oracle product installed, the installer will verify that dependencies related to this shared code are satisfied for the new product. The installer will upgrade the common software components only if required.

Next, the Oracle Installer copies the required files for every product. The files are placed in appropriate directories automatically. The Oracle Installer will allow the user to choose the directory in which a product is installed. However, all the executables are placed in a directory $ORACLE_HOME/bin.

# Important Installation Files

The Oracle Installer uses some key files. A brief description of these files is provided for your reference and understanding of the installation process. Even though all the files below are plain text files, *do not manually modify or delete these files at any time*. You are free to view them at any time to understand the installation process used by Oracle. If you are unable to find any of these files, try searching the contents of your installation media using the find utility.

### unix.prd

This file contains a listing of all products and their components available on the installation media. The installer reads this file to get a listing of available products on the media. It typically resides in a directory called **install** on the installation media. If you want to quickly determine the products available on any media for Oracle products on Solaris without invoking the installer, you can look at this file in an editor like **vi**.

In addition to **unix.prd** there are several **partial.prd** files that contain the components for each product. These files are under the product directories on the installation media.

### unix.ins

This file contains the Oracle installation script used by the installer. It is typically located in the install directory on the installation media. In addition to this file, every product typically has an installation script in its product directory on the media.

### unix.dei

This file contains the Oracle de-install script used by the installer. It is also located in the **install** directory on the installation media. It gets copied to the $ORACLE_HOME/orainst directory during installation. In addition to this file, every product typically has a de-install script in its product directory on the media.

### unix.stp

This file contains the script that initializes the environment variables for Oracle products on Solaris. It is read by the Oracle Installer at start up.

### prodinfo.ora

This file contains complete information on the product, such as the part number, version and operating system requirement. It is usually located in the root directory on the product media. Some older Oracle products might not have this file on the installation media.

### Files with an Extension .vrf

These files contain scripts that the installer uses for verification of some settings and dependencies.

### Files with an Extension .map

These files contain a listing of all the physical files for each product component, their source directory on the installation media, and their target directory. The size of the individual files is also documented here. The installer uses the information in these files to determine if the available disk space is sufficient.

### README

This file will contain information on any last minute changes and alerts for the user. It is recommended that you view the **README** file before beginning any installation. In fact, most Oracle installation procedures will automatically give you an opportunity to view the **README** file at the end of the installation. This file is typically located in the root directory of the installation media.

## Products and Components Available for Installation

When you start the Oracle Installer, you get a complete listing of Oracle products available on the product media. It is best that you select the high-level product (such as Developer/2000 Forms and SQL*Net) from the list of products to install. The installer will ensure that all dependent files such as Required Support Files are copied to your installation.

**NOTE**
*You might notice that some components like the Required Support Files are installed more than once. The version of the RSF usually corresponds with the version of the database. For example, Oracle7 Version 7.3 will use RSF 7.3 (only the first two digits are significant) and not RSF 7.2. Similarly SQL*Net Version 2.2 will use RSF 7.2 and not RSF 7.3. If you have both Oracle7 Version 7.3 and SQL*Net 2.2 installed, you will see both RSF 7.3 and RSF 7.2 installed. This is perfectly normal.*

## Installation Using the Oracle Installer

You can now use the Oracle Installer **orainst** to install the necessary products. We will not detail associated steps as complete instructions are available in your installation guide. Review carefully the **install.log** file created during the installation to identify any problems during the installation. We suggest that you create a separate **install.log** file for each of your installations and save them. These files can be very useful in diagnosing any problems that you might encounter. Be sure to execute the **root.sh** script after you have performed the installation. This is also documented in the installation guide.

Finally, follow the instructions documented in the section "Post Installation Tasks" in your installation guide.

## Re-linking Oracle Product Executables

At times you might need to re-link one or more of the Oracle product executables. If a re-link is required during installation, the Oracle Installer will warn you and even perform the necessary steps. However, there are times when you will need to manually re-link an executable. A good example of such a need is the installation of an additional SQL*Net protocol adapter. In such a situation, you will need to re-link the **oracle** executable as well as all tools like Developer/2000 Forms and SQL*Plus on the same machine so that they are made aware of the new protocol adapter. Oracle does provide convenient makefiles to help you re-link any executable. The makefiles are located in the *lib* subdirectory of the product. For example, a makefile called **ins_rdbms.mk** (this file was named **oracle.mk** in releases prior to Oracle Version 7.3) is available in $ORACLE_HOME/rdbms/lib to help you link the **oracle** executable. A makefile called **sqlplus.mk** is available in the $ORACLE_HOME/sqlplus/lib directory to create a new **sqlplus** executable.

In all situations where you need to recreate an executable, first ensure that all Oracle related processes (programs or executable) are terminated. Shut down the Oracle database and all client applications. Next, make a copy of the existing executable. In almost all the cases, the makefile will ensure that the old executable is backed-up before creating the new one, but it helps to be sure. Finally, build the executable using the **make** command after ensuring that /usr/ccs/bin is in your path. We illustrate the creation of a new **oracle** executable below:

Use the command

```
% su - oracle
```

to log in as the Oracle owner.

```
% cd $ORACLE_HOME/rdbms/lib
% make -f ins_rdbms.mk install
```

All Oracle makefiles have a variety of command line options that should be documented in the makefile itself. You can view the makefile in an editor before using **make** to create an executable.

# Two Types of Installation

There are two typical types of installations concerning Sun Solaris machines:

- **A stand-alone installation** This installation allows applications built with Oracle's client tools to be used with an Oracle7 server on the same computer running Sun Solaris 2.x.

■ **A client-server installation**  This installation enables applications built with Oracle's client tools to be used on a Sun Solaris machine, while the Oracle7 server resides on a separate machine.

We will give an example of each type to illustrate the installation process. The examples can easily be extended to cover every installation need of Oracle products on Sun Solaris.

# An Oracle Stand-Alone Installation

A stand-alone installation is one in which an Oracle tool is used to build an application by connecting to an Oracle7 database that is running on the same Sun Solaris server. We will illustrate a stand-alone installation by using Developer/2000 Forms 4.5 running under Motif on the Solaris server, to create an application that will connect to an Oracle7 server running on the same computer. Here are the necessary steps:

1. Install the Oracle7 server and verify the installation.

2. Install Developer/2000 Forms 4.5 for Motif.

3. Install database tables for Developer/2000 Forms 4.5.

4. Create a sample application using Developer/2000 Forms.

5. Run the sample application.

6. Ensure that database tables are properly installed.

## Step 1: Install the Oracle7 Server and Verify the Installation

Install the Oracle7 server on the Sun Solaris machine as per the instructions provided in the installation guide. Choose to install the Oracle RDBMS software and the database. You will get a starter database that can be easily tailored to suit your business needs at a later time.

Log in to the Solaris server as the *oracle* (owner of Oracle software) user. Start the Oracle7 database by using the Oracle Server Manager (on older versions you might have to use SQL*DBA, the executable is named **sqldba**).

```
% svrmgrl
Oracle Server Manager Release 2.1.3.0.0 - Production
Copyright (c) Oracle Corporation 1994,  1995.  All rights
     reserved.
Oracle7 Server Release 7.1.6.2.0 - Production Release
With the distributed, replication and parallel query options
PL/SQL Release 2.1.6.2.0 - Production
SVRMGR> connect internal
Connected.
SVRMGR> startup
ORACLE instance started.
Total System Global Area         4391216 bytes
Fixed Size                         48260 bytes
Variable Size                    3925164 bytes
Database Buffers                  409600 bytes
Redo Buffers                        8192 bytes
Database mounted.
Database opened.
SVRMGR> connect scott/tiger
Connected.
```

Be sure to leave the Oracle7 server running as we will need to create some database objects in order to run Developer/2000 Forms.

## Step 2: Install Developer/2000 Forms 4.5 for Motif

At this time, you are ready to install an Oracle application development tool of your choice. We will install the Developer/2000 Forms 4.5 product from the Developer/2000 product set.

Start the Oracle Installer again, and choose to install Developer/2000 Forms 4.5. The installer will copy all the files related to Developer/2000 Forms 4.5.

## Step 3: Install Database Tables for Developer/2000 Forms 4.5

We are now ready to create the database tables required by Developer/2000 Forms. Revert to the Oracle Installer and select the Create Database Objects option from the available Install Actions screen. Supply the password for the database user *system* if you are prompted for a password. The default password is *manager*. Pay special attention for any errors that you might see on the screen.

**NOTE**
*If you already have an earlier version of Developer/2000 Forms 4.x installed, you can select the option Upgrade Existing Database Objects.*

## Step 4: Create a Sample Application using Developer/2000 Forms

Before you start Developer/2000 Forms, ensure that you have the DISPLAY variable set in the UNIX environment.

```
% setenv DISPLAY ourclient:0.0
```

You might need to use the **xhost** command to authorize the X client to open a window on your machine.

```
% xhost + ourhost
ourhost being added to access control list
```

Start the Developer/2000 Forms Designer again and connect to the database. You can use the Oracle user *scott* and a password of *tiger* to connect to Oracle. You can leave the Connect String field blank. We will create a small sample application to ensure that the product is installed correctly. Double-click on Blocks in the Object Navigator of the Forms Designer. You should see a screen similar to the one shown in Figure 4-1. Next, click on the Select button next to the Base Table field. You will see a screen similar to the one shown here:

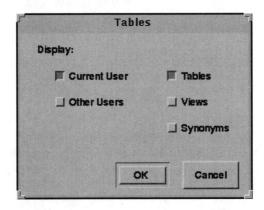

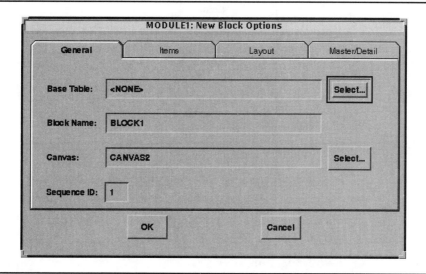

**FIGURE 4-1.** *New Block window in Developer/2000 Forms Designer*

Select the Current User, Other Users, and Tables check boxes that you see on screen, and click on the OK button. Now, pick any table from the list of tables you see and you will see a screen similar to the one shown in Figure 4-2. We have selected a table called DEPT owned by the current user SCOTT in our example. You can type any name for the Block Name field or take the default and click on the OK button. Your sample application is ready.

## Step 5: Run the Sample Application
Run the sample application by choosing File|Run.

## Step 6: Ensure that Database Tables Are Properly Installed
Now that we have managed to run a small application, we can try saving this to the database. First, ensure that you have selected the option to save to the database. Select Tools|Options and choose the Designer options as shown in Figure 4-3. Now select the option File|Save and choose the options shown next.

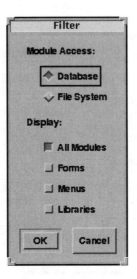

Click on the OK button to save the application to the database. If you do not get any errors, you have confirmed that Developer/2000 Forms and Personal Oracle7 are installed properly. Note that while it is easy to save an application to the file system, in a multi-user environment you typically will have to save applications to the database so that they can be shared by many users. If you are not concerned about saving applications to the database,

**FIGURE 4-2.** *Base Table and Block Name selection*

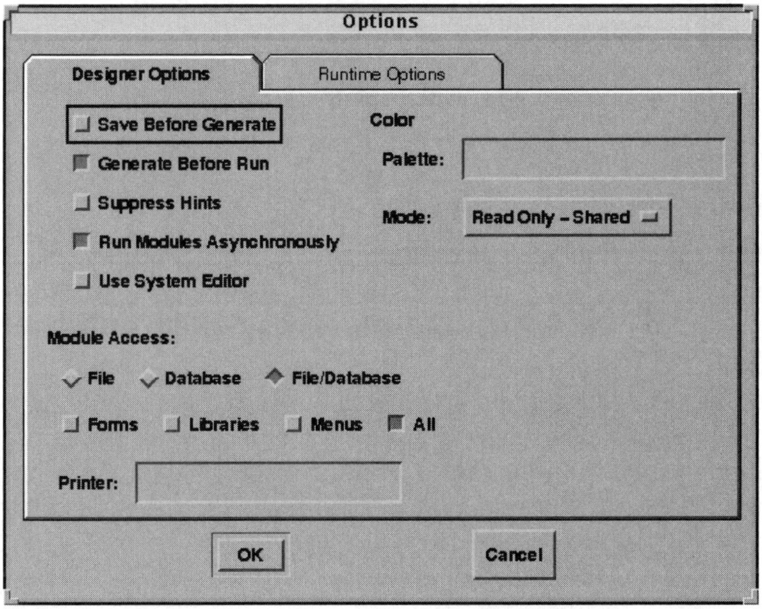

**FIGURE 4-3.** *Designer options in Developer/2000 Forms*

you can ignore the step to create the database tables (Step 3). However, if you are planning to save applications to the database this is a useful exercise.

# An Oracle Client-Server Installation

A client-server installation is one in which an Oracle tool is used to build an application by connecting to an Oracle7 database that is running on a separate machine. The connectivity is obtained by using Oracle's SQL*Net software. For more information on SQL*Net, please refer to Chapter 8.

We will illustrate a client-server installation with an application using Developer/2000 Forms 4.5 connecting to an Oracle7 database running on another Sun Solaris 2.5 machine across TCP/IP. The salient steps are listed below:

1. Verify network connectivity between the two Solaris machines.

2. Verify that SQL*Net is installed correctly on the Solaris server.

3. Install Developer/2000 Forms 4.5 for Motif on the Solaris client.

4. Install SQL*Net V2 for TCP/IP on the Solaris client.

5. Verify connectivity to Oracle7 on the Solaris server.

6. Install database tables for Developer/2000 Forms.

7. Create a sample application using Developer/2000 Forms.

8. Run the sample application and save it to the database.

## Step 1: Verify Network Connectivity Between the Two Solaris Machines

Oracle's SQL*Net relies on the underlying network layer to provide connectivity between the client and server. The first step in a client-server application must be to verify this network connectivity.

From the Solaris Client, use a Ping or Telnet utility to ensure that the Solaris server is visible on the network. Be sure to note down the server name and/or IP address of the Solaris machine.

## Step 2: Verify that SQL*Net Is Installed Correctly on the Solaris Server

Install SQL*Net V2 and the SQL*Net TCP/IP adapter on the Solaris server per the installation guide. Create the **tnsnames.ora**, **listener.ora**, and **sqlnet.ora** files per instructions. In the **tnsnames.ora** file, create a SQL*Net V2 alias definition for Oracle7 on the Solaris machine, called *mydb*.

### NOTE
*Sample SQL*Net configuration files are*
*provided in the media supplied with this book.*

Start the listener and ensure that it is running properly:

```
% lsnrctl start          /* Start the listener */
% lsnrctl stat           /* Status of the listener */
```

Now, attempt a loop-back test, i.e. use a tool such as Oracle Server Manager on the server and connect back to the same server using SQL*Net:

```
% svrmgrl
SVRMGR> connect scott/tiger
Connected.
```

If the above command lets you connect successfully, it shows that Oracle7 is running on the Solaris machine.

```
SVRMGR> connect scott/tiger@mydb
```

If the above command lets you connect successfully, it shows that SQL*Net is installed properly on the Solaris machine

## Step 3: Install Developer/2000 Forms 4.5 for Motif on the Solaris Client

At this time, you are ready to install an Oracle application development tool of your choice on the Solaris client. We will use Developer/2000 Forms 4.5.

Start the Oracle Installer **orainst** on the Solaris client, and choose to install Developer/2000 Forms 4.5. The installer will copy all the files related to Developer/2000 Forms 4.5.

## Step 4: Install SQL*Net V2 for TCP/IP on the Solaris Client

Since we are using TCP/IP, we now have to install SQL*Net V2 TCP/IP on the Solaris client. In the Oracle Installer, choose to install the components SQL*Net V2 (sometimes called SQL*Net V2 client) and the SQL*Net V2 TCP/IP Protocol Adapter.

Now, we need to create the SQL*Net configuration files **tnsnames.ora** and **sqlnet.ora** on the Solaris client. It is best to copy these files from the Solaris server using the ftp utility. The **tnsnames.ora** and **sqlnet.ora** on the Solaris machine are usually located in the $ORACLE_HOME/network/admin directory. Transfer these files using ftpfrom the Solaris server to the $ORACLE_HOME/network/admin directory on the Solaris client. The **tnsnames.ora** file should contain the SQL*Net V2 alias *mydb* that we created earlier.

## Step 5: Verify Connectivity to Oracle7 on the Solaris Server

Start Developer/2000 Forms Designer on the Solaris client and ensure that you can connect to the database. Choose the Connect option from the File menu, or press CTRL-N for the login screen. Type a user name and password for a valid Oracle user. If you are unsure, you may use an account created by Oracle. The user name is *scott* and the password is *tiger*. Type **mydb** in the field for the Connect String. You should see the status *<Con>* in the status bar at the bottom of the Developer/2000 Forms Designer screen. The item Disconnect should also now be available in the File menu.

Be sure to Exit from the Developer/2000 Forms Designer at this time.

## Step 6: Install Database Tables for Developer/2000 Forms

We are now ready to create the database tables required by Developer/2000 Forms. Revert to the Oracle Installer and select the Create Database Objects option from the available Install Actions screen. Supply the password for the database user *system* if you are prompted for a password. The default password is *manager*. Pay special attention for any errors that you might see on the screen.

**NOTE**
*If you already have an earlier version of Developer/2000 Forms 4.x installed, you can select the option Upgrade Existing Database Objects.*

At this time, you can quit the installer. We are ready to verify that the Developer/2000 Forms product is installed properly by creating a small sample application.

## Step 7: Create a Sample Application Using Developer/2000 Forms

Start the Developer/2000 Forms Designer again and connect to the database as in Step 5.

Create a sample application per instructions earlier in the section on stand-alone applications.

## Step 8: Run the Sample Application and Save It to the Database

Run the sample application and try saving it to the database per the instructions in the stand-alone applications section earlier in this chapter.

# Frequently Asked Questions (FAQ)

In this chapter we have presented some basic information that should be sufficient to get most installations completed. We will now present some FAQ to Oracle Worldwide Customer Support.

**Q.** When I try to start Oracle, I get an error message that says something about insufficient memory for SGA. How do I find out how much shared memory is available on my machine?

**A.** You can view the file **/etc/system** to look at your system configuration. In this file, you should see a section that provides information on shared memory. If you do not, you can add these lines after consulting with your system administrator. You should have something like:

```
set shmsys:shminfo_shmmax = 31457280
set shmsys:shminfo_shmmin = 1
set shmsys:shminfo_shmmni = 200
set shmsys:shminfo_shmseg = 50
set semsys:seminfo_semmns = 200
set semsys:seminfo_semmni = 70
set semsys:seminfo_semmsl = 100
```

Once these resources are in use, you can view the limits by using the **sysdef** command.

```
% sysdef
```

A sample excerpt from the output of **sysdef** is shown below:

```
IPC Shared Memory
31457280    max shared memory segment size (SHMMAX)
1           min shared memory segment size (SHMMIN)
200         shared memory identifiers (SHMMNI)
50          max attached shm segments per process (SHMSEG)
```

If you want to modify these settings, edit the **/etc/system** file and re-boot your machine.

**Q.** I have configured enough shared memory for Oracle; why am I still unable to start up the database?

**A.** Find out how shared memory is being used on your machine by using the **ipcs -m** command. You will need to log in as the Oracle owner. You need to configure sufficient shared memory for the SGA defined for Oracle in the **init.ora** in addition to the shared memory being used. See the section "Performance Tuning" in Chapter 7.

**Q.** I have completely shut down all Oracle databases running on this machine and yet **ipcs** is reporting that Oracle is using some shared memory. How is that possible?

**A.** If you are sure that all Oracle database instances are shut down and **ipcs** still reports some shared memory being used by Oracle, then it is possible that one of your databases was shut down abnormally. You can use the **ipcrm** command to free the shared memory segments in use.

```
% ipcs -m
IPC status from <running system> as of Mon Feb 24 12:49:31 1997
T    ID    KEY        MODE        OWNER     GROUP
Shared Memory:
m    400 0x0a1cadc7 --rw-r-----   oracle     dba
% ipcrm -m 400
```

In the above example, the **ipcrm** takes the ID of the shared memory segment returned from the **ipcs -m** command.

**Q.** I was trying to link Oracle and I got some warning. Are these critical?

**A.** All of the warnings that we have seen while linking Oracle products are not harmful and can be safely ignored. If you do not wish to see these messages, you can suppress them easily. We present a few common warnings that you might see:

```
ld: warning: option -YP appears more than once, first setting taken
ld: warning: option -Q appears more than once, first setting taken
```

You can edit your makefile and make the following changes if you wish to avoid these warnings. We *do not* recommend that you edit your makefile. If you choose to do so, be sure to first *make a backup copy*. We would like to again point out that Oracle Corporation does not support changes to its makefiles and you are taking a risk by editing them.

```
LDFLAGS= -L$(LIBHOME) to
LDFLAGS= -t $(LDSTRING) -L$(LIBHOME)
OTHERLIBS= 'cat $(ORACLE_HOME)/rdbms/lib/sysliblist' $(MLSLIBS)
```

$(LDSTRING) to
OTHERLIBS= 'cat $(ORACLE_HOME)/rdbms/lib/sysliblist' $(MLSLIBS)

You might see a warning while linking Developer/2000 Forms 4.5 similar to

```
ld : warning: symbol 'ui1064' has differing sizes:
   (file /home/oracle/Dev2000/forms45/lib/ui10.o value=0x90;
   file /home/oracle/Dev2000/lib/libtk21m.so value=0x1c);
```

Again, you can ignore these messages. You could edit the
**sqlforms45.mk** file and make the following change:

LDFLAGS= -L$(LIBHOME) to
LDFLAGS= -L$(LIBHOME) -t

You could also suppress these messages at the command line by using

```
% make -f sqlforms45.mk LDFLAGS="-L$ORACLE_HOME/lib -t"
```

**Q.** What about Motif libraries? I get a whole bunch of errors with **X11**, **XT**,
and **XM** files.
**A.** The GUI libraries on Solaris 2.3 and 2.4 are located in /usr/openwin/lib.
Some Oracle makefiles reference /usr/lib instead. You could also use the
run-time libraries available in /usr/dt/lib with Solaris 2.4 and above.

At times, on Solaris 2.4, you might also run into problems with
references to the static libraries **libx11.a** and **libxt.a**. If you run into this
problem, use the following workaround:

```
% cd /usr/openwin/lib
% cp libX11.so libX11.a
% cp libXt.so libXt.a
```

**Q.** I am trying to run an Oracle application on Motif. I have set the
DISPLAY variable properly. I still get a message that says something about
window system startup failure. What is the problem?
**A.** It is most likely that you are having trouble with opening a window on
your client. Ensure that the DISPLAY variable is set properly. You also may
have host-based security for programs enabled on your machine. Use the
**xhost** command to determine the current status.

```
% xhost
```

will report something like:

```
access control enabled, only authorized clients can connect
% xhost + ourhost
ourhost being added to access control list
```

This will add access control to the machine named "ourhost". If you want, you could provide blanket access to all clients with

```
% xhost +
access control disabled, clients can connect from any host
```

Table 4-2 provides a glimpse at the error messages and behavior from common Oracle tools when they fail to open a window on your client.

**Q.** I am having trouble with audio when I use Oracle products like Developer/2000 Reports. What do I do?
**A.** If you see an error message that indicates problems with audio capabilities, ensure that your audio devices have read and write permissions set.

```
% cd /dev/sound
% ls -l
total 4
lrwxrwxrwx   1 root      root          57 Nov 19 13:56 0 ->
../../devices/sbus@1f,0/SUNW,CS4231@d,c000000:sound,audio
lrwxrwxrwx   1 root      root          60 Nov 19 13:56 0ctl ->
../../devices/sbus@1f,0/SUNW,CS4231@d,c000000:sound,audioctl
```

| Product | Error | Error Description or Resultant Behavior |
|---|---|---|
| Developer/2000 Forms 4.5 | FRM-91111 | Internal error, window system startup failure. |
| Developer/2000 Reports 2.5 | REP-3000 | Internal error starting Oracle Toolkit. |
| Developer/2000 Reports 2.5 | None | Segmentation violation. |
| Oracle Procedure Builder | None | Program exits. |

**TABLE 4-2.** *Problems Associated with Window Start Up Failure for Oracle Tools*

The above commands should show you symbolic links to your audio devices. Ensure that read and write permissions are set:

```
% chmod 777 *
```

**Q.** I am running the Oracle Import Utility (**imp**). It ran for a while and imported some objects. Now it seems to be hanging. What is the problem?
**A.** It is most likely that the import is building indexes. All the objects have been imported successfully and indexes on some objects are being created. This can take a while. On some large objects, we have seen this task of building indexes take a few hours. Feel free to use the **truss -p** command to figure out if the *imp* process is doing something. In this case, the main *imp* process may be hung, but the server or shadow process associated with this import should be doing something.

**Q.** When I get a core dump and a file called **core** is created, is there something I can do with this file to figure out what is wrong?
**A.** In a majority of situations, **core** files are only useful to developers. Very advanced users may be able to get some useful information out of the **core** file by using a debugger like **adb** or **dbx** (we recommend **dbx** if it is available to you). If you get a core dump regularly on some task, we suggest that you contact Oracle Worldwide Customer Support and ask them to investigate the matter. Stack traces can help Oracle developers diagnose problems and provide faster bug fixes. In any case, if you are curious, you could try something like:

```
% dbx $ORACLE_HOME/bin/sqlplus core
```

In this example, a **core** file that was created by the **sqlplus** executable is available in the current directory.

**Q.** I am running into some weird errors. How can I get more information on what is wrong?
**A.** You can try using the **truss** command to figure out what is wrong. We recommend these utilities for very experienced UNIX users and administrators only.

We present an example here where we track an import task using **truss**.

```
% imp <command line options>
```

From another login session, you can use the **ps** command to get the *pid* of the **imp** task and then use **truss** to get a status of the import task.

```
% ps -ef|grep imp
oracle  3725  3720  0 13:43:07 pts/7    0:00 grep imp
oracle  3714  3663  0 13:42:27 pts/1    0:00 imp
% truss -p 3714
Received signal #20, SIGWINCH, in read() [default]
read(0, 0xEF655EA4, 1024)  (sleeping...)
read(0, " s c o t t\n", 1024)           = 6
lseek(3, 5120, SEEK_SET)                = 5120
read(3, "\0\f\0CE\0\0\0 P\0CF\0\0".., 512)  = 512
write(1, " P a s s w o r d :  ", 10)    = 10
ioctl(0, TCGETA, 0xEFFFF30C)            = 0
ioctl(0, TCGETS, 0xEFFFF384)            = 0
ioctl(0, TCSETSF, 0xEFFFF384)           = 0
...
```

At times, it is possible that the **imp** task is sleeping, but the shadow or server process associated with the **imp** is working actively. Try to use **truss** against the shadow process also. Continuing with our example, you can do this easily by using **ps** and **grep**. In our example, 3714 is the pid of the **imp** task.

```
% ps -ef|grep 3714
oracle  3714  3731  0 13:47:50 pts/1    0:00 imp
oracle  3743  3714  0 13:53:28 ?        0:00 mydb
(DESCRIPTION=(LOCAL=YES)(ADDRESS=(PROTOCOL=beq)))
oracle  3747  3706  0 13:56:58 pts/6    0:00 grep 3714
```

Very experienced administrators can also try the **snoop** command. We have found it especially useful when tracking communication between two machines. You can use syntax similar to **snoop -o /tmp/myfile myhost theirhost port 1521** to track packets between *myhost* and *theirhost* on port 1521.

**Q.** How do I record the activities in a long session? I want to keep track of what I am doing.
**A.** You can use the **script** command in these situations to record your session in a file. Here is a somewhat fantastic example:

```
% script /tmp/mysession.txt
% cd $ORACLE_HOME/bin
```

```
% sqlplus scott/tiger
SQL> select user from dual;
SQL > exit;
% mv sqlplus trying
% sqlplus scott/tiger
% mv trying sqlplus
% exit
% cat /tmp/mysession.txt
```

We definitely recommend using **script** to record your actions in critical situations like during backup and recovery or when performing an installation.

# CHAPTER
## 5

## Preventive Maintenance
## on UNIX

e looked at the Oracle installation process and issues relating to Oracle products on a typical UNIX implementation, Sun SPARC Solaris 2.x, in Chapter 4. We will now present some common issues that apply to Oracle products on almost all UNIX implementations. The topics covered in this chapter are common issues faced by Oracle users on UNIX.

# Configure Your UNIX Environment

It is critical that you ensure your UNIX environment is properly set before you use Oracle products. Many failures and errors are a direct result of improper settings of some necessary environment variables.

Ensure that you understand Oracle's requirements for environment variables such as PATH, ORACLE_HOME, ORACLE_SID, TWO_TASK, LD_LIBRARY_PATH and TNS_ADMIN. Once you have determined the necessary variables for your site, we suggest that you add these settings to your **.login**, **.cshrc**, or **.profile** files. Use commands like **echo** and **env** to ensure that your environment is set properly before you use an Oracle product.

Oracle provides shell scripts called **oraenv** (for **sh** or **ksh** users) and **coraenv** (for **csh** users) that can be modified to set the appropriate UNIX environment for Oracle users. These scripts can be placed in /usr/bin, /usr/local/bin or $ORACLE_HOME/bin.

If you are using a GUI tool from Oracle, also ensure that the environment variable DISPLAY is set properly.

 `% setenv DISPLAY ourhost:0.0`

# Re-linking Oracle Product Executables

At times you might need to re-link one or more of the Oracle product executables. In all situations where you need to recreate an executable, we recommend that all Oracle related processes (programs or executables) be terminated. Even though this is not necessary in many situations, we do recommend that you shut down the Oracle database and all client applications. Next, make a copy of your existing executable, if you have one.

All Oracle makefiles have an extension of **.mk**. There is sufficient documentation in the makefile itself. Take a few moments to review the makefile to get an understanding of the required files (mostly libraries) and their locations. This will help you provide proper settings for your path.

It is possible that you might see some warnings during the creation of your executable. These are mostly harmless and can be ignored safely. We present below an example of a warning that can be ignored.

```
ld: warning: option -YP appears more than once, first setting taken
ld: warning: option -Q appears more than once, first setting taken
```

Edit your makefile and make the following changes:

LDFLAGS= -L$(LIBHOME) to
LDFLAGS= -t $(LDSTRING) -L$(LIBHOME)
OTHERLIBS= 'cat $(ORACLE_HOME)/rdbms/lib/sysliblist' $(MLSLIBS)
$(LDSTRING) to
OTHERLIBS= 'cat $(ORACLE_HOME)/rdbms/lib/sysliblist' $(MLSLIBS)

# Configuring Shared Memory and Semaphores

Oracle uses UNIX resources like shared memory and semaphores extensively for Interprocess Communication (IPC). If you are low on these resources you could see a lot of problems during instance startup.

**NOTE**
*SQL\*Net V1 also uses shared memory to communicate between user processes and shadow processes.*

Before we take a look at the Oracle errors related to shared memory and semaphores, we will see how Oracle uses these resources.

Oracle uses shared memory for the *System Global Area (SGA)*. The SGA is an area that needs to be visible to all Oracle processes on the server. Oracle might use one or more segments in shared memory for the SGA. Oracle will try to obtain one segment for all shared memory requested (as defined in the **init.ora** file). If it cannot fit all shared memory requested in one segment, it will use multiple segments.

Semaphores are mostly used by Oracle for concurrency control. Various Oracle processes turn semaphores on and off to coordinate events. Unlike shared memory, semaphores are allocated when needed and not at instance start up.

We will now look at some common Oracle errors that are related to allocation of semaphores and shared memory.

ORA-7306, ORA-7336 and ORA-7329 are a direct result of a failed *shmget( )* call. In most cases, either there is insufficient virtual memory on the system or insufficient shared memory available. You might need to increase your swap space and also increase the value for the SHMMNI setting variables. It is also possible that shared memory is not configured on your system.

ORA-7307, ORA-7337 and ORA-7320 are reported if Oracle is unable to attach shared memory using the *shmat( )* system call. This usually indicates that the permissions to the allocated shared memory are bad or SHMSEG is too low. Ensure that the *setuid* bit is turned on for the **oracle** executable or increase SHMSEG to resolve these errors.

It is possible that Oracle needs more shared memory segments. You can increase SHMMAX to resolve Oracle errors ORA-7329 and ORA-7334.

If Oracle is unable to allocate a semaphore for any reason, you should see the errors ORA-7250, ORA-7279 and ORA-7252. You can increase SEMMNI or SEMMNS to resolve these errors.

Most of the above errors are accompanied by system errors such as ENOENT, ENOMEM, EINVAL, EMFILE, and ENOSPC.

Table 5-1 lists some critical system parameters that are related to shared memory and semaphores.

| Parameter | Description |
|-----------|-------------|
| SHMMAX | Maximum size of one shared memory segment |
| SHMMHI | Maximum number of shared memory segments |
| SHMSEG | Maximum number of segments that a process can attach |
| SEMMNS | Maximum semaphores on the system |

**TABLE 5-1.** *Critical UNIX System Parameters for Shared Memory and Semaphores*

If you encounter a crash of Oracle or perform an abnormal shutdown of Oracle, it is possible that the shared memory and semaphores allocated by Oracle are not returned to the system. Use the **ipcs** and **ipcrm** commands to view the IPC resources used by Oracle and free these resources. If you have multiple instances of Oracle on the same machine, we suggest that you perform a normal shutdown of the other instances before using **ipcrm**.

# Core Dumps

When an application terminates abnormally on UNIX you often get a file that contains an image of the state of the process at the instant it terminated. This file is named **core**. Most core dumps are caused when a process tries to access an area of memory that does not belong to it or when some required resource is exhausted. Unfortunately, core dumps are a part of life for all UNIX applications. If you are an experienced UNIX programmer, you can get some useful information out of the **core** file by using debuggers like **dbx**, **xdb**, or **adb** (we recommend **dbx** if it is available on your system). You need to determine the debugger available on your UNIX system. You also must know the command that was executed to start the offending program. The general syntax would be something like:

```
% <debugger> $ORACLE_HOME/bin/<program> core
```

where <debugger> is the debugger of your choice and <program> is the name of the offending program executable. Be sure to login as the user that created the core dump.

# Building a Permanent Staging Area

It is convenient to build a permanent staging area from which you can install Oracle products. We present the commands necessary to build a staging area from a CD-ROM and from tape. The exact commands on your UNIX system might vary. The following example shows commands that can be used to mount a CD-ROM on the mount point named *mount_point* on Sun SPARC Solaris 2.x or SunOS 4.1.3:

```
$ su
```

Provide the password to login as root.

```
# mkdir /mount_point
# chmod 555 /mount_point
# mount -r -F hsfs /dev/dsk/c0t6d0s0 /mount_point
# su - oracle
$ cd /mount_point/oracle/orainst
$ ./orainst
```

If you are using a tape device, you need to use the appropriate **cpio** command for your platform. Create a directory that will become your staging area. When you start **orainst**, you will be prompted for the name of your staging area. The Oracle installer will automatically copy the required files for your products into the specified staging area.

# Frequently Asked Questions (FAQ)

In this chapter, we have looked at topics that should be helpful to users of Oracle products on most implementations of UNIX. We will now look at some common questions that are asked by Oracle users and administrators on UNIX.

Q.   I have completely shut down all Oracle databases running on this machine and yet **ipcs** is reporting that Oracle is using some shared memory. How is that possible?
A.   If you are sure that all Oracle database instances are shut down and **ipcs** still reports some shared memory being used by Oracle, then it is possible that one of your databases was shut down abnormally. You can use the **ipcrm** command to free the shared memory segments in use.

```
% ipcs -m
IPC status from <running system> as of Mon Feb 24 12:49:31 1997
T     ID    KEY         MODE         OWNER      GROUP
Shared Memory:
m    400 0x0a1cadc7 --rw-r-----    oracle      dba
% ipcrm -m 400
```

In the above example, the **ipcrm** takes the ID of the shared memory segment returned from the **ipcs -m** command.

Q.  I am trying to run an Oracle application on Motif. I have set the DISPLAY variable properly. I still get a message that says something about window system startup failure. What is the problem?
A.  It is most likely that you are having trouble with opening a window on your client. Ensure that the DISPLAY variable is set properly. You also might have host-based security for programs enabled on your machine. Use the **xhost** command to determine the current status.

```
% xhost
```

will report something like:

```
access control enabled, only authorized clients can connect
% xhost + ourhost
ourhost being added to access control list
```

This will add access control to the machine named *ourhost*. If you want, you could provide blanket access to all clients with the following:

```
% xhost +
access control disabled, clients can connect from any host
```

Table 5-2 provides a glimpse at the error messages and behavior from common Oracle tools when they fail to open a window on your client.

| Product | Error | Error Description or Resultant Behavior |
|---|---|---|
| Oracle Forms 4.5 | FRM-91111 | Internal error, window system startup failure |
| Oracle Reports 2.5 | REP-3000 | Internal error starting Oracle Toolkit |
| Oracle Graphics 2.5 | None | Segmentation violation |
| Oracle Procedure Builder | None | Program exits |

**TABLE 5-2.**  *Problems Associated with Window Start Up Failure for Oracle Tools*

Q. I am running into some weird errors. How can I get more information on what is wrong?

A. You can try using the **truss** or the **trace** command to figure out what is wrong. We recommend these utilities for very experienced UNIX users and administrators only.

We present an example here where we track an import task using **truss**.

```
% imp <command line options>
```

From another login session, you can use the **ps** command to get the pid of the imp task and then use **truss** to get a status of the import task.

```
% ps -ef|grep imp
oracle  3725  3720  0 13:43:07 pts/7    0:00 grep imp
oracle  3714  3663  0 13:42:27 pts/1    0:00 imp
% truss -p 3714
Received signal #20, SIGWINCH, in read() [default]
read(0, 0xEF655EA4, 1024)   (sleeping...)
read(0, " s c o t t\n", 1024)             = 6
lseek(3, 5120, SEEK_SET)           = 5120
read(3, "\0\f\0CE\0\0\0 P\0CF\0\0".., 512)  = 512
write(1, " P a s s w o r d :  ", 10)      = 10
ioctl(0, TCGETA, 0xEFFFF30C)              = 0
ioctl(0, TCGETS, 0xEFFFF384)              = 0
ioctl(0, TCSETSF, 0xEFFFF384)             = 0
...
```

At times, it is possible that the imp task is sleeping, but the shadow or server process associated with the imp is working actively. Try to use **truss** against the shadow process also. Continuing with our example, you can do this easily by using **ps** and **grep.** In our example, 3714 is the pid of the imp task.

```
% ps -ef|grep 3714
oracle  3714  3731  0 13:47:50 pts/1    0:00 imp
oracle  3743  3714  0 13:53:28 ?        0:00 mydb
(DESCRIPTION=(LOCAL=YES)(ADDRESS=(PROTOCOL=beq)))
oracle  3747  3706  0 13:56:58 pts/6    0:00 grep 3714
```

Very experienced administrators can also try the **snoop** command. We have found it especially useful when tracking communication between two machines. You can use syntax similar to **snoop -o /tmp/myfile myhost**

**theirhost port 1521** to track packets between myhost and theirhost on port 1521.

Q. How do I record the activities in a long session? I want to keep track of what I am doing.

A. You can use the **script** command in these situations to record your session in a file. Here is a somewhat fantastic example:

```
% script /tmp/mysession.txt
% cd $ORACLE_HOME/bin
% sqlplus scott/tiger
SQL> select user from dual;
SQL > exit;
% mv sqlplus trying
% sqlplus scott/tiger
% mv trying sqlplus
% exit
% cat /tmp/mysession.txt
```

We definitely recommend using **script** to record your actions in critical situations like during backup and recovery or performing an installation.

Q. What about implementing RAID on Oracle?

A. It is hard to forecast the effect of implementing RAID on Oracle RDBMS files. If you are in a situation where you anticipate more read operations than write operations, we suggest that you place your data files on RAID-5 devices. RAID-5 provides performance benefits for read operations. We do not advise you to place Rollback Segments and Redo Logs on a RAID-5 device as write operations will be slower. Do not place data files belonging to temporary tablespaces on RAID-5 devices. Even in such cases it might be better to place your control files and log files on RAID-1 as RAID-1 provides for complete redundancy.

RAID-1 also guarantees complete redundancy of data as all data is mirrored. If disk space is not an issue, we suggest you implement RAID-1.

Q. What about raw devices? Will I get any benefits?

A. If I/O causes a bottleneck on your machine, you should get some benefit from using raw devices. In the case where I/O is a bottleneck, a write operation to a raw device bypasses the UNIX buffer cache and data is transferred directly from the Oracle buffer cache to the disk. Another benefit of raw devices is that no file system overhead is incurred as there are no inodes or free blocks to maintain. Some sites have reported performance improvement of up to 40 percent with raw devices.

In any case, we suggest that you use **sar** or **vmstat** to determine the I/O bottlenecks on your machine. If you already have an Oracle database, you could use **BSTAT** and **ESTAT** (refer to the "Performance Tuning Guide" for your platform for details on these utilities) to get I/O performance statistics to help you make your decision.

If you are using the Oracle Parallel Server, you must use raw partitions so that the database files, redo log files, and control files can be shared between the instances.

Q. If I decide to use raw devices, are there any precautions I should take with Oracle?
A. You must ensure that the raw device is owned by the Oracle owner. You should also ensure that the Oracle block size is a multiple of the physical block size. Another point to note is that you cannot use utilities like **tar** or **cpio** to create your backups. You must use the **dd** command. Of course, you have the option to use **dd** to copy the raw device file to a regular UNIX file system and then use **tar** or **cpio**. Archive log files cannot use raw device files, you must use a UNIX file system. You also cannot have more than one data file in a raw partition. It is more difficult to plan for growth of data. We also suggest that you place your raw partitions on separate disk devices to avoid contention.

Q. Can I use raw devices and RAID?
A. Absolutely! Again, we suggest that you look at your I/O characteristics and then decide on aspects like RAID and disk mirroring.

Q. Is the VOLSIZE feature of Export available on all platforms?
A. No, this is a UNIX feature designed to allow exporting to tapes or external media. Your port-specific documentation should have information on this feature, if available on your operating system.

Q. Can Export be run through *cron* jobs?
A. Absolutely!

Q.  When I run Export through shell scripts, what status codes should I expect? How can I use these return codes?

A.  An Export job can terminate with success, warnings, or errors. If an Export is successful or it terminates with warnings, you will get a return code of zero. If it returns with errors, you will get a return code of 1. Unfortunately, there is no clear indication of what constitutes a warning and what constitutes an error. An error is a result of a condition that is severe enough to stop the Export job, whereas a warning is not so severe. The Export continues despite the warning.

# CHAPTER
# 6

Preventive Maintenance
on OpenVMS

his chapter describes how to do a basic OpenVMS installation. The pre-installation setup and some of the post-installation tests are given. Some of the common mistakes that users make during installation are pointed out, and then we look at some of the frequently asked questions. Although we perform a 7.1.5 installation on a VAX machine in this chapter, we also discuss the new features of Oracle7 Release 7.3.2 on Alpha OpenVMS. A brief description of the Very Large Memory 64-bit feature is given in the FAQ section.

# Pre-Installation Tasks

Before we begin the installation, we need to ensure that we have the right privileges and sufficient disk space to install Oracle RDBMS and the database.

## Check Privileges

First we will examine the ORACLE7 account and make sure that proper privileges and process rights identifiers are given to the account. Then we look at the system resources, such as global pages, before proceeding with the installation.

```
    Welcome to openVMS VAX V6.2

Username: RVELPURI
Password:

    Welcome to openVMS VAX version V6.2 on node ORABLR
    Last interactive login on Monday, 13-JAN-1997 13:38
    Last non-interactive login on Monday, 13-JAN-1997 15:02

 $ set def sys$system
 $ run sys$system:authorize

UAF> show oracle7

Username: ORACLE7              Owner:  oracle
Account:                       UIC:    [377,100] ([ORACLE7])
CLI:      DCL                  Tables: DCLTABLES
Default:  DISK$USER:[ORACLE7]
LGICMD:
```

```
Flags:
Primary days:    Mon Tue Wed Thu Fri
Secondary days:                    Sat Sun
No access restrictions
Expiration:              (none)    Pwdminimum:  6   Login Fails:  0
Pwdlifetime:          90 00:00    Pwdchange:  16-NOV-1996 14:51
Last Login: 13-JAN-1997 15:20 (interactive), 13-JAN-1997 13:32
       (non-interactive)
Maxjobs:          0  Fillm:      300  Bytlm:        10240
Maxacctjobs:      0  Shrfillm:     0  Pbytlm:           0
Maxdetach:        0  BIOlm:       40  JTquota:       4096
Prclm:            2  DIOlm:       40  WSdef:         1024
Prio:             4  ASTlm:       40  WSquo:         1024
Queprio:          4  TQElm:       40  WSextent:      4096
CPU:         (none)  Enqlm:       50  Pgflquo:     102400
Authorized Privileges:
  NETMBX    TMPMBX
Default Privileges:
Identifier                      Value           Attributes
  ORA_DBINST_DBA                %X80010002
  ORA_IPEC_DBA                  %X80010004
  ORA_DBA                       %X80010003
```

   While looking at the quotas and privileges for account ORACLE7, you can see that the enque limit (enqlm), working set quota (wsquo), and buffered I/O limit (bytlm) are lower than recommended by Oracle Corporation. Also, not all the required privileges exist for this account. Later, we will create a database called **715** with the same SID and database name; so the proper *rights identifiers* need to be created as well. Let's increase the quotas and add the proper privileges and rights identifiers now. Please note that the enque limit (enqlm) should be set higher than 200 if you are using Oracle Parallel Server (OPS). Here we are assuming a non-OPS installation.

```
UAF> modify oracle7/enqlm=200

%UAF-I-MDFYMSG, user record(s) updated

UAF> modify oracle7/wsquo=2048

%UAF-I-MDFYMSG, user record(s) updated

UAF> modify oracle7/bytlm=32768
```

```
%UAF-I-MDFYMSG, user record(s) updated

UAF> modify oracle7/ defpriv=(cmkrnl,detach,world, -

_UAF> sysnam,prmmbx,netmbx,tmpmbx,log_io)

%UAF-I-MDFYMSG, user record(s) updated

 UAF> add/identifier ora_715_dba

%UAF-I-RDBADDMSG, identifier ORA_715_DBA value %X80010005 added
     to rights database

UAF> grant/identifier ora_715_dba oracle7

%UAF-I-GRANTMSG, identifier ORA_715_DBA granted to ORACLE7

UAF> add/identifier ora_715_oper

%UAF-I-RDBADDMSG, identifier ORA_715_OPER value %X80010006 added
     to rights database

UAF> grant/identifier ora_715_oper oracle7

%UAF-I-GRANTMSG, identifier ORA_715_OPER granted to ORACLE7

UAF> show oracle7


Username: ORACLE7                          Owner:  oracle
Account:                                   UIC:    [377,100]
([ORACLE7])
CLI:      DCL                              Tables: DCLTABLES
Default:  DISK$USER:[ORACLE7]
LGICMD:
Flags:
Primary days:   Mon Tue Wed Thu Fri
Secondary days:                    Sat Sun
No access restrictions
Expiration:             (none)   Pwdminimum:  6   Login Fails:  0
Pwdlifetime:        90 00:00     Pwdchange:   16-NOV-1996 14:51
Last Login: 13-JAN-1997 15:20 (interactive), 13-JAN-1997 13:32
       (non-interactive)
Maxjobs:        0  Fillm:      300  Bytlm:        32768
Maxacctjobs:    0  Shrfillm:     0  Pbytlm:           0
```

```
Maxdetach:       0   BIOlm:        40   JTquota:      4096
Prclm:           2   DIOlm:        40   WSdef:        1024
Prio:            4   ASTlm:        40   WSquo:        2048
Queprio:         4   TQElm:        40   WSextent:     4096
CPU:        (none)   Enqlm:       200   Pgflquo:    102400
Authorized Privileges:
  NETMBX  TMPMBX
Default Privileges:
  CMKRNL  DETACH  LOG_IO  NETMBX  PRMMBX  SYSNAM  TMPMBX  WORLD
Identifier                       Value            Attributes
  ORA_DBINST_DBA                 %X80010002
  ORA_IPEC_DBA                   %X80010004
  ORA_DBA                        %X80010003
  ORA_715_DBA                    %X80010005
  ORA_715_OPER                   %X80010006

UAF> exit

%UAF-I-DONEMSG, system authorization file modified
%UAF-I-RDBDONEMSG, rights database modified

$
```

Now let's examine the global pages and global sections available on the machine to do an Oracle installation by running the SYSGEN utility.

```
$ run sys$system:sysgen

SYSGEN>   USE CURRENT

SYSGEN>   SHOW GBLSECTIONS

Parameter Name      Current   Default    Min.     Max.     Unit  Dynamic
--------------      -------   -------   -------  -------    ----  -------
GBLSECTIONS            1000       250        60     4095 Sections

SYSGEN>


SYSGEN>   SHOW GBLPAGES

Parameter Name      Current   Default    Min.     Max.     Unit  Dynamic
--------------      -------   -------   -------  -------    ----  -------
GBLPAGES             70000     15000       512  4194176 Pages

SYSGEN>
```

```
SYSGEN>   SHOW VIRTUAL

Parameter Name      Current    Default    Min.     Max.     Unit  Dynamic
--------------      -------    -------    -------  -------   ----  -------
VIRTUALPAGECNT       139072     12032       512   4194304   Pages


SYSGEN>

SYSGEN>   SHOW MAXSYSGROUP

Parameter Name      Current    Default    Min.     Max.      Unit  Dynamic
--------------      -------    -------    -------  -------    ----  -------
MAXSYSGROUP              8          8         1     32768 UIC Group   D


SYSGEN>

SYSGEN>   EXIT

$
```

Note that you should also check the LOCKIDTBL and REHASHTBL values if you are doing an OPS installation. To see all the SYSGEN parameters, you need to check for OPS installation; refer to the *Oracle7 for Alpha OpenVMS Installation Guide* for Version 7.3. If any of the above parameters need to be changed, you should run the AUTOGEN utility. A procedure to do this is shown below. However, no changes have been made since we have sufficient system resources.

```
$ @sys$update:autogen savparams getdata

%AUTOGEN-I-BEGIN, SAVPARAMS phase is beginning.
%AUTOGEN-I-NEWFILE, A new version of SYS$SYSTEM:AGEN$FEEDBACK.DAT
    has been created. You may wish to purge this file.
%AUTOGEN-I-END, SAVPARAMS phase has successfully completed.
%AUTOGEN-I-BEGIN, GETDATA phase is beginning.
%AUTOGEN-I-NEWFILE, A new version of SYS$SYSTEM:PARAMS.DAT has
    been created.
        You may wish to purge this file.
%AUTOGEN-I-END, GETDATA phase has successfully completed.
$

$ type sys$system:params.dat
```

```
!
! This data file should NOT be modified. Users wishing to alter the
! data in this file should modify SYS$SYSTEM:MODPARAMS.DAT instead.
!
VERSION="V6.2     "
CPUTYPE=19
XCPUTYPE=4
CPUTYPE_SAVE=19
WSTYPE=7
MEMSIZE=131072
MICROVAX="true"
DISKSPEED= 4
DISKSIZE=2050860
```

Please note that the **PARAMS.DAT** file above is not completely shown. If you want to modify any of the parameters, you should do so in the **MODPARAMS.DAT** file and use the following command to reboot the machine:

 `$ @sys$sysupdate:autogen genparams reboot`

## Check Disk Space

Now let's look at the amount of disk space available to do our installation.

 `$ show device dka`

| Device Name | Device Status | Error Count | Volume Label | Free Blocks | Trans Count | Mnt Cnt |
|---|---|---|---|---|---|---|
| ORABLR$DKA0: | Mounted | 0 | USER | 2031980 | 3 | 1 |
| ORABLR$DKA100: | Online | 0 | | | | |
| ORABLR$DKA200: | Online | 0 | | | | |
| ORABLR$DKA300: | Mounted | 0 | OPENVMS062 | 1355589 | 279 | 1 |
| ORABLR$DKA500: | Online | 0 | | | | |

ORABLR$DKA0 is the device on which we will perform the installation. This disk (we will call it DKA0) has 2031980 free blocks available. Since each VMS block is 512 bytes, this is approximately equivalent to 1 GB of available disk space. After the installation is complete, we will see how much of that disk space is actually utilized by Oracle. Now let's create the root directory that will hold the oracle code tree and start the installation by copying the initial BOOT.BCK saveset from CD-ROM to the root directory.

```
$ set def disk$user:[oracle]

$ copy :== copy/noconfirm

$ create/dir [.715]

$ dir

Directory DISK$USER:[ORACLE]
715.DIR;1
Total of 1 file.

$ set def [.715]

$ show def

   DISK$USER:[ORACLE.715]
```

One important point to remember is that a lot of files are copied from one location to another, by Oracle, as part of the installation. Make sure that your COPY command at OS level doesn't have the CONFIRM option on. By default, the COPY command has the NOCONFIRM option set. Otherwise, set the NOCONFIRM option as shown above. Also, as shown above, DISK$USER:[ORACLE.715] is our oracle root directory. The next step is to mount the CD-ROM drive and copy the BOOT.BCK save set.

```
$ mount orablr$dka500:/override=id
%MOUNT-I-WRITELOCK, volume is write locked
%MOUNT-I-MOUNTED, OVAXRDBMS08  mounted on _ORABLR$DKA500:
$
$ backup/log orablr$dka500:[server]boot.bck/sav -
[]*.*/new_version/by_owner=parent

%BACKUP-S-CREATED, created DISK$USER:[ORACLE.715]BIN2HEX.ABJ;1
%BACKUP-S-CREATED, created DISK$USER:[ORACLE.715]BIN2HEX.OBJ;1
%BACKUP-S-CREATED, created DISK$USER:[ORACLE.715]CRT.CTL;1
%BACKUP-S-CREATED, created DISK$USER:[ORACLE.715]CRT.DEF;1
```

# Install Online Documentation

Before you start using the installer, we recommend that you install the online documentation. Oracle7 Version 7.3.2 includes online documentation for the following OpenVMS-specific guides:

- *Oracle7 for Alpha OpenVMS Installation Guide*

- *Oracle7 Server and Tools Administrator's Guide for Alpha OpenVMS*

- *SQL*Net Version 2.3.2 for OpenVMS Configuration and User's Guide*

Beginning with Version 7.3.2, online documents are distributed by Oracle Corporation in HyperText Markup Language (HTML) format. You should use an HTML browser on OpenVMS to view them. We recommend that you follow the following steps to install online documentation:

1. Create a directory called ORACLEDOC.

2. Set default to ORACLEDOC directory.

3. Use the following BACKUP command to restore the documentation saveset. Please note that **orablr$dka500** is the CD-ROM device in this example:

```
$ Backup/log orablr$dka500:[ORACLEDOC]ORACLEDOC.BCK/SAVE_SET -
[*...]/NEW_VERSION/BY_OWNER=PARENT
```

To view the Oracle document, invoke your HTML browser and use the following URL:

```
FILE:/disk_device/ORACLEDOC/INDEX.HTML
```

Now let's log out of the ORACLE7 account from the VAX/OpenVMS machine.

```
$ log
```

```
ORACLE7      logged out at 13-JAN-1997 15:56:20.13
```

Note that after you mount the CD-ROM, it is very important that you finish the installation without logging out of the session. This is a common mistake made by DBAs while doing installation. Above, we purposely logged out of the session after installing online documentation to show you what happens in the later part of the installation. Now we log back into the system and continue with the installation by running ORACLEINS.COM. Again, throughout the installation, our input is given in bold letters. **<CR>** means that we have pressed ENTER.

# The Oracle Installer (ORACLEINS.COM) on OpenVMS

The command procedure ORACLEINS.COM is supplied with the installation media and should be used to perform an installation on OpenVMS. This section shows some of the common mistakes made by users and how to rectify them. The below examples should help you avoid these mistakes.

```
Welcome to OpenVMS VAX V6.2

Username: ORACLE7

Password:
     Welcome to OpenVMS VAX version V6.2 on node ORABLR
     Last interactive login on Monday, 13-JAN-1997 15:46
     Last non-interactive login on Monday, 13-JAN-1997 13:32

$ set def disk$user:[oracle.715]

$ dir

Directory DISK$USER:[ORACLE.715]
```

| | | | |
|---|---|---|---|
| BIN2HEX.ABJ;1 | BIN2HEX.OBJ;1 | CRT.CTL;1 | CRT.DEF;1 |
| DDBEXT.CTL;1 | DDBEXT.DEF;1 | FINDVMSV.COM;1 | HEX2BIN.ABJ;1 |
| HEX2BIN.MAR;1 | HEX2BIN.OBJ;1 | INSLIB.OLB;1 | INSTALLUSER.COM;1 |
| LOGIN.SQL;1 | NETCONFIG.CTL;1 | NETCONFIG.DEF;1 | NLS.CTL;1 |
| NLS.DEF;1 | ORACLEINS.COM;1 | ORACRTL.OLB;1 | ORA_ADD_USER.COM;1 |
| ORA_BLD.COM;1 | ORA_BUILDLIST.COM;1 | ORA_CHECKTAPE.COM;1 | ORA_COMMONUSER.COM;1 |
| ORA_DATA.COM;1 | ORA_DECONC_PATH.COM;1 | ORA_DEINST.COM;1 | ORA_DEL_DIRTREE.COM;1 |
| ORA_INST.COM;1 | ORA_INSUTL.COM;1 | ORA_LINKINS.COM;1 | ORA_LOAD.COM;1 |
| ORA_LOGICALREG.COM;1 | ORA_MERGE.COM;1 | ORA_NOV6_COMPAT.COM;1 | ORA_PRDCTL.COM;1 |
| ORA_SYM.COM;1 | ORA_V6_COMPAT.COM;1 | PARREXT.CTL;1 | PARREXT.DEF;1 |
| PQOPT.CTL;1 | PQOPT.DEF;1 | PRODUCTS.TXT;1 | PROGINT.CTL;1 |

```
PROGINT.DEF;1          RDBMS.CTL;1          RDBMS.DEF;1          README.DOC;1
SHIPDATE.BOOT;1        SQLDBA.SQL;1         SQLNETASY.CTL;1      SQLNETASY.DEF;1
SQLNETATK.CTL;1        SQLNETATK.DEF;1      SQLNETDNT.CTL;1      SQLNETDNT.DEF;1
SQLNETLU62.CTL;1       SQLNETLU62.DEF;1     SQLNETTCP.CTL;1      SQLNETTCP.DEF;1
SQLPLUS.CTL;1          SQLPLUS.DEF;1        SQLREPORT.CTL;1      SQLREPORT.DEF;1
SVRMGR.CTL;1           SVRMGR.DEF;1         UTIL.CTL;1           UTIL.DEF;1
```

Total of 68 files.
$ **@oracleins**

```
    WARNING:   Your system is low on either contiguous free global
               pages or free global sections.  If you plan to install
               an additional version of the Oracle shareable image,
               or create a new database, please be aware of the
               following:

               Global pages (definition: page = 512 bytes = pagelets on
Alpha):
               -  You will need ~24,000 for every Oracle shareable installed
               -  You will need 2 for *every* kilobyte used by your SGA.
                  The default INIT.ORA will create an SGA needing about
                  10,200 global pages (5 Megabytes).

               Global sections:
               -  You will need ~16 for every Oracle shareable installed.

               Your system currently has the following resources:

               CONTIG_GBLPAGES=29766 pagelets/512 byte pages
               FREE_GBLSECTS=611 pagelets/512 byte pages

Press [RETURN] to continue:   <CR>




                   ORACLE Installation Startup Menu



Options:

  1) Create a new ORACLE system.

  2) Upgrade your system from an ORACLE distribution tape.

  3) Reconfigure existing products, manage the database,
     or load demo tables.
```

```
4) Exit.

Before attempting to upgrade, reconfigure, manage the database, or load
demo tables, please run ORA_UTIL:ORAUSER.COM or, if you created an
instance, ORA_DB:ORAUSER_<database name>.COM <SID> <setup_node>.
```

Choose an option please: **1**


               Create ORACLE from distribution media
               -------------------------------------

```
ORACLE Installation Version 1.0.12.7 - Production on 13-JAN-1997
16:06:08.04
```

Copyright (c) 1994, Oracle Corporation, California, USA.  All rights reserved.

Root directory? ( DISK$USER:[ORACLE.715] ) **<CR>**

The root directory will be DISK$USER:[ORACLE.715].

If you are loading products from save sets, enter the drive/directory where
the save sets are located (e.g. MUA0: or DISK$A:[ORACLE.SAVE_SETS]).  If
you are loading from a remote device, do not include a username and
password (you will be prompted instead).

If not loading save sets, press [RETURN].

Save set location or [RETURN]: **orablr$dka500:**


   ORA_INST:  The specified load location not a valid directory or tape drive.
   Please try again.

If you are loading products from save sets, enter the drive/directory where
the save sets are located (e.g. MUA0: or DISK$A:[ORACLE.SAVE_SETS]).  If
you are loading from a remote device, do not include a username and
password (you will be prompted instead).

If not loading save sets, press [RETURN].

Save set location or [RETURN]: **orablr$dka500:[server]**

```
ORA_INST:  The specified load location not a valid directory or tape
drive.
    Please try again.
```

The above error occurred, saying that the specified load location is not a valid directory or tape drive, because we logged out and logged in again during the installation. This dismounted the CD-ROM drive. Make sure that the CD-ROM drive is in *mounted* state during the installation. If you issue the command **show device** at the OS prompt, you should see that the CD-ROM drive is mounted, as shown below:

```
$ mount orablr$dka500:/override=id

%MOUNT-I-WRITELOCK, volume is write locked
%MOUNT-I-MOUNTED, OVAXRDBMS08  mounted on _ORABLR$DKA500:
$
$ show device dka
```

| Device Name | Device Status | Error Count | Volume Label | Free Blocks | Trans Count | Mnt Cnt |
|---|---|---|---|---|---|---|
| ORABLR$DKA0: | Mounted | 0 | USER | 2031944 | 3 | 1 |
| ORABLR$DKA100: | Online | 0 | | | | |
| ORABLR$DKA200: | Online | 0 | | | | |
| ORABLR$DKA300: | Mounted | 0 | OPENVMS062 | 1355589 | 280 | 1 |
| ORABLR$DKA500: | Mounted alloc wrtlck | 0 | OVAXRDBMS08 | 241395 | 1 | 1 |

```
$
```

# Installation

Now let's continue with the installation assuming that the CD-ROM drive is mounted. This involves loading the products that you want to install, configuring each product, and building the executables for each of the products.

## Loading Products

In this phase of the installation, you have to tell Oracle which products you want to load from the CD-ROM. Note that Oracle will not actually copy the files from the CD-ROM until you enter the *build* phase of the installation.

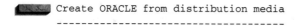 Create ORACLE from distribution media
------------------------------------

ORACLE Installation Version 1.0.12.7 - Production on 13-JAN-1997
16:15:18.78

Copyright (c) 1994, Oracle Corporation, California, USA.  All rights reserved.

Root directory? ( DISK$USER:[ORACLE.715] ) **<CR>**

The root directory will be DISK$USER:[ORACLE.715].

If you are loading products from save sets, enter the drive/directory where
the save sets are located (e.g. MUA0: or DISK$A:[ORACLE.SAVE_SETS]).  If
you are loading from a remote device, do not include a username and
password (you will be prompted instead).

If not loading save sets, press [RETURN].

Save set location or [RETURN]: **orablr$dka500:[server]**


The logical ORA_SOURCE now points to the default load location for
product save sets.  ORA_SOURCE has the following definition:
ORABLR$DKA500:[SERVER]

                    --- Doing some setup - please wait... ---


  - Creating ORA_UTIL:ORAUSER.COM.
  - Adding INSTALLUSER.COM to ORAUSER.COM.
  - Linking INSDRV.EXE for Install version 1.0.12.7 on VMS 6.2.

Press [RETURN] to continue: **<CR>**


                          Main Menu


                Oracle Product Installation and Upgrade
         _____


       1. Software Installation and Upgrade Menu

       2. Instance Creation, Startup, and Shutdown Menu

```
3. Build or Upgrade Database Tables Menu

Enter a number or (E)XIT to exit installation procedure:
1
```

In the main menu you should select the first option while installing code for the first time. However, if you are installing a new instance using the existing code tree, you should use the second option. Here we selected option 1 as we are installing the Oracle code for the first time.

```
              Software Installation and Upgrade Menu
         _____


    1. Select Products to Load

    2. Select Build Configuration Options

    3. Load and Build Selected Products

    4. Build Selected Products

              Enter a number or (E)XIT to return to the Main Menu:
1
```

The first option lets you select which products you want to load from the CD-ROM. The second option lets you configure each product that you have selected to load. The third option actually copies the code from the CD-ROM drive to the root directory and builds the products. The forth option just builds the products without copying the code from the CD-ROM. This last option is useful if you are trying to build the products after reconfiguring an existing product. For example, if you want to change the RDBMS installation from a *system* installation to a *group* installation, you can reconfigure the product using option 2 and then rebuild it by selecting option 4. We have selected the first option to decide which products we need. Let's proceed with the installation:

```
           Select Products to Load for Installation or Upgrade
      _____


  Product Name        Status          Product Name        Status
```

```
 1. CRT                    14. SQL*Plus
 2. DDBEXT                 15. SQL*Report
 3. NetConfig              16. SVRMGR
 4. NLS                    17. UTIL
 5. PARREXT
 6. PQOPT
 7. PROGINT
 8. RDBMS
 9. SQL*NetASY
10. SQL*NetATK
11. SQL*NetDNT
12. SQL*NetLU62
13. SQL*NetTCP


Enter (A)LL to select all products.

Enter (E)XIT to exit this menu with selected products.

Enter (Q)UIT to quit this menu with no action.

Enter the number of the product that you want to load:
1
Copy from ( ORA_SOURCE:CRT.BCK )
          > <CR>
```

A complete explanation of what these products mean and when you should select them is explained in Appendix A of the *Oracle7 for VAX OpenVMS Installation Guide.* Here, we are trying to install the RDBMS and the database extensions. To select a product, you need to type the product number and press ENTER when the copy prompt comes up as shown above. Then you will see the product screen with the status of the selected product as *load.* Since we chose to load product 1 above, you will see the screen as follows:

```
          Select Products to Load for Installation or Upgrade
          _____


   Product Name       Status        Product Name        Status

    1. CRT            - load         14. SQL*Plus
    2. DDBEXT                        15. SQL*Report
```

```
 3. NetConfig                    16. SVRMGR
 4. NLS                          17. UTIL
 5. PARREXT
 6. PQOPT
 7. PROGINT
 8. RDBMS
 9. SQL*NetASY
10. SQL*NetATK
11. SQL*NetDNT
12. SQL*NetLU62
13. SQL*NetTCP
```

```
Enter (A)LL to select all products.

Enter (E)XIT to exit this menu with selected products.

Enter (Q)UIT to quit this menu with no action.

Enter the number of the product that you want to load:
```

The following menu shows all the products that we have selected to load. A brief explanation of each product follows.

```
          Select Products to Load for Installation or Upgrade
          _____


    Product Name        Status        Product Name        Status

 1. CRT               - load       14. SQL*Plus          - load
 2. DDBEXT            - load       15. SQL*Report
 3. NetConfig         - load       16. SVRMGR            - load
 4. NLS                            17. UTIL              - load
 5. PARREXT           - load
 6. PQOPT             - load
 7. PROGINT           - load
 8. RDBMS             - load
 9. SQL*NetASY
10. SQL*NetATK
11. SQL*NetDNT        - load
12. SQL*NetLU62
13. SQL*NetTCP        - load
```

```
Enter (A)LL to select all products.

Enter (E)XIT to exit this menu with selected products.

Enter (Q)UIT to quit this menu with no action.

Enter the number of the product that you want to load:
e
```

CRT is used to set up terminal characteristics for Oracle products. CRT should be installed if you are using Oracle Applications. However, since CRT also defines some data dictionary views, you might want to install it even if you don't use Oracle Applications. DDBEXT specifies the distributed database option. If you want to use distributed transactions and two-phase commit, you should choose this option. In addition to this option, if you install PL/SQL, you can make remote procedure calls as well. PARREXT is the parallel server option. If you are running a VMS cluster with multiple instances of Oracle sharing the same database, then you should choose this option. If you intend to run only a single instance of Oracle, you don't need to install this option. The PQOPT is the parallel query option, which allows parallel query processing, index creation and data loading. Please note that installing this option doesn't automatically make queries parallel. You must explicitly alter the tables that you want to use for parallel query or use *hints* in your SQL statements.

PROGINT is the option that will allow you to use the precompilers such as Pro*C or other programmatic interfaces. NETCONFIG is a component that is used by all Oracle products. It contains the SQL*Net install scripts (SQL*Net 2.3 with Oracle 7.3), SQL*Net common code used by SQL*Net, and the drivers. It also contains the network utilities. SQL*Net DNT is the SQL*Net Version 2 DECnet adapter and SQL*Net TCP is the SQL*Net Version 2 TCP/IP adapter. Finally, UTIL is similar to NETCONFIG, it is a component that contains libraries and files, such as SQLLIB.OLB, that are accessed by several products. You should install and configure UTIL for every Oracle product installation.

**NOTE**
*With Oracle7 version 7.3.2 there are some new options available. AGENT is the Oracle Intelligent Agent. Use this only if you are using the Oracle Enterprise Manager. AROPT is the advanced replication option. SDOPT is the Spatial Data Option, which requires 10MB of free space in the SYSTEM tablespace. This happens automatically if you are installing Oracle7 version 7.3.2. If you are upgrading from 7.1.5, make sure you add 10MB of free space to the SYSTEM tablespace if you want to use the Spatial Data tables.*

## Configuring Products

Once the desired products are selected to load, you should configure them. Each product will have two basic options: First, you can decide whether to install it at a group level or system level. Whatever you decide, use the same value for all products. The second important option is to link it *shared* or *non-shared*. The S option means linking it shared. The T option stands for Independent Tools. There are some combinations of products and databases that don't work with the S option. For example, if you are using Oracle Version 6 tools with a 7.3 database, you have to use them in the client-server model. Let's configure some of the products that we have selected:

```
            Software Installation and Upgrade Menu
        _____


        1. Select Products to Load

        2. Select Build Configuration Options

        3. Load and Build Selected Products

        4. Build Selected Products

              Enter a number or (E)XIT to return to the Main Menu:
```

2

```
                    Select Configuration Options
          _____

        List of products available for installation or upgrade
configuration:

            1.  CRT                    14.  SQL*Plus
            2.  DDBEXT                 15.  SQL*Report
            3.  NetConfig              16.  SVRMGR
            4.  NLS                    17.  UTIL
            5.  PARREXT
            6.  PQOPT
            7.  PROGINT
            8.  RDBMS
            9.  SQL*NetASY
           10.  SQL*NetATK
           11.  SQL*NetDNT
           12.  SQL*NetLU62
           13.  SQL*NetTCP


Enter (A)LL to select all products.

Enter (E)XIT to exit this menu with selected products.

Enter (Q)UIT to quit this menu with no action.

Enter the number of the product that you want to configure:
1

                    CRT Configuration Options

Option                                        Current Value

 1. System or Group installation? [S/G]          S
 2. Which is the default crt?                     VT100
 3. Link Option? [S/T]                            S

Enter (A)LL to select all options.

Enter (E)XIT to exit this menu with selected options.

Enter (Q)UIT to quit this menu with no action.

Enter the number of the option that you want to change:
e
```

Select Configuration Options
_____

        List of products available for installation or upgrade
configuration:

|     |              |           |     |            |
| --- | ------------ | --------- | --- | ---------- |
| 1.  | CRT          | - rebuild | 14. | SQL*Plus   |
| 2.  | DDBEXT       |           | 15. | SQL*Report |
| 3.  | NetConfig    |           | 16. | SVRMGR     |
| 4.  | NLS          |           | 17. | UTIL       |
| 5.  | PARREXT      |           |     |            |
| 6.  | PQOPT        |           |     |            |
| 7.  | PROGINT      |           |     |            |
| 8.  | RDBMS        |           |     |            |
| 9.  | SQL*NetASY   |           |     |            |
| 10. | SQL*NetATK   |           |     |            |
| 11. | SQL*NetDNT   |           |     |            |
| 12. | SQL*NetLU62  |           |     |            |
| 13. | SQL*NetTCP   |           |     |            |

Enter (A)LL to select all products.

Enter (E)XIT to exit this menu with selected products.

Enter (Q)UIT to quit this menu with no action.

Enter the number of the product that you want to configure:
**2**

                    DDBEXT Configuration Options

Option                                          Current Value

 1. System or Group installation? [S/G]              S

Enter (A)LL to select all options.

Enter (E)XIT to exit this menu with selected options.

Enter (Q)UIT to quit this menu with no action.

Enter the number of the option that you want to change:
**e**

Select Configuration Options
_____

List of products available for installation or upgrade
configuration:

|     |            |           |     |            |
|-----|------------|-----------|-----|------------|
| 1.  | CRT        | - rebuild | 14. | SQL*Plus   |
| 2.  | DDBEXT     | - rebuild | 15. | SQL*Report |
| 3.  | NetConfig  |           | 16. | SVRMGR     |
| 4.  | NLS        |           | 17. | UTIL       |
| 5.  | PARREXT    |           |     |            |
| 6.  | PQOPT      |           |     |            |
| 7.  | PROGINT    |           |     |            |
| 8.  | RDBMS      |           |     |            |
| 9.  | SQL*NetASY |           |     |            |
| 10. | SQL*NetATK |           |     |            |
| 11. | SQL*NetDNT |           |     |            |
| 12. | SQL*NetLU62|           |     |            |
| 13. | SQL*NetTCP |           |     |            |

Enter (A)LL to select all products.

Enter (E)XIT to exit this menu with selected products.

Enter (Q)UIT to quit this menu with no action.

Enter the number of the product that you want to configure:
**8**

RDBMS Configuration Options

| Option | Current Value |
|--------|---------------|
| 1. System or Group Installation? [S/G] | S |
| 2. ORACLE Image Identifier? | V715 |
| 3. SGA Base Address (Bytes)? | 512 |
| 4. Size of SGA Pad (KBytes)? | 5120 |
| 5. Link Option for Tools located in ORA_ROOT:<RDBMS>? [S/T] | S |
| 6. Include distributed database option? [Y/N] | N |
| 7. Include Parallel Server option? [Y/N] | N |
| 8. Include parallel query option? [Y/N] | N |

Enter (A)LL to select all options.

```
Enter (E)XIT to exit this menu with selected options.

Enter (Q)UIT to quit this menu with no action.

Enter the number of the option that you want to change:
4


Size of SGA Pad (KBytes)?
   Original Default:  5120
   Current Value   :  5120
   New Value       >
3000
```

```
                         RDBMS Configuration Options


Option                                          Current Value

   1. System or Group Installation? [S/G]          S
   2. ORACLE Image Identifier?                     V715
   3. SGA Base Address (Bytes)?                     512
   4. Size of SGA Pad (KBytes)?                     3000
   5. Link Option for Tools located in             S
      ORA_ROOT:<RDBMS>? [S/T]
   6. Include distributed database option? [Y/N]   N
   7. Include Parallel Server option? [Y/N]        N
   8. Include parallel query option? [Y/N]         N

Enter (A)LL to select all options.

Enter (E)XIT to exit this menu with selected options.

Enter (Q)UIT to quit this menu with no action.

Enter the number of the option that you want to change:
6
```

Note one important point above: We have changed the SGAPAD size from the default value to 3000 K. This will have serious ramifications as we will see later on. This is a common mistake made by customers doing an installation for the first time. We have selected all the database extensions shown in the above menu in options 6, 7, and 8. The final RDBMS configuration looks as follows:

```
                    RDBMS Configuration Options

Option                                        Current Value

1. System or Group Installation? [S/G]        S
2. ORACLE Image Identifier?                   V715
3. SGA Base Address (Bytes)?                  512
4. Size of SGA Pad (KBytes)?                  3000
5. Link Option for Tools located in           S
   ORA_ROOT:<RDBMS>? [S/T]
6. Include distributed database option? [Y/N] Y
7. Include Parallel Server option? [Y/N]      Y
8. Include parallel query option? [Y/N]       Y


Enter (A)LL to select all options.

Enter (E)XIT to exit this menu with selected options.

Enter (Q)UIT to quit this menu with no action.

Enter the number of the option that you want to change:
e


                    Select Configuration Options
          _____


     List of products available for installation or upgrade
configuration:

        1.  CRT             - rebuild    14. SQL*Plus
        2.  DDBEXT          - rebuild    15. SQL*Report
        3.  NetConfig                    16. SVRMGR
        4.  NLS                          17. UTIL
        5.  PARREXT
        6.  PQOPT
        7.  PROGINT
        8.  RDBMS           - rebuild
        9.  SQL*NetASY
       10.  SQL*NetATK
       11.  SQL*NetDNT
       12.  SQL*NetLU62
       13.  SQL*NetTCP


Enter (A)LL to select all products.
```

```
Enter (E)XIT to exit this menu with selected products.

Enter (Q)UIT to quit this menu with no action.

Enter the number of the product that you want to configure:
e
```

```
                  Software Installation and Upgrade Menu
      _____


         1. Select Products to Load

         2. Select Build Configuration Options

         3. Load and Build Selected Products

         4. Build Selected Products

Enter a number or (E)XIT to return to the Main Menu:
3
```

This starts the loading process, which involves copying various files
from the CD-ROM to the root directory. A portion of the code is given
below and its not complete.

```
  - Creating CRT directories.
  - Loading CRT files into ORA_ROOT:[CRT].
%BACKUP-S-CREATED, created ORA_ROOT:[CRT]CRT.CTL;1
%BACKUP-S-CREATED, created ORA_ROOT:[CRT]CRT.DEF;1
%BACKUP-S-CREATED, created ORA_ROOT:[CRT]CRT.DOC;1
..
..
%BACKUP-S-CREATED, created ORA_ROOT:[UTIL]UTLIB.OLB;1
12 products have been successfully loaded.

    The products you requested have been loaded.

    You have the following options:

    1.  Build the Oracle products loaded.

    2.  Return to the Software Installation and Upgrade Menu (to
```

```
      choose new configuration values or to load additional
      products from another tape or directory).
```

```
Enter the number of the option you want [2]: 1
```

# Building Executables

Note that after loading all the necessary files and before building the executables, the installation script gives you one last chance to reconfigure if you have done something wrong or forgotten to configure a product. Once you select option 1 as shown above, Oracle starts running a lot of .COM files and creates the necessary executables (.EXE files) as shown below. Note that the listing below is not complete.

```
    - Creating list of products to rebuild.

    - Running ORA_SQLNETDNT_BLD.COM.
    - Adding SQLNETDNTUSER.COM to ORAUSER.COM.
    ..

    ..
    - Linking LSNRCTL.EXE
    - Linking TNSLSNR.EXE
    - Adding NETCONFIGUSER.COM to ORAUSER.COM.

    - Running ORA_PARREXT_BLD.COM.
    - Adding PARREXTUSER.COM to ORAUSER.COM.

    - Running ORA_PQOPT_BLD.COM.
    - Adding PQOPTUSER.COM to ORAUSER.COM.

    - Running ORA_DDBEXT_BLD.COM.
    - Adding DDBEXTUSER.COM to ORAUSER.COM.

    - Running ORA_RDBMS_BLD.COM.
    - Building ORACLE with the following configuration parameters
        RDBMS image                 : ORACLEV715
        Root directory              : DISK$USER:[ORACLE.715]
        RDBMS Tools Link option     : S
        Parallel Server option      : Y
        Distributed database option : Y
```

```
        Parallel query option        : Y
        SGA base address             : 512
        SGA size                     : 3000
        Accessible by                : SYSTEM
- Linking Oracle utilities
- Linking shared ORACLE image (ORACLE)

- Scanning map file for symbols.

- 11268 symbols read from ora_map:oracle.map
- Writing symbol file.

- Running SYM2STB

    Reading symbols from file: ora_common:oracle.sym

    Writing symbols to file:   ora_common:oracle.stb

- Linking shared ORA*CORE image
- Linking shared UPI image
- Linking SRV.EXE
- Linking SQLDBA.EXE
..
..
- Running ORA_SQLPLUS_BLD.COM.
 - Linking SQLPLUS.EXE
 - Adding SQLPLUSUSER.COM to ORAUSER.COM.
12 products have been successfully built.

 NOTE:  If you wish to create known file entries for some of the
        linked products using the VMS INSTALL utility, run
ORA_INSTALL:ORA_INSUTL.COM.
        Refer to the appropriate ORACLE for OpenVMS
        Administrator's Guide for details.

Press [RETURN] to continue: <CR>

                   Software Installation and Upgrade Menu
                   _____

        1. Select Products to Load

        2. Select Build Configuration Options
```

```
3. Load and Build Selected Products

4. Build Selected Products

        Enter a number or (E)XIT to return to the
Main Menu:
e


                        Main Menu


            Oracle Product Installation and Upgrade
    _____

    1. Software Installation and Upgrade Menu

    2. Instance Creation, Startup, and Shutdown Menu

    3. Build or Upgrade Database Tables Menu

  Enter a number or (E)XIT to exit installation procedure:
2
```

Note that we have successfully finished the code installation from the main menu. Next, we have to create an instance and a database. Therefore, we have selected option 2 from the main menu.

```
            Instance Creation, Startup, and Shutdown Menu
    _____

  1. Create a New Instance and Database

  2. Startup an Existing Instance

  3. Set up a Parallel Server Instance

  4. Shutdown an Existing Instance

            Enter a number or (E)XIT to return to Main Menu:
1

            Currently known database SIDs:
```

<NONE>

Press [RETURN] to quit with no action.

NOTE:   The SID can be a maximum of 6 characters in length.

What is the SID for the instance you want to create?
**715**

NOTE:   The database name can be a maximum of 8 characters in length.

What is the name of the database you want to create?
**715**

RDBMSDB Configuration Options

Option                                                    Current Value

1. System or Group Installation? [S/G]                    S
2. Root directory for database administration             ORA_ROOT:[000000]
   directory (ORA_DB)?
3. Initial database file for SYSTEM Tablespace?           ORA_DB:ORA_SYSTEM.DBS
4. Initial size of SYSTEM Tablespace?                     10M
5. Log File 1?                                            ORA_DB:ORA_LOG1.RDO
6. Log File 1 Size?                                       500K
7. Log File 2?                                            ORA_DB:ORA_LOG2.RDO
8. Log File 2 Size?                                       500K
9. Control File 1 Name?                                   ORA_DB:ORA_CONTROL1.CON
10. Control File 2 Name?                                  ORA_DB:ORA_CONTROL2.CON
11. Value for MAXDATAFILES   (1..1022)?                   32
12. Value for MAXLOGFILES    (2..254)?                    32
13. Value for MAXINSTANCES   (1..63)?                     16
14. Value for MAXLOGMEMBERS (1..5)?                       2
15. Value for MAXLOGHISTORY (0..5000)?                    1600
16. Value for CHARACTER SET?                              US7ASCII

Enter (A)LL to select all options.

Enter (E)XIT to exit this menu with selected options.

Enter (Q)UIT to quit this menu with no action.

```
Enter the number of the option that you want to change:
4

Initial size of SYSTEM Tablespace?
   Original Default:  10M
   Current Value    :  10M
   New Value        >
5m
```

**NOTE**

*Although the Oracle7 for VAX OpenVMS Installation Guide* says that six alphanumeric characters or fewer should be entered for the instance SID and eight alphanumeric characters or fewer should be used for the database name, we recommend that the SID and database names start with an alpha character (and not numeric character as shown in the above installation) since there have been some problems when the SID and database names start with a number.

Please note that the default sizes for the online log files and the SYSTEM data file are quite reasonable. Since this is a test installation, we have changed the sizes of the SYSTEM data file and the log files. More importantly, the MAX*parameters* shown above from options 11 through 15 are worth modifying. While the values you select depend on your business needs (How fast will your data grow? How fast do you generate redo? Will you be running multiple instances? How many log file members do you want to maintain for fault tolerance? etc.), the default values provided (at least for some options) are small. Our experience shows that the default values provided by Oracle for MAXDATAFILES and MAXLOGMEMBERS is small. Below, we show the final configuration for the database after modifying all of the MAX*parameter* options.

```
                        RDBMSDB Configuration Options


Option                                          Current Value

 1. System or Group Installation? [S/G]              S
```

```
 2. Root directory for database administration    ORA_ROOT:[000000]
    directory (ORA_DB)?
 3. Initial database file for SYSTEM Tablespace?   ORA_DB:ORA_SYSTEM.DBS
 4. Initial size of SYSTEM Tablespace?             5M
 5. Log File 1?                                    ORA_DB:ORA_LOG1.RDO
 6. Log File 1 Size?                                100K
 7. Log File 2?                                    ORA_DB:ORA_LOG2.RDO
 8. Log File 2 Size?                                100K
 9. Control File 1 Name?                           ORA_DB:ORA_CONTROL1.CON
10. Control File 2 Name?                           ORA_DB:ORA_CONTROL2.CON
11. Value for MAXDATAFILES   (1..1022)?            200
12. Value for MAXLOGFILES    (2..254)?             50
13. Value for MAXINSTANCES   (1..63)?              16
14. Value for MAXLOGMEMBERS (1..5)?                4
15. Value for MAXLOGHISTORY (0..5000)?             1600
16. Value for CHARACTER SET?                       US7ASCII

Enter (A)LL to select all options.

Enter (E)XIT to exit this menu with selected options.

Enter (Q)UIT to quit this menu with no action.

Enter the number of the option that you want to change:
e


      A directory has been created for database 715, which contains
scripts to create the database, start it, shut it down, and define
instance-specific and database-specific logicals.  In addition, a node-
specific file (ORABLR_715_INIT.ORA) has been created for the
instance 715 that will call the database-specific INIT.ORA
and INITPS.ORA files, which are also included in this directory.

NOTES:
   - ORA_PARAMS has been set to point to ORABLR_715_INIT.ORA
   - The directory that contains these files is located at:
     DISK$USER:[ORACLE.715.db_715]

Continuing will initialize your database.

Do you want to continue (Y/N)? [Y]   <CR>

Now creating the initial data file, control files, and log files
of your database...
```

```
SQL*DBA: Release 7.1.5.2.4 - Production on Mon Jan 13 16:49:24 1997

Copyright (c) Oracle Corporation 1979, 1994.  All rights reserved.

Oracle7 Server Release 7.1.5.2.4 - Production Release
With the distributed, parallel query and Parallel Server options
PL/SQL Release 2.1.5.2.0 - Production

SQLDBA>
File DISK$USER:[ORACLE.715.DB_715]CREATE_715.LOG opened Mon Jan 13
16:49:25 1997.

SQLDBA>

SQLDBA>
remark - This will take some time, please wait.

SQLDBA>

SQLDBA>
connect internal

Connected.

SQLDBA>
startup nomount

ORA-07639: smscre: SGA pad area not large enough (4621824 bytes required)
 - %SYSTEM-S-NORMAL, normal successful completion

SQLDBA>
create database "715" controlfile reuse
2>
        datafile 'ORA_DB:ORA_SYSTEM.DBS' size 5M reuse
3>
        logfile   'ORA_DB:ORA_LOG1.RDO' size 100K reuse,
4>
                  'ORA_DB:ORA_LOG2.RDO' size 100K reuse
5>
        maxdatafiles    200
6>
        maxlogfiles     50
7>
        maxinstances    16
8>
```

```
        maxlogmembers   4
9>
        maxloghistory   1600
10>
        character set   US7ASCII;

DBA-00342: unable to complete internal login

ORA-01034: ORACLE not available
ORA-07625: smsget: $MGBLSC failure
%SYSTEM-W-NOSUCHSEC, no such (global) section

SQLDBA>

SQLDBA>
set termout off

SQLDBA>
SQL*DBA complete.

Press [RETURN] to continue: <CR>
```

Note that the above installation has failed while trying to start up the database with the error *ORA-07639: smscre: SGA pad area not large enough (4621824 bytes required)*. The INIT.ORA file supplied by Oracle creates a minimum SGA size of about 4.7 megabytes as indicated in the error. This shows that modifying the SGAPAD size, while configuring the RDBMS, has caused the above failure. The SGAPAD is a file on the disk that maps the SGA. The SGAPAD size should always be greater than the SGA size. Having said this, now we have two options to rectify this problem: One, we can modify the INIT.ORA file size supplied by Oracle and reduce some of the parameter sizes to reduce the SGA size so that it is less than 3 megabytes (since our SGAPAD is 3 megabytes). However, this is a bad option since Oracle recommends a minimum size for the SGA of about 4.7 MB. The second option is to go back and reconfigure the RDBMS and set the SGAPAD size back to 5 MB (which is the default). Unfortunately, this is time-consuming since we have to rebuild the RDBMS after reconfiguring. This exercise is done to show users how important it is *not* to modify (especially reduce) the size of the SGAPAD. Now let's go ahead and reconfigure the RDBMS and re-link it before creating the instance.

```
                        Instance Creation, Startup, and Shutdown Menu
            _____

            1. Create a New Instance and Database

            2. Startup an Existing Instance

            3. Set up a Parallel Server Instance

            4. Shutdown an Existing Instance

                    Enter a number or (E)XIT to return to Main Menu:
    e


                            Main Menu


                    Oracle Product Installation and Upgrade
            _____

            1. Software Installation and Upgrade Menu

            2. Instance Creation, Startup, and Shutdown Menu

            3. Build or Upgrade Database Tables Menu

        Enter a number or (E)XIT to exit installation procedure:
    1


                        Software Installation and Upgrade Menu
            _____

            1. Select Products to Load

            2. Select Build Configuration Options

            3. Load and Build Selected Products

            4. Build Selected Products

        Enter a number or (E)XIT to return to the Main Menu:
    2


                            Select Configuration Options
            _____
```

List of products available for installation or upgrade configuration:

```
 1. CRT                          14. SQL*Plus
 2. DDBEXT                       15. SQL*Report
 3. NetConfig                    16. SVRMGR
 4. NLS                          17. UTIL
 5. PARREXT
 6. PQOPT
 7. PROGINT
 8. RDBMS
 9. SQL*NetASY
10. SQL*NetATK
11. SQL*NetDNT
12. SQL*NetLU62
13. SQL*NetTCP
```

Enter (A)LL to select all products.

Enter (E)XIT to exit this menu with selected products.

Enter (Q)UIT to quit this menu with no action.

Enter the number of the product that you want to configure:
**8**


RDBMS Configuration Options


| Option | Current Value |
| --- | --- |
| 1. System or Group Installation? [S/G] | S |
| 2. ORACLE Image Identifier? | V715 |
| 3. SGA Base Address (Bytes)? | 512 |
| 4. Size of SGA Pad (KBytes)? | 3000 |
| 5. Link Option for Tools located in ORA_ROOT:<RDBMS>? [S/T] | S |
| 6. Include distributed database option? [Y/N] | Y |
| 7. Include Parallel Server option? [Y/N] | Y |
| 8. Include parallel query option? [Y/N] | Y |

Enter (A)LL to select all options.

Enter (E)XIT to exit this menu with selected options.

Enter (Q)UIT to quit this menu with no action.

```
Enter the number of the option that you want to change:
4

Size of SGA Pad (KBytes)?
   Original Default:  5120
   Current Value   :  3000
   New Value       >
5120
```

RDBMS Configuration Options

| Option | Current Value |
|--------|---------------|
| 1. System or Group Installation? [S/G] | S |
| 2. ORACLE Image Identifier? | V715 |
| 3. SGA Base Address (Bytes)? | 512 |
| 4. Size of SGA Pad (KBytes)? | 5120 |
| 5. Link Option for Tools located in<br>   ORA_ROOT:<RDBMS>? [S/T] | S |
| 6. Include distributed database option? [Y/N] | Y |
| 7. Include Parallel Server option? [Y/N] | Y |
| 8. Include parallel query option? [Y/N] | Y |

```
Enter (A)LL to select all options.

Enter (E)XIT to exit this menu with selected options.

Enter (Q)UIT to quit this menu with no action.

Enter the number of the option that you want to change:
e
```

Select Configuration Options
_____

List of products available for installation or upgrade configuration:

| | | | |
|---|---|---|---|
| 1. | CRT | 14. | SQL*Plus |
| 2. | DDBEXT | 15. | SQL*Report |
| 3. | NetConfig | 16. | SVRMGR |
| 4. | NLS | 17. | UTIL |
| 5. | PARREXT | | |
| 6. | PQOPT | | |
| 7. | PROGINT | | |

```
 8.  RDBMS                     - rebuild
 9.  SQL*NetASY
10.  SQL*NetATK
11.  SQL*NetDNT
12.  SQL*NetLU62
13.  SQL*NetTCP

Enter (A)LL to select all products.

Enter (E)XIT to exit this menu with selected products.

Enter (Q)UIT to quit this menu with no action.

Enter the number of the product that you want to configure:
e


             Software Installation and Upgrade Menu
             _____


       1. Select Products to Load

       2. Select Build Configuration Options

       3. Load and Build Selected Products

       4. Build Selected Products


            Enter a number or (E)XIT to return to the Main Menu:
4


 - Creating list of products to rebuild.

 - Running ORA_RDBMS_BLD.COM.
 - Building ORACLE with the following configuration parameters
       RDBMS image                : ORACLEV715
       Root directory             : DISK$USER:[ORACLE.715]
       RDBMS Tools Link option    : S
       Parallel Server option     : Y
       Distributed database option : Y
       Parallel query option      : Y
       SGA base address           : 512
       SGA size                   : 5120
       Accessible by              : SYSTEM
```

```
- Linking Oracle utilities
- Linking shared ORACLE image (ORACLE)
..

..
- Running ORA_SQLPLUS_BLD.COM.
- Linking SQLPLUS.EXE
6 products have been successfully built.

NOTE:  If you wish to create known file entries for some of the linked
       products using the VMS INSTALL utility, run
ORA_INSTALL:ORA_INSUTL.COM.
       Refer to the appropriate ORACLE for OpenVMS Administrator's Guide
       for details.


Press [RETURN] to continue: <CR>

                  Software Installation and Upgrade Menu
           _____


        1. Select Products to Load

        2. Select Build Configuration Options

        3. Load and Build Selected Products

        4. Build Selected Products

                Enter a number or (E)XIT to return to the Main Menu:
e
```

Please note that we tried to rebuild only the RDBMS, but you can see that a total of six products have been rebuilt. Oracle Installer does this automatically, as it understands product dependencies when you rebuild the RDBMS.

# Creating a New Instance and Database

In this section, we will choose the second option from the main menu and will demonstrate how to create a new instance and a database.

```
                              Main Menu


                Oracle Product Installation and Upgrade
          _____

       1. Software Installation and Upgrade Menu

       2. Instance Creation, Startup, and Shutdown Menu

       3. Build or Upgrade Database Tables Menu

   Enter a number or (E)XIT to exit installation procedure:
 2

                Instance Creation, Startup, and Shutdown Menu
          _____

       1. Create a New Instance and Database

       2. Startup an Existing Instance

       3. Set up a Parallel Server Instance

       4. Shutdown an Existing Instance

                  Enter a number or (E)XIT to return to Main Menu:
 1

                  Currently known database SIDs:

                              715
```

### NOTE
*Even though the instance creation failed the*
*first time, the SID we tried* to create is still
stored by Oracle.

```
                  Press [RETURN] to quit with no action.

          NOTE:  The SID can be a maximum of 6 characters in length.

   What is the SID for the instance you want to create?
 715
```

```
        NOTE:  The database name can be a maximum of 8 characters in length.

What is the name of the database you want to create?
715

                    RDBMSDB Configuration Options


Option                                        Current Value


 1. System or Group Installation? [S/G]       S
 2. Root directory for database administration ORA_ROOT:[000000]
    directory (ORA_DB)?
 3. Initial database file for SYSTEM Tablespace? ORA_DB:ORA_SYSTEM.DBS
 4. Initial size of SYSTEM Tablespace?        5M
 5. Log File 1?                               ORA_DB:ORA_LOG1.RDO
 6. Log File 1 Size?                          100K
 7. Log File 2?                               ORA_DB:ORA_LOG2.RDO
 8. Log File 2 Size?                          100K
 9. Control File 1 Name?                      ORA_DB:ORA_CONTROL1.CON
10. Control File 2 Name?                      ORA_DB:ORA_CONTROL2.CON
11. Value for MAXDATAFILES   (1..1022)?       200
12. Value for MAXLOGFILES    (2..254)?        50
13. Value for MAXINSTANCES   (1..63)?         16
14. Value for MAXLOGMEMBERS (1..5)?           4
15. Value for MAXLOGHISTORY (0..5000)?        1600
16. Value for CHARACTER SET?                  US7ASCII

Enter (A)LL to select all options.

Enter (E)XIT to exit this menu with selected options.

Enter (Q)UIT to quit this menu with no action.

Enter the number of the option that you want to change:
e
```

Again note above that the database options are stored by the installation even though the previous instance creation had failed. Now, Oracle starts creating the database for you.

```
ORA_RDBMS_CDB:
    The directory ORA_DB (DISK$USER:[ORACLE.715.db_715])
    and/or the data files for database 715 already exist.
```

```
     If you continue, you will destroy any existing data files.

Do you want to continue (Y/N)? [N] y

  ORA_RDBMS_CDB:  The SID 715 is already in use on this
     node (ORABLR) by another instance of this database (715).

     If you continue, you will override this other instance (careful!).

Do you want to continue (Y/N)? [N] y


     A directory has been created for database 715, which contains
  scripts to create the database, start it, shut it down, and define
  instance-specific and database-specific logicals.  In addition, a node-
  specific file (ORABLR_715_INIT.ORA) has been created for the
  instance 715 that will call the database-specific INIT.ORA
  and INITPS.ORA files, which are also included in this directory.

  NOTES:
     - ORA_PARAMS has been set to point to ORABLR_715_INIT.ORA
     - The directory that contains these files is located at:
       DISK$USER:[ORACLE.715.db_715]

  Continuing will initialize your database.

  Do you want to continue (Y/N)? [Y]  y

  Now creating the initial data file, control files, and log files
  of your database...

%DCL-I-SUPERSEDE, previous value of ORA_SID has been superseded

SQL*DBA: Release 7.1.5.2.4 - Production on Mon Jan 13 16:59:17 1997

Copyright (c) Oracle Corporation 1979, 1994.  All rights reserved.

Oracle7 Server Release 7.1.5.2.4 - Production Release
With the distributed, parallel query and Parallel Server options
PL/SQL Release 2.1.5.2.0 - Production

SQLDBA>
File DISK$USER:[ORACLE.715.DB_715]CREATE_715.LOG opened Mon Jan 13
16:59:18 1997.
```

```
SQLDBA>

SQLDBA>
remark - This will take some time, please wait.

SQLDBA>

SQLDBA>
connect internal

Connected.

SQLDBA>
startup nomount

ORACLE instance started.

SQLDBA>
create database "715" controlfile reuse
     2>
        datafile 'ORA_DB:ORA_SYSTEM.DBS' size 5M reuse
     3>
        logfile   'ORA_DB:ORA_LOG1.RDO' size 100K reuse,
     4>
                  'ORA_DB:ORA_LOG2.RDO' size 100K reuse
     5>
        maxdatafiles   200
     6>
        maxlogfiles    50
     7>
        maxinstances   16
     8>
        maxlogmembers  4
     9>
        maxloghistory  1600
    10>
        character set  US7ASCII;

Statement processed.

SQLDBA>

SQLDBA>
set termout off
```

```
ORABLR::ORACLE7 17:15:42 SQLDBA       CPU=00:09:31.82 PF=298104 IO=110050
MEM=12708
ORABLR::ORACLE7 17:15:47 SQLDBA       CPU=00:09:32.34 PF=298112 IO=110052
MEM=12711
ORABLR::ORACLE7 17:16:19 SQLDBA       CPU=00:09:37.96 PF=298176 IO=110513
MEM=12771

SQLDBA>
SQL*DBA complete.



Press [RETURN] to continue: <CR>
```

This completes the creation of the new instance of SID 715 and the database called 715. Note that creating the database will take some time and you need to be patient. If you want to make sure that the process is working, you can press CTRL-T to make sure of this. This will give you information about CPU, Page faults and I/O information. In the above instance creation, you will see that a CTRL-T was issued three times. When the instance creation is done, the database is left in an **open** state. The following test proves this:

```
              Instance Creation, Startup, and Shutdown Menu
         _____


         1. Create a New Instance and Database

         2. Startup an Existing Instance

         3. Set up a Parallel Server Instance

         4. Shutdown an Existing Instance

                 Enter a number or (E)XIT to return to Main Menu:
2

                 Currently known database SIDs:

                            715

            Press [RETURN] to quit with no action.

      NOTE:  The SID can be a maximum of 6 characters in length.
```

```
What is the SID for the instance you want to startup?
715

%DCL-I-SUPERSEDE, previous value of ORA_SID has been superseded

SQL*DBA: Release 7.1.5.2.4 - Production on Mon Jan 13 17:17:30 1997

Copyright (c) Oracle Corporation 1979, 1994.  All rights reserved.

Oracle7 Server Release 7.1.5.2.4 - Production Release
With the distributed, parallel query and Parallel Server options
PL/SQL Release 2.1.5.2.0 - Production

SQLDBA>
File DISK$USER:[ORACLE.715.DB_715]STARTUP_EXCLUSIVE_715.LOG opened Mon Jan
13 17:17:31 1997.

SQLDBA>
connect internal

Connected.

SQLDBA>
startup open "715"

ORA-01081: cannot start already-running ORACLE - shut it down first

SQLDBA>

SQLDBA>
SQL*DBA complete.

Press [RETURN] to continue: <CR>


                 Instance Creation, Startup, and Shutdown Menu
            _____


        1. Create a New Instance and Database

        2. Startup an Existing Instance

        3. Set up a Parallel Server Instance
```

```
        4. Shutdown an Existing Instance

              Enter a number or (E)XIT to return to Main Menu:
e


                            Main Menu


              Oracle Product Installation and Upgrade
          _____

        1. Software Installation and Upgrade Menu

        2. Instance Creation, Startup, and Shutdown Menu

        3. Build or Upgrade Database Tables Menu

    Enter a number or (E)XIT to exit installation procedure:
e

                    ---- ORACLEINS Completed ----
$
```

# Post Installation Tasks

Post-installation tasks include creating the demo tables, testing the database installation, selecting ARCHIVELOG mode, and testing the installation of Oracle shared images.

## Creating Demo Tables

Once the instance and database are created, you should use the third option "Build or Upgrade Database Tables Menu" from the main menu to build demo tables. This will show you a list of all the products. Enter the item number of each product whose database tables you want to create. Next, enter **I** to initialize (**U** to upgrade for existing system tables) the system tables for the new products you just installed. When asked whether you want to create demo tables, press **Y**. We recommend that you create the demo tables.

## Test Database Installation

Once the basic installation and instance creation are done, we need to do some simple tests to make sure that the database has been installed correctly. So let's connect to the database and select from a few common tables:

```
$ sqldba lmode=y

SQL*DBA: Release 7.1.5.2.4 - Production on Mon Jan 13 17:18:00 1997

Copyright (c) Oracle Corporation 1979, 1994.  All rights reserved.

Oracle7 Server Release 7.1.5.2.4 - Production Release
With the distributed, parallel query and Parallel Server options
PL/SQL Release 2.1.5.2.0 - Production

SQLDBA>
connect internal

Connected.

SQLDBA>
select username, user_id, default_tablespace from dba_users;

USERNAME             USER_ID    DEFAULT_TABLESPACE
-------------------- ---------- -----------------------------

SYS                  0          SYSTEM

SYSTEM               5          SYSTEM

2 rows selected.


SQLDBA>
select file_name, file_id, tablespace_name from dba_data_files;

FILE_NAME                                      FILE_ID    TABLESPACE_NAME
---------------------------------------------- ---------- ----------------

DISK$USER:[ORACLE.715.DB_715]ORA_SYSTEM.DBS 1             SYSTEM

1 row selected.
```

```
SQLDBA>
select * from v$logfile;

GROUP#     STATUS   MEMBER
---------- -------  -------------------------------------------------------

        1            DISK$USER:[ORACLE.715.DB_715]ORA_LOG1.RDO

        2            DISK$USER:[ORACLE.715.DB_715]ORA_LOG2.RDO

2 rows selected.

SQLDBA>
select tablespace_name, initial_extent, pct_increase, status from
dba_tablespaces;

TABLESPACE_NAME          INITIAL_EX PCT_INCREA STATUS
--------------------     ---------- ---------- ----------

SYSTEM                   10240      50         ONLINE

1 row selected.

SQLDBA>

SQLDBA>
show sga

Total System Global Area      4621348 bytes
            Fixed Size          42940 bytes
         Variable Size        4447336 bytes
      Database Buffers         122880 bytes
          Redo Buffers           8192 bytes
```

# Selecting ARCHIVELOG Mode

Note that the database has been created with the data file, log file sizes, and SGA size as we have configured. The next important thing to consider is to decide whether to run the database in ARCHIVELOG mode or not. If you decide to run the database in NOARCHIVELOG mode, you can skip this section. However, this may have severe consequences should you have a media failure and need to recover the database from a backup. Refer to the *ORACLE7 Server Administrator's Guide* or *ORACLE Backup and Recovery Handbook, edition 7.3* (Osborne/McGraw-Hill) for more information. The following procedure shows how to use the database in ARCHIVELOG mode:

```
SQLDBA>
archive log list

Database log mode            NOARCHIVELOG
Automatic archival           DISABLED
Archive destination          ORA_ARCHIVE:
Oldest online log sequence   178
Current log sequence         179

SQLDBA>
shutdown

Database closed.
Database dismounted.
ORACLE instance shut down.

SQLDBA>
exit

SQL*DBA complete.

$ show def

  DISK$USER:[ORACLE.715]
$ set def ora_db

$ edt init.ora
```

At this point you should edit the INIT.ORA file located in the directory, DISK$USER:[ORACLE.715.DB_715]. You should set the parameter LOG_ARCHIVE_START to TRUE to enable automatic archiving. Enabling automatic archiving is always recommended by Oracle (versus *manual* archiving). This will start a process called ARCH when you start the database. The ARCH process archives the online log files automatically every time the LGWR process switches the log files. Also, you should set the ARCHIVE_LOG_DEST parameter to point to a directory where you would like Oracle to create the archive log files. We have set this parameter to the directory ORABLR$DKA0:[ORACLE.715.DB_715.ARCHIVE]. Note that this directory doesn't exist yet, so we need to create this directory before

starting the database and putting the database in ARCHIVELOG mode. The
following procedure shows how to set the database in ARCHIVELOG mode:

```
$ show def

  DISK$USER:[ORACLE.715.DB_715]

$ create/dir [.archive]

$

$ sqldba lmode=y

SQL*DBA: Release 7.1.5.2.4 - Production on Mon Jan 13 17:26:53 1997

Copyright (c) Oracle Corporation 1979, 1994.  All rights reserved.

Oracle7 Server Release 7.1.5.2.4 - Production Release
With the distributed, parallel query and Parallel Server options
PL/SQL Release 2.1.5.2.0 - Production

SQLDBA>
connect internal

Connected.

SQLDBA>
startup mount

ORACLE instance started.
Database mounted.

SQLDBA>
alter database archivelog;

Statement processed.

SQLDBA>
archive log list

Database log mode              ARCHIVELOG
Automatic archival             ENABLED
Archive destination            ORABLR$DKA0:[ORACLE.715.DB_715.ARCHIVE]
Oldest online log sequence     178
```

```
Next log sequence to archive    179
Current log sequence            179

SQLDBA>
alter system switch logfile;

ORA-01109: database not open

SQLDBA>
alter database open;

Statement processed.

SQLDBA>
alter system switch logfile;

Statement processed.

SQLDBA>
exit

SQL*DBA complete.

$ show def

   DISK$USER:[ORACLE.715.DB_715.ARCHIVE]

$ dir

Directory DISK$USER:[ORACLE.715.DB_715.ARCHIVE]

T0001S0000000179.ARC;1

Total of 1 file.
$
```

# Testing Installation of Oracle Shared Images

As a final test we will demonstrate how to look at the OS level to see if the shared images of Oracle are installed or not. If the command procedure INSORACLE.COM is run, it installs the Oracle shared images. Similarly, running REMORACLE.COM removes the shared images of Oracle.

**NOTE**
*You should especially use REMORACLE.COM
to de-install the images and reinstall with
INSORACLE.COM when you re-link the kernel
to pick up the new kernel.*

You can use the INSTALL utility of VMS to look at the installed images
on OpenVMS. Also, note that REMORACLE and INSORACLE are symbols
that run the command procedures REMORACLE.COM and
INSORACLE.COM respectively. These symbols are set when you run the
ORA_USER*.COM file. The following procedure demonstrates how to use
the symbols:

```
$ sqldba lmode=y

SQL*DBA: Release 7.1.5.2.4 - Production on Mon Jan 13 17:33:47 1997

Copyright (c) Oracle Corporation 1979, 1994.  All rights reserved.

Oracle7 Server Release 7.1.5.2.4 - Production Release
With the distributed, parallel query and Parallel Server options
PL/SQL Release 2.1.5.2.0 - Production

SQLDBA>
connect internal

Connected.

SQLDBA>
shutdown

Database closed.
Database dismounted.
ORACLE instance shut down.

SQLDBA>
exit

SQL*DBA complete.

$ set def ora_rdbms

$ dir *oracle*.com
```

```
Directory DISK$USER:[ORACLE.715.RDBMS]

INSORACLE.COM;2        REMORACLE.COM;2

Total of 2 files.
$ remoracle

$ sqldba lmode=y

%DCL-W-ACTIMAGE, error activating image ORA_UPISHRV715
-CLI-E-IMAGEFNF, image file not found
ORABLR$DKA300:[SYS0.SYSCOMMON.][SYSLIB]ORA_UPISHRV715.EXE;
$ install

INSTALL> list

DISK$OPENVMS062:<SYS0.SYSCOMMON.SYSEXE>.EXE
   ACS;1             Open Hdr Shar
   ADA;1             Open Hdr Shar
..
..
DISK$OPENVMS062:<SYS0.SYSCOMMON.SYSLIB>.TPU$SECTION
   EVE$SECTION;1    Open Hdr Shar            Lnkbl

DISK$OPENVMS062:<SYS0.SYSCOMMON.SYSMSG>.EXE
   ADAMSG;2         Open Hdr Shar            Lnkbl
..
..
INSTALL> exit

$ insoracle

$ install

INSTALL> list

DISK$USER:<ORACLE.715.RDBMS>.EXE
   COREV715;2       Open Hdr Shar            Lnkbl
   ORACLEV715;2     Open Hdr Shar       Prot Lnkbl
   UPISHRV715;2     Open Hdr Shar            Lnkbl

DISK$USER:<ORACLE.715.UTIL>.EXE
   SQLLIBSHRV715;2  Open Hdr Shar            Lnkbl
```

```
DISK$OPENVMS062:<SYS0.SYSCOMMON.SYSEXE>.EXE
   ACS;1              Open Hdr Shar
..
..

INSTALL> exit

$ logout

   ORACLE7       logged out at 13-JAN-1997 17:42:45.67
```

A very common question asked by users is, "How much disk space does an Oracle installation take?" Let's look at the free space available on DKA0:

$ **show dev dka**

| Device Name | Device Status | Error Count | Volume Label | Free Blocks | Trans Count | Mnt Cnt |
|---|---|---|---|---|---|---|
| ORABLR$DKA0: | Mounted | 0 | USER | 1866200 | 32 | 1 |
| ORABLR$DKA100: | Online | 0 | | | | |
| ORABLR$DKA200: | Online | 0 | | | | |
| ORABLR$DKA300: | Mounted | 0 | OPENVMS062 | 1355544 | 281 | 1 |
| ORABLR$DKA500: | Online wrtlck | 0 | | | | |

If you recall, in the "Check Disk Space" section of this chapter, the same query showed that the available free blocks for disk DKA0 were 2031980. So the Oracle installation has used 165780 OpenVMS blocks. Each OpenVMS block is 512 bytes, which means this installation has taken approximately 85 MB of disk space. Note that if you take the default data file and log file sizes, this would be slightly more. Also, we have installed only the RDBMS here. If you install other Oracle products such as Developer/2000, you would consume more space.

# Frequently Asked Questions (FAQ)

**Q.** I was installing Oracle V7.1.3 on VAX/VMS and received the error: "%SYSTEM-F-NOPRIV, no privilege for attempted operation". What should I do?

**A.** The ORACLE VMS account requires GRPNAM as well as SYSNAM privilege to install Oracle V7.1.3. This is Bug #250057. If you do not have

GRPNAM privilege on the ORACLE account, you will get the above VMS error (depending on your OpenVMS version) when building the shared SQLLIB in ORA_UTIL_BLD.COM.

**Q.** I get undefined symbol errors while installing Oracle V7.1.3. Why is this, and what should I do?
**A.** If your site uses default user libraries to the VMS Linker (i.e., if you define LNK$LIBRARY logical names to tell the VMS Linker to automatically search one or more default user libraries to resolve undefined symbolic references), you should DEASSIGN these logicals for the duration of the Oracle V7.1.3 installation.

**Q.** I need to upgrade from Oracle 7.0 to 7.1. I also need to upgrade from SQL*Net V1 to V2. Is there anything I should be concerned about?
**A.** If you are upgrading from Oracle V7.0 to V7.1 or from SQL*Net V1 to V2 in the same Oracle code tree, you must configure the RDBMS and/or NETCONFIG a second time to get the correct configuration options for V7.1. Refer to Page 5-3 in the *Oracle7 for VAX (or Alpha AXP) OpenVMS Installation Guide Version 7.1* for more information. If you are upgrading from Oracle V7.0.x to Oracle V7.1.3, you should remove obsolete products from ORA_UTIL:PRODUCTS.TXT and ORA_UTIL:ORAUSER.COM. In particular, remove PROGINT15 from ORA_UTIL:PRODUCTS.TXT and PROGINT15USER.COM from ORA_UTIL:ORAUSER.COM. PROGINT has replaced PROGINT15 in Oracle V7.1.3.

**Q.** I get undefined symbol errors while linking the RDBMS on OpenVMS. What should I do?
**A.** If you get the following 4 undefined symbols (CMA$TIS_ERRNO_GET_ ADDR, CMA$TIS_ERRNO_SET_ADDR, CMA$TIS_VMSERRNO_ GET_ ADDR, and CMA$TIS_VMSERRNO_SET_ADDR) when linking the RDBMS on VAX/OpenVMS, then don't continue building the products. Exit out of ORACLEINS to the VMS DCL prompt ("$" prompt). Set your default directory to ORA_RDBMS and copy the file VAXCRTLLIB6.OPT to VAXCRTLLIB.OPT. Invoke ORACLEINS and select NETCONFIG to *configure and build* to start the re-link of Oracle.

**Q.** How long has Oracle V7.1.3.2 been shipping for OpenVMS?
**A.** Oracle V7.1.3.2 has been shipping for OpenVMS systems since October 1994.

**Q.** Which version(s) of OpenVMS are certified with Oracle V7.1.5?
**A.** Oracle V7.1.5 has been certified on the following OpenVMS versions:

| VAX | Alpha |
|---|---|
| OpenVMS V5.5 | OpenVMS V6.1 |
| OpenVMS V6.0 | OpenVMS V6.2 |
| OpenVMS V6.1 | |
| OpenVMS V6.2 | |

**NOTE**

*As of VMS V5.4, VMS has been renamed "OpenVMS" to indicate that OpenVMS is a "POSIX-compliant" operating system.*

**Q.** Which version(s) of OpenVMS are certified with Oracle V7.3.2?
**A.** Oracle V7.3.2 requires OpenVMS version 7.0 or greater.

**Q.** Which OpenVMS compilers are supported with Oracle V7.1.3?
**A.** The following OpenVMS compilers were used in certifying the precompilers (PROGINT V1.6.4) which was shipped with Oracle V7.1.3:

| Language | VAX | Alpha |
|---|---|---|
| ADA | V2.3-2 | V3.0A-7 |
| C | VAXC V3.2-05 | DECC V4.0-000 |
| COBOL | V5.1-10 | V2.0-271 |
| FORTRAN | V6.0-1 | V6.2 |
| Pascal | V4.4-89 | V5.2-19-274F |
| PL/I | V3.5-124 | V4.0-5 |

**Q.** Can I upgrade directly from Oracle V6 to Oracle V7.1.3?
**A.** Yes.

**NOTE**

*If you have precompiled programs developed under ORACLE V6, you may have to modify them to be able to run them under Oracle V7. Refer to the bulletin titled "Porting Pro-Language Programs from V6 to Oracle7" on the enclosed CD-ROM.*

**Q.** What are the various options in upgrading from Oracle V7.0.x to V7.1.3.2?

**A.** There are three ways of upgrading from Oracle V7.0.x to V7.1.3.2. The main factor in determining how to upgrade is whether you wish to keep your existing V7.0.x instances running along with V7.1.3.2.

**NOTE**

*Regardless of the way the upgrade is performed, you MUST install the new versions of any Oracle product(s) (e.g., SQL\*Forms, SQL\*Menu, etc.) that you are currently using. You must upgrade to the new versions of the products because Oracle V7.1.3.2 has changed the locations of numerous object libraries, and the product link scripts have been updated to reflect these changes. Failure to install the new versions of the products will result in fatal errors when linking the products.*

**Option 1: Overwriting Existing Oracle V7.0.x with V7.1.3.2**

This is the easiest way to perform the upgrade. All your Oracle V7.0.x code will be overwritten with the Oracle V7.1.3.2 code. Contrary to the instructions in the V7.1.3.2 installation guide, you MUST restore the BOOT.BCK savesets into the ORA_INSTALL directory, *not* ORA_ROOT.

**Pre-upgrade checklist:**

■ Make a complete backup of your Oracle V7.0.x code.

■ Make sure that all your Oracle V7.0.x instances are shut down.

■ Make sure to remove *all* Oracle shareable images, by invoking:

- ORA_RDBMS:REMORACLE.COM to remove Oracle shareable images

- ORA_UTIL:REMUTILITY.COM if you have installed any of the tools as shareable images

**Option 2: Installing Oracle V7.1.3.2 in a New Directory Tree and then Moving Existing V7.0.x Databases to the V7.1.3.2 Code Tree**

This is a bit tricky and you should be careful while doing this kind of installation. For this option, you will create a new Oracle directory which will become the new ORA_ROOT. Set your default to this new directory and run ORACLEINS as a "new" installation. After you have successfully installed the Oracle V7.1.3.2 code, execute the following steps:

1. Invoke ORACLEINS.

2. Select Option 3 *Reconfigure existing products, manage the database, or load demo tables.*

3. Make sure *Root directory* points to your new ORA_ROOT directory.

4. Press ENTER when prompted for saveset location.

5. From the main menu, select Option 2 *Instance Creation, Startup, and Shutdown Menu.*

6. From the *Instance Creation, Startup, and Shutdown Menu*, Select Option 1 *Create a New Instance and Database.*

7. Enter the same *SID* and *database name* as your existing V7.0.x instance and database.

At this point you should see text similar to the following:

```
A directory has been created for database xxxx, which contains
scripts to create the database, start it, shut it down, and
define instance-specific and database-specific logicals.  In
addition, a node-specific file (nodename_xxxx_INIT.ORA) has been
created for the instance xxxx that will call the
database-specific INIT.ORA and INITPS.ORA files, which are also
included in this directory.

NOTES:
    - ORA_PARAMS has been set to point to nodename_xxxx_INIT.ORA
```

```
    - The directory that contains these files is located at:
      disk$a:[ORACLE.7010302.db_xxxx]

Continuing will initialize your database.

Do you want to continue (Y/N)? [Y] N
```

Make sure you enter **N** for No for the above question and exit ORACLEINS. Copy your control files and *nodename_sid*_INIT.ORA file from your Oracle V7.0.x database administration directory to the newly-created database administration directory in the Oracle V7.1.3 code tree. You should now be able to bring up your V7.0.x database under Oracle V7.1.3. Once the instance is up, make sure to run the catalog scripts documented in Section 1.2 of the ORA_RDBMS:README.DOC file. Also run CATEXP.SQL to rebuild the Export utility views. Then upgrade all base tables for all other Oracle products you have installed.

### Option 3: Installing Oracle V7.1.3 in a New Directory Tree and Keeping Existing V7.0.x Instances Running

For this option, you will create a new Oracle directory which will become the new ORA_ROOT. Set your default to this new directory and run ORACLEINS as a "new" installation. After you have successfully installed the Oracle V7.1.3 code, run ORACLEINS to create a new instance. The SID and database name *must* be different than any existing SID or database name on this node. To toggle between your V7.0.x and V7.1.3 instances, simply run the instance-specific ORAUSER_*dbname*.COM located in the database administration directory for the particular database.

**Q.** I cannot get Server Manager to function properly after installing Oracle V7.1.5. What is the matter?
**A.** The version of Server Manager that shipped with Oracle V7.1.3 and V7.1.5 has numerous bugs. Customers should continue to use SQLDBA to manage their databases until Oracle V7.3.2 is released.

**Q.** I cannot link Oracle Network Manager or Oracle Names Server. The system cannot find file SYS$SHARE:DECW$XMLIBSHR.EXE. What is wrong?
**A.** You need DEC Motif installed, preferably DEC Motif V1.2. If you are running DEC Motif V1.1, you will need to obtain the following patches from DEC:

| OpenVMS Version | VAX |
|---|---|
| All | CSCPAT_1091 |
| 5.4 | CSCPAT_1035 and CSCPAT_1053 |
| 5.5-2 | CSCPAT_1053 |
| **OpenVMS Version** | **Alpha** |
| All | CSCPAT_2010 and CSCPAT_2012 |

**Q.** How long has Oracle V7.3.2.3 been shipping for Alpha OpenVMS?
**A.** Oracle V7.3.2.3 has been shipping for Alpha OpenVMS systems since September 1996.

**Q.** Which version(s) of OpenVMS are certified with Oracle V7.3.2.3?
**A.** As mentioned earlier, Oracle V7.3.2.3 has been certified and requires Alpha OpenVMS V7.0. Oracle V7.3.2.3 will not run on the following Alpha systems, which are not supported to run OpenVMS V7.0:

- Alphastation 255

- Alphaserver 1000a

- Alphastation 500

- Alphaserver 2000a

- Alphaserver 4100

- Any system which contains a KZPSC-BA triple-port SCSI RAID controller for Storageworks arrays is not supported to run OpenVMS V7.0.

**Q.** Which Alpha OpenVMS compilers are supported with Oracle V7.3.2.3?
**A.** The following Alpha OpenVMS compilers were used in certifying the precompilers that shipped with Oracle V7.3.2.3:

| Programmatic Interface | Certification Version |
|---|---|
| Pro*Ada | DEC Ada V3.0 |
| Pro*C and SQL*Module C | DEC C V5.3 |
| Pro*Cobol | DEC COBOL V2.0 |
| Pro*Fortran | DEC Fortran V6.1 |

| | |
|---|---|
| Pro*Pascal | DEC Pascal V5.1 |
| Pro*PLI | DEC PL/I V4.0 |

**Q.** Any precautions while migrating from 7.1.5 to 7.3.2?

**A.** If you plan to configure the Advanced Replication option in 7.3, you need 20 MB of free space in your SYSTEM tablespace. Similarly, for Spatial Data option, you require 10 MB in the SYSTEM tablespace. Add enough space to your SYSTEM tablespace before migrating from 7.1.5 to 7.3.2.

**Q.** What is the Oracle 64-bit feature? Is this an option? What does it give me?

**A.** The 64-bit feature is a standard feature of Oracle7 for Alpha OpenVMS and cannot be de-installed. This feature primarily can support Very Large Memory (VLM) for systems that are configured with large amounts of RAM. The performance will improve because the number of calls to the disk are reduced due to large amounts of data being stored in memory. This feature will improve scalability to support a large number of users since swapping data in and out of memory is eliminated.

Oracle version 7.3.2.3.2 and higher of Oracle7 for Alpha OpenVMS supports the Very Large Memory 64-bit feature. Note that there is no longer an SGAPAD, and process startup times will be faster since Oracle doesn't calculate the maximum SGA size during installation.

# CHAPTER
## 7

Problem Solving RDBMS

racle7 Server is the heart of all business solutions based on Oracle software. In this chapter we present a wide variety of tips and techniques that will cover many issues, from creating a database to performance tuning. We would like to emphasize that the content of this chapter is intended to supplement the information in the *Oracle7 Server Administrator's Guide*, *Oracle7 Server Concepts*, *Oracle7 Server SQL Reference*, *Oracle7 Server Utilities*, and *Oracle7 Server Messages* manuals provided by Oracle Corporation.

We begin the chapter by providing basic information on creating and maintaining an Oracle database. We will then cover issues concerning user management, space management, and performance tuning. Next, we will provide a section on backup and recovery before moving on to the Oracle utilities, such as Import and Export and the Enterprise Manager. After this, we will provide information on the diagnostic capabilities of Oracle. We will then provide a listing of common errors encountered by users and fixes for these errors. Finally, like all the other chapters in this book, we have a Frequently Asked Questions (FAQ) section that has been compiled from real-life support calls that Oracle Worldwide Customer Support (WWCS) received from Oracle customers.

New users of Oracle are often overwhelmed by the complexity and amount of information in the Oracle documentation set. If you are a new user to Oracle, we suggest you spend some time reviewing the *Oracle7 Server Concepts* documentation; it is important to understand the terminology defined there. Also, pay special attention to the section titled *Reading Guide to the Oracle7 Server Library*. This section contains a flowchart that will help Database Administrators (DBAs), Application Developers, and almost any Oracle user determine the order in which they should read the Oracle documentation.

# Creating a Database

The easiest method of creating a database is to use the Oracle Installer. You can run the Oracle Installer and choose to create a database (called the *seed* database). The installation guide for your platform will have specific instructions for this purpose. Please note that the seed database created by Oracle has a fixed schema (platform dependent).You can change the schema of the seed database by adding tablespaces and other objects, such as rollback segments. Alternatively, you can create a database with your own schema, using the *Create Database* script that is provided with the Oracle installation. The name and location of this script vary with the operating system. On Windows 95, you can use the **BUILDALL.SQL** and **BUILD_DB.SQL** SQL scripts as a starting point to create your own database. On UNIX systems, you should find a similar script named **crdb**<sid>**.sql**. On OpenVMS, you should find a SQL file named **CREATE**<sid>**.SQL** in the ORA_DB directory.

We will illustrate the process of creating a new database on our sample Solaris 2.5 installation. We begin by making copies of the **crdb\*.sql** scripts and the **init.ora**. We will make appropriate changes to these files to create a database named *test.*

```
% cd $ORACLE_HOME/dbs
% mkdir test
% cp init.ora test/inittest.ora
% cp crdb* test/.
```

Now edit the **inittest.ora** file and set the *db_name* parameter.

```
db_name = test
```

You need to set the ORACLE_HOME and ORACLE_SID variables before running the create database scripts.

```
% setenv ORACLE_HOME /home1/oracle
% setenv ORACLE_SID test
```

Ensure that the ORACLE_SID variable matches the db_name parameter in the **init.ora**. Our sample scripts **crdbtest.sql** and **crdb2test.sql** are shown below along with their output:

```
REM  crdbtest.sql
REM * Set terminal output and command echoing on; log output of this script.
spool /home1/oracle/dbs/test/crdbtest.lst
REM * Start the <sid> instance (ORACLE_SID here must be set to <sid>).
connect internal
startup nomount pfile=/home1/oracle/dbs/test/inittest.ora
REM * Create the <dbname> database.
REM * SYSTEM tablespace configuration guidelines:
REM *    General-Purpose ORACLE RDBMS          10Mb
REM *    Additional dictionary for applications  10-50Mb
REM * Redo Log File configuration guidelines:
```

```
REM * Use 3+ redo log files to relieve ``cannot allocate new log...'' waits.
REM * Use ~100Kb per redo log file per connection to reduce checkpoints.
REM *
create database "test"
    maxinstances 8
    maxlogfiles  32
    character set "US7ASCII"
    datafile
    '/home1/oracle/dbs/test/systtest.dbf'  size   50M
    logfile
    '/home1/oracle/dbs/test/log1test.dbf'  size 500k,
    '/home1/oracle/dbs/test/log2test.dbf'  size 500k,
    '/home1/oracle/dbs/test/log3test.dbf'  size 500k;
disconnect
spool off


REM * crdb2test.sql
REM * Run this after crdbtest.sql
REM * This script takes care off all commands necessary to create
REM * an OFA compliant database after the CREATE DATABASE command has
REM * succeeded.
REM * Set terminal output and command echoing on; log output of this script.
REM *
spool 2-rdbms.lst
REM * The database should already be started up at this point with:
REM * pfile=/home1/oracle/dbs/test/inittest.ora
connect internal
REM * install data dictionary views:
@/home1/oracle/rdbms/admin/catalog.sql
REM * Create additional rollback segment in SYSTEM before creating tablespace.
REM *
connect internal
create rollback segment r0 tablespace system
storage (initial 16k next 16k minextents 2 maxextents 20);
REM * Use ALTER ROLLBACK SEGMENT ONLINE to put r0 online without shutting
REM * down and restarting the database.
REM *
alter rollback segment r0 online;
REM * Create a tablespace for rollback segments.
REM * Rollback segment configuration guidelines:
REM *   1 rollback segment for every 4 concurrent xactions.
REM *   No more than 50 rollback segments.
REM *   All rollback segments the same size.
REM *   Between 2 and 4 homogeneously sized extents per rollback segment.
REM * Attempt to keep rollback segments to 4 extents.
```

```
REM *
create tablespace rbs datafile
    '/home1/oracle/dbs/test/rbstest.dbf'    size   8M
default storage (
    initial          128k
    next             128k
    pctincrease       0
    minextents        2
);
REM * Create a tablespace for temporary segments.
REM * Temporary tablespace configuration guidelines:
REM * Initial and next extent sizes = k * SORT_AREA_SIZE, k in {1,2,3,...}.
REM *
create tablespace temp datafile
    '/home1/oracle/dbs/test/temptest.dbf'  size   5m
default storage (
    initial      256k
    next         256k
    pctincrease  0
    optimal      1M
);
REM * Create a tablespace for database tools.
REM *
create tablespace tools datafile
    '/home1/oracle/dbs/test/tooltest.dbf'    size   1m;
REM * Create a tablespace for miscellaneous database user activity.
REM *
create tablespace users datafile
    '/home1/oracle/dbs/test/usrtest.dbf'    size   1m;
REM * Create rollback segments.
REM *
create rollback segment r01 tablespace rbs;
create rollback segment r02 tablespace rbs;
create rollback segment r03 tablespace rbs;
create rollback segment r04 tablespace rbs;
REM * Use ALTER ROLLBACK SEGMENT ONLINE to put rollback segments online
REM * without shutting down and restarting the database.  Only put one
REM * of the rollback segments online at this time so that it will always
REM * be the one used.  When the user shuts down the database and starts
REM * it up with initSID.ora, all four will be brought online.
REM *
alter rollback segment r01 online;
REM * alter rollback segment r02 online;
REM * alter rollback segment r03 online;
REM * alter rollback segment r04 online;
```

```
REM * Since we've created and brought online 2 more rollback segments, we
REM * no longer need the second rollback segment in the SYSTEM tablespace.
alter rollback segment r0 offline;
drop rollback segment r0;
REM * Alter SYS and SYSTEM users.
REM *
alter user sys temporary tablespace temp;
#revoke resource from system;
#revoke resource on system from system;
#grant resource on tools to system;
alter user system default tablespace tools temporary tablespace temp;
REM * For each DBA user, run DBA synonyms SQL script.  Don't forget that EACH
REM * DBA USER created in the future needs dba_syn.sql run from its account.
REM *
connect system/manager
@/home1/oracle/rdbms/admin/catdbsyn.sql
spool off
```

# User Management

The Oracle RDBMS is widely used in a multi-user environment. As a DBA, you will be frequently required to manage users in the database. Even though the *Oracle7 Server Administrator's Guide* and the *Oracle7 Server SQL Reference* document the syntax and commands related to user management, we have found that Oracle customers frequently contact WWCS for assistance. We have therefore included some common user management tasks in this section.

## Creating a New Oracle User

You can create a new Oracle user with the **CREATE USER** command in SQL. When you create a new user, you have to consider quotas, permissions, default tablespaces, temporary tablespaces, and roles. The **CREATE USER** command has many variations in syntax. We provide some common user tasks here for your ready reference:

We assume that *system* is an Oracle DBA account with *manager* as the password. We will create an Oracle user called *robbie* and grant appropriate *CONNECT* and *READ/WRITE* permissions to a tablespace named USERS. To create the user, connect to the database as a DBA and issue the **CREATE USER** command as follows:

```
SQL> CONNECT system/manager
SQL> CREATE USER robbie IDENTIFIED BY kooldog DEFAULT TABLESPACE USERS;
User Created.
```

Now, if you try to connect as the user *robbie*, you will get an error message, as shown below, since you still do not have permission to create a session on Oracle.

```
SQL> CONNECT robbie/kooldog
ERROR: ORA-01045: user ROBBIE lacks CREATE SESSION privilege; logon denied
Warning: You are no longer connected to ORACLE.
```

You can issue an **ALTER USER** command to rectify this situation from *system*.

```
SQL> CONNECT system/manager
SQL> GRANT CONNECT TO robbie;
Grant succeeded.
```

The user *robbie* still has no permission to create objects in Oracle. You need to provide the *RESOURCE* privilege to this user, or else you will see an ORA-1950 error.

```
SQL> CONNECT robbie/kooldog
SQL> CREATE TABLE shay (col1 number);
ERROR at line 1:
ORA-01950: no privileges on tablespace 'USERS'
SQL> CONNECT system/manager
SQL> GRANT RESOURCE TO robbie;
Grant succeeded.
```

We will now alter the tablespace used for temporary segments for the user*robbie.* If you do not do this, Oracle will use the SYSTEM tablespace by default while creating temporary segments.

```
SQL> ALTER USER robbie TEMPORARY TABLESPACE TEMP;
User altered.
```

You can verify the creation and setup of all Oracle users by querying the ALL_USERS view.

```
SQL> SELECT * FROM ALL_USERS WHERE USERNAME='robbie';
USERNAME                          USER_ID CREATED
------------------------------- ---------- --------
ROBBIE                                 15 01-05-97
```

The user can also get such information by querying the USER_USERS view.

```
SQL> CONNECT robbie/kooldog
SQL> SELECT * FROM USER_USERS;
USERNAME        USER_ID    DEFAULT_TABLESPACE  TEMPORARY_TABLESPACE  CREATED
------------    ---------- ------------------  --------------------  --------
ROBBIE          15         USERS               TEMP                  01-05-97
```

## Dropping an Oracle User

If you want to stop an Oracle user from connecting to the database, you can use the **REVOKE** command to accomplish this task. This will ensure that the objects owned by the user will still be available in the database.

```
SQL> CONNECT system/manager
SQL> REVOKE CONNECT FROM robbie;
Revoke succeeded.
```

If you want to completely drop a user from the database, you must use the **DROP USER** command.

```
SQL> DROP USER robbie;
```

If the user owns any objects in the database, you will see the following error message as Oracle will not let you drop a user who owns objects.

```
ORA-01922: CASCADE must be specified to drop 'ROBBIE';
```

You must use the **CASCADE** option for the **DROP USER** command. This will drop the user and all objects owned by the user permanently.

```
SQL> DROP USER robbie CASCADE;
User dropped.
```

## Changing an Oracle User's Password

At times, it is necessary to change or reset a user's password. You can use the **ALTER USER** command to accomplish this task. You can do this as a DBA or as the user itself.

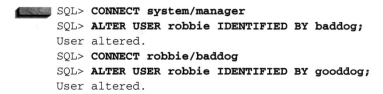

```
SQL> CONNECT system/manager
SQL> ALTER USER robbie IDENTIFIED BY baddog;
User altered.
SQL> CONNECT robbie/baddog
SQL> ALTER USER robbie IDENTIFIED BY gooddog;
User altered.
```

The **ALTER USER** command provides additional options that allow you to change profiles and roles. You can refer to the *Oracle7 Server SQL Reference* for details.

# Profiles

Oracle permits a mechanism that allows the DBA to put limitations on system resources available to a user. Using *profiles*, you can control the number of concurrent sessions a user can have, the CPU time allotted to a user, the amount of I/O performed by a user, and even the time a user is connected to Oracle. The idea is to create a set of profiles and assign them to users as necessary. We would like to point out the following difference: Roles are used to manage *privileges* of related users, while profiles are used to manage *resource limits* of related users.

You must first categorize the types of users on your database in terms of need for system resources. Once you have done this, you must determine values for the resource limits. You must also keep in mind the resource usage on your database and the availability of resources. The MONITOR utility will give you the necessary information. Finally, assign profiles to users as appropriate. We present an example of the creation of a profile:

```
SQL> CREATE PROFILE test LIMIT
sessions_per_user      2
cpu_per_session        unlimited
connect_time           30;
Profile created.
SQL> ALTER USER scott PROFILE test;
User altered.
```

In order to use profiles, you must set the **init.ora** parameter RESOURCE_LIMIT:

```
RESOURCE_LIMIT=true
```

# Rebuilding Database Schema and Objects

It is necessary to rebuild database objects such as rollback segments, redo logs, tables, tablespaces, and control files from time to time. Some of the reasons to rebuild a database schema or object might be to provide for additional growth of the database, reduce fragmentation, or even improve performance. In this section we provide techniques that DBAs can use to rebuild Oracle objects in a clean, safe, and efficient manner.

## Rollback Segments

Rollback Segments may need to be recreated in order to resize them. If your users are experiencing the ORA-1555 (refer to the section "Common Oracle Errors" later in this chapter for more information) error frequently, it is necessary to add or recreate rollback segments. It is critical that you ensure there are no active transactions in the rollback segment before dropping it. You can do this by bringing the rollback segment offline. Once the rollback segment in question is offline, you can drop it and rebuild it with the required storage parameters. As an example, we will rebuild a rollback segment called *myrbs* here:

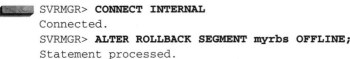

```
SVRMGR> CONNECT INTERNAL
Connected.
SVRMGR> ALTER ROLLBACK SEGMENT myrbs OFFLINE;
Statement processed.
```

It is important to ensure that the rollback segment is really offline using the query below.

```
SVRMGR> SELECT STATUS FROM DBA_ROLLBACK_SEGS WHERE SEGMENT_NAME = 'MYRBS';
STATUS
----------------
OFFLINE
1 row selected.
```

If the query returns the status "OFFLINE", you can proceed safely. If it returns a status "ONLINE" or "PARTLY AVAILABLE", it means there are still pending transaction entries in the rollback segment. You must wait until the corresponding transactions are completed. You can run the above query repeatedly until the status is "OFFLINE".

```
SVRMGR> DROP ROLLBACK SEGMENT myrbs;
Statement processed.
```

You can now recreate the rollback segment with appropriate storage parameters.

```
SVRMGR> CREATE ROLLBACK SEGMENT myrbs TABLESPACE rbs STORAGE (INITIAL 20
    NEXT 20);
Statement processed.
SVRMGR> ALTER ROLLBACK SEGMENT myrbs ONLINE;
Statement processed.
```

We suggest that you also add the newly created rollback segment to the listing in the ROLLBACK_SEGMENTS parameter of the **init.ora** file. Similarly, if you drop a rollback segment, you must remember to delete the entry for the dropped rollback segment from the ROLLBACK_SEGMENTS in the **init.ora**. If you forget, you will get an error, *ORA-01534: rollback segment doesn't exist.*

# Redo Logs

Performance can degrade if redo log switches are occurring too frequently on your database, since log switches trigger checkpoints. It is a good idea to recreate the redo log groups with members of larger sizes, or even add a few new redo log groups. We recommend that you keep all the redo log groups of the same size and that you have at least 2 members in each group. If you have only two redo log groups, you need to create a third one before you can drop and recreate the original redo log groups. It is necessary for Oracle to have a minimum of two redo log groups at any time. We present a safe procedure to recreate redo log groups here:

First, create a third redo log group. This step is a must if you have only two redo log groups.

```
SVRMGR> CONNECT INTERNAL
SVRMGR> ALTER DATABASE ADD LOGFILE '/home1/oracle/dbs/newlog.ora' SIZE 500k;
Statement processed.
```

Next, you need to mount the database in RESTRICT mode.

```
SVRMGR> SHUTDOWN IMMEDIATE
Database closed.
Database dismounted.
ORACLE instance shut down.
SVRMGR> STARTUP RESTRICT MOUNT
```

```
ORACLE instance started.
Database mounted.
```

Determine if you are running the database in ARCHIVELOG mode by issuing the following command:

SVRMGR> **ARCHIVE LOG LIST**
```
Database log mode              ARCHIVELOG
Automatic archival             ENABLED
Archive destination            /home1/oracle/dbs/arch
Oldest online log sequence     254
Next log sequence to archive   256
Current log sequence           256
```

If the database log mode shows ARCHIVELOG, then you must force archiving by issuing the following command:

SVRMGR> **ARCHIVE LOG ALL**

Next, you need to determine the status of the log files. A log file that has the status CURRENT is in use and must be recreated last. It is safe to drop and recreate a log file that has the status INACTIVE.

To find the status of the log files, use the following query:

SVRMGR> **SELECT GROUP#, STATUS FROM V$LOG;**
```
GROUP#     STATUS
---------- --------
         1 CURRENT
         2 INACTIVE
         3 INACTIVE
         4 UNUSED
```

You can drop the inactive redo groups safely at this point and recreate them at the desired location with appropriate size.

SVRMGR> **ALTER DATABASE DROP LOGFILE GROUP 3;**
```
Statement processed.
```
SVRMGR> **ALTER DATABASE ADD LOGFILE GROUP**
    **'/home1/oracle/newlog.ora' SIZE 500K**
REUSE;
```
Statement processed.
```

You can rebuild all the log files by following the same procedure in sequence. Once you are finished with all the log files, you can open the database for normal use and ensure that the redo log files are properly created.

```
SVRMGR> ALTER DATABASE OPEN;
Statement processed.
SVRMGR> ALTER SYSTEM SWITCH LOGFILE;
Statement processed.
SVRMGR> SELECT GROUP#, STATUS, ARCHIVED FROM V$LOG;
GROUP#      STATUS   ARC
---------- -------- ---
         1 INACTIVE YES
         2 INACTIVE YES
         3 INACTIVE YES
         4 CURRENT  NO
4 rows selected.
```

If the database is in ARCHIVELOG mode, we suggest that you ensure that the redo groups have been archived properly. The STATUS needs to be INACTIVE and ARCHIVED needs to be YES. You can use the following query separately to determine this:

```
SVRMGR> SELECT ARCHIVED, STATUS FROM V$LOG;
ARC STATUS
--- --------
YES INACTIVE
YES INACTIVE
YES INACTIVE
NO  CURRENT
4 rows selected.
```

Repeat the process of switching log files until all the log files are archived.

# Tablespaces

At times, it might be necessary to rebuild a tablespace to reduce fragmentation or to resolve a problem with the tablespace approaching its MAXEXTENTS limit. The steps to rebuild tablespaces depend on the type of the tablespace. We will present techniques to build some common types of tablespaces in this section.

## Rebuilding the SYSTEM Tablespace

The SYSTEM tablespace cannot be rebuilt in any manner as it is required to be available all the time. You must rebuild your entire database if you want to create a new SYSTEM tablespace.

## Rebuilding the Rollback Segment Tablespace

Before you rebuild a tablespace that contains only rollback segments, you must ensure that the database is running in RESTRICT mode. This will ensure that no user transactions need to use rollback segments when the tablespace is being rebuilt. The following steps will ensure that you perform this operation in a safe manner:

```
SVRMGR> CONNECT INTERNAL
SVRMGR> SHUTDOWN IMMEDIATE
SVRMGR> STARTUP RESTRICT MOUNT
```

Get a complete listing of all the rollback segments belonging to the tablespace that needs to be recreated.

```
SVRMGR> SELECT SEGMENT_NAME, TABLESPACE_NAME FROM
    DBA_ROLLBACK_SEGS WHERE TABLESPACE_NAME = 'RBS';
SEGMENT_NAME                      TABLESPACE_NAME
------------------------------    ------------------------------
R01                               RBS
R02                               RBS
R03                               RBS
R04                               RBS
```

Next, bring all the rollback segments that belong to the tablespace in question offline. Drop them after ensuring that they are offline.

```
SVRMGR> ALTER ROLLBACK SEGMENT r01 OFFLINE;
SVRMGR> ALTER ROLLBACK SEGMENT r02 OFFLINE;
SVRMGR> ALTER ROLLBACK SEGMENT r03 OFFLINE;
SVRMGR> ALTER ROLLBACK SEGMENT r04 OFFLINE;
SVRMGR> SELECT STATUS FROM DBA_ROLLBACK_SEGS WHERE SEGMENT_NAME LIKE 'R%';
SEGMENT_NAME                      STATUS
------------------------------    ----------------
R01                               OFFLINE
R02                               OFFLINE
R03                               OFFLINE
R04                               OFFLINE
SVRMGR> DROP ROLLBACK SEGMENT R01;
Statement processed.
SVRMGR> DROP ROLLBACK SEGMENT R02;
Statement processed.
SVRMGR> DROP ROLLBACK SEGMENT R03;
Statement processed.
SVRMGR> DROP ROLLBACK SEGMENT R04;
Statement processed.
```

Bring the tablespace offline, drop it and recreate it.

```
SVRMGR> ALTER TABLESPACE rbs OFFLINE;
SVRMGR> SELECT STATUS FROM DBA_TABLESPACES WHERE TABLESPACE_NAME ='RBS';
STATUS
---------
OFFLINE
```

If the STATUS is OFFLINE, drop the tablespace and recreate it.

```
SVRMGR> DROP TABLESPACE rbs INCLUDING CONTENTS;
SVRMGR> CREATE TABLESPACE rbs DATAFILE '/home1/oracle/rbs.ora'
     DEFAULT STORAGE (INITIAL 500 NEXT 500);
```

Finally, recreate the rollback segments in the tablespace. In the above example, we have opened the database in RESTRICT mode to simplify the procedure. In most of the production shops, it is necessary to keep the database open and available for users and it is not permissible to run in RESTRICT mode. In this case you can use a slightly more complex approach. Create a few temporary rollback segments. Add these to the **init.ora** file on a separate line from the permanent rollback segments and manipulate the ROLLBACK_SEGMENTS parameter as required before starting the database. In this case, your **init.ora** will have two ROLLBACK_SEGMENTS parameters as illustrated below:

```
# These are the permanent rollback segments
ROLLBACK_SEGMENTS = (r01,r02,r03,r04)
# These are the temporary rollback segments. Un-comment the
# following statement and comment out the statement above as necessary
# ROLLBACK_SEGMENTS = (temp01,temp02)
```

## Rebuilding the Index Tablespace

First, ensure that you can recreate the contents of the index tablespace in question. You can do this by using the Oracle Export utility and choosing the option to create indexes. Alternatively, you could create dynamic SQL using the USER_IND_COLUMNS view to generate a SQL script that has the appropriate CREATE INDEX statements as shown below:

```
set echo off
set heading off
set termout off
set pagesize 0
```

```
spool cr_index.sql
select 'create index ' || index_name || ' on ' || table_name
    ||'('|| column_name || ');' from user_ind_columns;
spool off
```

You can run the **cr_index.sql** created from the above script to recreate your indexes at any time. Note that this script will not work for concatenated indexes. Once you have accomplished this, you can bring the tablespace offline, drop it, and recreate it. Finally, recreate all the objects in this tablespace.

```
SVRMGR> ALTER TABLESPACE ourindextb OFFLINE;
SVRMGR> SELECT STATUS FROM DBA_TABLESPACES WHERE TABLESPACE_NAME =
    'OURINDEXTB';
STATUS
---------
OFFLINE
```

If the STATUS is OFFLINE, drop the tablespace and recreate it.

```
SVRMGR> DROP TABLESPACE ourindextb INCLUDING CONTENTS CASCADE CONSTRAINTS;
SVRMGR> CREATE TABLESPACE ourindextb DATAFILE'/home1/oracle/index.ora'
    SIZE 2M REUSE;
```

We recommend that you back-up the datafile associated with the newly created tablespace and the control file.

# Tables

Sometimes it is necessary to recreate a table in a production environment. The most common reasons to recreate tables are to change their storage parameters, to eliminate fragmentation, to move them from one tablespace to another, or to change their ownership. There are three methods for recreating a table: export/import, the **CREATE AS SELECT** command, and the SQL*Plus **COPY** command.

## Export/Import

If you need to rebuild a table with new storage parameters, this method is recommended. This procedure involves four steps:

1. Export the table.

**2.** Verify that the export file is valid by using the Import utility with the SHOW=Y option.

**3.** Drop the table. We suggest that you rename the source table using the **RENAME** command if you have room in the database. You can drop this table after ensuring that the import in the next statement is successful.

**4.** Import the table.

Some details will vary depending on the objective behind recreating the table. If the goal is to change storage parameters or eliminate fragmentation, you will need to set the COMPRESS option to an appropriate value. If you want to combine all the existing extents of a table into one initial extent, then use COMPRESS=Y. This will eliminate fragmentation. You can modify the storage parameters after the import using the **ALTER TABLE** command. Alternatively, you could create the table manually with the desired storage parameters and then perform the import with the IGNORE=Y option.

If the goal is to move the table from one tablespace to another, you could simply create the table in the new tablespace before the import. Again, you must use the IGNORE=Y option.

If the objective is to change the owner of the table, you need to use the import command line options FROMUSER and TOUSER.

```
% exp userid=system/manager file=emp.dmp tables=scott.emp
% imp userid=system/manager file=emp.dmp fromuser=scott touser=doublea
```

## Create as Select

This is the simplest method to recreate a table. First, you can create a copy of the source table using the **CREATE TABLE** command. Then drop the source table and use the **RENAME** command to change the name of the newly created table to the original one.

```
SQL> CREATE TABLE newtable AS SELECT * FROM oldtable;
SQL> DROP TABLE oldtable;
SQL> RENAME newtable TO oldtable;
```

Again, depending on the objective behind recreating the table, you could create the new table with appropriate storage parameters and then

use the **INSERT INTO** command instead of the **CREATE TABLE AS**
command. For example:

```
SQL> CREATE TABLE tempempno (empno number) storage (initial 500 next 500);
SQL> INSERT INTO tempempno (select * from aaempno);
```

We also suggest that you use the **PARALLEL CREATE TABLE AS SELECT**
(PCTAS) feature, which is available with Oracle7 Release 7.2 and later, for
large production tables.

```
SQL> CREATE TABLE emp_sal (empno, comm CHECK (comm < 2000), sal NOT NULL)
         PARALLEL (DEGREE 3) AS SELECT empno, comm, sal FROM emp;
Table created.
```

## Copy

This is the easiest method to change the ownership of a table. This
command is available only with the SQL*Plus product and requires
SQL*Net. The syntax is defined in the *SQL*Plus User's Guide and
Reference.* The **COPY** command neither permits you to change storage
parameters, nor allows you to create the table in a non-default tablespace.
We will provide below an example that will copy the table EMP belonging
to SCOTT from the current database into JOE's schema at a database
defined by the SQL*Net alias *foo*:

```
SQL> CONNECT scott/tiger
SQL> COPY TO joe/lion@foo CREATE JOE_EMP USING SELECT * FROM EMP;
```

# Space Management

Oracle allows dynamic allocation of space to datafiles. If you choose to use
this option, space is added to datafiles automatically, when needed. In this
case, a file can grow *unlimited* until the disk it resides in runs out of space
or the filesystem fills up. This option can be turned on or off using
commands similar to the ones shown below:

```
SQL> ALTER DATABASE DATAFILE datafile AUTOEXTEND OFF;
SQL> ALTER DATABASE DATAFILE datafile AUTOEXTEND ON NEXT 100K MAXSIZE 250M;
```

Irrespective of whether you use this option, careful planning is a must
for creating and maintaining any database. Much thought must be given to

sizing and growth-rate of tables and data. Sizing information is especially essential for implementing a database that will have a long life. The space requirements for database objects should be carefully calculated and planned for before the database goes into production. Accurate sizing of the data dictionary, user tables, user indexes, rollback segments, and redo logs depends on accurate estimates of the number and size of rows stored in user tables and the transaction sizes. Considerations should be made for the larger tables that will reside in the database as well as for tables that will grow considerably over time. When calculating this space it is important to remember that the RDBMS deals more efficiently with a table or index stored in a single extent than one stored in multiple extents.

The type of transactions executed on your database also impact space management and objects such as rollback segments to a large extent. Short update transactions affect relatively small amounts of data and require small rollback segments. Long-running update transactions that alter significant amounts of data require large rollback segments. It becomes even more difficult to plan for transactions if the type of transactions varies during a 24-hour period. You may have short transactions during the day and long transactions during the night.

In any case, it is necessary to gather row and transaction information before estimating proper object sizes for the database. In this section, we will look at several aspects of space management.

**NOTE**
*Oracle may change the "space estimation" in future versions. All the methods described here are approximations and are applicable to Oracle7.*

# Managing Space in the Data Dictionary

The data dictionary resides in the SYSTEM tablespace and usually requires a small percentage of space when compared with application requirements. It is critical to allow enough room for the data dictionary to grow and for other objects, such as deferred rollback segments, to exist in the SYSTEM tablespace. (When the database is in operation, the Oracle RDBMS will update the data dictionary in response to every DDL statement, reflecting changes in database structures, auditing, grants, and data.) To ensure that space remains available for the data dictionary and other objects that must reside in the SYSTEM tablespace, place all user tables, indexes, temporary segments, and rollback segments in other tablespaces. In addition, make the SYSTEM tablespace large enough so that it has at least 50 to 75 percent free space. Finally, ensure that your users do not have resource privileges on the SYSTEM tablespace for creating objects or temporary segments.

In addition to the data dictionary, extra space in the SYSTEM tablespace is required for new functionality in Release 7.3. For example, on OpenVMS, the Spatial Data Option (SDOPT), requires 10MB of free space in the SYSTEM tablespace. This space is automatically used if you are installing Oracle7 Release 7.3. You must ensure that sufficient free space is available in the SYSTEM tablespace for all your options before upgrading to Oracle7 Release 7.3.

## Managing Space for Tables

Table size is defined by the number of rows in the table and the average row length. We provide a formula below that will provide sufficient insight into space requirements for both small and large tables. This procedure estimates only the initial amount of space required for the table. It is also important to note that the methods provided here are approximations. We suggest that you assume a 10 to 20 percent margin of error. You will also need to refer to your installation guide, as some of the numbers used in these calculations are platform-specific.

Each table has a segment header and is made up of two or more blocks (every table has at least one header block and one body block). Each of the blocks in turn has a block header. We will first calculate the total block header size:

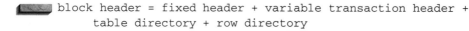
```
block header = fixed header + variable transaction header +
        table directory + row directory
```

where:

> fixed header = 57 bytes;
> variable transaction header = 24 * $i$, where $i$ is the value of INITRANS for the table (and grows dynamically up to MAXTRANS);
> table directory = 4 * $n$, where $n$ is the number of tables in the cluster;
> row directory = 2 * $x$, where $x$ is the number of rows in the block.

The variable transaction header in the block header contains 24 bytes that hold information about transactions accessing the block. By default, space is reserved for only one transaction (INITRANS = 1) in the block header. As more transactions access the block, space for additional transaction entries is allocated out of the free space in the block or an old entry is reused. As rows are inserted, the 2 bytes for each row in the row directory is also allocated out of the free space. Once allocated, this space becomes part of the block header. This space is not reclaimed when the row is deleted but is reused when new rows are inserted.

Using the above formula, the initial block header size for a non-clustered table with INITRANS = 1 is:

```
block header = 57 + (24 * 1) + (4 * 1) + (2 * x) = (84 + 2x) bytes
```

The space reserved for data within the block, as specified by PCTFREE, is calculated as a percentage of the block size minus the block header.

```
available data space = (block size - total block header) -
        ((block size - total block header) * (PCTFREE/100))
```

Continuing with our example, with PCTFREE = 10 and a block size of 2048, the total space for new data in a block is:

```
available data space = (2048 - (84 + 2x)) - ((2048 - (84 + 2x)) *
        (10/100))
= (1768 - 1.8x) bytes
```

Now, calculate the combined data space required for an average row. Calculating this depends on the following:

■ The number of columns in the table definition.

■ The datatypes used for each column.

■ The average value size for variable length columns.

To calculate the combined data space for an average row in a table, use the following query:

```
SQL> SELECT AVG(NVL(VSIZE(column 1), 1)) +
        AVG(NVL(VSIZE(column 2), 1)) +
        ... +
        AVG(NVL(VSIZE(column n), 1))
        FROM table;
```

**NOTE**
*This formula assumes that columns containing nulls are not trailing columns.*

We will illustrate this with an example here:

```
SQL> CREATE TABLE test (A CHAR(10), B DATE, C NUMBER(10, 2));
Table created.
SQL> INSERT INTO TEST VALUES ('ABCDEFGHIJ', '10-05-97', 23000000.1);
1 row created.
SQL> SELECT AVG(NVL(VSIZE(A), 1)) +  AVG(NVL(VSIZE(B), 1)) +
AVG(NVL(VSIZE(C), 1)) FROM test;
AVG(NVL(VSIZE(A),1))+AVG(NVL(VSIZE(B),1))+AVG(NVL(VSIZE(C),1))
--------------------------------------------------------------
                                                            23
```

Using the results from above, you can calculate the total average row size (or the minimum amount of space required by a row) in a non-clustered table with this formula:

```
average row size = row header + F + V + D bytes per row
```

where:

row header = 3 bytes per row of a non-clustered table;
F = total length in bytes of all columns with 1-byte column lengths having CHAR, NUMBER, DATE, and ROWID types;
V = total length in bytes of all columns with 3-byte column lengths having CHAR, LONG, RAW, and LONG RAW datatypes;
D = combined data space of all columns in average row (from the query).

For example, the total average row size for table "test" is:

```
average row size = (3 + (3 * 1) + (3 * 0) + 23)
                 = 29 bytes
```

**NOTE**
*The minimum row size for a non-clustered table is 9 bytes. Therefore, if the calculated value for an average row size is less than this absolute minimum row size, use the minimum value as the average row size.*

Once the average row size is determined, you can calculate the average number of rows that can fit into a database block using:

```
average number of rows per block =  floor(available data space /
       average row size)
```

where available data space and average row size are calculated above.
    So, for the example we used above:

```
average number of rows per block, x = (1768 - 1.8x)/29 bytes
```

The average number of rows is 57. Ensure that you round $x$ or the average number of rows per block DOWN. Once you know the number of rows that can fit inside the available space of a database block, you can calculate the number of blocks required to hold the proposed table using:

```
number of blocks for the table = number of rows / average number
       of rows per block
```

Using 10,000 rows for table "test":

```
number of blocks for table test  = 10000 rows / 57 rows per block
  = 176 blocks
```

You can also multiply the number of blocks with the DB_BLOCK_SIZE parameter to get a value in terms of bytes.
    It is also useful to determine the number of rows that begin in each block of a table and the number of blocks that contain data. To determine the number of rows that begin in a block, you can use:

```
SQL> select substr(rowid,1,8) || substr(rowid,15,4)
      block,count(*) from emp group by substr(rowid,1,8)||substr
      (rowid,15,4);
BLOCK               COUNT(*)
------------        ----------
000016400001            14
```

To determine the number of blocks that contain data, use:

```
SQL> select
     count(distinct(substr(rowid,1,8)||substr(rowid,15,4))) from emp;
COUNT(DISTINCT(SUBSTR(ROWID,1,8)||SUBSTR(ROWID,15,4)))
------------------------------------------------------
                                                     1
```

# Managing Space for Indexes

Indexes increase in size at a faster rate than the corresponding table. We will now describe a method that can be used for calculating the size of an index.

First, calculate the space required by the database block header of a block to contain index data. To calculate the total block header size:

```
block header size = fixed header + variable transaction header
```

where:

fixed header = 113 bytes;
variable transaction header = 24 * *i* where *i* is the value of INITRANS for the index.

So for an INITRANS = 2 (the default for indexes), the previous formula can be reduced to:

```
block header size = 113 + (24 * 2) = 159 bytes
```

The space reserved in each database block for index data, as specified by PCTFREE, is calculated as a percentage of the block size minus the block header.

```
available data space = (block size - block header size) -
                       ((block size - block header size) *
                         (PCTFREE/100))
```

Assuming a block size of 2048 bytes and PCTFREE of 10:

```
available data space = (2048 bytes - 159 bytes) - (2048 bytes -
      159 bytes) * (10/100))
= 1700 bytes
```

The calculation of the combined column lengths of an average index value is the same as the calculation for table size described in the previous section, except you only need to calculate the average combined column lengths of the columns in the index.

Once the combined column length of an average index entry has been calculated, the total average entry size can be calculated, using this formula:

```
bytes per entry = entry header + ROWID length + F + V + D
```

where:

> entry header = 1 byte;
> ROWID length = 6 bytes;
> F = total length in bytes of all columns with 1-byte column lengths having CHAR, NUMBER, DATE, and ROWID types;
> V = total length in bytes of all columns with 3-byte column lengths having CHAR and RAW datatypes;
> D = combined data space of all columns.

For example, given that D is calculated to be 22 bytes (from the table in the previous section), and that the index is comprised of three CHAR columns, the total average entry size of the index is:

```
bytes per entry = 1 + 6 + (3 * 1) + (3 * 0) + 22 bytes
                = 32 bytes
```

To calculate the number of blocks and bytes required for the index, use:

```
number of blocks for index  = 1.1 * ((number of not null rows *
     avg. entry size)
/
               ((floor (avail. data space / avg. entry size)) *
     (avg. entry size))
```

**NOTE**
*The 10 percent is added to account for the extra space required for branch blocks of the index.*

```
number of blocks for index = 1.1 * ((10000 * 32 bytes) / ((floor
     (1700/32 bytes)) * (32 bytes)) = 208 blocks
```

The number of bytes can also be calculated by multiplying the result by the database block size.

Storing indexes for large tables in separate tablespaces makes space management more efficient. This makes it easy to recreate an index or recover an index datafile. If an index datafile is lost, it is sufficient to perform a *tablespace recovery* on the lost datafile.

# Managing Space for Temporary Segments

The amount of temporary segment space needed for a sort grows proportionally with the amount of data being sorted. Most SQL operations do not require data to be sorted; however, the few SQL operations that do require sorting are:

| | |
|---|---|
| CREATE INDEX | SELECT ... ORDER BY |
| SELECT ... DISTINCT | SELECT ... GROUP BY |
| SELECT ... UNION | SELECT ... INTERSECT |
| SELECT ... MINUS | un-indexed joins |
| certain correlated sub-queries | |

The SORT_AREA_SIZE parameter in the **init.ora** sets an upper limit on the size of a sort that can be performed in memory. Common settings of this parameter range between 64K and 256K for larger systems. Sorts exceeding the SORT_AREA_SIZE limit transparently acquire a temporary segment in the database. Temporary segments have storage clauses of the tablespace that they reside in. To ensure that the temporary segments can grow to handle large transactions, the INITIAL EXTENT should be greater than SORT_AREA_SIZE and NEXT EXTENT and MAXEXTENTS should be large (we suggest setting this to the operating system limit). A PCTINCREASE of zero may reduce fragmentation in the temporary tablespace. Temporary segments are allocated as needed during a user session. The storage characteristics for the extents of the temporary segment are determined by the defaults of the tablespace in which the temporary segment is created. Temporary segments are dropped when the statement completes.

A sort may require up to twice the amount of space needed to store the data being sorted. Most statements issued by interactive transactions will not generate sorts requiring a temporary segment, and of those that do, few will require a large amount of temporary segment space. Reports and index creations, however, often require large temporary segments. Setting aside a separate tablespace for temporary segments may help you measure more accurately the temporary segment requirements of different parts of your applications. To monitor the temporary segment usage, query the data dictionary views USER_SEGMENTS, ALL_SEGMENTS, or DBA_SEGMENTS, where the value for the column SEGMENT_TYPE equals *TEMPORARY*. Measurements will be inflated because temporary segment space will not be reclaimed until needed or until database startup.

# Managing Rollback Segments

Rollback segments are used to store undo transactions in case the actions need to be "rolled back" or the system needs to generate a read-consistent state from an earlier time. As the amount of data and number of rows being modified by a statement increase, the amount of rollback segment space required for the statement will increase in size proportionally. A larger rollback segment is required when generating a lot of undo information. Therefore, it is wise to allocate more space than the initial estimates may suggest because support for long-running transactions may be needed. For sizing rollback segment extents, Oracle strongly recommends that each extent be of the same size. The number of extents for an individual segment should be between 10 and 30. Oracle documents the requirements for rollback segments as shown in Table 7-1.

You now have some good base estimates for the size and number of rollback segments needed for normal data processing. After calculating the size and the number of rollback segments required, it is time to plan for the configuration of the rollback segment tablespace. To do this, you first need to understand the amount of undo that is being generated and the kind of transactions being executed.

You can estimate the amount of undo generated by a transaction with the help of the following script (note that this script should be run from SQL*Plus only).

```
set   feedback off
set termout  off
column name format A40
define undo_overhead = 54
DROP TABLE undo$begin;
DROP TABLE undo$end;
CREATE TABLE undo$begin ( writes number );
CREATE TABLE undo$end ( writes number );
INSERT INTO undo$begin;
SELECT sum(writes) FROM v$rollstat;
INSERT INTO undo$send;
SELECT sum(writes) FROM v$rollstat;
SELECT  ( ( e.writes - b.writes) - &undo_overhead) " number of
     bytes generated"
FROM undo$begin b, undo$end e;
DROP TABLE undo$begin;
DROP TABLE undo$end;
```

The value reported by this script is the undo generated during the transaction. You need to make sure that this is the only running transaction in the database. The UNDO_OVERHEAD defined in the script is a constant that compensates for the unavoidable overhead of the **insert into undo$begin** statement.

| Number of Concurrent Transactions (n) | Number of Rollback Segments |
|---|---|
| n < 16 | 4 |
| 16 <=n < 32 | 8 |
| n >= 32 | n/4 (maximum 50) |

**TABLE 7-1.** *Rollback Segments Based on Concurrent Transactions*

In the rollback segment storage clause for Oracle7, the PCTINCREASE parameter has been replaced by a parameter called OPTIMAL. This parameter specifies the optimal size of a rollback segment in bytes (also kilobytes or megabytes). The RDBMS tries to keep the segment at its specified optimal size. The size is rounded up to the extent boundary, which means that the RDBMS tries to have the fewest number of extents such that the total size is greater than or equal to the size specified as OPTIMAL. If additional space is needed beyond the optimal size, it will eventually deallocate extents to shrink back to this size. The process of deallocating extents is performed when the head moves from one extent to the next. At this time, the segment size is checked and the RDBMS determines if the next extent should be deallocated. The extent can only be deallocated if there are no active transactions in it. If necessary, the RDBMS will deallocate multiple extents at one time until the segment has shrunk back to its optimal size. The RDBMS always deallocates the oldest inactive extents as they are the least likely to be used for read consistency.

The optimal size can be set on the SYSTEM rollback segment as well. This is important because the SYSTEM rollback segment can grow like any other rollback segment but can never be dropped by the DBA since it belongs to the user SYS. There are two important reasons why SYSTEM rollback segments can grow: If there are no non-SYSTEM rollback segments created by the DBA, or the user has specifically requested Oracle to use the SYSTEM rollback segment by issuing the following command before executing the transaction:

```
SQL> SET TRANSACTION USE ROLLBACK SEGMENT system;
```

We would like to point out that the SET TRANSACTION USE only works for DML statements. In either case, the SYSTEM rollback segment will grow and the only way to shrink it is to use the OPTIMAL parameter. However, it's very important to note that the OPTIMAL parameter should not be set too small for the SYSTEM rollback segment. The initial size of the SYSTEM rollback segment is 100K, and the OPTIMAL for it should not be smaller than that. If the OPTIMAL value is set less than the MINEXTENTS size, you will get an error. Setting the OPTIMAL parameter too small for the SYSTEM rollback segment (or any rollback segment) may degrade the system's performance because the rollback segment keeps shrinking too often, which is an expensive operation.

At times it is also possible that there is some contention for rollback segments. You can use the following queries to determine if there is contention for rollback segments.

```
SQL> SELECT CLASS,COUNT FROM V$WAITSTAT WHERE UPPER(CLASS) IN
        ('SYSTEM UNDO HEADER','SYSTEM UNDO BLOCK','UNDO HEADER',
        'UNDO BLOCK');
CLASS                      COUNT
------------------    ----------
system undo header         0
system undo block          0
undo header                0
undo block                 0
SQL> SELECT SUM(VALUE) FROM V$SYSSTAT WHERE UPPER(NAME) IN ('DB
        BLOCK GETS','CONSISTENT GETS');
SUM(VALUE)
----------
     17445
```

For each of the categories in the first query, try to achieve a ratio of < 0.01 against the value returned from the second query.

## Managing Redo Log Files

The issues in sizing redo log files are very different from the issues in other objects discussed in this chapter. The online redo logs should be on devices that are not loaded with other database files. Ensure that enough redo log space is available for the LGWR process to write out bursts of information during heavy processing times, and for the ARCH process to catch up later if necessary. Otherwise, database operations will be suspended until the ARCH can make a redo log available. You can either add more redo log groups or create bigger redo logs to ensure that sufficient redo log space is available.

One efficient way to monitor how effectively your redo logs are performing is to look for messages about switching logs, archiving logs, and checkpointing in your alert log. Every time Oracle does a log switch it is recorded in the alert log. Your alert log will have entries similar to the following:

```
Mon May 5 13:53:31 1997
Thread 1 advanced to log sequence 68
  Current log# 2 seq# 68 mem# 0: /u05/dbs/log2ween.dbf
```

The rate at which the redo logs are switching reflects the activity on the database. If you feel that the redo logs are switching too frequently, examine the activity on the database. Hot backups can impact redo logs. If a table is being written to, and it belongs to a tablespace that is currently under hot backup, a lot of redo is generated. In this case it is recommended that you create larger redo logs and remove the smaller ones.

Recording of checkpoints can also impact redo log files. The LGWR is responsible for recording checkpoints in the datafile headers. If checkpoints are occurring frequently and you have many datafiles, system performance can be degraded as the LGWR can get overloaded. We suggest that you enable the checkpoint process, CKPT to separate the work of performing a checkpoint from other work performed by LGWR. You can accomplish this by setting the **init.ora** parameter CHECKPOINT_PROCESS.

```
# Value of false disables CKPT and value of true enables CKPT
checkpoint_process = true
```

## Managing Growth of the Database

Once the database is up and running, it is always good practice to monitor the growth of the system. If you can anticipate how much more space a particular database object will need, then you can plan where to acquire the additional space. This will eliminate the inconvenience to users from error messages in the range ORA-1652 to ORA-1655. Of course, you can always use the AUTOEXTEND feature on the datafile for dynamic space allocation. However, this will not resolve the MAXEXTENTS problem. We provide a SQL script that can be used to monitor space usage and extents on the system. You could also use the Monitor facility.

```
SQL> SELECT  TO_CHAR(SYSDATE,'DY DD-MON-YY HH:MI PM') SYS_DATE,
        DS.OWNER , DS.SEGMENT_NAME , DS.SEGMENT_TYPE ,
```

```
           DS.BYTES/1024   KBYTES , DS.EXTENTS, DS.MAX_EXTENTS
FROM       SYS.DBA_SEGMENTS        DS
WHERE      DS.EXTENTS > x
ORDER BY DS.EXTENTS DESC , DS.OWNER
```

In the above query, you should replace x with the number of extents that you want to be warned about. Note that the MAXEXTENTS value depends on the DB_BLOCK_SIZE of your database and your operating system. Table 7-2 provides information on the relationship between the database block size and MAXEXTENTS.

For example, if you have a block size of 2048, your MAXEXTENTS would be 121. In this case, we recommend that you substitute a value such as 100 for x in the query provided to warn you about approaching MAXEXTENTS.

# Performance Tuning

While tuning an Oracle RDBMS is an iterative task that can warrant a lot of time and effort, there are some basic tuning tips and techniques that we want to present for the average DBA. We would like to caution that it is most beneficial to consider tuning during the design and development of the application itself. It is very expensive and time consuming to tune an application in production. We will not touch upon tuning issues related to hardware or the operating system in this section. However, we will provide information that should help Oracle users get started with their Oracle RDBMS tuning tasks.

| Database Block Size (bytes) DB_BLOCK_SIZE | Maximum number of Extents MAXEXTENTS |
|---|---|
| 512 | 25 |
| 1024 | 57 |
| 2048 | 121 |
| 4096 | 249 |
| 8192 | 505 |

**TABLE 7-2.**  *Relationship Between DB_BLOCK_SIZE and MAXEXTENTS*

# Tuning Memory

It is important to distribute fast access and expensive memory between Oracle structures. We recommend that you attempt tuning operations related to memory after tuning your application and before tuning I/O. Moreover, it is important that you tune the operating system first, and then consider the private SQL and PL/SQL areas before dealing with the shared pool.

It is important to avoid paging or swapping at all costs. You must fit the System Global Area (SGA) into physical memory at all times. You can connect to the database using server manager and issue the **SHOW SGA** command to determine the size of your SGA.

```
SVRMGR> connect internal
Connected.
SVRMGR> show sga
Total System Global Area        4438144 bytes
Fixed Size                        48260 bytes
Variable Size                   3972092 bytes
Database Buffers                 409600 bytes
Redo Buffers                       8192 bytes
```

Alternately, you could query the V$SGA view.

```
SVRMGR> SELECT * FROM V$SGA;
NAME                    VALUE
-------------------- ----------
Fixed Size                 48260
Variable Size            3972092
Database Buffers          409600
Redo Buffers                8192
4 rows selected.
```

We also suggest that you pre-load the SGA into physical memory by setting the PRE_PAGE_SGA parameter in the **init.ora** file.

```
pre_page_sga = yes
```

In addition to the SGA, it is important to keep the SQL and PL/SQL areas tuned properly. You must try to ensure that *Parse* calls are kept to a minimum. You can generate a SQL trace for a transaction and then look at the ratio of *Parse* to *Execute* calls (the count statistic shows this). This ratio must be as low as possible. We provide an extract from a sample SQL trace file below:

| call | count | cpu | elapsed | disk | query | current | rows |
|------|-------|-----|---------|------|-------|---------|------|
| Parse | 4 | 0.00 | 0.00 | 0 | 0 | 0 | 0 |
| Execute | 7 | 0.00 | 0.00 | 0 | 0 | 0 | 0 |
| Fetch | 0 | 0.00 | 0.00 | 0 | 0 | 0 | 0 |
| total | 11 | 0.00 | 0.00 | 0 | 0 | 0 | 0 |

In this example, the ratio of *Parse* calls to *Execute* calls is 4/7. You must try to tune your applications in a manner that drives this ratio as low as possible.

It is also important to control private SQL areas via the OPEN_CURSORS parameter in the **init.ora** file. This parameter determines the maximum number of cursors that one user can have at any time. This parameter does not control the entire system, and only determines the memory space used by each process.

You must also keep the library cache and the data dictionary cache in the shared pool tuned optimally. The library cache contains SQL and PL/SQL areas. Again, the idea is to ensure that there are minimum reloads in the library cache. You should try to reduce the number of ad-hoc queries against your database to ensure that the library cache is used optimally. You can use the following query to determine the performance of your library cache:

```
SQL> SELECT SUM(PINS),SUM(RELOADS) FROM V$LIBRARYCACHE;
  SUM(PINS) SUM(RELOADS)
---------- ------------
      5787           36
```

You must try to keep the ratio of reloads to pins as small as possible. In order to tune the library cache you must increase the SHARED_POOL_SIZE and/or the OPEN_CURSORS parameter in the **init.ora** file.

Another issue with the library cache is the way in which cursors are cached in a session. You must try to ensure that a SQL area is never de-allocated while an associated application cursor is open. In addition, you must ensure that the maximum number of cursors open in a session get cached. You can use the following **init.ora** parameters to tune the cursors cached in a session:

```
# The following parameter will ensure that a shared SQL area will
      never be de-allocated
# when an associated cursor is open
cursor_space_for_time = true
# The following parameter determines the number of session
```

```
        cursors that can be cached
# We have specified that a maximum of 50 cursors can be cached
        for a user session
session_cached_cursors = 50
```

In order to determine a proper value for SESSION_CACHED_CURSORS, you can use a query similar to the one shown below:

```
SQL> SELECT SID, USERNAME,PROGRAM FROM V$SESSION WHERE
        USERNAME='scott';
SID   USERNAME           PROGRAM
----- -------------- -------------------------------------------
    8 SCOTT                sqlplus@insun289 (TNS interface)
```

Now, use the SID returned from the above query on V$SESSTAT.

```
SQL> SELECT VALUE FROM V$SESSTAT WHERE SID = 8 AND STATISTIC# =
        (SELECT STATISTIC# FROM V$STATNAME WHERE NAME = ''session
        cursor cache hits');
    VALUE
----------
    2
```

You must try to ensure that the ratio of the value returned from this query to the total *Parse* count from the SQL trace is close to 1.

We have looked at some key aspects of the library cache. The issues related to the data dictionary cache are very similar. The goal is to keep as many of the database blocks in the data dictionary cache as possible. You can use the following query to determine your performance.

```
SQL> SELECT SUM(GETS), SUM(GETMISSES) FROM V$ROWCACHE;
 SUM(GETS) SUM(GETMISSES)
---------- --------------
     13263            725
```

You must try to keep the ratio of getmisses to gets close to 0. In order to tune the performance, you can increase the SHARED_POOL_SIZE and/or the DB_BLOCK_BUFFERS parameters in the **init.ora**.

# Tuning I/O

We have looked at some key issues with tuning memory in the previous section. We will now address tuning issues with I/O. We again wish to point out that an attempt to tune I/O must be made after tuning memory.

We recommend that you do not put Oracle files on the same disks as non-Oracle files. In addition, you should also keep redo log files and database files on separate disks. We also suggest that tables and indexes associated with those tables are kept in tablespaces that have datafiles on separate disks. The general idea is to minimize concurrent access to a disk.

The V$FILESTAT view provides information on the physical reads and physical writes (physical I/O happens to a disk whereas logical I/O happens in memory).

```
SQL> SELECT NAME,PHYRDS,PHYWRTS FROM V$DATAFILE A, V$FILESTAT B
        WHERE A.FILE# = B.FILE#;
NAME                                    PHYRDS          PHYWRTS
---------------                      ----------       ----------
/home1/oracle/dbs/systweb.dbf          1150              155
/home1/oracle/dbs/rbsweb.dbf             19              112
/home1/oracle/dbs/tempweb.dbf             0                0
/home1/oracle/dbs/toolweb.dbf             0                0
/home1/oracle/dbs/usrweb.dbf              0                0
```

You must keep the total number of physical reads and writes within the optimal limits of your hardware and the operating system.

Another common I/O bottleneck is caused by chained rows (rows that are chained across multiple blocks). You can eliminate chained rows by using the procedure described below.

First run the **utilchain.sql** script from your installation ($ORACLE_HOME/rdbms/admin directory) to create the CHAINED_ROWS table. Use the **ANALYZE TABLE** command to get a listing of chained rows in the CHAINED_ROWS table.

```
SQL> @$ORACLE_HOME/rdbms/admin/utlchain.sql
SQL> create table CHAINED_ROWS (
  2      owner_name      varchar2(30),
  3      table_name      varchar2(30),
  4      cluster_name    varchar2(30),
  5      head_rowid      rowid,
  6      timestamp       date
  7  );
Table created.
SQL> describe chained_rows;
 Name                           Null?     Type
 --------------------------    --------  ----
 OWNER_NAME                              VARCHAR2(30)
 TABLE_NAME                              VARCHAR2(30)
```

```
CLUSTER_NAME              VARCHAR2(30)
HEAD_ROWID               ROWID
TIMESTAMP                DATE
SQL> ANALYZE TABLE EMP LIST CHAINED ROWS;
Table analyzed.
SQL> SELECT * FROM CHAINED_ROWS;
no rows selected
```

If you do get records listed in the CHAINED_ROWS table, you can create a temporary table using the **CREATE TABLE AS SELECT** syntax, DROP the rows from the existing table, and INSERT them back from the temporary table.

## Tuning Sorts

Sorting is a very expensive operation and can impact performance to a large extent. It is important to complete most of the sorting operations in memory and not sort on disk. In order to determine the number of sorts in memory and the number of sorts on disk, use the following query:

```
SQL> SELECT NAME, VALUE FROM V$SYSSTAT WHERE UPPER(NAME) IN
('sorts(memory)','sorts(disk)');
```

If you see high values for sorts on disk, you can increase the SORT_AREA_SIZE parameter in the **init.ora** file.

## Tuning Index Builds

Index builds can consume a lot of time. Oracle 7.3 provides a new syntax for index creation called **ALTER INDEX REBUILD**. This is much quicker than dropping and recreating an index. If your data is also sorted, you can use the NOSORT option while building the index.

```
SQL> ALTER INDEX emp_primary_key REBUILD;
SQL> CREATE INDEX myidx ON emp(ename) NOSORT;
```

# Backup and Recovery

In this section, we assume that you are familiar with the fundamentals of backup and recovery. We assume that you know the difference between hot (online) backups and cold (offline) backups. Similarly, we assume you are familiar with the following recovery commands:

```
recover database
recover datafile
recover tablespace
```

In the first section, we give tips on when to take backups of which files during database maintenance. Then we provide a flowchart that shows what files to back up and when to back them up. In the second section, we give a flowchart to determine what type of recovery is required based on the kind of failure.

# Tips on Backup

During media failure, if you want to recover fully without losing any data, the following tips are very important:

## Tip #1: Always run your database in ARCHIVELOG mode

This will ensure that any changes made to your database are always stored in the archived log files. Archive log files are essential while recovering your database from backups. In server manager, use the **ARCHIVE LOG LIST** command to see if your database is in ARCHIVELOG mode or not. If not, there are two essential steps you need to do to set your database to ARCHIVELOG mode:

1. Shut down and mount your database and issue the command:

   SVRMGR> **alter database archivelog;**

2. Enable the automatic archiving facility by using the following command after the database is open:

   SVRMGR> **log archive start;**

   You have to do Step 2 every time you open the database. A preferred method of accomplishing Step 2 is to set the **init.ora** parameter LOG_ARCHIVE_START to true. This will ensure that automatic archiving is enabled every time you start the database.

### Tip #2: Never back up online log files

Irrespective of taking online or offline backups, you should never take backups of your online log files. There is one special case where you are required to copy the online log files. WWCS will tell you when appropriate. So, for any kind of physical backup, you need to back up only your datafiles, control files and archive log files. Many times, we have seen customers (who take backups of online log files) run into problems because they accidentally apply those logs while doing recovery.

### Tip #3: Always mirror online log files

Oracle7 provides the capability of multiplexing online log files. This protects you from the single point of failure of losing online log files because of media failures.

### Tip #4: Take full backups when you start the database with RESETLOGS option

In the unlikely event that you have to open the database with the RESETLOGS option, we suggest that you take a full database backup immediately. This is because the current backups you have (which were taken before the RESETLOGS point) cannot be used to recover through the RESETLOGS point. If you do not have backups after a RESETLOGS point and another media failure occurs, immediately contact WWCS.

### Tip #5: Take a backup of the control file after schema changes

Many times, while doing database management, you might be changing the schema of your database. Note that you don't need to take full backups of your database for every schema change. Various examples are given below:

**NOTE**
*We make the basic assumption that you have an automated process to take regular backups once a week or so.*

■ If you change datafiles from READ ONLY mode to READ/WRITE mode, you should always take a backup of the control file only;

there is no need to back up the datafiles. This is because, if you are doing recovery using a backup control file, the control file should recognize that the datafile is in READ/WRITE mode. Otherwise, changes to this file are not applied as part of recovery.

■ If you have added or deleted log groups, you don't need to take a full backup of the database. However, since the schema change affects the control file, you should take a backup of the control file immediately.

■ If you have added a new datafile to the database, you should take a backup of the new datafile as well as the control file. However, it's not necessary for you to take a full backup of the database.

■ If you have deleted a tablespace from the database, just take a backup of the control file.

### Tip #6: Use current control file

We recommend that you use the current control file whenever possible and avoid using the backup control file. If you use the backup control file to do recovery, you have to open the database with the RESETLOGS option. Then you have to do a full backup of the database (see Tip #4 above). If you lose your current control file, but have all your online log files and datafiles intact, you should use the **CREATE CONTROL FILE** command with NORESETLOGS option and create a new control file instead of using a backup control file.

Finally, Figure 7-1 gives a flowchart of when and how to take backups.

# Recovery

You have a lot of options, as a DBA, to do recovery for a given failure. DBAs are often overwhelmed by the options that Oracle provides. First you need to determine whether you can do complete recovery or incomplete recovery. Next you need to decide whether to do online recovery or offline recovery. Similarly, you need to decide on the kind of recovery command to use—**RECOVER DATABASE**, **RECOVER TABLESPACE**, or **RECOVER DATAFILE**. Figure 7-2 gives a flowchart to determine the kind of recovery you should do. For details on recovery concepts and recovery procedures, we recommend that you read *Oracle Backup and Recovery Handbook Edition 7.3* published by Osborne/McGraw-Hill.

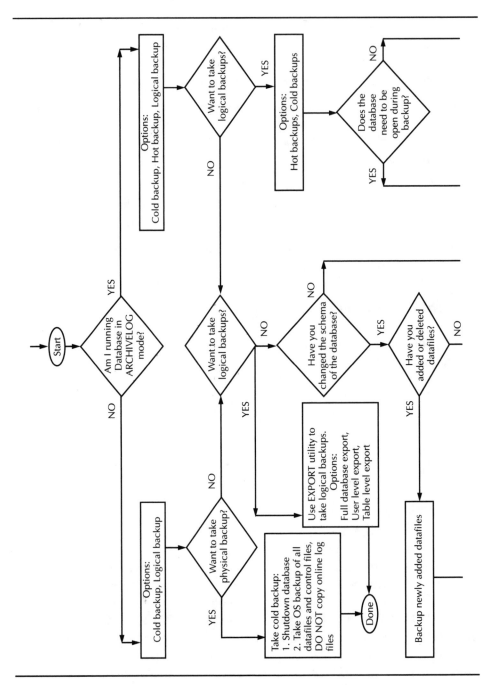

**FIGURE 7-1.** *Backup flowchart* (continued on next page*)*

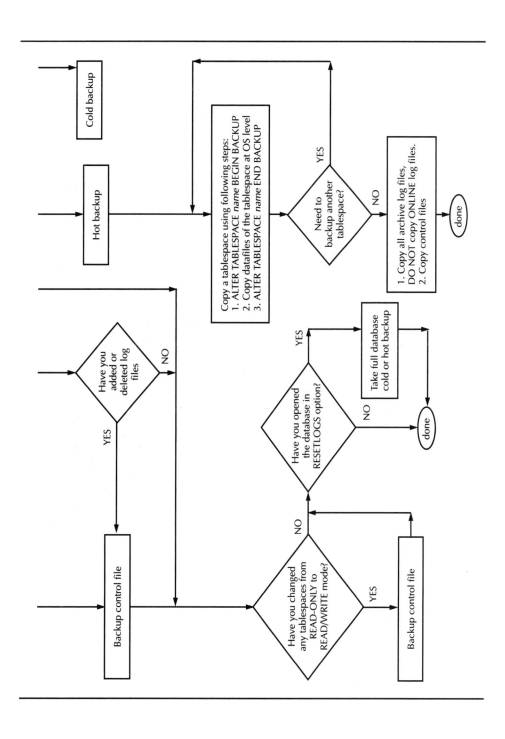

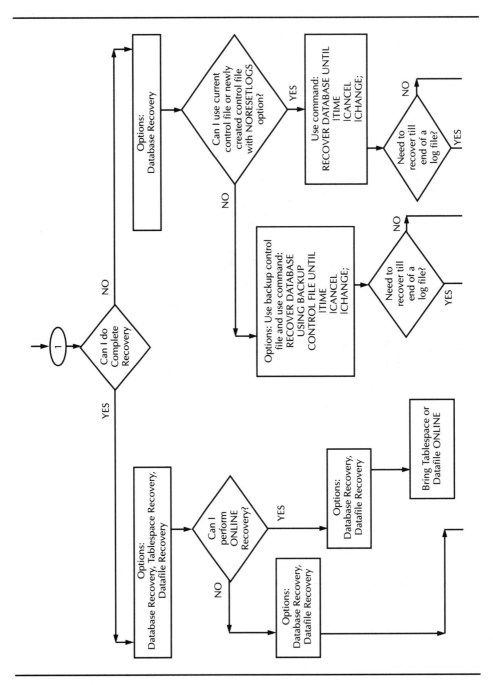

**FIGURE 7-2.** *Recovery flowchart (continued on next page)*

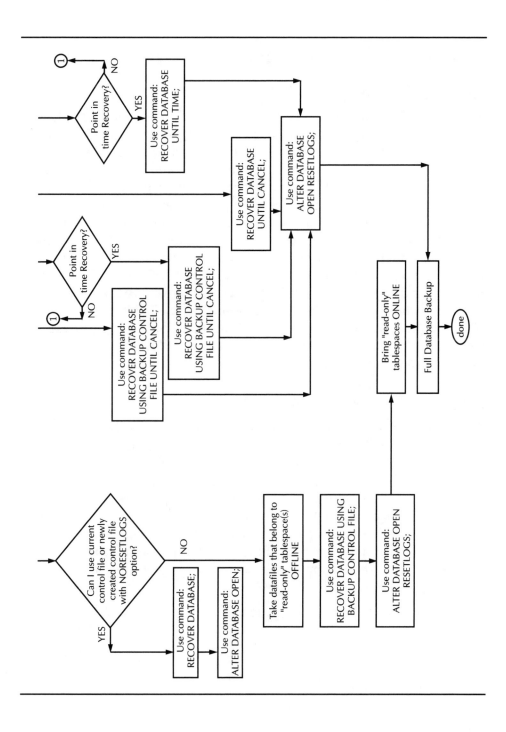

# Diagnostic Features of the Oracle7 Server

We will now familiarize you with the diagnostic facilities that are available in Oracle7. In order for you to diagnose any RDBMS-related problems, you should be familiar with the debugging utilities that are provided by Oracle. In addition, certain concepts, such as reading file dumps or reading trace files, might be necessary. All the information recorded in a trace file might not be useful to the DBA or the user. But this information will be specifically useful to WWCS analysts and the Oracle development teams. You will be able to get better support if you can provide the Oracle support analyst with the right information. We will first discuss the various trace files that are generated by Oracle automatically. We will then take a look at the common diagnostic tools available to debug the RDBMS. Note that this section is dedicated to learning the diagnostic tools pertaining to the RDBMS only. Tools to debug and tune applications such as *SQL_TRACE* and *TKPROF* or database tuning scripts such as *UTLBSTAT / UTLESTAT* are not discussed in this chapter.

## Oracle Trace Files

The alert log file (the actual name is operating system dependent) is very helpful in pointing the DBA toward the trace files with crucial information, and should usually be the first file you look at when diagnosing a database problem. The ability to use the information contained in a trace file is very dependent on your experience with the various messages printed in the file. We would like to point out that there will also be many messages that are printed to log information not associated with any error conditions.

During start up of the database, if the alert log file doesn't exist, Oracle will create one for you. Following is a partial alert log file created on Windows NT using Oracle7 Release 7.3:

```
Dump file D:\ORANT\RDBMS73\trace\orclALRT.LOG
Wed May 07 15:40:30 1997
ORACLE V7.3.2.2.1 - Production Release vsnsta=0
vsnsql=b vsnxtr=3
Windows NT V4.0, OS V5.101, CPU type 586
Wed May 07 15:40:30 1997
Shutting down instance (normal)
```

```
License high water mark = 2
Wed May 07 15:40:30 1997
ALTER DATABASE CLOSE NORMAL
Wed May 07 15:40:31 1997
SMON: disabling tx recovery
SMON: disabling cache recovery
Wed May 07 15:40:32 1997
Thread 1 closed at log sequence 139
  Current log# 1 seq# 139 mem# 0: D:\ORANT\DATABASE\LOG2ORCL.ORA
Wed May 07 15:40:32 1997
Completed: ALTER DATABASE CLOSE NORMAL
Wed May 07 15:40:32 1997
ALTER DATABASE DISMOUNT
Completed: ALTER DATABASE DISMOUNT
Starting up ORACLE RDBMS Version: 7.3.2.2.1.
System parameters with non-default values:
  processes               = 50
  shared_pool_size        = 6500000
  control_files           = D:\ORANT\DATABASE\ctl1orcl.ora,
D:\ORANT\DATABASE\ctl2orcl.ora
  compatible              = 7.3.0.0.0
  log_buffer              = 8192
  log_checkpoint_interval = 10000
  db_files                = 20
  sequence_cache_hash_buckets= 10
  remote_login_passwordfile= SHARED
  mts_servers             = 0
  mts_max_servers         = 0
  mts_max_dispatchers     = 0
  audit_trail             = NONE
  sort_area_retained_size = 65536
  sort_direct_writes      = AUTO
  db_name                 = oracle
  text_enable             = TRUE
  snapshot_refresh_processes= 1
  background_dump_dest     = %RDBMS73%\trace
  user_dump_dest           = %RDBMS73%\trace
  max_dump_file_size       = 10240
```

When the database is started, all the **init.ora** parameters and messages indicating that the background processes have started are recorded in the alert log file. The thread that this instance is using, as well as the log sequence number that *LGWR* is currently writing to, is recorded. In general, the alert log file keeps a log of all database startups, shutdowns, tablespace creations, rollback segment creations, a few **alter** statements issued, information regarding log switches, and error messages. Each entry has a timestamp associated with it, and for non-error messages, there is usually an entry for the beginning of an action plus an entry indicating its successful completion. It is very important for DBAs to regularly check this file for error messages. If there is an error message in the alert log file, it will often direct you to a specific trace file for more information.

In addition to the alert log file, there are two types of trace files that Oracle generates automatically. One type is the *background trace files* created by background processes such as *DBWR* and *LGWR*. The background trace files might or might not be created on startup, depending on whether there is any information that the background process needs to write at that time. Initially, when the file is created, it contains some header information indicating the version numbers of the RDBMS and the operating system. These files are created in a directory specified by the **init.ora** parameter, **background_dump_dest**.

The second type of trace file is produced by the user connection to Oracle and is known as the *user trace file*. These files are only created when the user session encounters an error condition and information can be dumped to the trace files. In addition, if a user session requests a trace file by using the **ALTER SESSION** command, then one is created as a user trace as well. The user trace files are created in a directory specified by the **init.ora** parameter, **user_dump_dest**.

The names of the trace files give information that can help users locate the correct one more easily. The naming convention is operating system specific. In the UNIX environment, the background trace file will look something like: **ORA_PID_PROCESS_ID.trc** and the user trace file has the name **PROCESS_ID.trc**. The ORA_PID is the Oracle process ID and the PROCESS_ID is the system process ID for the process creating the trace file. On OpenVMS, the file has the name **IMAGE_NAME_SID_PROCESS_ID.TRC**. The IMAGE_NAME is the name of the executable image that created the trace file. The SID is the system identifier of the instance. The PROCESS_ID is the process ID of the process that created the trace file. Note that all messages written to the user trace files might not be critical, but it is always good practice for the DBA to monitor the trace files at periodic intervals.

There is a lot of information contained in the trace files that the DBA can use to resolve some problems. Later in this chapter, we will discuss in detail some of the common errors, causes, and resolutions. But before we do that, we need to examine some of the diagnostic features and better understand how to read the information in certain dump files.

# Setting Trace Events

Oracle provides various diagnostic tools for debugging the RDBMS. Certain events can be set to dump diagnostic information of various data structures to trace files. Next, some special **init.ora** parameters are available that can be used while diagnosing memory and disk corruption. These parameters are not set during the normal operation of the database, as these diagnostic tools affect performance. We strongly suggest that you use trace events only under the supervision of an Oracle support analyst. The purpose of this section is to help you save time while collecting event information required by Oracle. We are only documenting a few event settings here. In addition to these, there are many events available, which may be used by Oracle support personnel as and when the situation demands.

There are two ways to turn on the event trace. The first way is to set the required event in the **init.ora** file, which will turn on event trace for all the sessions. The second way is to enter the **ALTER SESSION SET EVENTS** command, usually from the Oracle server manager. This will turn on event trace for just the current session.

The syntax while using **init.ora** is:

```
EVENT = "event syntax | ,LEVEL n|: event syntax | ,LEVEL n|.."
```

The syntax while using SQL is:

```
SQL> ALTER SESSION SET EVENTS 'event syntax LEVEL n: event syntax
     LEVEL n :...';
```

For example, to dump the complete contents of the control file, the syntax is:

```
SQL> ALTER SESSION SET EVENTS 'IMMEDIATE TRACE NAME CONTROLF
     LEVEL 10';
```

The *event syntax* contains multiple keywords. The first keyword of the event syntax can be an *event number* or a special keyword, **IMMEDIATE**. Event numbers can be Oracle error numbers (those prefixed by "ORA-" in the *Oracle7 Server Messages and Codes Manual* ) or internal *event codes* defined in the Oracle RDBMS. The event codes are implemented by logic in the kernel, which takes some action depending on its value. These internal event codes can be found in the rdbms/mesg/**oraus.msg** file on UNIX, or in the **ERROR.MSG** file in the ORA_RDBMS directory on OpenVMS. In some operating systems, including Microsoft Windows, this file might be in binary format and not text. The internal events codes are in the range 10000-20000.

If the keyword **IMMEDIATE** is specified as the first word in the event syntax, it is an indication to Oracle that it is an unconditional event, and the structure specified should be dumped to trace immediately after the command is issued. This keyword is issued in the **ALTER SESSION** command (it doesn't make sense to use it in the **init.ora** file).

The second and third keywords in the event syntax are almost always **TRACE** and **NAME**, respectively. The keyword **TRACE** indicates that the output will be dumped to a trace file and the keyword **NAME** comes before the actual *event name*. There are qualifiers other than **TRACE** that can be used as well, but are used only by the Oracle development team for internal use. The last keyword of the event syntax is the *event name*, which is the actual structure that you want to dump.

If you are not using the **IMMEDIATE** option as the first keyword in the event syntax, then you need to specify how long the specified tracing should be enabled. Specifying the keyword **FOREVER** will keep the event active for the life of the session or instance, depending on whether the event is set from **init.ora** or at a session level.

After the event syntax, the **LEVEL** keyword is specified for most events. An exception would be while dumping the **errorstack** where there is no level (**errorstack** is discussed later in this section). Usually the **LEVEL** needs to be set between 1 and 10. A value of 10 would mean to dump all the information for that event. So, for example, setting **LEVEL** to 1 while dumping the control file would dump only the control file header, whereas setting **LEVEL** to 10 would dump the entire contents of the control file. **LEVEL** has a special meaning while using the **BLOCKDUMP** keyword to dump a data block. Here, the **LEVEL** is the actual address of the datablock, specified in decimal form. In all cases, WWCS would advise you on what the value of **LEVEL** should be depending on the structure you are dumping to trace.

Putting all this together, here are some examples. The following are examples that can be implemented while using the **init.ora** file to set events:

```
EVENT = "604 TRACE NAME ERRORSTACK FOREVER"
EVENT = "10210 TRACE NAME CONTEXT FOREVER, LEVEL 10"
```

The above two lines need to be typed in the **init.ora** file exactly as shown. The first statement would dump the error stack every time a process encounters the ORA-604 error. The second statement is a block-checking event that would check every block's integrity when read from disk to cache. Remember that setting these events in the **init.ora** file would create a trace when the above conditions occur from any session in the database.

The following are examples that can be implemented while using SQL to set events:

```
SQL> ALTER SESSION SET EVENTS 'IMMEDIATE TRACE NAME BLOCKDUMP
     LEVEL 67109037';
SQL> ALTER SESSION SET EVENTS 'IMMEDIATE TRACE NAME CONTROLF
     LEVEL 10';
SQL> ALTER SESSION SET EVENTS 'IMMEDIATE TRACE NAME SYSTEMSTATE
     LEVEL 10';
```

The first statement would dump the datablock 67109037 to a trace file. Every datablock in the Oracle database is uniquely identified by a block number and a file number combination. In the above example, 67109037 is the decimal representation of the file number and the block number. This information is operating system-dependent. The second statement would dump the entire contents of the control file to trace. The third statement would dump the *system state* to trace, which includes all *process state* dumps (a system state will give information about objects currently held by the Oracle RDBMS while a process state dump will show objects held by a particular process). This system state dump will be useful while diagnosing *system hang* problems.

## Event Names

There is a wide variety of event names available. We again emphasize that Oracle support personnel should guide you with event names and while setting trace events. We present a few event names here to give you a feel of the type of events available.

**ERRORSTACK**    Oracle will create a stack called the "error stack" in which to store information related to a particular error that a process has encountered. The Oracle foreground process gets an error message. While running some applications (Developer/2000 Forms) the foreground process will not get all the information related to the error. This event dumps the entire error stack to trace, and this is very useful for debugging any Oracle error. For example, if an application is failing with the ORA-604 error,

```
SQL> alter session set events '604 trace name errorstack forever';
```

would dump the error stack to the trace file.

**SYSTEMSTATE**    This event dumps the entire system state, which includes all processes' state dumps. This event is very useful for diagnosing problems when experiencing performance degradation, process hangs, or system hangs. For example,

```
SQL> alter session set events 'immediate trace name systemstate
        level 10';
```

would dump the system state to trace.

**EVENT CODES 10013 AND 10015**    These event codes are used while diagnosing problems induced by a corrupted rollback segment. In such cases, the database cannot be started and gives the ORA-1578 error, indicating that a block in the database is corrupted for whatever reason. If WWCS determines the cause to be a rollback segment, setting the above events in the **init.ora** file would create a trace file that will be helpful in determining the bad rollback segment. The syntax for setting this event in the **init.ora** file is:

```
event = "10015 trace name context forever"
```

**EVENT CODES 10210 AND 10211**    These are *block-checking* and *index-checking* events, respectively. Normally when a block is read from disk to cache, some basic integrity checks are performed. By setting these events, Oracle does additional checks, which could be crucial while diagnosing some block corruption. PMON always has block checking turned on. It is good practice to use the block-checking and index-checking events even during normal operation of the database, but there is an overhead involved. Running the database with these events turned on is especially advisable for customers running a VLDB shop with high availability requirements. For example,

```
event = "10210 trace name context forever, level 10"
```

would turn on block checking for every data block read into the SGA.

**EVENT CODES 10231 AND 10232** These are probably the most important event codes. Assume that because of a physical outage, one of the blocks on disk is zeroed out, i.e., all the data in that block is gone. To salvage the remaining data in that table, one needs to export the table. However, a full table scan would fail when the bad block is read. To work around the corruption, event 10231 needs to be set. This event would skip corrupted blocks during full table scans. If event 10232 is set, these corrupted blocks are dumped to a trace file. There are certain conditions that need to be met in order for this event to work:

- This block should be *soft-corrupted* by Oracle. This means that, when Oracle detects a corrupt block, it marks the block as corrupt by setting certain bits in the block. In order for Oracle to soft-corrupt the block, you have to use the event 10210. So using event 10231 along with event 10210 is recommended.

- The **LEVEL** should be set correctly. WWCS can provide this information to you.

- Accessing the blocks through an index wouldn't work. Only full table scans should be done on the table. Note that if this event is set in a session, it would work only if that session does the full table scan. If you need to export the table, then this event should be set in the **init.ora** file.

Two examples are given below, the first one is used with SQL and the other in the **init.ora** file.

```
SQL> alter session set events '10231 trace name context off';
event = "10231 trace name context forever, level 10"
```

The first statement would turn off block-checking for that session. The second statement would turn on block-checking database-wide for all data blocks read into the SGA by any process.

# V$ Views

Oracle maintains a set of tables called dynamic performance tables. The data in these tables keep changing during normal operation of the database. Though most of these tables contain data related to the performance of the database, there are some tables that contain information regarding the control file, data files, log files, and back-up information. There are a set of views called V_$ views created for these tables along with public synonyms on top of these views that are prefixed with V$. Some of the V$ objects (commonly referred to as V$ views) are extremely useful while diagnosing common problems on a day-to-day basis, and to monitor the normal database activity and its status. Some V$ views are very useful while diagnosing problems related to backup and recovery. A list of some of the important V$ views is given below:

| | | |
|---|---|---|
| V$ACCESS | V$ARCHIVE | V$BACKUP |
| V$BGPROCESS | V$CONTROLFILE | V$DATABASE |
| V$DATAFILE | V$DB_OBJECT_CACHE | V$INSTANCE |
| V$LOCK | V$LOG | V$LOGFILE |
| V$LOG_HISTORY | V$PROCESS | V$RECOVERY_LOG |
| V$RECOVERY_FILE | V$ROLLNAME | V$ROLLSTAT |
| V$SESSION | V$SESSION_WAIT | V$THREAD |
| V$WAITSTAT | | |

# Lock Utility

Locking is an essential aspect of any dynamic system where there are many users or many processes sharing access to a single object or resource. Depending on the applications being used, or on the circumstances of process termination, there are situations that can cause processes to hang while waiting for a particular resource. For many DBAs, determining which process is "holding up" the rest involves intense analysis of the MONITOR LOCK screen.

There are two types of locks managed by the Oracle RDBMS: internal locks and data (DML) locks.

The two categories of internal locks are *latches* and *enqueues*. Both latches and enqueues protect shared-memory data structures. Enqueues, however, protect other objects as well, such as access to control files, redo logs, and rollback segments. Latches are internal locks that are only held for short periods of time. Structures such as the LRU (Least Recently Used) chain in the buffer cache are protected by this latch, meaning processes that modify the LRU chain need to acquire this latch before doing so.

When a process must acquire a latch, most of the time it tries to acquire it with a *willing to wait* request. This means that it will retry in the event that it cannot acquire the latch on the first try. The overall assumption here is that, since latches will be held for very short periods of time, a short wait followed by a retry will be successful. Enqueues are also internal locks, but they differ from latches in that there is a built-in mechanism for processes to wait in line for the resource. Enqueues can be held in shared or exclusive mode, depending on the degree of sharing allowed for the given transaction. Two of the most common types of enqueues are row wait (RW) and row cache enqueues.

Data locks, which are present to protect the consistency of the data, can be held in exclusive or shared mode at the row or table level. With row-level locking, this category of locks is the most common source of contention.

To diagnose locking problems, or systems hung on locks, Oracle provides a script called **UTLLOCKT.SQL**. This script can be quite useful for filtering out relevant information from the MONITOR LOCK screen, especially when there may be many other users whose shared locks are not really interesting to the problem at hand. The **UTLLOCKT.SQL** script normally resides in the $ORACLE_HOME/rdbms/admin directory and has instructions that clearly describe how to use this script and interpret the output.

# Oracle Errors and Resolution

This section is divided into three parts. The first part focuses on common errors that a DBA might encounter on a day-to-day basis in the areas of space management and general database administration. These common errors, their background, resolution, and some proactive measures are discussed. The second part discusses Oracle internal errors. Oracle internal errors are uncommon, yet severe, and cause production database or applications downtime. Such internal errors are usually due to various data structure corruption caused by hardware and software failures. It is best to seek immediate assistance from Oracle support personnel for internal errors. Finally, we also categorize problems related to databases and suggest some minimal diagnostic actions to DBAs.

## Common Oracle Errors

You have likely been in a situation where a user has approached you to say that rows cannot be added to a table because Oracle is giving an error. This is a very common scenario, and one of the less stressful situations compared to others that DBAs face. In this section, we discuss some of the typical problems that DBAs face on a day-to-day basis, such as space management issues with tables and indexes. Errors due to memory fragmentation problems with shared pool area, problems with snapshots, and finally rollback segment management are also discussed in this section. Problem resolution or workarounds are suggested where applicable.

## ORA-604

```
604, 00000, "error occurred at recursive SQL level %s"
// *Cause:  An error occurred while processing a recursive SQL statement
//          (a statement applying to internal dictionary tables).
// *Action: If the situation described in the next error on the stack
//          can be corrected, do so; otherwise contact Oracle Support.
```

Normally, an ORA-604 comes with a secondary error, such as ORA-1652. If you can't find the source of the error in any of the trace files, try setting the following event in **init.ora** and restart the database.

```
event="604 trace name errorstack forever"
```

You should get a trace file in the directory specified by USER_DUMP_DEST when an ORA-604 occurs. The trace file should provide more information on the error, which might help you resolve the problem.

## ORA-1000

```
01000, 00000, "maximum open cursors exceeded"
// *Cause:
// *Action:
```

This error is usually encountered in OCI programs, Pro*C programs, Visual Basic, Developer/2000 applications, etc. This error could also occur at the database level, with regular INSERTS, UPDATES, DELETES SQL (PL/SQL). The reason you receive this error is that Oracle has reached the set limit for open cursors allowed for that executable or that user session. We will provide a brief discussion of cursors before going into the solution.

There are two kinds of open cursors: *implicit* and *explicit.* Implicit cursors are created and managed automatically by Oracle. An implicit cursor is declared for all data definition and data manipulation statements. Explicit cursors are created and managed entirely by users. Users can control the number of cursors created in their application. However, if there is a bug in the application and the cursors do not get closed properly, this will result in a large number of simultaneous open cursors. Cursors are stored in a work area called the *Private SQL Area*. As a result of this, the number of cursors that can be created is limited by parameters in the **init.ora**.

There are two ways to solve an ORA-1000 error. You can tune cursor usage at the database level and at the application level. At the database level, you can use the OPEN_CURSORS parameter in the **init.ora** file to define the number of cursors that a user can open in a session. The default value on most operating systems is 50 which might not be sufficient. You should set this to a higher value, such as 255. Please refer to the *Oracle7 Server Administrator's Guide* for details on this parameter.

**NOTE**
*You can also do some tuning for cursors at the application level. If you are using a pre-compiler program, there are three parameters that affect handling cursors at the application level: RELEASE_CURSOR, HOLD_CURSOR, and MAXOPENCURSORS. For more details refer to the* Programmer's Guide to Precompilers.

## ORA-1110 or ORA-1122 or ORA-120x

```
ORA-01122, 00000, "database file %s failed verification check
// *Cause:  The information in this file is inconsistent with information
//          from the control file. See accompanying message for reason.
// *Action: Make certain that the db files and control files are the
//          correct files for this database.
ORA-.01110, 00000, "data file %s: '%s'"
// *Cause:  Reporting file name for details of another error
// *Action: See associated error message

and one of the following ORA errors:

01201, 00000, "file size %s in header does not match size %s in control file"
// *Cause:  The file sizes in the control file and in the file header do not
//          match. One of them is probably a corrutped value.
```

```
// *Action: Replace the corrupted file with a good one and do recovery as
//          needed.
01202, 00000, "wrong incarnation of this file - wrong creation time"
// *Cause:  The creation time in the file header is not the same as the
//          creation time in the control file. This is probably a copy
//          of a file that was dropped.
// *Action: Restore a current copy of the data file and do recovery as
//          needed.
01203, 00000, "wrong incarnation of this file - wrong creation SCN"
// *Cause:  The creation SCN in the file header is not the same as the
//          creation SCN in the control file. This is probably a copy of
//          a file that was dropped.
// *Action: Restore a current copy of the data file and do recovery as
//          needed.
01204, 00000, "file number is %s rather than %s - wrong file"
// *Cause:  The file number in the file header is not correct. This is
//          probably a restored backup of the wrong file, but from the
//          same database.
// *Action: Restore a copy of the correct data file and do recovery as
//          needed.
01205, 00000, "not a data file - type number in header is %s"
// *Cause:  The file type in the header is not correct for a data file.
//          This is probably a log file or control file. If the type is
//          not a small non-zero positive number then the header is
//          corrupted.
01206, 00000, "file is not part of this database - wrong database id"
// *Cause:  The database id in the file header does not match the
//          database id in the control file. The file may be from a
//          different database, or it may not be a database file at all.
//          If the database was rebuilt, this may be a file from before
//          the rebuild.
// *Action: Restore a copy of the correct data file and do recovery as
//          needed.
```

These errors, when encountered, are always during the startup of a database. In most of the cases, these errors are reported when you are attempting to recover from a backup, or when the previous shutdown was not complete. In any case, these errors usually indicate that the file indicated in the error has a bad header and cannot be read by Oracle.

Usually this occurs when the file has been touched at the operating system level by a user, another application, or a UNIX command such as **dd** or **cp** or **mv**. The solution in most cases involves restoring from a backup. In order to get a better understanding of why the file in question is corrupted, you can use the following procedure.

First, startup the database using **STARTUP MOUNT**. You can then query the status of the datafiles by using the V$DATAFILE view.

```
SVRMGR> CONNECT INTERNAL
SVRMGR> STARTUP MOUNT
SVRMGR> SELECT file#, status, enabled, name FROM V$DATAFILE;
FILE#      STATUS  ENABLED     NAME
---------- ------- ----------- ------------------------------------
         1 SYSTEM  READ WRITE  /home1/oracle/dbs/systemweb.dbf
         2 ONLINE  READ WRITE  /home1/oracle/dbs/rbsweb.dbf
         3 OFFLINE READ WRITE  /home1/oracle/dbs/tempweb.dbf
         4 ONLINE  READ WRITE  /home1/oracle/dbs/toolweb.dbf
         5 ONLINE  READ WRITE  /home1/oracle/dbs/usrweb.dbf
```

Make a note of all the datafiles that have the status OFFLINE. You need to recover those database files. Occasionally, the file that is being reported in the error message may have the status ONLINE. In this case, you can bring the file OFFLINE using the **ALTER DATABASE DATAFILE OFFLINE** command and then try to start up the database.

If you want to investigate the matter further, you can get a dump of the file header and contact WWCS. You can collect a dump of the header using the **ALTER SESSION** command. A trace file will be generated in the directory specified by USER_DUMP_DEST.

```
SVRMGR> ALTER SESSION SET EVENTS 'IMMEDIATE TRACE NAME FILE_HDRS LEVEL 10';
```

Finally, you will need to make a decision on how you can recover the corrupted file.

## ORA-1427

```
01427, 00000, "single-row subquery returns more than one row"
// *Cause:
// *Action:
```

An ORA-1427 occurs when a sub-query returns more than one value than expected by the main query. Let us examine the following query:

```
SELECT * FROM emp WHERE deptno = (SELECT deptno FROM dept);
```

If the sub-query returns more than one value for *deptno* you will get an ORA-1427. The solution is to rewrite the query with an IN instead of an equal sign.

```
SELECT * FROM emp WHERE deptno IN (SELECT deptno FROM dept);
```

## ORA-1545

```
01545, 00000, "rollback segment '%s' specified not available"
// *Cause: Either:
//            1) An attempt was made to bring a rollback segment online that is
//               unavailable during startup; for example, the rollback segment
//               is in an offline tablespace.
//            2) An attempt was made to bring a rollback segment online that is
//               already online.  This is because the rollback segment is
//               specified twice in the ROLLBACK_SEGMENTS parameter in the
//               initialization parameter file or the rollback segment is
//               already online by another instance.
//            3) An attempt was made to drop a rollback segment that contains
//               active transactions.
// *Action: Either:
//            1) Make the rollback segment available; for example, bring an
//               offline tablespace online.
//            2) Remove the name from the ROLLBACK_SEGMENTS parameter if the
//               name is a duplicate or if another instance has already
//               acquired the rollback segment.
//            3) Wait for the transactions to finish, or, if the rollback
//               segment needs recovery, discover which errors are holding up
//               the rolling
//               back of the transactions and take appropriate actions.
```

When we see a rollback segment with NEEDS RECOVERY status, it means precisely that the rollback segment needs to be recovered. Here is some useful information on the issue and how to work around it.

Oracle performs crash recovery automatically on startup. This leaves the database in a state in which the roll forward is complete and there is no more redo to be applied. Then the rollback segments (containing undo information) are scanned to roll back all the uncommitted or active transactions that are detected by looking at the transaction table of the rollback segments. If undo can be applied to all the uncommitted transactions, the rollback will be successful and complete. If Oracle cannot, for any reason, apply the undo, then the rollback segment is not recovered completely and will be put in the NEEDS RECOVERY state. The best way to detect this is to set the diagnostic events 10013 and 10015 as discussed earlier in this chapter. When these events are set, the transaction table is dumped to the trace file for all the rollback segments both before and after recovery. For rollback segments that are completely recovered, there will be a dump for both—that is, before and after recovery of the rollback segment. But for irrecoverable rollback segments, there will be a *before image* dump with a stack trace. By scanning the transaction table before recovery, you should see active transaction entries. In the trace file, there will also be an Oracle error, ORA-1135, at some point after the transaction table dump. The error indicates that a particular data file is offline, and looks something like the following:

```
ORA-01135 file name accessed for DML/query is off-line
```

This indicates that there is a data file that is offline and undo needs to be applied to this file. If the **init.ora** file specifies a rollback segment to be acquired for the instance, which is marked as NEEDS RECOVERY, you will get the ORA-1545 error which says:

```
ORA-01545 rollback segment #'name' was not available
```

Unfortunately, the message doesn't say why it is unavailable. By simply taking the rollback segment name off the ROLLBACK_SEGMENTS parameter list, in **init.ora**, you should be able to start up the database, if that is the only segment that needs recovery. The DBA might find that there is more than one rollback segment in NEEDS RECOVERY state, but this gets you over the problem temporarily. The important question you might ask is, "why can't undo be applied while rolling back?" The most probable reason is that the DBA either has taken a tablespace offline using the IMMEDIATE option, or has made a file offline before opening the database, while mounted. This problem can be permanently resolved in two ways:

- Bring the tablespace online so that the online command will cause the undo to be applied and change the status of the rollback segment.

- Drop the tablespace so that the drop command will trash the undo, as it is no longer required. Obviously, this action can be taken only if the tablespace can be rebuilt.

Both of the above actions can be taken while the database is open. If neither can be used, then bringing the database up without the rollback segments specified in the **init.ora** and leaving the database open for a while (maybe 30 minutes) will change the rollback segment's status from NEEDS RECOVERY to AVAILABLE. This undercover job is done by SMON which, among other things, looks at the rollback segments and copies the unapplied undo to *saveundo* (a deferred rollback segment). The DBA needs to make sure that there is sufficient free space in the SYSTEM tablespace for this to happen. The save undo will stay there until the tablespace in question is available again. If the system rollback segment has a transaction that is active, and can't be rolled back because of a tablespace being offline, then the DBA needs to go back to a backup. Needless to say, this should be a rare case and possible only if this database contains a single rollback segment.

## ORA-1652 - ORA-1655

The ORA-165x error message simply says that there is no more space available to allocate in a specific tablespace. (In Release 7.0 and some versions of 7.1 this used to be ORA-1547.)

```
ORA-1652: No more space is available to allocate to a temporary segment
ORA-1653: No more space available to allocate to a table
ORA-1654: No more space available to allocate to an index
ORA-1655: No more space available to allocate to a cluster
```

The ORA-165x error is possibly the most common Oracle error message a DBA would see. You need to understand the circumstances in which these errors arise, and the options you have when resolving these errors. Essentially, Oracle uses the logical tablespace unit; however, the physical aspect of the tablespace unit is the data file. The data file, which is created physically on disk, is where all objects within that tablespace reside. In order to add space to the tablespace, you must add a data file. When the ORA-165x error arises, the problem is due to lack of space in a particular tablespace. The error message gives two parameters: *SIZE*, which tells the DBA how many Oracle blocks the system was not able to find, and *TABLESPACE*, which tells the DBA where the space is needed. Oracle will always try to allocate contiguous space. Although the tablespace may have enough free space, if it is not contiguous, the error will still occur.

In order to see the free space available for a particular tablespace (say, USERS ), you must use the view SYS.DBA_FREE_SPACE. Within this view, each record represents one fragment of free space. For example:

```
SQL> SELECT FILE_ID, BLOCK_ID, BLOCKS, BYTES FROM
  SYS.DBA_FREE_SPACE WHERE TABLESPACE_NAME='USERS';

FILE_ID    BLOCK_ID    BLOCKS    BYTES
--------   ---------   -------   -------
4          2           20        40960
4          1465        72        147456
4          22          25        51200
4          147         1318      2699264

4 rows selected.
```

The above query tells you that there are four chunks of free space within the tablespace USERS and it shows each of their sizes, in Oracle blocks and bytes. The above query, however, doesn't properly display the contiguous chunks of free space. If you alter the query a bit by adding an ORDER BY clause, the output will be easy to read.

```
SQL> SELECT FILE_ID, BLOCK_ID, BLOCKS, BYTES FROM
  DBA_FREE_SPACE WHERE TABLESPACE_NAME='USERS' ORDER BY BLOCK_ID;

FILE_ID    BLOCK_ID    BLOCKS    BYTES
--------   ---------   -------   -------
4          2           20        40960
4          22          25        51200
4          147         1318      2699264
4          1465        72        147456

4 rows selected.
```

You can see that there are really two chunks of contiguous space instead of four. If you carefully examine the output, you see that at block 2, there are 20 blocks of free space. The next chunk of free space starts with block 22, which would make those two chunks contiguous. The same thing applies to block 147. When you add the number of blocks at that location, you see that they end at block 1464, which is adjacent to the next chunk of space.

Using the same example from above, if you try to create a table of 1325 Oracle blocks (or 2650K, assuming a block size of 2K), the free space is coalesced:

```
SQL> CREATE TABLE bulletin (y NUMBER) STORAGE (INITIAL 2650K)
     TABLESPACE users;

Table created.

SQL> SELECT FILE_ID, BLOCK_ID, BLOCKS, BYTES FROM DBA_FREE_SPACE
     WHERE TABLESPACE_NAME='USERS' ORDER BY BLOCK_ID;

FILE_ID  BLOCK_ID  BLOCKS  BYTES
-------  --------  ------  -----
4        2         45      92160
4        1472      65      133120

2 rows selected.
```

It is equally important to understand how the space algorithm works within Oracle. The RDBMS initially tries to find an exact-sized extent. If this doesn't exist, it will then break up an extent of a larger size. Finally, if it still is not able to find space, it will coalesce. Note that dropping the object has no effect on coalescing. Consider the following example:

```
SQL> DROP TABLE bulletin;

Table dropped.

SQL> SELECT FILE_ID, BLOCK_ID, BLOCKS, BYTES FROM
DBA_FREE_SPACE WHERE TABLESPACE_NAME='USERS' ORDER BY BLOCK_ID;

FILE_ID  BLOCK_ID  BLOCKS  BYTES
-------  --------  ------  -----
4        2         45      92160
4        147       1325    2713600
4        1472      65      133120

3 rows selected.
```

A simpler approach is to simply determine the biggest chunk of free space available, and see if it is smaller than the size the error is giving. This is the only approach needed for Oracle7.

Perform the following query:

```
SQL> SELECT MAX(BLOCKS) FROM SYS.DBA_FREE_SPACE WHERE
     TABLESPACE_NAME = name;
```

This will return one record that shows the biggest chunk of space free in the tablespace in question. This number will be lower than the one returned by the error. If you wish to compare the contiguous space with total space, perform the following query:

```
SQL> SELECT SUM(BLOCKS) FROM SYS.DBA_FREE_SPACE WHERE
     TABLESPACE_NAME = name;
```

This also returns one record. This value can be compared to the above to see how much of the total space is contiguous. Note that if there is no space in a tablespace, no records will be retrieved from the SYS.DBA_FREE_SPACE view.

Sometimes a user might try to do an insert into one tablespace and get an error on another tablespace. To understand this, let's examine the objects that can grow in the database.

**DATA DICTIONARY**    The ORA-165x error will occur if the data dictionary objects need to extend but there is not enough space in the SYSTEM tablespace for them to do so. This situation presents itself with the ORA-604 error before the ORA-165x error. For example, if creating a table forces the dictionary table **tab$** to extend and if the SYSTEM tablespace doesn't have enough space, the create table will receive the ORA-604 error followed by the ORA-165x error.

**TABLES AND INDEXES**    The ORA-165x error will occur if additional space is needed to satisfy an insert or update of an object. If this error arises on the creation of an index or table, the specified storage or tablespace default storage parameters need to be investigated.

**ROLLBACK SEGMENTS**    If the error occurs with a rollback segment, the ORA-1650 error will always precede the ORA-165x error. The ORA-1650 error indicates that it couldn't extend the rollback segment and the reason is the lack of space described by the ORA-165x error. The ORA-1650 error message is shown below:

```
ORA-1650 "unable to extend rollback segment"
```

**NOTE**
*Oracle versions prior to 7.1 displayed an*
*ORA-1562 instead of an ORA-1650.*

**TEMPORARY SEGMENTS**     Temporary segments are created by the Oracle kernel to do a sort on behalf of the user. Users can tell that they are running out of space for a temporary table, based on the operation they are performing (such as creating an index, doing a query with an ORDER BY clause, or a lengthy *join* statement). In this case, the temporary tablespace of the user needs to be found using the following query:

```
SQL> SELECT TEMPORARY_TABLESPACE FROM SYS.DBA_USERS WHERE
         USERNAME = username;
```

If the space being used seems excessive, you may want to investigate the default storage for the temporary tablespace, as it is possible that the defaults are too large. To see the default storage, perform the following query:

```
SQL> SELECT INITIAL_EXTENT, NEXT_EXTENT, MIN_EXTENTS,
         PCT_INCREASE FROM SYS.DBA_TABLESPACES WHERE TABLESPACE_NAME
         = name;
```

The default storage of the temporary (or any) tablespace can be altered using the following SQL command:

```
SQL> ALTER TABLESPACE name DEFAULT STORAGE (INITIAL xxx NEXT yyy);
```

Rather than add space to the temporary tablespace, you may opt to alter the user so that the user uses a tablespace that you know has more free space. If you wish to change the temporary tablespace for the user, issue the following command:

```
SQL> ALTER USER username TEMPORARY TABLESPACE new_tablespace_name;
```

Space can be added to a tablespace using the **ALTER TABLESPACE** command. This statement will create a database file on disk, and add the file to the tablespace. The **ALTER TABLESPACE** command can be performed on all tablespaces (including system) without shutting down the database or taking the tablespace offline. Immediately following the completion of the statement, the space is available for the DBA. Please note that once a data file is added, it cannot be deleted. The tablespace needs to be dropped.

While adding a data file to a tablespace, a DBA might accidentally add a bigger file than needed. In such cases, some DBAs tend to shut the database down, mount it, and use the **ALTER DATABASE** command to take the file offline and then open the database. Then they drop the data file they just added. This is a very dangerous operation. It will work as long as Oracle doesn't allocate any space from this data file. Note that even if the file is taken offline, Oracle will still try to allocate space to it as the free space is seen by Oracle in the **fet$** table. So the only solution to such problems is to export the data in that tablespace, drop the tablespace, recreate the tablespace with the right file sizes and finally import the data back. A data file can be added to the tablespace using the following SQL command:

```
SQL> ALTER TABLESPACE tablespace_name ADD DATAFILE filename SIZE
        size_of_file;
```

To get an idea of the naming conventions, or locations for existing files, perform the following query:

```
SQL> SELECT FILE_NAME FROM SYS.DBA_DATA_FILES WHERE
        TABLESPACE_NAME=name;
```

Sometimes, users receive the ORA-165x error while running an import. Some of the common reasons are discussed here:

**EXPORT AND THE ORA-165X**    Exporting with COMPRESS=Y modifies the *initial extent* storage parameter to be equal to the space that the table has allocated at the time of export. If a user tries to import specific tables into an existing database, the import often fails because it cannot find contiguous space. Consider the scenario where a table is spread across 4 extents of 10MB each. When this table is exported with COMPRESS=Y, the initial extent for this table is now 40MB. The user drops the table, then tries to import and the RDBMS cannot find 40MB of contiguous space, which causes an ORA-165x error. Although the table existed in the tablespace, import can no longer create it.

To work around this problem without adding space to the tablespace, the DBA can do one of the following:

- Export the table and specify COMPRESS=N. This preserves the table's original storage parameters.

- Create the table with specific storage parameters before importing.

- Truncate the table before importing the data rather than dropping it.

**IMPORT AND THE ORA-165X**    By default, the Import utility commits at the end of each table; therefore, it is very likely that your rollback segments will run out of space. To work around this problem, without adding space to the rollback segment tablespace, you can specify the COMMIT=Y option on import. This overrides the default and commits at the end of each *buffer* (also an import parameter), rather than at the end of the table. This will impact performance considerably as every commit forces the LGWR process to write the commit record to the log file on disk. This means more I/O.

We would like to point out that some new concepts in space management have been introduced in Release 7.2 that should reduce the administrative overhead while doing space management. One of these is the concept of dynamically resizing data files. Without adding a data file, the DBA can manually extend a file to add more space or shrink a file to reclaim the free space in the database using the **ALTER DATABASE DATAFILE RESIZE** command. Please refer to Oracle documentation for information on resizing data files.

**INDEXES AND THE ORA-165X**    If the import fails when creating the indexes, you need to modify your temporary tablespace. The solution is to create enough space for the RDBMS to do the sorting for the index. One workaround is to create the table and index before importing. This should only be used if it is not possible to add the space, even for a short period of time. This method also has a grave effect on the import's performance because every time a row is inserted, the index tree needs to be traversed to insert the key. If you are using SQL*LOADER to load data, a better workaround is to create the index with the NOSORT option before importing. Then you need to sort the data using some other utility before loading it into the table.

## ORA-1555

```
01555, 00000, "snapshot too old (rollback segment too small)"
// *Cause: rollback records needed by a reader for consistent read are
//     overwritten by other writers
// *Action: Use larger rollback segments
```

There are various reasons why users get the ORA-1555 error. The most common reason is that the rollback segments are too small, but there are other reasons as well. The following discussion gives a complete summary of all the situations that would cause the ORA-1555 error and how to resolve them. In order to understand the discussion, you need to be familiar with some of the internal mechanisms of Oracle, so a brief explanation about read consistency and block cleanouts is given.

Oracle always enforces statement-level read consistency. This guarantees that the data returned by a single query is consistent with respect to the time when the query began. Therefore, a query never sees the data changes made by transactions that commit during the course of execution of the query.

Oracle maintains something called a System Change Number (SCN). An SCN can be defined as the state of the database at any given point in time. To produce read consistency, Oracle marks the current SCN as the query enters the execution phase. The query can only see the snapshot of the records from that SCN onwards. Oracle uses rollback segments to reconstruct the read-consistent snapshot of the data. Whenever a transaction makes any changes, a snapshot of the record before the changes were made is copied to a rollback segment and the data block header is marked appropriately with the address of the rollback segment block where the changes are recorded. The data block also maintains the SCN of the last committed change to the block. As data blocks are read on behalf of the query, only blocks with lower SCNs than the query SCN will be read. If a block has uncommitted changes of other transactions, or changed data with more recent SCNs, then the data is reconstructed using the saved snapshot from the rollback segments. In some rare situations, if the RDBMS is not able to reconstruct the snapshot for a long-running query, the query results in the ORA-1555 error.

A rollback segment maintains the snapshot of the changed data as long as the transaction is still active (as long as a commit or rollback has not been issued). Once a transaction is committed, the RDBMS marks it with the current SCN and the space used by the snapshot becomes available for reuse. Therefore, the ORA-1555 error will result if the query is looking for a snapshot that is so old the rollback segment doesn't contain it because of wrap around or overwrite.

Now that we have looked at how rollback segments are used, we will address the four main reasons for ORA-1555 errors.

**FEW AND SMALL ROLLBACK SEGMENTS** If a database has many concurrent transactions changing data and committing very often, then the chances of reusing the space used by a committed transaction are higher. A long-running query then may not be able to reconstruct the snapshot because of wrap around and overwrite in rollback segments. Larger rollback segments in this case will reduce the chance of reusing the committed transaction slots.

**CORRUPTED ROLLBACK SEGMENTS** Corrupted rollback segments can cause this error as well. If the rollback segment is corrupted and cannot be read, then a statement needing to reconstruct a before image snapshot will result in this error.

**FETCH-ACROSS COMMITS** A *fetch-across commit* is a situation in which a query opens a cursor, loops through fetching, changes data, and commits the records on the same table. For example, suppose a cursor was opened at an SCN value of 10. The execution SCN of the query is then marked as SCN=10. Every fetch by that cursor now needs to get the read-consistent data from SCN=10. Let's assume that the user program fetches *x* number of records, changes them, and then commits them with an SCN value of 20. If a later fetch happens to retrieve a record that is in one of the previously-committed blocks, then the fetch will see that the SCN there is 20. Since the fetch has to get the snapshot from SCN=10, read consistency needs to be performed on the data using the rollback segment. If it cannot roll back to SCN 10, the ORA-1555 error occurs. Committing less often in this case will result in larger rollback segments and *reduce* the probability of getting the error.

**FETCH-ACROSS COMMITS WITH DELAYED BLOCK CLEANOUT**
When a data or index block is modified in the database and the transaction is committed, Oracle does a fast commit by marking the transaction as committed in the rollback segment header, but does not clean the locks in

the data blocks that were modified. The next transaction that does a select on the modified blocks will do the actual cleanout of the block. This is known as a *delayed block cleanout.*

Now let's take the same example as with fetch-across commits, but instead of assuming one table, let's assume that there are two tables that the transaction uses. In other words, the cursor is opened, and then in a loop, fetches from one table and changes records in another, and commits. Even though the records are getting committed in another table, it could still cause the ORA-1555 error because cleanout has not been done on the table from which the records are being fetched. This is possible because some other transaction has modified this table before we did the select. For this case, a full table scan before opening and fetching through the cursor will help.

Note that fetch-across commits, as explained in the last two cases, are not supported by ANSI SQL standards. According to the standard, a cursor is invalidated when a commit is performed and should be closed and reopened before fetching again. Though not ANSI SQL standard, Oracle, unlike some other database vendors, allows users to do fetch-across commits, but users should be aware that this might result in the ORA-1555 error.

## ORA-1594

```
01594, 00000, "attempt to wrap into rollback segment (%s) extent (%s) which
is being freed"
// *Cause:  Undo generated to free a rollback segment extent is attempting
//          to write into the same extent due to small extents and/or too
//          many extents to free
// *Action: The rollback segment shrinking will be rollbacked by the system;
//          increase the optimal size of the rollback segment.
```

The most probable cause of the ORA-1594 error is small extent sizes. Shrinking of extents is started when a request is made for an undo block and the kernel detects that the current extent of the rollback segment is reaching the end of its free space. If several extents are to be freed, this can generate substantial undo, which may eventually wrap into the extent that is being freed up. This will cause the ORA-1594 error to occur. Having a smaller number of larger extents is a good way to deal with this problem.

## ORA-1628 or ORA-163x

```
01628, 00000, "max # extents (%s) reached for rollback segment %s"
// *Cause:  Tried to extend rollback segment already at maxextents value
// *Action: If maxextents storage parameter less than system allowable max,
//          raise this value. Consider upping the pctincrease value as well.
```

Sometimes, you may also see the following ORA error with ORA-1628:

```
ORA-01562, 00000, "failed to extend rollback segment (id = %s)"
// *Cause: Failure occurred when trying to extent rollback segment
// *Action: This is normally followed by another error message that caused
//          the failure. Shutdown, restart and then take appropriate action
//          for the error the caused the failure. If starting up the system
//          again doesn't solve the problem, it is possible that there is
//          an active transaction in the rollback segment and the system
//          can't roll it back for some reasons. Check the trace file
//          generated by the PMON process for more information.
```

Other errors related to the same issue are:

```
01630, 00000, "max # extents (%s) reached in temp segment in tablespace %s"
// *Cause:  A temp segment tried to extend past max extents.
// *Action: If maxextents for the tablespace is less than the system
//          maximum, you can raise that. Otherwise, raise pctincrease for
//          the tablespace
01631, 00000, "max # extents (%s) reached in table %s.%s"
// *Cause:  A table tried to extend past maxextents
// *Action: If maxextents is less than the system maximum, raise it.
//Otherwise,you must recreate with larger initial, next or pctincrease params
01632, 00000, "max # extents (%s) reached in index %s.%s"
// *Cause:  An index tried to extend past maxextents
// *Action: If maxextents is less than the system max, raise it. Otherwise,
//          you must recreate with larger initial, next or pctincrease params.
```

All of these errors indicate that an object in Oracle has reached the MAXEXTENTS limit. This error can occur at the database or the application level. The MAXEXTENTS parameter defines the maximum number of extents that an object in Oracle can allocate. When you hit this pre-defined limit, you will see one of these errors. The error can be reported for a segment or a tablespace itself. We will first discuss an example of a table that has reached the maximum number of extents.

Let us assume that you attempted to issue the below SQL statement and you get the subsequent ORA-1631 error shown:

```
SQL> INSERT INTO mytab SELECT * FROM mytab;
ORA-01631: max # extents (2) reached in table MYTAB
```

You must first query the USER_TABLES view to verify the problem.

```
SQL> SELECT INITIAL_EXTENT, NEXT_EXTENT, MAX_EXTENTS FROM
     USER_TABLES WHERE TABLE_NAME = 'MYTAB';
INITIAL_EXTENT NEXT_EXTENT MAX_EXTENT
-------------- ----------- ----------
        6144       10240          2
```

Note that the MAXEXTENT limit for the object is 2 extents, but that is not the *hardcoded* limit. The hardcoded limit for the maximum number of extents depends on the value of the DB_BLOCK_SIZE parameter in the **init.ora** that should be specified when the database is created. We have presented this information in Table 7-2 earlier in this chapter.

> **NOTE**
> *An attempt to specify a storage clause with a MAXEXTENT value larger than the LARGEST MAXEXTENT VALUE will result in an ORA-02226.*

In order to resolve an ORA-1628 if the platform limit for MAXEXTENTS is not reached, you can use the **ALTER TABLE ... STORAGE (MAXEXTENTS *n*)** SQL command to increase MAXEXTENTS. Note that *n* must be larger than the count specified in the error message, but not larger than the LARGEST MAXEXTENT value. However, if you have reached the LARGEST MAXEXTENT VALUE, then the only way to resolve this is to recreate the object with larger extent sizes and fewer extents so that the MAXEXTENT limit will not be reached. You must first export the table using the Oracle Export utility with the COMPRESS=Y option. If room is available in your tablespace, we also recommend that you rename the original table to have a backup. Finally import the table back into the database. You can also change the STORAGE clause for this new table using the **ALTER TABLE** command.

We will now present your options if you have hit MAXEXTENTS for rollback segments, indexes, and temporary tablespaces. If the error is occurring on a rollback segment or an index, then you can just drop and recreate the object. If the error is occurring on the temporary tablespace, then altering the storage clause for the temporary tablespace will solve the problem as temporary segments always use the default storage parameters of the tablespace when they are created.

```
SQL> ALTER TABLESPACE temp tablespace STORAGE (INITIAL n NEXT n)
```

## ORA-3113 or ORA-3114

```
03113, 00000, "end-of-file on communication channel"
// *Cause:
// *Action:
03114, 00000, "not connected to ORACLE"
// *Cause:
// *Action:
```

An ORA-03113 is a fairly common error that is reported when a client loses its connection to the server. It basically means that communications were lost for an unexpected reason. It is usually followed by an ORA-03114. The most common reason for an ORA-3113 is that the Oracle server (shadow) process on the server died unexpectedly. The alert log on the server should have more information on this error. Another common cause of ORA-03113 (mostly on UNIX platforms) is that the Oracle executable is not linked with the appropriate SQL*Net. In such cases the SQL*Net listener successfully received a connect request and passed it to an Oracle server process that was unable to handle this type of a request. Obviously, network or machine failures on the server side will also result in these errors.

## ORA-4031

```
04031, 00000, "unable to allocate %s bytes of shared memory
(\"%s\",\"%s\",\"%s\")"
// *Cause:  More shared memory is needed than was allocated in the shared
//          pool.
// *Action: Either use the dbms_shared_pool package to pin large packages,
//          reduce your use of shared memory, or increase the amount of
//          available shared memory by increasing the value of the
//          init.ora parameter "shared_pool_size".
```

Fragmentation of shared pool memory area is a common problem that application programmers and DBAs often face, and the ORA-4031 error is commonly a result of such fragmentation. Here, we will discuss some of the workarounds that are available today and future enhancements that are under consideration. The text of an ORA-4031 is provided here for your reference.

Imagine the *shared pool* being similar to a tablespace. While you may get the ORA-165x error when you cannot get sufficient contiguous free space in the tablespace, you will get the ORA-4031 error when you cannot get contiguous free space in the shared pool (in the SGA). Application programmers usually get this error while attempting to load a big package or while executing a very large procedure and there is not sufficient contiguous free memory available in the shared pool. This may be due to fragmentation of the shared pool memory or insufficient memory in the shared pool.

If it is due to fragmentation, one needs to flush the shared pool and/or break up the package or procedure into smaller blocks. If the shared pool is badly fragmented, even using small packages or procedures can result in this error. Flushing the shared pool might not help all the time because it will not flush the PINNED buffers (containing information on on-going SQL statements) that are being changed at that time.

If it is due to insufficient memory, the SHARED_POOL_SIZE should be increased from the default value, which is 3.5MB in the **init.ora** file. Increasing the shared pool might not be a viable solution in some shops that have high availability requirements, because you allocate the size of the shared pool during start-up time, and increasing this means shutting down and restarting the database. Unfortunately, this size is fixed and cannot be extended while the database is up.

We therefore recommend that you increase the SHARED_POOL_SIZE, as the current default tends to be a low estimate when utilizing the procedural option.

## ORA-4091

```
ORA-04091, 00000, "table %s.%s is mutating, trigger/function may not see it"
// *Cause: A trigger (or a user defined plsql function that is referenced in
//         this statement) attempted to look at (or modify) a table that was
//         in the middle of being modified by the statement which fired it.
// *Action: Rewrite the trigger (or function) so it does not read that table.
```

ORA-4091 is a very common error that occurs when database triggers are not managed properly. A full understanding of triggers will help you avoid this error.

A mutating table is a table that is currently being modified by an update, delete, or insert statement. You will encounter the ORA-4091 error if you have a row trigger that reads or modifies the mutating table. For example, if your trigger contains a SELECT statement or an UPDATE statement referencing the table it is triggering, you will receive the error.

Another way this error can occur is if the trigger has statements to change the primary, foreign, or unique key columns of the table the trigger is currently triggering. If you must have triggers on tables that have referential constraints, the workaround is to enforce the referential integrity through triggers as well.

## ORA-12004

```
12004, 00000, "REFRESH FAST cannot be used"
// *Cause:  The snapshot log does not exist or cannot be used.
// *Action: Use just REFRESH, which will reinstantiate the entire table.
//          If a snapshot log exists and the form of the snapshot allows the
//          use of a snapshot log, REFRESH FAST will be available starting
//          the next time the snapshot is refreshed.
```

You need to understand the concepts of *snapshots* and *procedures* before you read this section. Please refer to the *Oracle7 Server Application Developer's Guide* for details on snapshots and procedures. This section gives some debugging information on snapshots. Most of the snapshot problems can be approached this way.

An ORA-12004 occurs when you try to do a *fast refresh* and the attempt failed because Oracle could not use the snapshot log.

For example, assume that the procedure **dbms_snapshot.set_up** is executed (remotely) at the master site. One query in the procedure is:

```
SELECT log, oldest, youngest+1/86400
FROM  mlog$ WHERE master = :2 and mowner = :1 FOR UPDATE;
```

This procedure retrieves the log name and updates the timestamps in the snapshot log. If the update fails, if you are not able to get the log name, or if any other error occurs, then this procedure does not return a log name and the ORA-12004 error is signaled.

Consider the scenario where the procedure **dbms_snapshot.get_log_age** is executed (again, remotely at the master site). This procedure returns a date defined by:

```
SELECT oldest INTO oldest FROM sys.mlog$ WHERE mowner = mow AND
       master = mas;
```

This date (call it log_date) is then compared to the date of this snapshot's most recent refresh (call it snap_date). The value of snap_date is given by the snaptime column in the **snap$** base data dictionary table. If snap_date is earlier than log_date, then the ORA-12004 error is signaled.

To summarize, there are two possible causes of the ORA-12004 error. Either you were unable to retrieve the name of the log file (from

**dbms_snapshot.set_up**), or the log is out of date, possibly because the snapshot log has been purged (snapshot logs can be purged manually using **dbms_snapshot.purge_log**; Oracle also purges the log automatically after refreshes, but the automatic purge shouldn't "age out" any other snapshots).

To debug this problem, you can run **dbms_snapshot.set_up** manually. The name of the log table is an OUT variable. So consider the following procedure:

```
CREATE TABLE foo (a varchar(30));
DECLARE
owner varchar(30);
master varchar(30);
log varchar(30);
snapshot date;
snaptime date;
BEGIN
    snapshot := SYSDATE;
    snaptime := SYSDATE;
    owner := 'SCOTT';
    master := 'EMP';
    dbms_snapshot.set_updblink(owner, master, log, snapshot, snaptime);
    INSERT INTO foo(a) VALUES (log);
END;
```

After executing this, the log name for the master table should be in *foo*. This can be verified as follows:

```
SVRMGR> select * from foo;
A
-------------------
MLOG$_EMP
1 row selected.
```

As a side effect, this procedure will cause the master site (and mlog$ and snapshot logs) to believe that a snapshot has occurred, and will result in future refreshes, possibly returning the ORA-12004 error for out-of-date reasons. So, be prepared to do full refreshes on your snapshots after running this test.

If **dbms_snapshot.set_up** appears to be running correctly, then you can attempt to figure out why your log tables are outdated using the above queries.

# Oracle Internal Errors

Most of the high priority problems reported to WWCS are kernel-related. These kinds of problems need to be diagnosed as soon as possible, and some initial diagnostic tests can be performed by DBAs. This section first discusses Oracle internal errors, such as the ORA-600 error. Next, the section presents an overview of the various categories of priority 1/priority 2 problems and the diagnostic information a DBA can collect before calling WWCS. Lastly, some examples illustrate how to deal with memory or block corruption.

## ORA-600

As discussed earlier in this chapter, the main purpose of trace files is to record information when error conditions occur. All errors signaled by Oracle have a code associated with them. While some common errors are displayed on the screen to users, some fatal or internal errors are recorded in the alert file, and create a trace file. For example, the ORA-1578 error means that a block has been corrupted. All of the ORA- errors are documented either in the *Oracle7 Server Messages and Codes Manual* or the *Oracle Installation and User's Guide* for a specific platform. There is a special Oracle error code that has meaning only to WWCS and development. The ORA-600 error is signaled when a sanity check fails within the Oracle code. To illustrate what is meant by a sanity check, examine the following pseudo-code:

```
/* Pseudo-code to get file# F, block# B from the database */
GET(F,B)
BEGIN
     IF (F > MAX_NUMBER_OF_FILES)
          signal ("ORA 600 [2858] [F]");
          exit ( )
     ENDIF;
     ......
END;
```

In this code segment, the *if* statement tests the validity of the file number requested. If the file number requested is out of range, the program will signal the error and exit. Note that this is not the complete meaning of the actual ORA-600 [2858] error, but an illustration of a sanity check.

The first argument in the ORA-600 error is used as a tag for the location in the code where the error is signaled. Each first argument is unique to one section of the code. The second through fifth arguments are used to give additional information such as the file number in the previous example.

The ORA-600 error message informs WWCS where the error occurred in the code, but doesn't indicate what the RDBMS was doing when it entered the routine containing the error. The *stack trace dumps* help to determine what was happening at the time the error occurred. The stack trace is a dump of the execution stack of a process. It contains the names of all active routines and the values of the arguments passed to those routines. Stack traces are read from the bottom up, with the top routine usually being the routine that prints out the stack trace. The arguments on the stack trace of an Oracle process are usually not very helpful, since they are mostly address pointers and not the values of actual data structures. But the routine names help WWCS determine what type of activity led up to this error. For example, it can be determined that a corrupted block was found during the act of building a consistent read block if the routine that builds consistent read blocks is on the stack.

The dump of a stack trace is done by making a call to the operating system that Oracle is currently running on. This causes the appearances of stack traces to look different from one platform to another. On UNIX platforms, the dump of the stack trace will include the routine names, whereas on OpenVMS the stack trace is dumped with the routine names encrypted as addresses in the code. To make the stack trace readable, the DBA should format the trace file using the **TRCFMT** command on the machine on which the trace file is created. This will convert the addresses to routine names and will be in a human-readable format.

The ORA-600 error is often followed by state dumps in the trace files. There are two types of state dumps, *system state* and *process state.* A system state dump will contain information about objects currently held by the Oracle RDBMS. A process state dump will show objects held by a particular process. These dumps are usually large in size and difficult to decipher. But one of the key pieces of the information contained in these dumps is the blocks held by each process. When a process hits an error condition, it is often due to some information it has extracted from a block it is holding. If we know the blocks held by the errant process, it is easier to track down the source of the problem. By using the data block addresses in the system or process state dump, we can see what objects are encountering the signaled errors. If more information is required, WWCS will request that the DBA dump more information concerning a block, or a process state, or system state, depending on the error (the syntax for dumping the system state and the process state are discussed earlier in this chapter).

# Categories of Priority I/Priority 2 Problems and Diagnostic Actions

Following are the various categories of problems that could impact the availability of the database or question the data integrity of the database. This information is provided to help you accurately describe your problem to WWCS. It will be necessary to get assistance from the support analyst in these situations.

- Data corruption

- Logical corruption

- System hangs

- Performance problems

- System crashes

- Critical functionality not available

- Memory corruption

## Data Corruption

*Data corruption* includes all block format corruption, invalid index entries and corruption of meta-data (e.g., the data dictionary). An example is a user getting the ORA-600 [3339] error on a system data file when selecting from a table. There are various reasons why data corruption occurs. For example, it could be the hardware vendor's operating system problem with clustered disks. Standard or typical diagnostic actions for these kinds of problems include:

- Collecting trace files (and formatting them where applicable) if the corruption is reported as an internal error.

- Dumping the redo logs corresponding to the time of corruption. If you are not sure how many log files to dump, save all the redo log files and contact WWCS.

- Asking the system manager for complete hardware diagnostics to be carried out if there is a reason to suspect a vendor operating system problem.

- Where appropriate, determining whether the problem is generic or port-specific.

## Logical Corruption

*Logical corruption* refers to the case where data (either as stored or as returned by a query) is incorrect, although it isn't necessary that an error is returned externally. Phantom rows in a table after updating a column to null, or a query returning different results when using different types of optimizer would be typical examples of a logical corruption. Logical corruptions are very dangerous, as they are difficult to detect. Standard diagnostic actions for DBAs include:

- Trying to create a reproducible test case.

- Collecting trace files (and formatting them where applicable) if the corruption is reported as an internal error (e.g., ORA-600 [13004]).

- When appropriate, determining whether the problem is generic or port-specific.

## System Hangs

*System hangs* can be defined as users unable to log on to the database or to execute operations. System hangs could also mean that the database hangs on open after media or crash recovery. For example, a process holding a latch on a crucial data structure and spinning might cause a system hang. Standard diagnostic actions during system hangs are as follows:

- In the case of a hang on database open, set events and diagnose at which stage of recovery the database is stuck, and dump the diagnostic information (e.g., the header of the undo segment if spinning while doing transaction recovery). In the case of a system hang, take the system state dumps at appropriate intervals, either using a tool such as ORADBX or by using the **ALTER SESSION** command. Monitor CPU and I/O activity of background and foreground processes.

■ When appropriate, determine if the problem is generic or port-specific.

■ If reproducible, create a test case.

■ If reproducible only at your site with reasonable frequency, set up a modem for WWCS personnel to dial in and monitor.

## Performance Problems

*Performance problems* can be classified into two kinds. General cases of deterioration in response time or batch completion times are one kind. The other is performance degradation on increase in concurrent activity. These kinds of problems are generally time consuming and require patience. Poor response times can sometimes be due to waits for library cache pins. Standard diagnostic actions include:

■ Documenting performance degradation in terms of specific indicators, such as response time, batch completion time, number of concurrent logins supported, efficiency of shared pool management, and so on.

■ Providing a reproducible test case, if possible, or documenting in detail the environment and factors leading to poor performance. For example, in the case where reproducibility depends on concurrency in a production environment, it is appropriate to document circumstances surrounding degradation, such as number of logins, average memory usage, typical functionality invoked, I/O activity, and dynamic statistics on Oracle activity.

■ Setting up a modem for WWCS personnel to dial in and monitor, if the problem is reproducible only at your site with reasonable frequency.

■ When appropriate, determining whether the problem is generic or port-specific.

## System Crashes

*System crashes* include cases where the database crashes because one of the background processes died. These kinds of problems are not common, but if the database crashes, DBAs should take the following diagnostic actions:

- Check the alert file to see if any ORA-600 errors have occurred. If so, get the trace files and format them if necessary.

- Find out what the users were doing at the time of the crash, and which applications were running at that time. If a specific application is isolated, try reproducing the problem by running the application on a test machine.

- When appropriate, determine whether the problem is generic or port-specific.

## Critical Functionality Not Available

*Critical functionality not available* refers to all situations where functionality or vital features that rely on a production application become unavailable, typically because of a bug in the database software or any third party software that runs on top of Oracle. Some examples that fall under this category include cases where Oracle utilities core dump or the applications error out. In some cases, a function not available might affect the availability of the database indirectly. For example, a database is being recovered from a full database export, and import from multiple tapes doesn't work correctly, thereby preventing a database rebuild of a production database. Again, the standard diagnostic actions in this case include:

- Collecting trace files and dumping relevant redo log files (under WWCS guidance) depending on the error, and documenting the circumstances leading up to the error.

- Providing a reproducible test case if possible.

- Providing detailed information, such as utilities used, storage structures accessed, DDL/DML performed, and procedures or packages executed during the time the error occurred, especially if providing a reproducible test case is not possible.

- When appropriate, determining whether the problem is generic or port-specific.

### Memory Corruption

*Memory corruption* includes internal errors that signal memory leaks, corruption of memory data structures, and cache corruption. Diagnostic actions include:

- Collecting trace files, if the error produces them.

- Providing a reproducible test case if possible, or documenting circumstances, such as the following, that caused the error:

  - Details of OCI or the Oracle tool/utility or the pre-compiler used in application

  - Operating system tools or third-party tools used in conjunction with the application

  - Triggers fired by application

  - Packages or procedures executed

# Frequently Asked Questions (FAQ)

In this section we present questions and answers that cover various categories of the database. These include general availability questions related to Oracle7 Release 7.3, user management, space management, backup and recovery, and the Export/Import utilities.

**Q.**   I want to assign a bunch of my users uniform object privileges for a particular application. Is there some way I can do this without repeating **GRANT** commands for a lot of users?

**A.**   The easiest way to ensure that a set of users gets similar access to a set of objects is to create appropriate roles and then assign new users to those roles. We present an example below that provides read access to a table called EMP owned by SCOTT.

```
SQL> CONNECT system/manager
Connected.
SQL> CREATE ROLE empread;
Role created.
SQL> CONNECT scott/tiger
Connected.
SQL> GRANT SELECT ON emp TO empread;
Grant succeeded.
SQL> CONNECT system/manager
Connected.
SQL> GRANT empread TO aa;
Grant succeeded.
```

In the above example, we create the role as a DBA to illustrate system-wide privileges. It is also possible for the schema *scott* to create and maintain the role EMPREAD as shown below.

```
SQL> CONNECT scott/tiger
Connected.
SQL> CREATE ROLE empread;
Role created.
SQL> GRANT SELECT ON emp TO empread;
Grant succeeded.
SQL> GRANT empread TO aa;
Grant succeeded.
```

**Q.** I am trying to insert some records into an existing table and I get an *ORA-1653 "unable to extend table* table *in tablespace* tablespace_name*"*. What is wrong?

**A.** This error appears when the tablespace does not have room to hold the new extents required to grow the table. You must add a new datafile to the tablespace in question to resolve the error. Look carefully at the error statement for the name of the tablespace that is full, and then use the **ALTER TABLESPACE** command to allocate a new datafile to this tablespace.

```
SQL> ALTER TABLESPACE name ADD DATAFILE file SIZE size;
```

Be sure to include the complete path to the file specification in the above command. Alternatively, you can enable dynamic allocation of space by using the command **ALTER DATABASE DATAFILE name AUTOEXTEND ON**.

**Q.**  I have added new rollback segments with the **CREATE ROLLBACK SEGMENT** command to account for increased transactions on my database. My users are still having problems with DML statements. I think it is contention for rollback segments. What is the problem?
**A.**  You need to ensure that the new rollback segments you created are brought online.

```
SQL> CONNECT system/manager
Connected.
SQL> SELECT SEGMENT_NAME, STATUS FROM DBA_ROLLBACK_SEGS;
SEGMENT_NAME                 STATUS
-------------------------    ----------------
SYSTEM                       ONLINE
R01                          ONLINE
R02                          ONLINE
R03                          ONLINE
R04                          OFFLINE
```

Use the **ALTER ROLLBACK SEGMENT** command to bring OFFLINE segments ONLINE.

```
SQL> ALTER ROLLBACK SEGMENT r04 ONLINE;
Rollback segment altered.
```

We also suggest that you add these newly created rollback segments to the ROLLBACK_SEGMENTS parameter in the **init.ora** file if you wish to keep them permanently.

```
rollback_segments = (r01, r02, r03, r04)
```

**Q.**  I have added a lot of new users to a new department in our shop. I want to designate a fixed tablespace for all their objects and temporary segments. How do I do this?
**A.**  You can user the **ALTER USER** command to assign a default tablespace for objects created by a user and also to assign a tablespace for temporary segments.

```
SQL> ALTER USER aa DEFAULT TABLESPACE users TEMPORARY TABLESPACE
     temp;
```

You can determine the currently assigned tablespaces by querying the DBA_USERS view.

```
SQL> SELECT USERNAME,DEFAULT_TABLESPACE,TEMPORARY_TABLESPACE FROM DBA_USERS;
USERNAME                DEFAULT_TABLESPACE          TEMPORARY_TABLESPACE
----------------------  --------------------------  --------------------
SYS                     SYSTEM                      TEMP
SYSTEM                  TOOLS                       TEMP
WWW_DBA                 SYSTEM                      SYSTEM
SCOTT                   USERS                       TEMP
```

**Q.** I created a new Oracle user on my database and assigned suitable default and temporary tablespaces using the **CREATE USER** command. My user is still unable to log on. Why?

**A.** You are probably seeing the error *ORA-1045: User lacks CREATE SESSION privilege; logon denied.* You need to grant the **CREATE SESSION** privilege to the user using the **GRANT** command before the user can connect to Oracle.

```
SQL> GRANT CONNECT TO newuser;
Grant succeeded.
```

**Q.** I am unable to change some data on my Oracle database. I issue an update command and it just hangs. What is the problem?

**A.** You are probably trying to change a set of records that are locked by another transaction. Ensure that you do not have another Oracle session from which you have a pending transaction. You must complete the pending transaction by issuing a COMMIT or a ROLLBACK before you can proceed with the new transaction. This type of a situation is common when you open multiple sessions to Oracle from different windows using the same Oracle user or when you use EXPLICIT locks on objects via SQL statements such as LOCK and SELECT FOR UPDATE.

**Q.** I was reviewing my alert log file and I noticed that there are a lot of entries that say something like "Thread 1 cannot allocate new log sequence number" or something like that. What should I do?

**A.** You are probably running into a situation where you are waiting for a redo log group to be available. Try adding one or two more redo log groups to your database. You can use the **ALTER DATABASE ADD LOGFILE** command to accomplish this. Be sure to review the "Rebuilding Database Schema and Objects" section earlier in this chapter for more information on redo log groups.

**Q.** In a nut shell, can you tell us all the new features of Oracle7
Release 7.3?
**A.** The following list provides this information:

■ New features of 7.3.3 are:

Direct load to cluster    Can use backup from before RESETLOGS

■ New features of 7.3 (before 7.3.3) are:

| | | |
|---|---|---|
| Histograms | Hash Joins | Star Join Enhancement |
| Standby Databases | Parallel UNION-ALL | Dynamic **init.ora** Configuration |
| Direct Path Export | Compiled Triggers | Fast Create Index |
| Multiple LRU Latches | Updateable Join Views | LSQL Cursor Variable Enhancement |
| Replication Enhancement | OPS Processor Affinity | Net 2 Load Balancing |
| XA Scaling / Recovery | Thread Safe Pro*C/OCI | DB Verify |
| New PLSQL Packages | New PLSQL Features | Bitmap Indexes |

**Q.** What are the new Parallel features in Oracle7 Release 7.2 and 7.3?
**A.** Operations parallelized by Oracle7 Parallel Query are:

■ **Parallel Data Loading:** conventional and direct-path, to the same
table or multiple tables concurrently

■ **Parallel Query:** table scans, sorts, joins, aggregates, duplicate
elimination, UNION and UNION ALL (7.3)

■ **Parallel Subqueries:** in INSERT, UPDATE, DELETE statements

■ **Parallel Execution:** of application code (user-defined SQL functions)

■ **Parallel Joins:** nested loop, sort-merge, star join optimization
(creation of Cartesian products plus the nested loop join), hash joins
(7.3)

■ **Parallel Anti-Joins:** NOT IN (7.3)

■ **Parallel Summarization (CREATE TABLE AS SELECT):** query and
insertion of rows into a rollup table

■ **Parallel Index Creation (CREATE INDEX):** table scans, sorts, index
fragment construction

**Q.** What were the optimizations introduced in Releases 7.2 and 7.3?

**A.** They are:

■ **Direct Database Reads:** Parallel query processes must scan very large tables to perform filtering, sorting, joins, etc. Direct Database Reads enable direct contiguous disk to contiguous memory reads for improved read efficiency and performance. They also bypass the buffer cache to eliminate contention with concurrent OLTP activity.

■ **Direct Database Writes:** Parallel query processes must often write results back to disk, such as for intermediate sort runs, summarization (CREATE TABLE AS SELECT), and index creation (CREATE INDEX). Direct Database Writes enable direct contiguous memory to contiguous disk writes for improved efficiency and performance. They also bypass the buffer cache to eliminate contention with concurrent OLTP activity and the database writer (DBWR) process. Direct Database Reads and Writes make it possible to tune the Oracle7 server separately and optimally, supporting a mixed workload of concurrent OLTP and DSS activity.

■ **Asynchronous I/O:** Oracle7 already employs asynchronous write facilities for sorts, summarization, index creation, and direct-path loading (where supported by the underlying operating system). Beginning with Release 7.3, Oracle7 will also employ asynchronous read-ahead to maximize the overlap of processing and I/O for further improvements in performance.

■ **Parallel Table Creation:** Databases often create temporary tables (CREATE TABLE ... AS SELECT ...) to hold summarized or interim results of queries run against large tables of detailed data. This functionality is commonly used during "drill-down" analysis to hold the results of intermediate operations.

■ An option exists that will suppress the generation and writing of log records to further improve performance and scalability. This option is similarly available for index creation and direct-path data loading.

**NOTE**
*This is unrelated to parallel insert/update/delete.*

■ **Support for the Star Query Optimization:** Oracle7 automatically recognizes cases where a star schema exists and invokes the star query optimization to yield dramatic improvements in performance. A star query first joins multiple small tables, then joins the results to a single large table.

■ **Intelligent Function Shipping:** Beginning with Release 7.3, the coordinator process for a parallel query will understand the "affinity" of disks (and hence data) to processing nodes within a non-shared memory machine (cluster or MPP). Based upon this information, the coordinator can intelligently assign parallel query operations to processes running on particular node-disk pairs (a.k.a. function shipping) such that data need not pass across the machine's shared interconnect. This improves efficiency, performance, and scalability, yielding all the benefits of a "shared nothing" software architecture without the associated costs and overhead.

■ **Histograms:** Beginning with Release 7.3, the Oracle optimizer is able to take advantage of more granular information about the distribution of data values within a table's columns. A "histogram" of values and their relative frequencies gives the optimizer a better idea of the relative "selectivity" of indexes and allows it to better decide whether to use an index. The right choice can mean a difference of several minutes or even hours in query processing time.

■ **Parallel Hash Joins:** Beginning with Release 7.3, Oracle7 can employ hash joins to provide dramatic—in some cases, orders of magnitude—improvements in join processing times. Hashing techniques do not require Oracle7 to sort data to perform joins, and can be employed "on-the-fly" without requiring pre-existing indexes. This technique will again speed small-to-large table joins which are typical with star schema databases.

■ **Parallel UNION and UNION ALL:** Beginning with Release 7.3, Oracle7 can fully parallelize the execution of queries involving the set operators UNION and UNION ALL. This will make it easier to manage large tables as a manually partitioned set of smaller tables (one table per month of sales data, rather than a single large table, for example). Queries retain full flexibility while executing in parallel against each individual leg of a UNION or UNION ALL view of the underlying manually partitioned tables.

**Q.** What products are in Release 7.3.3? Give us a list.

**A.** This is the generic product listing for Oracle7 Server release 7.3.3. Please note that not all platforms release all products in the list.

| Product | Revision |
| --- | --- |
| Advanced Replication Option | 7.3.3.0.0 |
| Parallel Query Option | 7.3.3.0.0 |
| Parallel Server Option | 7.3.3.0.0 |
| Oracle7 Server | 7.3.3.0.0 |
| Distributed Database Option | 7.3.3.0.0 |
| Oracle*XA | 7.3.3.0.0 |
| Oracle Spatial Data Option | 7.3.3.0.0 |
| PL/SQL | 2.3.3.0.0 |
| ICX | 7.3.3.0.0 |
| OWSUTL | 7.3.3.0.0 |
| Slax | 7.3.3.0.0 |
| ConText Option | 2.0.4.0.0 |
| Pro*C | 2.2.3.0.0 |
| Pro*PL/I | 1.6.27.0.0 |
| Pro*Ada | 1.8.3.0.0 |
| Pro*COBOL | 1.8.3.0.0 |
| Pro*Pascal | 1.6.27.0.0 |
| Pro*FORTRAN | 1.8.3.0.0 |
| PRO*CORE | 1.8.3.0.0 |
| Sqllib | 1.8.3.0.0 |
| Codegen | 7.3.3.0.0 |
| Oracle CORE | 2.3.7.2.0 |
| SQL*Module Ada | 1.1.5.0.0 |
| SQL*Module C | 1.1.5.0.0 |
| Oracle CORE | 3.5.3.0.0 |
| NLSRTL | 2.3.6.1.0 |
| Oracle Server Manager | 2.3.3.0.0 |

| Product | Revision |
|---|---|
| Oracle Toolkit II | (Dependencies of svrmgr) |
| DRUID | 1.1.7.0.0 |
| Multi-Media APIs (MM) | 2.0.5.4.0 |
| OACORE | 2.1.3.0.0 |
| Oracle*Help | 2.1.1.0.0 |
| Oracle7 Enterprise Backup Utility | 2.1.0.0.2 |
| NLSRTL | 3.2.3.0 |
| SQL*Plus | 3.3.3.0.0 |
| Oracle Trace Daemon | 7.3.3.0.0 |
| Oracle MultiProtocol Interchange | 2.3.3.0.0 |
| Oracle DECnet Protocol Adapter | 2.3.3.0.0 |
| Oracle LU6.2 Protocol Adapter | 2.3.3.0.0 |
| Oracle Names | 2.0.3.0.0 |
| Advanced Networking Option | 2.3.3.0.0 |
| Oracle TCP/IP Protocol Adapter | 2.3.3.0.0 |
| Oracle Remote Operations | 1.3.3.0.0 |
| Oracle Named Pipes Protocol Adapter | 2.3.3.0.0 |
| Oracle Intelligent Agent | 7.3.3.0.0 |
| SQL*Net APPC | 2.3.3.0.0 |
| SQL*Net/DCE | 2.3.3.0.0 |
| Oracle OSI/TLI Protocol Adapter | 2.3.3.0.0 |
| Oracle SPX/IPX Protocol Adapter | 2.3.3.0.0 |
| NIS Naming Adapter | 2.3.3.0.0 |
| NDS Naming Adapter | 2.3.3.0.0 |
| Oracle Installer | 4.0.1 |

**Q.** A group of 50 users will be accessing the database this afternoon for training purposes. I don't use the Multi-Threaded Server option. What do I need to do?

**A.** The **init.ora** parameter PROCESSES must be properly set. This parameter specifies the maximum number of operating system user processes that can simultaneously connect to the database. Make sure you add the background processes while calculating the number of processes.

**Q.** I'm trying to access a table with degree of parallelism defined at 8, but I can't. Why?

**A.** Make sure that the **init.ora** parameter PARALLEL_MAX_SERVERS is set appropriately.

**Q.** I have users who are writing new PL/SQL applications. Before they start running them, I would like to increase the shared pool size. What should I do?

**A.** Increase the **init.ora** parameter SHARED_POOL_SIZE. This parameter is the shared pool size in bytes.

**Q.** I was trying to add a new datafile but had problems doing it. I realized I have reached my limit of MAXDATAFILES. How can I modify this parameter?

**A.** The MAXDATAFILES parameter is not an **init.ora** parameter. All the MAX*parameters* are set when the database is created. To see what parameters your database has been created with, use the following command:

```
SVRMGR> alter database backup controlfile to trace;
```

This command creates a SQL script that contains a few database commands. A partial listing of the file is given below:

```
CREATE CONTROLFILE REUSE DATABASE "733" NORESETLOGS ARCHIVELOG
      MAXLOGFILES 16
      MAXLOGMEMBERS 2
      MAXDATAFILES 30
      MAXINSTANCES 1
      MAXLOGHISTORY 100
LOGFILE
   GROUP 1 '/home/orahome/data/733/redo01.log'  SIZE 500K,
   GROUP 2 '/home/orahome/data/733/redo02.log'  SIZE 500K,
   GROUP 3 '/home/orahome/data/733/redo03.log'  SIZE 500K
DATAFILE
   '/home/orahome/data/733/system01.dbf' SIZE 500K,
   '/home/orahome/data/733/rbs01.dbf' SIZE 500K,
   '/home/orahome/data/733/tools01.dbf' SIZE 500K,
   '/home/orahome/data/733/users01.dbf' SIZE 500K,
   '/home/orahome/data/733/test1.dbf' SIZE 500K,
   '/home/orahome/data/733/temp.dbf' SIZE 500K
;
```

From the above file you can see the MAX*parameter* values of your database. The only way you can change these parameters is by recreating the database or recreating the control file. Obviously, the first option is very drastic so we recommend the latter. The **CREATE CONTROLFILE** command should be used to recreate the control file. Use the new MAX*parameter* values while creating the new control file.

**Q.** I want to run my database in ARCHIVELOG mode. So I shut down my database, mounted it, and put the database is ARCHIVELOG mode. After a few hours, my users started calling me saying the database is hanging. Why did this happen and what should I do?

**A.** There are two steps involved in switching the database to ARCHIVELOG mode. You have done the first one. After this, you have to enable automatic archiving. Otherwise, Oracle expects you to do manual archiving. Until you do this, you can't create new redo. Please refer to Tip 1 of the section "Backup and Recovery" in this chapter.

**Q.** What precautions should I take while using the command **ALTER DATABASE CREATE DATAFILE**?

**A.** Make sure you have a current control file that recognizes the datafile you are trying to create. If you are using a backup control file, make sure this control file was backed up after the datafile in question was created. In other words, always take a backup of the control file after adding new datafiles.

**Q.** What is **CATEXP.SQL**?

**A.** Export is responsible for generating SQL statements for all objects in the database. In order to do this, Export must query the data dictionary to find out all the relevant information about each object. Since a lot of the information is spread across multiple data dictionary tables, Export uses the view definitions in **CATEXP.SQL** to get the information it needs. There is at least one view per type of object in **CATEXP.SQL** (for example: EXU7TBS enumerates all the tablespaces, EXU7ROL enumerates all the roles, etc.). This file was called **EXPVEW.SQL** prior to Release 7.1.

**Q.** When I run Export I get the error ORA-942. What does that mean?

**A.** ORA-942 is the generic message indicating that a table or view does not exist. This probably means **CATEXP.SQL** has not been run to install the Export views. If **CATEXP.SQL** *has* been run, then it is possible the wrong version was used. Please see the questions in the compatibility section below.

**Q.** Do you also need to run **CATEXP.SQL** for Import?
**A.** Yes. Import shares some views with Export and these views are loaded by running **CATEXP.SQL**. Since they are the same views, a separate **CATIMP.SQL** was not created. As of Oracle7 Release 7.2, the few views in common have been moved to the top of the **CATEXP.SQL** script, so that a user using only Import does not have to run **CATEXP.SQL** in its entirety, and can remove the non-Import portion of the script into a separate script.

**Q.** Do you need to run **CATALOG.SQL** before running **CATEXP.SQL**?
**A.** No. While it is true that **CATEXP.SQL** is called from within **CATALOG.SQL**, there is no view in **CATEXP.SQL** that depends on views defined in **CATALOG.SQL**. The **CATEXP.SQL** views are based on tables owned by SYS (these objects are primarily defined in **SQL.BSQ**) and thus can be run on their own.

**Q.** Who should own the views in **CATEXP.SQL**?
**A.** User SYS should own them. This is documented at the top of the script.

**Q.** I can't seem to find my Export and/or Import executables. What should I do?
**A.** The executables are called *exp* and *imp.* They can be created manually if they are not present. They should be in the same directory as the oracle executable. For example, on UNIX systems, they should be in the $ORACLE_HOME/bin directory. Please refer to your platform-specific documentation for more information.

**Q.** What are the compatibility issues that one should be concerned about when using Export and Import?
**A.** Since Export and Import are user-side (client-side) utilities, the version of the utility used may be different from the database revision. There are essentially four possibilities when discussing mixing revisions. Assume the database (and thus Export) versions are X and Y and that Y > X. The issues involved are the following:

- It should be possible to use Export version X to export from database X and use Import version X to import back to database X.

This is the simplest case and is called *base compatibility* where all versions are identical.

■ It should be possible to use Export version X to export from database X and use Import version Y to import into database Y. This is *upward compatibility*.

■ It should be possible to use Export version Y to export from database Y and use Import version X to import into database X. This is *downward compatibility*.

■ It should be possible to use Export version X over a two-task connection (like SQL*Net) to export from database Y and import back into either X or Y (using the appropriate Import utility). This is *cross compatibility*.

Upward compatibility must always be maintained and every effort is also made to maintain downward compatibility within a major release.

Cross compatibility is more difficult to maintain because the views may not be synchronized with the Export code. For example, if you use Export Y against database X, then there may be a new view or an extra column (of an old view) that Export Y expects but the **CATEXP.SQL** script that has been run on the database corresponds to database X and is thus an older version (this older version would have been the script for Export X). The solution would be to try to set up your Export usage such that the revision of the views at least matches that of the executable.

Every effort is made so that the script always grows. Views or columns of views are not deleted, even if they are redundant. As a result, older Export revisions will still work.

**Q.** Why is cross compatibility an issue?
**A.** Cross compatibility is an issue because some customers run in a data center type of environment where there are several different machines, each with different Oracle revisions. The DBA may want to run all the exports on one centralized machine for convenience. As a result, the Export revision may be different with respect to the database version.

**Q.** I want to import a file created using an later version of Export. What happens to the new features available in the later release?
**A.** This was described previously as downward compatibility. Since the new features cannot be used by the earlier release, they will cause a

warning error to occur. The export will continue and process the remaining contents of the export file. It will ultimately terminate with warnings, but that is the intended behavior.

**Q.** Can you provide an example of a feature that fails during downward compatibility?
**A.** In Oracle7 Release 7.2, there is an option called *hash cluster expressions* which allows users to specify their own hash function when creating a hash cluster. This was not available with Releases 7.1 and 7.0. As a result the CREATE CLUSTER statement for Release 7.2 hash clusters will fail in Releases 7.1 and 7.0 if they are specified with this option. Clusters created in Release 7.2 that don't have this option specified can still be imported into Releases 7.1 and 7.0.

Another example is job queues, which were added in Release 7.1. When importing into Release 7.0, the DDL used to create job queues will fail (as expected).

**Q.** I ran Export and I got an ORA-904. What does that mean?
**A.** ORA-904 generally means that a column in a view is missing. This is probably due to the fact that **CATEXP.SQL** was not run to prepare the views for the version of Export being used. Please run the **CATEXP.SQL** script that matches the Export revision.

**Q.** When I do an export, I sometimes get EXP-37, which says that the Export views are not compatible with the database. What does this mean?
**A.** This means that there is a cross-compatibility problem, in that the views currently in the database are of an earlier version than that expected by Export. The solution is to install the correct version of the views. This compatibility message was added in 7.1 to avoid the ORA-904 message.

**Q.** How do I take the contents of an Oracle7database back to a Version 6 database?
**A.** Use Export Version 6 against an Oracle7 database. When this is done, Export Version 6 generates an export file that can be imported into a Version 6 database using Import Version 6. It is not possible to do the export using an Export Oracle7 and then import the file into Version 6. This is because the file format changed between Version 6 and Oracle7 and this new format is not understood by Import Version 6.

**Q.**  Does Export Version 6 extract the new Oracle7 features like triggers, procedures, roles, etc.?
**A.**  No. Export Version 6 will only export the objects that it knows about.

**Q.**  What is **CATEXP6.SQL**?
**A.**  **CATEXP6.SQL** contains the set of views that are understood by Export Version 6. If you run this script against an Oracle7 database, Export Version 6 will "see" the Oracle7 database as a Version 6 database. **CATEXP6.SQL** was called **EXPVEW6.SQL** prior to Release 7.1.

**Q.**  Is it possible to export from V5 and import to Oracle7?
**A.**  Yes. If the export file was created using Export V5, Import Oracle7 can import that file. Old statements like CREATE SPACE DEFINITION generated by V5 are converted to equivalent Oracle7 statements.

**Q.**  Does the export file format change between releases?
**A.**  Yes, the export file can change across major releases. However, every effort is made to keep the file compatible within a release to aid downward compatibility. If the format is ever changed, you will still be able to use your old files.

**Q.**  What is in the export file?
**A.**  The exact contents of the export file cannot be disclosed, but the export file does contain a header followed by SQL and other DDL statements interspersed with table data.

**Q.**  Is the file readable and portable?
**A.**  Although the file is a binary file, parts of it can be deciphered if brought up in an editor like emacs or by using "od" on a UNIX system. The file is portable because all data is exported in Oracle format which is portable across platforms, and any numbering information is stored in a byte-independent format.

**Q.**  How are export files transported?
**A.**  Since the files are binary files, you can use FTP in binary mode or some equivalent protocol.

**Q.**  Can the export file be edited?
**A.**  No. Editing the export file is not supported.

**Q.** Typically, Export and Import are run using the positional or keyword method. What is the difference between these two methods?
**A.** The keyword method allows the user to specify the keyword along with each value on the command line. For example:

```
exp userid=system/manager recordlength=1024 buffer=102400
file=test.dmp
```

In this example, each keyword (USERID, RECORDLENGTH, BUFFER, FILE) has been specified along with the user-specified value for that keyword. The following command is equivalent to the above:

```
exp system/manager 1024 102400 test.dmp
```

This is the positional method. If no keywords are specified then the parameter values are assigned in the order that Export expects them. For example, positionally, Export expects BUFFER to be the third parameter, hence the value of 102400 is applied to BUFFER in the example above.

Oracle recommends that you *not* use the positional method, however. This is because it requires prior knowledge of the ordering, which is not documented. A miscalculation can lead to parameters being assigned incorrectly leading to "less than desirable" results.

A little bit of extra typing to qualify the keywords will save a lot of grief.

**Q.** When I run Export or Import and I am exporting or importing table data, I can't seem to tell how many rows have been processed so far. It looks like the process is just hung. What do I do?
**A.** Use the FEEDBACK option, which displays a simple progress meter using dots across the display. Each dot on the screen corresponds to a user-specified number of rows. This option is available starting with Release 7.2.

**Q.** Is there more than one type of user-mode Export?
**A.** Yes and no. Essentially, a user export comes in two flavors:

- A user exports his own objects:

  ```
  exp scott/tiger file=myexp.dmp
  ```

- A DBA like SYSTEM/MANAGER exports a set of users:

  ```
  exp system/manager owner=(scott,raghu) file=user.dmp
  ```

Both of these exports are classified as a user export. In the latter case, the import must also be done by a DBA since the export was done by a DBA. The FROMUSER/TOUSER option can be used on import with export files generated in the second scenario.

**Q.** Is there more than one type of table-level export?
**A.** Again, the answer is yes and no. A table export can be one of two methods:

■ A user exports his or her own tables:

```
exp donald/duck tables=(huey,dewey,louie)
```

■ A DBA like SYSTEM/MANAGER exports an assortment of tables belonging to a set of users:

```
exp system/manager tables=(scott.emp, humpty.dumpty)
```

Both of these exports are classified as table-level exports. In the latter case, the import must also be done by a DBA since the export was done by a DBA.

**Q.** Does a user have to be a DBA to do a full database export?
**A.** No. This was true in Version 6; however, this behavior has changed with the introduction of roles in Oracle7. Essentially, any user that has been granted the EXP_FULL_DATABASE role can do a full export. This role is granted to DBA. So, it is possible for someone to own this role but still not be a DBA. The privileges that accompany this role are defined in **CATEXP.SQL**. After examining the privileges, one can see that a user who has this role may as well be a DBA.

**Q.** What is the order in which objects are exported?
**A.** Here is the order in which objects are exported in Oracle7. Please read the following information by rows from left to right.

| | | | |
|---|---|---|---|
| Tablespaces | Profiles | Users | Roles |
| System Privilege Grants | Role Grants | Default Roles | Tablespace Quotas |
| Resource Costs | Rollback Segments | Database Links | Sequences (includes grants) |

| Snapshots (includes grants, auditing) | Snapshot Logs | Job Queues | Refresh Groups |
|---|---|---|---|
| Cluster Definitions | Tables (constraints, grants, indexes, comments, audits) In 7.3.4 the order for tables will be changed to: (indexes, constraints, grants, comments, and audits) | Referential Integrity | POSTTABLES actions |
| Synonyms | Views | Stored Procedures | Triggers |
| Default and System Auditing | | | |

**Q.** Is the order important? If so, why?

**A.** Yes, the order is very important. It is important to realize that Import is a serial session that issues the SQL statements against the database. Some objects depend on the existence of others so the dependent objects must come later. For example, triggers depend on tables and therefore tables must be imported before their triggers. There are some objects that can exist alone, like procedures and views. These objects can be loaded into the database with compilation errors and they will be validated when first used.

**Q.** Export uses a mechanism called array fetch. What is that?

**A.** Export issues SELECT statements to retrieve table data. The data must be shipped from the database to the user side. If Export were to retrieve only one row at a time, there would be too many round trips to make to the database. As a result, Export fetches a set of rows each time and the total time is decreased. Array fetch is the concept of fetching multiple rows per trip from the database.

**Q.** What is the purpose of the BUFFER parameter in Export?

**A.** As mentioned in the previous answer, Export fetches multiple rows at a time. This information is retrieved into memory on the user side before it is put out to the file. The amount of memory allocated on the user side to retrieve this information corresponds to the value of the BUFFER parameter.

**NOTE**
*This parameter is often confused with the*
*RECORDLENGTH parameter explained below.*

**Q.** What is the RECORDLENGTH parameter in Export?
**A.** When Export writes information out to the export file, it does not write it out one character at a time. Rather it writes a buffer of information at a time and RECORDLENGTH is the size of this buffer. It is best to keep this a multiple of the operating system block size.

This is often confused with the BUFFER parameter, which, as explained previously, is used for retrieving data only. The reason there are two buffers is because the write buffer can also contain SQL statements. Also, when the data is retrieved from the database, it is not in the format that ends up in the export file. There is some massaging of data that needs to be performed to get the data in the right format.

**Q.** How do I know how many rows are being fetched per cycle?
**A.** This value can be determined by dividing the size of the buffer (as defined by the BUFFER parameter) by the size of a single row. The size of a single row is approximated as follows:

( sum of all internal columns sizes) + 4x( number of columns)

**Q.** Does LONG data work the same way?
**A.** No. In the case of LONG data, only single-row fetches are currently performed. This is because a LONG can be potentially 2GB in length and so it is not feasible to use that upper bound for LONGs in the above formula.

**Q.** Can I run multiple exports in parallel?
**A.** Yes, as long as they are not incremental exports. This is because incremental exports record information in the dictionary and running multiple sessions will cause the information to conflict.

**Q.** What is the RECORD parameter?
**A.** This applies to incremental exports. In incremental exports, the idea is to be able to export only objects that have changed since the previous incremental/cumulative/complete export. In order to do this, the object modification timestamp in the data dictionary is compared with a

timestamp stored in the INCEXP table. When the object is exported, the new timestamp is reflected in the INCEXP table.

By specifying RECORD=Y, the information in the INCEXP table will be kept current. Otherwise no information is kept, which would mean that all objects are effectively exported with RECORD=N.

This parameter is often confused with the RECORDLENGTH parameter which has to do with the size of the write buffer and nothing to do with incremental exports.

**Q.** What are some of the things that cause a table to be flagged as "modified", thus requiring it to be in the next incremental export?
**A.** Obviously any change to the data using INSERT, DELETE, or UPDATE will declare the object to be modified. Any DDL change such as modifying a column to not null or altering the storage clause will also cause the table to be modified. Even adding a grant or a comment to a table will flag it as modified.

**Q.** When data is exported, is all the data consistent as of the time of the export? What is the "snapshot too old" error?
**A.** Export extracts data by issuing a series of SELECT statements and the snapshot time of each table's data corresponds to when the SELECT statement was issued for that table. If there is no database activity, then this is not an issue. However, it is possible to manipulate the table after the export has started, in which case the snapshot of the data may be a factor. Export does not get an exclusive lock on any table.

There is an option called CONSISTENT=Y. When this is enabled, Export first issues a SET TRANSACTION READ ONLY command before doing the export. There is a risk of running out of rollback segment space and getting a "snapshot too old" error when doing a long running export. Please refer to the error number ORA-1555 earlier in this chapter.

**Q.** What are pre-table and post-tables actions?
**A.** Pre-table actions are PL/SQL routines that get executed before a table is imported. Post-tables actions are PL/SQL routines that get executed after *all* the tables have been imported. The procedures may thus make modifications after table data is imported. These options will be opened up in some future release to allow customers to specify routines that they would like to run. This would allow modification of data from within the Import session.

**Q.** Import uses array inserts. What is that?
**A.** Just as Export selects table data, Import inserts them back into the database. Inserting one row at a time is resource intensive. The number of trips to the database can be decreased by inserting multiple rows per trip. This is the concept of *array insert*.

**Q.** When importing a table with a LONG column, I am seeing one row being inserted at a time. Is it correct?
**A.** Yes. With LONGs, the array size defaults to 1. Again, this is because Export needs contiguous memory to hold the entire LONG before inserting it, and so there is no way to come up with a reasonable upper bound. This behavior will be changed when there is database support for piecemeal insertion of LONGs.

**Q.** What is the Import BUFFER parameter?
**A.** This parameter specifies the amount of memory allocated on the user side to store table rows before they are sent to the database.

**Q.** Can I commit with each array insert?
**A.** Yes. That is what COMMIT=Y does. The exact number of rows committed per trip will depend on the size of the buffer and how many rows can fit into that buffer.

**Q.** What is the RECORDLENGTH parameter?
**A.** Import does not read information from the export file one character at a time. Instead, it reads a buffer's worth of information into memory. RECORDLENGTH is the size of this read buffer. It is best to keep this as a multiple of the operating system block size.

   This parameter is often confused with the BUFFER parameter, which, as explained previously, affects table data only. It is necessary to have separate buffers since there are SQL statements interspersed in the table data and the data thus needs to be separated out.

**Q.** Can you clarify what the DESTROY option does on import?
**A.** The syntax for CREATE TABLESPACE has a REUSE clause, which allows users to reuse existing data files. You should, however, use caution, since this can have the undesirable effect of allowing the user to inadvertently destroy a file that belongs to some other tablespace. Using DESTROY=N will cause Import to run the CREATE TABLESPACE statement without the REUSE clause (this is the default).

**Q.** When I run Import, I sometimes get the message "seals don't match". What is a seal?

**A.** A seal is another name for the header of the export file that contains information about the export session.

**Q.** When I run Import, I sometimes get an "abnormal end of file" message (IMP-09). What does this mean?

**A.** This usually means that the Export file is corrupted in some way. Usually Import is trying to get to a certain point in the file and if the file is corrupted then Import may be erroneously trying to seek ahead somewhere. As a result, it thinks the file ended abnormally.

   Your Export file may have been corrupted if it was not transported correctly from one machine to another. The file may need to be sent again from the exporting machine. One thing to verify is that your file transport protocol is in binary mode.

**Q.** I am using the FROMUSER/TOUSER feature and I specify more users in the FROMUSER clause than the TOUSER clause. What happens to the extra users?

**A.** Import will map as many FROMUSERs as it can to appropriate TOUSERs. The extra users will map back to themselves so they may as well not have been specified in the first place.

**Q.** I am using the FROMUSER/TOUSER feature and I have more TOUSERs than FROMUSERs. What happens to the extra TOUSERs?

**A.** They are ignored.

**Q.** How does Import deal with character set conversion?

**A.** Assume that the exporting database has been created with character set A. The Export session is in character set B. As a result, there is a conversion of data from A to B, which is done by the two-task layer. The data in the export file is now in character set B. The file is then transferred to another machine where the file is about to be imported. The Import session is in, say, character set C. Note that the data in the export file is still in character set B. The destination database is in character set D. The conversion from C to D is done via two-task. However, the conversion from B to C must be performed by Import.

   Here are a few points worth noting:

■ Character sets B and C must have a ratio of 1. If the ratio between B and C is *n* it means that the length of a string in character set C will be at most *n* times the length of the same string in the source character set B. The reason we expect the ratio to be 1 is because of the current memory management model used on the Import side. This will be changed at some point in the future. The strings are converted from B to C by Import and then sent through the two-task layer for possible conversion to character set D.

■ Not all characters may be convertible between B and C. This is very data-dependent and is the responsibility of the user.

■ When doing the export, any special characters stored in database A must be captured in character set B (for the export file). Otherwise, you will lose information.

■ If you are concerned about this information please pay special attention to the following:

   ■ The database character encoding is specified when issuing the CREATE DATABASE for the source database.

   ■ The client character encoding is specified with NLS_LANG when the data was inserted.

   ■ The client character encoding is done when the data was exported. This should be able to capture all the special characters you want.

   ■ The database character encoding is specified when issuing the CREATE DATABASE for the destination database.

   ■ The client character encoding is done when the data was imported.

**Q.** I am unable to make the conversion from character set B to C. What do I do?
**A.** Set your NLS_LANG for the Import session to character set B. Now B=C and it should work.

**Q.** What is the CHARSET option?
**A.** The idea behind the CHARSET option is to let the user specify the character set of the Export file. Let's say, that would be character set B. However, sometimes the user wants to specify a different character set (call

it E). Since the export file is still in B, in theory there should be a conversion from B to E and then from E to C. Data may get lost in this translation. Currently CHARSET can only be set to B. This will change in the future.

**Q.** What is the "8-bit problem"?
**A.** The user has the option to specify the character set when creating a database as part of the CREATE DATABASE command. If the user did not specify a character set then the default is US7ASCII. Users have been putting 8-bit data like umlauts into a database in US7ASCII. They were able to select it because there was no manipulation of the high bit and so it worked as a side-effect.

The 8-bit problem now is that users would like to migrate this 8-bit data to another database. One of two things happens.

The user specifies character set B to be US7ASCII. No conversion occurs on export so the 8-bit data comes out as is, but the file is tagged as US7ASCII. As a result, when importing to a true 8-bit database, the high bit is lost.

Alternatively, the user specifies character set B to be 8-bit. In this case when extracting the data, the high bit is lost before it reaches the export file.

So either the information is lost or the file is tagged incorrectly. The solution to this problem is to enhance the CHARSET feature.

**Q.** How do I find out what the database character set is?
**A.** Issue the following query:

```
select * from props$ where name = 'NLS_CHARACTERSET';
```

PROPS$ is owned by SYS.

**Q.** I would like to create an identical copy of my database but with no data. How do I do that?
**A.** Just run a full database export with the option ROWS=N:

```
exp system/manager full=Y rows=N file=full.dmp
```

Alternatively, run a full database import with ROWS=N:

```
imp system/manager full=Y rows=N file=full.dmp
```

If you are going to put the duplicate database on the same machine, then the new tablespaces will have to be pre-created because the old data files are already in use.

**Q.**  I want to replace my existing data with new data on Import. Can I do this directly?
**A.**  No. Import does not have a replace option like SQL*Loader. You must manually delete all the rows first.

**Q.**  Why are objects owned by SYS not exported?
**A.**  While it is possible for a user to connect as SYS and create any object, SYS also owns the dictionary tables like OBJ$, USER$, etc. It also owns the catalog views and other dictionary objects.

Exporting SYS would involve finding all the objects that are not dictionary objects. This is because the new database would already have its own dictionary tables. While it is possible to determine this, it is a considerable bookkeeping effort for Export as new dictionary objects get created. As a result, SYS was excluded.

Also, users should not be connecting as SYS to do any private work. A DBA should be given his or her own account and objects should be created in their own schema. SYS is a very powerful account and is best left relatively unused.

**Q.**  Are grants on SYS's objects exported?
**A.**  No, for the same reason as above.

**Q.**  Are the passwords for SYS and SYSTEM exported? What about other users?
**A.**  Yes. The passwords for these two users will be altered to match the values in the export file. It is thus possible for a DBA to get locked out if he or she forgot the password. A way around this is to connect as INTERNAL. Other user passwords are not altered.

**Q.**  Are the passwords decipherable from looking at the export file?
**A.**  No. They are encrypted. However, they are portable so that they will work on any database.

**Q.**  Can I do a full export by doing a bunch of user exports in parallel?
**A.**  A user-level export only contains objects owned by a particular user or set of users. A full database export contains information about other

dictionary objects like tablespaces, profiles, roles, auditing, etc. These are items that will not show up in a user export.

So, in theory, a collection of user exports is not equivalent to a full export. However, there is some validity to just exporting users because it saves time to do them in parallel. The user should just keep an extra full export (without rows) around to recreate the other objects.

**Q.** Can Export and Import be run at the same time while there is other database activity?
**A.** Yes. In the case of Export, the snapshot time of each table will be different as explained previously (unless CONSISTENT=Y is used).

In the case of Import, table data is committed after each table (implicitly by executing the next DDL statement). Foreign key relationships are not established until all the tables have been imported. Applications that depend on these relationships may not work until the import is complete.

**Q.** My tablespace is corrupted beyond repair. I want to get whatever data I can and replace the tablespace. Can this be done?
**A.** Yes. Please contact Oracle Worldwide Customer Support.

**Q.** How is referential integrity done on Import?
**A.** All foreign key relationships are established after ALL the tables have been imported. Other constraints like CHECK and PRIMARY KEY are established after the particular table's data has been imported.

**Q.** I exported a table called EMP. I want to import it into a table called TEST. Can I do that?
**A.** No. The table has to be imported as EMP. However, you can manually rename the table later.

**Q.** Do we have a tablespace-level export/import?
**A.** Currently no, although this is something we are looking at implementing. Currently Export and Import run in three modes: full, user, and table. Each level is a superset of the next. Tablespaces are orthogonal to these modes and don't fit cleanly in the hierarchy. For now, a possible (although not necessarily convenient) "workaround" is to identify all the objects in the tablespace and export in table mode.

This "workaround" assumes that the indexes and their associated tables are in the same tablespace. This will not support exporting indexes whose associated table is in a different tablespace.

**Q.** I am importing data into a table that already exists. This table has indexes and triggers on it. Why doesn't Import disable these to speed up the insertion process?

**A.** The user may have multiple triggers and constraints on a table and it is possible that the user may have selectively disabled some of these for other reasons. As a result, Import will have to keep track of which ones are enabled and which ones are not and then re-establish them later. Since constraints and triggers enforce business rules, this responsibility was left to user control.

**Q.** I have a table that is part of a cluster. I want to do a table-level export of the table. Do I still get the cluster definition with it?

**A.** No. The table will be created on import without the cluster information.

**Q.** I would like to pin a particular rollback segment before starting an export. Can I do this?

**A.** Currently, no.

**Q.** Has the behavior for exporting views changed between Version 6 and Oracle7?

**A.** In Version 6, views were exported in the order of their creation timestamp. So, if view B is based on view A, then view A is exported first because it is older. However, it was possible for both views to be created at the exact same time (via a script); then the order in which these views were exported was indeterminate. As a result, the creation of view B would fail if it appeared before view A in the export file.

This problem is solved in Oracle7 because views are now exported in order of "level". View B is now always exported last because it is at a higher level than view A. The level information is determined by examining DEPENDENCY$.

**Q.** When importing table data, are the indexes already there?

**A.** If the table is new, then no. The indexes get created after all the table data has been imported. Thus, there is no hit on the index. If the table already exists, then the index is not disabled.

**Q.** How are grants exported?

**A.** All grants with the WITH GRANT OPTION are exported first. This is then followed by regular grants in order of their creation.

**Q.** How are synonyms exported?

**A.** Synonyms are exported in the order of their creation.

**Q.** How does Import compress extents? What value do you use for the NEXT extent if the table is compressed? What are the advantages and disadvantages of using the COMPRESS option?

**A.** Actually, Import does not compress any extents, Export does. When COMPRESS=Y is specified, Export determines the current size of the table by summing up all the allocate extents and sets the initial extent in the CREATE TABLE statement in the export file to this value. The value for NEXT is the true size of the second extent. This will prevent compressed tables from growing out of control after they are imported.

It should be pointed out that if the table was large at export time and COMPRESS=Y was specified, then it is possible that Import cannot create the table because the initial extent is too large. The solution for this is to pre-create the table with a smaller initial extent prior to running Import.

**Q.** How do I defragment a table?

**A.** The purpose of defragmentation is to reclaim space lost due to fragmentation. To defragment a table:

1. Export the table with COMPRESS=Y. This will set the initial extent to the size of the table.

2. Drop the table (you should first back up your database just to be safe).

3. Import the table. This will put all the contents of the table into one extent.

If you do a user level export, then all indexes on the table not owned by the user are not exported. These will get dropped when the table is dropped.

It is possible that the table is large in size but relatively empty due to some prior large deletes. In this case, it is worth pre-creating the table with a smaller initial extent prior to Import.

**Q.** Can I export tables that have lowercase names?

**A.** Yes. The recommendation here is not to create table names in lowercase. Lowercase table names are created by using quotes around the table name. For example:

```
create table "mytab" (col1 number);
```

This table will be stored in the dictionary as mytab rather than MYTAB. You can select from the above table by issuing:

```
select * from "mytab";
```

Notice that the quotes are always needed. As a result, when trying to do a table-level export of a lowercase table, the operating system shell may interpret the quotes differently at the command line.

**Q.** When exporting stored procedures, packages, and package bodies, where is the text for these obtained?
**A.** The text is obtained from SOURCE$ and is exported as is.

**Q.** I have some wrapped stored procedures. Is the text for these also obtained from SOURCE$?
**A.** Yes. The wrapped format is portable, so this is no problem.

**Q.** I have a table owned by user A. The index on the table is owned by user B. I do a user-level export as user A. Is the index exported?
**A.** No. The index does not belong to user A and is therefore not exported. However if a DBA did a user-level export of user A, the index would be exported. This is because the import would then be done by a DBA who has the privilege to recreate the index in another schema.

**Q.** Can you give me some basic tips to speed up performance during an export?
**A.** First check to see if there are any machine load issues. Also verify that the disk Export is writing to is not overloaded. Since Export issues a sequence of dictionary queries (against the views in **CATEXP.SQL**) it is possible that one of the queries is running slowly. More information can be obtained by running sql_trace.

**Q.** I installed my database without PL/SQL. What will Export do when it tries to export PL/SQL-dependent objects like job queues and refresh groups?
**A.** Export ignores them. This was a bigger issue with Release 7.0 since it was possible to purchase Oracle without PL/SQL. Starting with Release 7.1, PL/SQL comes bundled, but the user still has the option not to install it.

**Q.** When exporting procedures and packages, are creation timestamps preserved?

**A.** The creation timestamp is preserved to avoid unnecessary recompilations.

**Q.** After exporting my packages and procedures, I sometimes find some of them are invalid. Is this a problem?

**A.** No. Since procedures can depend on each other, it is possible that one procedure may get created first before its dependent procedure has been created. These objects will be validated when they are used.

**Q.** I am doing a full database export. Somebody dropped one of my tables before Export had a chance to export it. Is this possible?

**A.** Yes. Export does not get locks on all the tables at the start of the session. Export first gets a list of all the tables at the start of the session. It is possible that the table may be dropped between the time that Export generated the table list and the time that the table was to be exported. Export will skip the table and continue. This is a warning condition.

**Q.** I have a read-only tablespace. After an export/import cycle, will it still be read-only?

**A.** Currently, no. The tablespace will be read/write. The reason for this is because tablespaces are created before the table data is imported. If the tablespace was created read-only then none of the table data can be imported. An option would be to import the data and then to automatically make the tablespace read-only later, but it is possible that the user pre-created the tablespace and does not want it to become read-only. This decision is thus left to the user.

**Q.** I currently have an offline tablespace. Will Export extract the data in this tablespace? Will the tablespace stay offline after an export/import cycle?

**A.** No on both counts.

**Q.** My rollback segment is currently offline. Will it stay offline after an export/import cycle?

**A.** No.

**Q.** What is the "backup any table" privilege given to the EXP_FULL_DATABASE role?

**A.**   This privilege is necessary to allow a user to do an incremental export. The whole idea behind an incremental export is to only export those tables that have *changed* since the last incremental export. When a table is changed, a modification bit is set and Export looks for this bit. If the bit is set, it then exports the table and issues a statement that clears the bit so that this table won't get exported on the next incremental export (unless it got changed again by other means).

In order to issue this statement, the exporting user needs the "backup any table" privilege. Usually, only a DBA runs an incremental export, but in reality, anyone with the EXP_FULL_DATABASE role can also run an incremental export. If a DBA did the export, then this privilege is irrelevant because a DBA can do anything to the database anyway.

However, it is possible to have a user who is *not* a DBA but has the EXP_FULL_DATABASE role. Then this privilege becomes relevant because this is how a non-DBA can clear the modification bit.

**Q.**   I have a snapshot that is based on two tables belonging to two different users (call them A and B). I export my snapshots and then want to move them to another user using the FROMUSER/TOUSER option such that I also move A and B to C and D. Is this feasible using FROMUSER/TOUSER feature on import?
**A.**   No. The idea behind FROMUSER/TOUSER is simply to move the objects that a user owns to another user. Dependent definitions are not covered in this definition.

**Q.**   When I export a table, will the constraint indexes also retain their storage characteristics from the time of the export?
**A.**   Yes. This is done using the USING INDEX STORAGE clause with the **ALTER TABLE** command.

**Q.**   I would like my data to be pre-sorted in a particular way before importing it. Is there a feature to do this?
**A.**   Currently, no, although there is some attention being given to this issue.

**Q.**   I have a full database export and am about to perform a full database import. Is there a particular set of objects that are worth pre-creating?
**A.**   Yes. It is worth pre-creating the tablespaces and rollback segments so that you have them in the right place. This will especially be necessary if the full export came from a different operating system (like OpenVMS to UNIX). Although not necessary, it is also worth pre-creating those users

whose attributes, such as quotas and default/temporary tablespaces, are intended to be different. Using Import with SHOW=Y first will show you the statement currently in the export file.

**Q.** I would like user A's tables to be diverted to his or her default tablespace rather than the one specified in the export file. The original tablespace also exists in the new database. What do I need to do to make this happen?

**A.** You can either revoke resource on that tablespace selectively or set user A's quota on that tablespace to zero. In both cases the table will get diverted.

**Q.** I would like to prevent user JOE from running exports. JOE is not a DBA. What do I do?

**A.** The only role associated with export is the EXP_FULL_DATABASE role, which if enabled allows a user to do a full database export. Disabling this role still allows a user to do a user- or table-level export of his or her own objects. There is no role or privilege within the database to disallow a user to do exports entirely. This is best achieved at the operating system level by not providing access to the Export executable or implementing something equivalent.

**Q.** I have many data files in my SYSTEM tablespace. Will the information about these data files and their sizes be exported?

**A.** No. No information about tablespace SYSTEM is exported. The reason is that since the database has to be up to do an import, the new database must already have its own SYSTEM tablespace. It is thus best to keep your objects in tablespaces other than SYSTEM and leave the SYSTEM tablespace to contain catalog information. If you have added extra files to the SYSTEM tablespace in the source database, then they will have to be manually created in the target database before importing the file.

**Q.** The combination of options COMPRESS=Y and ROWS=N does not make sense to me because why would someone not want to export rows in this situation?

**A.** COMPRESS=Y merely modifies the storage clause so that the initial extent is now the sum of all current extents. It has no bearing on whether there is any data in the table or not. It is conceivable that the user would want to create a table of identical size in a new database but have no data.

**Q.** I would like to generate a SQL script that contains all the DDL in the export file. Can I do this?

**A.** Yes, although not directly. Using the SHOW=Y option on import will give you a listing of all statements that will be run. This can be sent to a log file using the LOG option. This log file can then be manually edited, or an appropriate operating system tool (on UNIX, using SED, AWK will suffice) can reformat it into a SQL script. There will be a direct option to do this in the future.

**Q.** How can I determine which objects have been analyzed after an export/import cycle and which haven't?

**A.** There is a three-level hierarchy when determining which ANALYZE statements are written to the export file:

- Cluster

- Table

- Index

This is a description of the algorithm that Export uses:

- If the cluster is analyzed, then no ANALYZE statements are generated for tables or indexes in the cluster because they will be automatically analyzed.

- If the cluster is not analyzed, but only certain tables are analyzed, then only those ANALYZE TABLE statements are written to the file on a per-table basis. The indexes for the analyzed tables will be automatically analyzed so there is no ANALYZE INDEX statement written to the file.

- It is possible that there is an index on a clustered table, but neither the cluster or the table has been analyzed. In this case, if the index was analyzed, then an ANALYZE INDEX statement is written to the export file.

# CHAPTER
# 8

## Problem Solving
## Connectivity Issues

racle Corporation has adopted the client-server architecture in almost all its software. This allows tremendous flexibility, because the database application and the RDBMS can reside on separate computers, yet communicate over a wide variety of network protocols. In this chapter, we will first provide an overview of SQL*Net and then discuss the installation procedures and common issues concerning SQL*Net. We will then follow this with a section on ODBC. As with every chapter in this book, we will conclude with a FAQ section.

**NOTE**
*Throughout this chapter we will only discuss SQL\*Net V2, as SQL\*Net V1 has been obsolete for several months now.*

Oracle's SQL*Net is a layer of Oracle software that allows communication between an Oracle client program and an Oracle7 RDBMS over an intermediate medium such as a network using some protocol. Almost all Oracle tools are capable of communicating with SQL*Net. There are some third-party applications that are also capable of communicating with SQL*Net directly using Oracle's API. In addition, there are third-party applications that can communicate with Oracle using the Open Database Connectivity standard (ODBC).

**NOTE**
*The term server in this chapter could mean the server computer or the Oracle7 RDBMS server, depending on the context.*

**NOTE**
*All our discussions in this chapter will be of a generic nature (not restricted to an operating system or network protocol) unless explicitly specified. For purposes of understanding, it does help to look at SQL\*Net in terms of its implementation on UNIX. At times we use terms like 'processes' which can be understood in the same vein as UNIX. Obviously, SQL\*Net software is implemented differently on different operating systems, but the architecture and concepts are very similar on all operating systems.*

# An Overview of SQL*Net

As mentioned earlier, SQL*Net allows for communication between an
Oracle client and an Oracle RDBMS. SQL*Net software allows this
communication to occur seamlessly across most of the industry's common
network protocols. Oracle has created networking technology called
Transparent Network Substrate (TNS), which permits a single application
interface to industry-standard networking protocols. Several protocol
adapters are also available to help this standard application interface
communicate with all major network protocols available in the industry.
An Oracle protocol adapter translates function calls of specific network
protocols into equivalent function calls in Oracle's TNS. The Oracle
protocol adapter also translates TNS function calls into calls for the
underlying network protocol. Figure 8-1 illustrates this architecture.

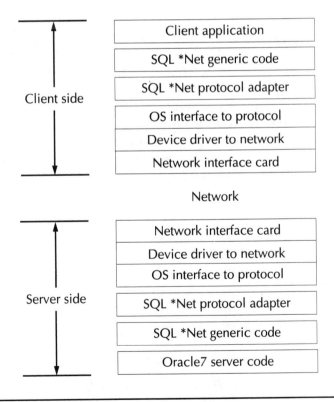

**FIGURE 8-1.**   *Oracle client-server model and SQL*Net*

It is apparent from Figure 8-1 that SQL*Net resides on both the client as well as the server side. In addition, it is also clear that there is a generic layer of SQL*Net code and a protocol adapter that matches the network protocol on both sides. This is necessary since the implementation of SQL*Net varies with the operating system. The client might be using Windows 95 and communicating with a server running Sun SPARC Solaris 2.x across TCP/IP. It is therefore necessary to install SQL*Net for Windows 95 and SQL*Net TCP/IP Protocol Adapter on the client and SQL*Net for Sun Solaris on the server along with the SQL*Net TCP/IP Protocol Adapter.

# Major Components of SQL*Net

We will provide a description of some of the components and terminology relating to SQL*Net before we discuss troubleshooting techniques for SQL*Net.

## Listener

All connections to Oracle7 on a different computer require a *listener* process running on the server machine. The listener is the single point of contact for all incoming connection requests. It has the task of passing connect information (Oracle user and password) to the Oracle server process, which either rejects the connection request if the connect information is invalid or sets up a valid connection. A valid connection is handed over to a dedicated server, a pre-spawned server, or a dispatcher. It must be noted that the listener is only responsible for processing the connection request. Once this has been completed, it is no longer responsible for any communication between the client and the server.

## Listener Configuration File

The listener configuration file is called **listener.ora** by default. This file provides three sets of information to the listener:

- Where the listener should "listen" for connection requests. This information describes the host on which the listener is running. For example, if you are using TCP/IP, this information will include the host and the port number for the listener.

- Available services on the server. The available Oracle instances on the host are listed in the **listener.ora** file as the SID_NAME or KEY.

There are other types of services in the Multi-Threaded Server (MTS) configuration. We will leave details on such services for the section on MTS later in this chapter.

■ Tracing, time-outs, logs, etc. Parameters defining level of trace, target directory for trace files, time-outs, and passwords for the listener startup and shutdown are specified in this section.

We will take a more detailed look at the **listener.ora** file later in this chapter when we discuss troubleshooting techniques for the listener.

## Connect Requests to the Listener

When a connect request is received by the listener, it needs to decide whether the requested service is available. The list of available services is obtained from the **listener.ora** or from a dispatcher process in the MTS. If the requested service is available, a server process is spawned. This is accomplished using the bequeath operation, which is also described later in this chapter. In the case of MTS, an alternate address for the requested service is handed back. If the service being requested is unknown, the connect request is rejected.

## Connect Requests from a Client

A client application can make a connect request by sending connect information consisting of an Oracle user/password combination along with a SQL*Net alias that defines the location of the server. For example, you can attempt a SQL*Plus connection by issuing a command similar to

```
% sqlplus scott/tiger@myloopback
```

where SCOTT is the Oracle user, *tiger* is the password for scott, and *myloopback* is the SQL*Net alias. The alias definition is resolved in this case by information provided in a SQL*Net client configuration file called **tnsnames.ora**. There are other methods of resolving aliases, such as Oracle Names, which will be discussed in more detail in a separate section. In all our discussions throughout this chapter on aliases and resolution of aliases, we will use the **tnsnames.ora** file for the sake of better understanding.

## SQL*Net Client Configuration Files

The client configuration file is called **sqlnet.ora**. In addition, a **tnsnames.ora** (Again it must be noted that there are other, more complex methods to configure clients, such as using Oracle Names. We will describe the **tnsnames.ora** here as it is the simplest method to configure a client in our opinion.) is used to resolve aliases. The **sqlnet.ora** and **tnsnames.ora** files are usually located in the $ORACLE_HOME/network/admin directory. The **tnsnames.ora** file defines the aliases that can be used in a connection. These aliases provide information on the location of the target listener and the name of the service that can be requested on the server. The requested service could be the name of an Oracle instance on the host defined by the SID. We will review these client files in greater detail when we describe client troubleshooting techniques later in this chapter.

## Bequeath Protocol Adapter

The *bequeath* protocol adapter is the default SQL*Net driver for Oracle7 (mostly on UNIX). It has two main purposes:

- To spawn sub-processes and mediate messages to and from these sub-processes.

- To provide a default SQL*Net connection layer for a connection request originating from the same machine. A SQL*Net protocol adapter is not required for such "local" connection requests.

Here is an example of how the bequeath adapter works with a local SQL*Plus connection in a UNIX environment:

```
% sqlplus scott/tiger
```

If you now execute a **ps** you should see something similar to:

```
% ps -ef|grep sqlplus
    oracle    942    935  1 10:45:43 pts/3    0:00 sqlplus scott/tiger
% ps -ef|grep 942
    oracle    943    942  1 10:45:44 ?        0:00 oraclemydb
(DESCRIPTION=(LOCAL=YES)(ADDRESS=(PROTOCOL=beq)))
    oracle    942    935  0 10:45:43 pts/3    0:00 sqlplus scott/tiger
```

### Multi-Threaded Server (MTS)

By default, every client connect request makes the listener spawn another process termed the dedicated server process. This server process acts as the point of contact for all communication between the client and the Oracle7 server during that session. MTS allows for a configuration that shares server processes between client requests. A detailed description is provided in a separate section on MTS later in this chapter.

Now that we have some notion of the various components of SQL*Net, we can concentrate on the installation and troubleshooting of SQL*Net.

# Installing SQL*Net

The installation procedures for SQL*Net on all platforms are very similar. We will describe the installation process and the configuration of SQL*Net on common operating systems. We will illustrate the installation and configuration of SQL*Net server and SQL*Net client using UNIX (Sun SPARC Solaris 2.x ) and also Windows NT. We will use TCP/IP on the Sun Solaris machine and Named Pipes on Windows NT since they are the native network protocols. In addition, we will also illustrate a SQL*Net client on Windows 95. We will restrict ourselves to the normal use of SQL*Net and not touch more complex areas such as Multi-Protocol Interchange.

## SQL*Net on UNIX (Sun Solaris 2.5)

We will configure SQL*Net server on a Sun Solaris machine and then illustrate a SQL*Plus client connection through SQL*Net on the same computer (termed a *loop-back*). Once this is successfully illustrated, we will use a Windows 95 client to connect to Oracle7 running on this Solaris server over TCP/IP.

### Step 1: Install SQL*Net V2 Generic Software

Login to the Solaris server as the Oracle owner (usually *oracle)*. Ensure that your install medium, such as CD-ROM or tape, is mounted properly. Run the Oracle installer executable $ORACLE_HOME/bin/**orainst**. Select to install the SQL*Net V2 component from the list of available components in the left pane of the installer. Follow the instructions provided by the Oracle Installer and complete the installation.

## Step 2: Install the SQL*Net V2 TCP/IP Protocol Adapter

After SQL*Net V2 is installed, you are ready to install the TCP/IP Protocol Adapter. Choose the SQL*Net TCP/IP Protocol Adapter component and install it. You are free to install as many protocol adapters as you need. Many adapters can sit on top of one generic layer.

If you are not sure whether SQL*Net is already installed on your server, then execute the following commands:

```
% grep -i v2 $ORACLE_HOME/orainst/unix.rgs
150 network    root "network" "2.1.6.1.0"  "SQL*Net V2"
43823869 "08/26/96 07:26:45 PM" [network,tcppa,rdbms,plus,svrmgr]
"Product files loaded."   true false ""   [] [] ""   [] "" [] "" []
 155 tcppa       root "tcppa"   "2.1.6.1.0"  "TCP/IP Protocol Adapter (V2)"
3191000 "08/26/96 07:28:42 PM" [tcppa]
"Product files loaded."   true false "pa" [] [] "pa" [] "" [] "" []
% cd $ORACLE_HOME/bin
% adapters tnslsnr
SQL*Net V2 Protocol Adapters linked with tnslsnr are:
    V2 BEQ Protocol Adapter
    V2 IPC Protocol Adapter
    V2 TCP/IP Protocol Adapter
Network security products linked with tnslsnr are:
```

## Step 3: Create SQL*Net Server Configuration Files

Oracle provides a utility called the Oracle Network Manager (ONM) to create the configuration files. This utility is available on Windows 3.1 with all SQL*Net versions (a version of Oracle Network Manager was available on Motif with SQL*Net 2.1). If you do not have access to ONM, you can use the sample configuration files provided by Oracle as a starting point.

If you choose to use ONM, you will see a dialog box similar to Figures 8-2. ONM will automatically detect the available protocols on your computer. You are also free to add protocols that you do not have.

ONM will walk you through the utility and create configuration files automatically:

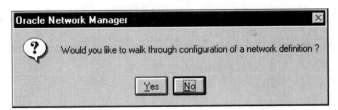

You can also configure multiple protocols as shown in Figure 8-3.

We will not go into further details of using ONM. We suggest that you look at the online documentation for help with ONM.

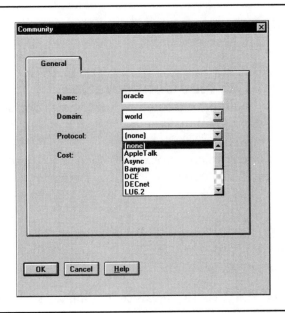

**FIGURE 8-2.** *ONM detection of available protocol*

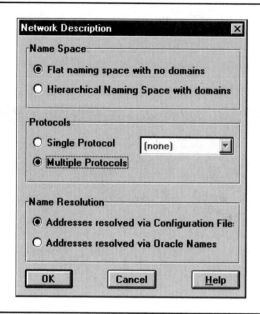

**FIGURE 8-3.** *Describing your network for ONM*

## Step 4: Verify SQL*Net Configuration

Even though ONM should have created proper **listener.ora**, **sqlnet.ora**, and **tnsnames.ora** files, we suggest that you take a few moments to view them to ensure that they have been created properly.

Bring up **sqlnet.ora** in an editor of your choice. You should have something similar to:

```
AUTOMATIC_IPC = OFF
TRACE_LEVEL_CLIENT = OFF
sqlnet.expire_time = 2147483647
names.default_domain = world
name.default_zone = world
```

If the parameter AUTOMATIC_IPC is set to ON, we suggest you change it to OFF. If the parameter is missing, we suggest that you add it. More information about this is given in the FAQ section found at the end of the chapter.

**CAUTION**
*Oracle Corporation does not support manual editing of SQL\*Net configuration files. While we do not encourage or advise you to edit any of these files manually, in exceptional circumstances you might need to edit a file and change the setting of a parameter. Be sure to maintain the formatting, as even white spaces could be significant. We recommend that you use a **search and replace** type of operation (such as **cw** or **c$** in the 'vi' editor) in the editor. You should maintain a backup of these files at all times for safety.*

Next, bring up the **listener.ora** file in an editor. It should look something like this:

```
LISTENER =
    (ADDRESS_LIST =
        (ADDRESS =
            (PROTOCOL = TCP)
            (Host = ourhost)
            (Port = 1521)
        )
STARTUP_WAIT_TIME_LISTENER = 0
CONNECT_TIMEOUT_LISTENER = 10
TRACE_LEVEL_LISTENER = ADMIN
SID_LIST_LISTENER =
    (SID_LIST =
      (SID_DESC =
        (SID_NAME = mydb)
      )
    )
```

Ensure that the host and port information is accurate. Also verify that the name of your Oracle instance (the SID) is accurate.

Finally, view the **tnsnames.ora** file in an editor. Ensure that you have something similar to this:

```
myloopback.world =
    (DESCRIPTION =
      (ADDRESS_LIST =
```

```
      (ADDRESS =
        (COMMUNITY = tcp.world)
        (PROTOCOL = TCP)
        (Host = ourhost)
        (Port = 1521)
      )
    )
    (CONNECT_DATA = (SID = mydb)
    )
  )
```

Verify the host and port information. Also take note of the alias definition (myloopback.world in this example). You will need this alias information later.

## Step 5: Start and Verify Listener

We are now ready to start the SQL*Net listener and verify that it is functioning properly. Ensure that you are logged into the UNIX system as the Oracle owner and start the listener.

```
% lsnrctl start
LSNRCTL for SVR4: Version 2.1.6.1.0 - Production on 03-MAR-97
      11:06:10
Copyright (c) Oracle Corporation 1994.  All rights reserved.
Starting /home1/oracle/bin/tnslsnr: please wait...
TNSLSNR for SVR4: Version 2.1.6.1.0 - Production
System parameter file is /home1/oracle/network/admin/listener.ora
Log messages written to /home1/oracle/network/log/listener.log
Listening on:
(DESCRIPTION=(CONNECT_TIMEOUT=10)(ADDRESS=(PROTOCOL=TCP)(HOST=
      ourhost)(PORT=1521)))
Connecting to (ADDRESS=(PROTOCOL=TCP)(HOST=ourhost)(PORT=1521))
STATUS of the LISTENER
------------------------
Alias                     LISTENER
Version                   TNSLSNR for SVR4: Version 2.1.6.1.0 -
      Production
Start Date                03-MAR-97 11:06:14
Uptime                    0 days 0 hr. 0 min. 1 sec
Trace Level               off
Security                  OFF
Listener Parameter File   /home1/oracle/network/admin/listener.ora
Listener Log File         /home1/oracle/network/log/listener.log
Services Summary...
```

```
   mydb         has 1 service handlers
The command completed successfully
```

## Step 6: Loopback Test

Now that your SQL*Net listener is running properly, you can verify the server-side configuration by running a loopback test. The idea behind a loopback test is to use an application on the server itself to connect to the Oracle7 RDBMS using SQL*Net. This is accomplished somewhat easily by issuing a SQL*Net connect string during the connect request. We will demonstrate this technique using SQL*Plus.

```
% sqlplus scott/tiger@myloopback
```

The above command should connect you to the database. Execute a couple of sample SQL queries to double-check this connection.

## Step 7: Verify Client Configuration

We have looked at the installation of SQL*Net on a Sun Solaris Server. We will now install and configure SQL*Net on a Windows 95 client and connect to the Oracle7 RDBMS on the same Sun Solaris server.

First, we need to ensure that the PC is configured to use TCP/IP on Windows 95 (look at your Windows 95 documentation if you need help with this process). Go to the DOS shell on Windows 95 and issue a **ping** command to test connection to the network.

```
C:\WINDOWS> ping ourhost
Pinging ourhost.com [196.15.16.23] with 32 bytes of data:


Reply from 196.15.16.23: bytes=32 time=1ms TTL=254

Reply from 196.15.16.23: bytes=32 time=2ms TTL=254

Reply from 196.15.16.23: bytes=32 time=2ms TTL=254

Reply from 196.15.16.23: bytes=32 time=2ms TTL=254
```

If you get an error here, *stop*! There is no point in continuing until you have ensured that the PC is connected properly to the network.

Next, use the Oracle Installer for Windows 95 to install SQL*Net Client V2 and SQL*Net V2 TCP/IP Protocol Adapter. You should see a folder C:\ORAWIN95\NETWORK\ADMIN after this installation.

We can now create SQL*Net client-side configuration files for Windows 95. You can use the SQL*Net Easy Configuration utility under the group Oracle for Windows 95 to create the client-side **tnsnames.ora**. When you start the SQL*Net Easy Configuration utility, you should see something similar to Figure 8-4.

Select Add Database Alias to see a dialog similar to this one:

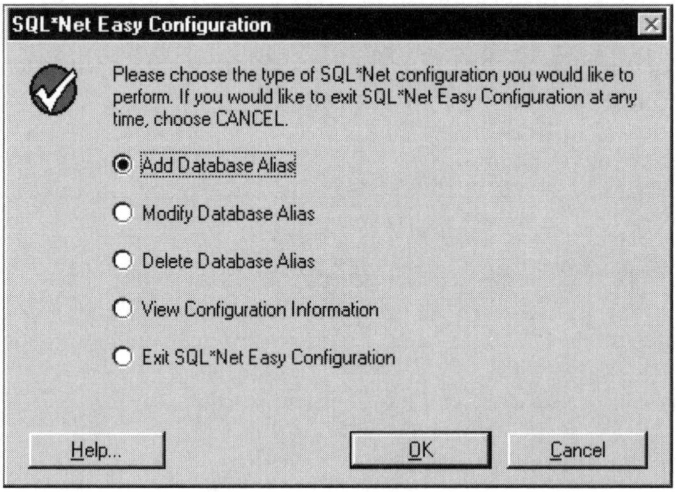

FIGURE 8-4. *SQL*Net Easy Configuration utility*

Provide any alias for your connection. This string will be the SQL*Net alias that you use in your connect information. We will create an alias called *myloopback* for a TCP/IP connection to our Solaris host called *ourhost*. Provide the information in the dialog boxes to follow as shown here:

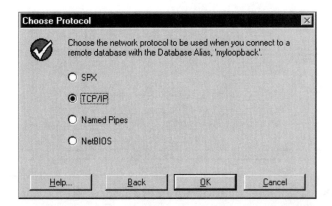

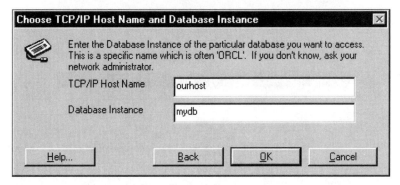

Finally, confirm the creation of an alias as shown in Figure 8-5.

Alternatively, you could just copy the **sqlnet.ora** and **tnsnames.ora** files from your Solaris server to the C:\ORAWIN95\NETWORK\ADMIN directory using the **FTP** utility.

We can now test a connection from the PC to the Solaris server. We will illustrate this using SQL*Plus on Windows 95.

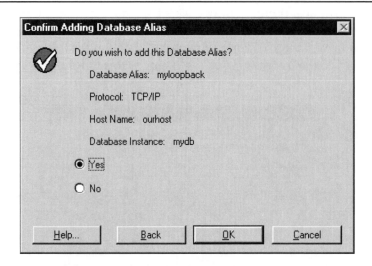

**FIGURE 8-5.** *Confirm creation of SQL*Net alias*

Start SQL*Plus and you should see a logon screen similar to this one:

Type the connect information as shown in the figure and click OK. You should connect successfully.

# SQL*Net on Windows NT

We have just discussed a configuration where a Windows 95 client is connecting to a Sun Solaris server using SQL*Net TCP/IP. We will now take a look at SQL*Net configuration on a Windows NT server. We will configure a Windows NT server for both the SQL*Net Named Pipes and TCP/IP protocols to provide variety and a better understanding of SQL*Net configuration.

## Step 1: Install SQL*Net V2 Software

Shut down all Oracle applications running on your Windows NT machine. You can verify this by using the Services applet in the Control Panel. Now use the Oracle Installer on Windows NT to install the SQL*Net V2 Server, the Named Pipes Protocol Adapter, and the TCP/IP Protocol Adapter. You should see a directory C:\ORANT\NETWORK after this installation is complete.

## Step 2: Create SQL*Net Server Configuration Files

Run the Oracle Network Manager (ONM) to create the configuration files. You can refer to Step 3 of the section "SQL*Net on UNIX" earlier in this chapter for information on ONM. If you do not have access to ONM, you can use the sample files provided with your Oracle installation in the folder C:\ORANT\NETWORK\ADMIN\SAMPLE as a starting point.

## Step 3: Verify SQL*Net Configuration

Spend a few moments to view the **listener.ora**, **sqlnet.ora**, and **tnsnames.ora** files created by ONM. These files should be located in the C:\ORANT\NETWORK\ADMIN folder.

Your **sqlnet.ora** should look similar to this:

```
AUTOMATIC_IPC = OFF
TRACE_LEVEL_CLIENT = OFF
names.directory_path = (TNSNAMES)
names.default_domain = world
name.default_zone = world
```

If the parameter AUTOMATIC_IPC is set to ON, we suggest you change it to OFF. More information about this is given in the FAQ section of the chapter.

Next, bring up the **listener.ora** file in an editor. It should look something like:

```
LISTENER =
    (ADDRESS_LIST =
        (ADDRESS=
            (COMMUNITY= NMP.world)
            (PROTOCOL= NMP)
            (SERVER= ournt)
            (PIPE= ORAPIPE)
        )
        (ADDRESS=
            (COMMUNITY= TCP.world)
            (PROTOCOL= TCP)
            (Host= ntserver)
            (Port= 1521)
        )
    )
STARTUP_WAIT_TIME_LISTENER = 0
CONNECT_TIMEOUT_LISTENER = 10
TRACE_LEVEL_LISTENER = ADMIN
SID_LIST_LISTENER =
    (SID_LIST =
        (SID_DESC =
            (SID_NAME = ORCL)
        )
    )
PASSWORDS_LISTENER = (oracle)
```

Note that we have an ADDRESS definition for each network protocol. The default database SID on Windows NT is *ORCL*.

Finally, view the **tnsnames.ora** file in an editor. Ensure that you have something similar to:

```
ourtcp.world =
    (DESCRIPTION =
        (ADDRESS_LIST =
            (ADDRESS =
                (COMMUNITY = tcp.world)
                (PROTOCOL = TCP)
                (Host = ntserver.in.oracle.com)
                (Port = 1521)
            )
        )
```

```
      (CONNECT_DATA = (SID = ORCL)
      )
  )
ournmp.world =
  (DESCRIPTION =
    (ADDRESS_LIST =
        (ADDRESS =
          (COMMUNITY = nmp.world)
          (PROTOCOL = NMP)
          (Server = OURNT)
          (Pipe = ORAPIPE)
        )
    )
    (CONNECT_DATA = (SID = ORCL)
    )
  )
```

Verify that the server name is set properly in the named pipes alias definition and that the host and port information is set correctly for the TCP/IP alias. Also take note of the alias definition (*ournmp* and *ourtcp* in this example*)*. You will need this alias information later.

## Step 4: Start and Verify Listener

We are now ready to start the SQL*Net listener and verify that it is functioning properly. Use the Services applet in the Windows NT Control Panel to start the OracleTNSListener service, as shown in Figure 8-6. It is best to set the Startup property of this service to Automatic.

We suggest that you also use the *lsnrctl* utility to check the status of your listener. From the DOS command prompt, issue the command

```
C:> lsnrctl status
LSNRCTL for 32-bit Windows: Version 2.3.2.1.4 - Production on
    03-MAR-97 09:23:57
Copyright , 1996(c) Oracle Corporation 1994.  All rights reserved.
Connecting to (ADDRESS=(PROTOCOL=IPC)(KEY=oracle.world))
STATUS of the LISTENER
------------------------
Alias                     LISTENER
Version                   TNSLSNR for 32-bit Windows: Version
    2.3.2.1.4 -
Production
Start Date                03-MAR-97 09:23:35
Uptime                    0 days 0 hr. 0 min. 22 sec
```

```
Trace Level              admin
Security                 ON
SNMP                     OFF
Listener Parameter File  C:\ORANT\network\admin\listener.ora
Listener Log File        C:\ORANT\network\log\listener.log
Listener Trace File      C:\ORANT\network\trace\listener.trc
Services Summary...
   ORCL          has 1 service handler(s)
The command completed successfully
```

Pay special attention to the Listener Parameter File being used. Ensure that this is the file that you intend to use. It is also best to get a listing of services *known* to the listener:

```
C:> lsnrctl services
LSNRCTL for 32-bit Windows: Version 2.3.2.1.4 - Production on
    03-MAR-97 09:37:58
Copyright , 1996(c) Oracle Corporation 1994.  All rights reserved.
Connecting to (ADDRESS=(PROTOCOL=IPC)(KEY=oracle.world))
Services Summary...
   ORCL          has 1 service handler(s)
    DEDICATED SERVER established:0 refused:0
The command completed successfully
```

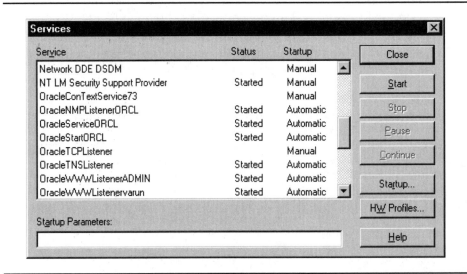

**FIGURE 8-6.** *Oracle services screen on Windows NT*

## Step 5: Loopback Test

Now that your SQL*Net listener is running properly, you can verify the server-side configuration by running a loopback test. The idea behind a loopback test is to use an application on the server itself to connect to the Oracle7 RDBMS using SQL*Net. This is accomplished easily by issuing a SQL*Net connect string during the connect request. We will demonstrate this technique using SQL*Plus. Start SQL*Plus and provide proper connect information in the login window. You can use the connect string **ournmp** to connect to Oracle using Named Pipes and the connect string **ourtcp** to connect over TCP/IP.

## Step 6: Verify Client Configuration

We just took a look at the installation and verification of SQL*Net server on Windows NT. We will now install and configure SQL*Net on a Windows 95 client and connect to the Oracle7 RDBMS on the same Windows NT machine. Follow the instructions in Step 7, Verify Client Configuration, of the section "SQL*Net for UNIX" earlier in this chapter.

## Common SQL*Net Listener Errors

Now that we have seen how to configure and start the listener, let us look at some common errors associated with this process. Most errors associated with the listener are due to bad content in the **listener.ora** file. Use the Oracle Network Manager to create this file and avoid editing it manually. A majority of the errors associated with the listener are encountered when you attempt to start the listener. We present the errors, their causes and solutions below.

| | |
|---|---|
| **Error** | NL-00462: Error loading parameter file /../**listener.ora** |
| | NL-00427: Bad list |
| **Cause** | Mismatched parenthesis in the **listener.ora**. |
| **Solution** | Use the % key in an editor like 'vi' to match parentheses. |
| **Error** | NL-00462 : Error loading parameter file /../**listener.ora** |
| | NL-00405: Cannot open listener file |
| **Cause** | listener.ora could not be found or is unreadable. |
| **Solution** | Ensure that the file is available. Set the environment variable TNS_ADMIN to point to the directory where the file is located. This error mostly applies to UNIX platforms. |

| | |
|---|---|
| **Error** | TNS-01155: Incorrectly specified SID_LIST_LISTENER in **listener.ora** |
| | NL-00303: syntax error in NV string |
| **Cause** | listener.ora has an error in an assignment. |
| **Solution** | Ensure that all assignments are in the form (X=Y) in the **listener.ora** file. |
| **Error** | TNS-12537 TNS: connection closed |
| | TNS-12560 TNS: protocol adapter error |
| | TNS-00507 TNS: connection closed |
| **Cause** | An invalid protocol adapter is referenced in the **listener.ora**. |
| **Solution** | Ensure that the PROTOCOL parameter in the **listener.ora** has the correct protocol reference. If it does, ensure that you have installed the protocol adapter. On UNIX, you could use the **adapters** command provided by Oracle. |

```
% cd $ORACLE_HOME/bin
% adapters tnslsnr
```

If your adapter shows up in this listing, try re-building the **oracle** executable. Shut down all Oracle instances and do the following:

```
% cd $ORACLE_HOME/rdbms/lib
% make -f oracle.mk install
```

## Common SQL*Net Client Errors

It is possible that your listener is configured correctly and you are still unable to connect to this listener from a client. Most client errors are caused by an invalid **tnsnames.ora** file or an improper SQL*Net alias definition. We will present a few common client errors along with suggested solutions here:

| | |
|---|---|
| **Error** | TNS-12203 : TNS: unable to connect to destination |
| **Cause** | Unable to find the specified protocol adapter, or the listener is not running on the server. |
| **Solution** | First, verify that the listener is running on the server by using the command **lsnrctl** *status*. Next, ensure that the protocol adapter specified by your SQL*Net alias is installed on your client. Also ensure that you have a proper **tnsnames.ora** file available on the client. Look at the ADDRESS parameter in the **tnsnames.ora** file. On Windows-based operating systems, ensure that you have a proper setting for the ORACLE_HOME variable in the **ORACLE.INI** or the Windows registry. |

| | |
|---|---|
| **Error** | TNS-12154 : TNS: could not resolve service name |
| **Cause** | The SQL*Net alias information is not available in the **tnsnames.ora** file |
| **Solution** | Either the SQL*Net alias specified during the connection request is not available or there is a problem with the definition of that alias in the **tnsnames.ora**. If you have edited the **tnsnames.ora** file, look for mismatched parentheses. You can also try to comment out the parameter NAMES.DEFAULT_ZONE. You can use the '#' character to do so. If you are using TCP/IP, try replacing the host name with the IP address. On UNIX platforms, make sure that you are using the correct **tnsnames.ora**. SQL*Net can use a **tnsnames.ora** file in the /etc directory, $HOME directory, or $ORACLE_HOME/network/admin directory. We suggest that you add an environment variable called TNS_ADMIN and point it to the location of your **tnsnames.ora**. This is often the safest bet: |

```
% setenv TNS_ADMIN $ORACLE_HOME/network/admin/tnsnames.ora
```

| | |
|---|---|
| **Error** | TNS-12545 : TNS: name lookup failure |
| **Cause** | The host name provided in the TCP/IP alias definition could not be resolved. |
| **Solution** | First ensure that the host name in the alias definition is specified correctly. Next, use the **ping** or **telnet** utility on the client to verify if the host name can be resolved by the client. If all fails, use the IP address instead of the host name in the **tnsnames.ora** file. |
| **Error** | TNS-12533 : TNS: illegal ADDRESS parameters |
| **Cause** | The information provided in the ADDRESS parameter of the **tnsnames.ora** file is incorrect |
| **Solution** | Verify that the ADDRESS parameter is properly specified. If you manually created the **tnsnames.ora** alias definition, ensure that the syntax for the alias definition is correct. We suggest that you avoid editing the **tnsnames.ora** file and use Oracle SQL*Net Easy Configuration instead. |

# Multi-Threaded Server (MTS)

By default, the SQL*Net listener spawns a server (also called the dedicated server process) after validating a connection request for each client process. This server process is responsible for all communication between the client and the Oracle7 server during that session. This is not very desirable in situations where the client process is sporadically active. The server process is unnecessarily idling during such inactive phases. To overcome this, SQL*Net V2 provides the ability to configure the MTS. The idea is to create a pre-determined number of server processes and then share these processes among many clients. Such server processes are called shared server processes. It must be noted that these server processes are not a part of SQL*Net, but a part of the Oracle7 RDBMS. The messaging between the clients and the shared server processes is handled by *dispatchers*. Dispatchers are also pre-determined and can be tuned for specific network protocols. We will look at some major aspects of MTS in more detail.

## Configuration of MTS

The configuration of MTS is done in the parameter file **init.ora** (on UNIX, the default parameter file is **init<SID>.ora**) and not in any of the SQL*Net configuration files. Information on dispatchers and shared servers is defined using parameters in the **init.ora**. We will take a look at the widely used MTS parameters first and then look at a sample configuration of MTS.

### MTS_SERVICE

This is the name of the service that dispatchers will use to register services with the SQL*Net listener. As pre-configured services in the **listener.ora** use the ORACLE_SID for the service name, there are two options for setting this parameter.

If you choose the same name as the ORACLE_SID, clients requesting a connection to a particular SID will get an MTS connection, if available. Otherwise, they will get a dedicated server connection. You can override this by requesting a dedicated connection, which is done by specifying *(SERVER=DEDICATED)* in the SQL*Net alias definition.

If you choose a value different from the ORACLE_SID, clients can request MTS and non-MTS connections by using different aliases. This obviously means that you need two different aliases in the **tnsnames.ora** (unless you are using something like Oracle Names). One problem with this is that you will *not* get a default dedicated connection if the MTS connect request fails.

### MTS_DISPATCHERS

This parameter is used to configure the number of dispatchers. In fact, you can configure dispatchers by the network protocol. For example, if you have a site with a majority of users connecting to the Oracle7 server using TCP/IP and a few users connecting over IPX/SPX, you can configure a total of 10 dispatchers, eight dedicated to TCP/IP and two dedicated to IPX/SPX.

### MTS_MAX_DISPATCHERS

This sets the ceiling on the maximum number of dispatchers.

### MTS_SERVERS

This parameter defines the initial number of shared servers the Oracle instance starts with.

### MTS_MAX_SERVERS

This sets the maximum number of shared servers for the Oracle instance.

### MTS_LISTENER_ADDRESS

Since dispatchers have to register or make known their services to the SQL*Net listener, the address for the listener itself needs to be advertised using this parameter.

## Registering with the Listener

On start up, dispatchers *register* themselves as a service with the SQL*Net listener. This is done by using a random address to register with the listener. We will describe this process using the TCP/IP protocol.

As the SQL*Net listener is started, it is aware of the services listed in the **listener.ora**. So, for TCP/IP, this service is *addressed* by the *port* information.

When an Oracle instance configured for MTS is started, each dispatcher acquires its own listen point. For TCP/IP, this will be a random available port.

Each dispatcher now locates the SQL*Net listener by using the MTS_LISTENER_ADDRESS parameter. It then advertises its listen point to the listener (along with the protocol information). The listener is able to redirect requests to the dispatcher using these listen points.

# Client Connections

Now that we have an idea of the process used on the Oracle server side, let us see how clients use MTS.

The client makes a connect request to the listener. The listener processes the service request and does a look-up of available (registered) services. If the requested service is registered with the listener, the listener redirects the connection request to the address associated with the registered service.

The client now establishes a connection with this service. The dispatcher is now responsible for this client connection. It also continues to listen for more connection requests.

If the client sends a SQL statement to the dispatcher, the dispatcher places this SQL statement onto a queue in the System Global Area (SGA). An available shared server process will pick up this request from the SGA, process it, and return the results to a separate queue, also in the SGA, defined for the dispatcher.

The dispatcher picks up the response message from the SGA, converts it into a SQL*Net message and returns it to the client.

## A Sample MTS Configuration

Now that we have looked at various aspects of MTS, let us put it all together in a sample configuration. We will assume a UNIX server for the purpose of this discussion. We will use the following **init.ora** parameters:

```
# We will use the default MTS Service name LISTENER
# An address where the SQL*Net listener can be located
mts_listener_address = "(ADDRESS=(PROTOCOL=IPC)(KEY=MYDB))"
# We will start with 1 IPC dispatcher and 1 TCP dispatcher
mts_dispatchers = "ipc, 1"
mts_dispatchers = "tcp, 1"
# We will define a ceiling of 10 dispatchers and 10 shared servers
mts_max_dispatchers = 10
mts_max_servers = 10
# We will choose to start 2 out of 10 shared servers
mts_servers = 2
```

The **listener.ora** file should look something similar to:

```
LISTENER =
   (ADDRESS_LIST =
```

```
            (ADDRESS =
               (PROTOCOL = IPC)
(KEY = mydb)
            )
            (ADDRESS =
               (PROTOCOL = TCP)
               (Host = ourhost)
               (Port = 1521)
            )
STARTUP_WAIT_TIME_LISTENER = 0
CONNECT_TIMEOUT_LISTENER = 10
TRACE_LEVEL_LISTENER = ADMIN
SID_LIST_LISTENER =
   (SID_LIST =
     (SID_DESC =
        (SID_NAME = mydb)
     )
   )
```

Once we have added the MTS parameters to the **init.ora** file for our instance, and started the listener, we can verify the MTS configuration with a sample connection. Before we do that, we will *bounce* the database so the changes in the **init.ora** take effect. Use the **ps** command to verify that you have the shared servers and dispatchers:

```
% ps -ef|grep oracle
oracle   1205     1  0 13:36:43 ?           0:01 ora_s000_mydb
oracle   1208     1  0 13:36:49 ?           0:00 ora_d001_mydb
oracle   1203     1  0 13:36:41 ?           0:00 ora_reco_mydb
oracle   1202     1  0 13:36:38 ?           0:00 ora_smon_mydb
oracle   1207     1  0 13:36:47 ?           0:00 ora_d000_mydb
oracle    935   932  0 10:45:38 pts/3       0:01 -csh
oracle   1201     1  0 13:36:36 ?           0:00 ora_lgwr_mydb
oracle   1199     1  0 13:36:32 ?           0:00 ora_pmon_mydb
oracle   1229     1  0 13:56:41 ?           0:00 /home1/oracle/bin
       /tnslsnr LISTENER -inherit
oracle   1200     1  0 13:36:34 ?           0:00 ora_dbwr_mydb
oracle   1206     1  0 13:36:45 ?           0:00 ora_s001_mydb
oracle    950   947  0 10:45:52 pts/4       0:00 -csh
```

The processes with the names ora_sNNN_<SID> and ora_dNNN_<SID> are the shared servers and dispatchers.

Now we can try a connection using MTS. Note that a SQL*Net alias is required to use MTS as it will not work without SQL*Net V2.

```
% sqlplus scott/tiger@myloopback
SQL> select username,program,server from v$session where audsid
     2  =userenv('sessionid');
USERNAME                  PROGRAM                       SERVER
-----------------------------------------------------------------
SCOTT          sqlplus@ourhost(TNS interface)          SHARED
```

This should return the value *SHARED* for the SERVER column. If it returns the value *DEDICATED*, MTS is not configured properly.

You can also verify that the dispatchers have registered services with the listener by issuing this command:

```
% lsnrctl services
LSNRCTL for SVR4: Version 2.1.6.1.0 - Production on 03-MAR-97
     14:20:39
Copyright (c) Oracle Corporation 1994.  All rights reserved.
Connecting to (ADDRESS=(PROTOCOL=IPC)(KEY=mydb))
Services Summary...
  mydb           has 3 service handlers
    DEDICATED SERVER established:1 refused:0
    DISPATCHER established:0 refused:0 current:0 max:60
    state:ready
      D000 (machine: ourhost, pid: 1276)
      (ADDRESS=(PROTOCOL=ipc)(DEV=8)(KEY=#1276.1))
    DISPATCHER established:2 refused:0 current:2 max:60
    state:ready
      D001 (machine: ourhost, pid: 1277)
      (ADDRESS=(PROTOCOL=tcp)(DEV=8)(HOST=196.15.17.34)
      (PORT=33750))
The command completed successfully
```

## Common Issues While Using MTS

We will now look at some frequent issues while using the MTS configuration. Here, we will provide an excerpt of the error or problem and then suggest a solution:

**Error**    ORA-00101 - invalid specification for parameter mts_dispatchers

ORA-00102 - network protocol <protocol> cannot be used by the dispatcher

**Cause**    Your **ORACLE** executable is not aware of the protocol you are using or your network protocol does not support MTS.

**Solution**    Ensure that the MTS_DISPATCHERS parameter in the **init.ora** file is valid. Start the Oracle Installer and ensure that the protocol adapter for your network protocol is installed. For example, if you are using TCP/IP, ensure that SQL*Net TCP/IP Protocol Adapter is installed. Ensure that the **ORACLE** executable is aware of your adapter. On UNIX, use:

```
% cd $ORACLE_HOME/bin
% adapters oracle
```

If you do not see your adapter in the listing, then shut down all Oracle instances on your machine and re-link **ORACLE** like this:

```
% cd $ORACLE_HOME/rdbms/lib
% make -f oracle.mk install
```

If MTS still does not work, your network protocol adapter does not support MTS.

**Problem**    A lsnrctl services does not list MTS Service

**Cause**    The dispatcher(s) have not registered with the SQL*Net listener

**Solution**    Ensure that your MTS_LISTENER_ADDRESS is matching the listener. You can also look at $ORACLE_HOME/rdbms/log/alert_SID.log for more errors. You might want to use a utility such as **grep**:

```
% cd $ORACLE_HOME/rdbms/log
% grep -i dispatcher alert*.log
```

**Problem**    A connection is made, but it shows up as DEDICATED in *V$SESSION*

**Solution**    Ensure that the alias definition does not have *(SERVER=DEDICATED)*. Try setting AUTOMATIC_IPC=OFF in the **sqlnet.ora** file. Ensure that you do not have the parameter *USE_DEDICATED_SERVER = ON* in the **sqlnet.ora** file.

In addition to the above solutions, also ensure that the alias being used is coming from the correct **tnsnames.ora**. A lot of installations have many copies of this file and your alias definition could have been resolved by the wrong **tnsnames.ora** file. For example, on UNIX, the **tnsnames.ora** is located by looking at the TNS_ADMIN environment variable, then in the **/etc** directory and finally in **$ORACLE_HOME/network/admin**.

# Oracle Names

We have discussed the resolution of SQL*Net aliases on the client side via the **tnsnames.ora** file so far. Oracle provides another sophisticated feature called Oracle Names that simplifies the administration of network configuration by removing the need for changes on clients when Oracle server configurations are modified. Oracle Names is a name service that makes network addresses of servers and database links available to all clients on the network (the concepts behind Oracle Names are very similar to the idea of Domain Name Server—DNS—used by TCP/IP). The idea is to assign a unique Global Database Name to every database in the network. This Global Database Name consists of a database name and a domain name. Clients access databases using Service Names (SQL*Net aliases) which are globally unique names that establish services (usually a database) available to the client. Please refer to the *Oracle Names Administrator Guide* for details on configuration of Oracle Names. All configuration can be done using the Oracle Network Manager. We will, however, bring some tips to your attention.

If you have multiple protocols on your network, we suggest that you have at least one Oracle Names Server for each protocol community. If you have a large number of clients, it is advisable to install back-up Oracle Names Servers and avoid a single point of failure. Oracle Names requires minimal memory and disk space and does allow for replication. Finally, if you feel the need for a more descriptive Global Database Name than that allowed by the DB_NAME parameter in the **init.ora**, you can use the *ALTER DATABASE RENAME GLOBAL_NAME* command to specify a database name longer than eight characters.

# SQL*Net Tracing

SQL*Net provides a facility for creating trace information on the client as well as the server. This might be useful for advanced users to solve problems with connections as well as in tuning. We would like to point out that SQL*Net trace files can grow very quickly and can slow down your application considerably. We therefore recommend that you use SQL*Net tracing for diagnostic purposes only. We also caution you that SQL*Net trace files are very complicated and are not subject to easy interpretation.

In order to enable client tracing, you need to add the following parameters to the **sqlnet.ora** file:

```
trace_level_client=admin
trace_file_client=cli
trace_directory_client=$ORACLE_HOME/network/trace
trace_unique_client=true
```

The TRACE_UNIQUE_CLIENT=TRUE parameter can be used to get the pid of the process added to the trace file name. A trace file with the name **cli_<pid>.trc** will be created in the directory specified by TRACE_DIRECTORY_CLIENT (the pid might not be added on some older versions of SQL*Net). The TRACE_LEVEL_CLIENT=ADMIN setting provides detailed tracing. You can set this parameter to *USER* if you do not want detailed trace information.

You can enable server-side tracing to get a trace of the SQL commands being executed by a client. Server-side tracing for SQL*Net is not useful for SQL*Net debugging itself, as a connection has already been established by this time. You need to add the following parameters to the **sqlnet.ora** file on the server to enable SQL*Net tracing on the server:

```
trace_level_server=admin
trace_file_server=serv
trace_directory_server=$ORACLE_HOME/network/trace
```

You will get a file named **serv_<pid>.trc** in the directory specified by TRACE_DIRECTORY_SERVER.

At times, it is also useful to diagnose problems with the listener by enabling listener tracing. You can do this by adding the following parameters to the **listener.ora** file:

```
trace_level_listener=admin
trace_file_listener=list
trace_directory_listener=$ORACLE_HOME/network/trace
```

You should get a trace file in the directory specified by TRACE_DIRECTORY_LISTENER. You will need to re-start the listener for this setting to take effect.

```
% lsnrctl reload
```

On Windows-based platforms, use DOS file naming conventions to set values for SQL*Net tracing. You can also get an additional level of tracing at the Virtual Socket Library level. Edit the C:\WINDOWS\**VSL.INI** file, and enable this level of tracing by adding the statement

```
trace=4
```

to this file. In fact, this statement should already be present in the file. You just need to "un-comment" this statement by removing the semicolon in front of it. Trace information is written to C:\**MSOCKLIB.TXT.** Again, the trace information might not provide any useful information to the less-experienced user.

## Trace Levels

You can essentially set four levels of tracing for SQL*Net. The following settings are valid:

    OFF or number 0
    USER or number 4
    ADMIN or number 10
    SUPPORT or number 16

The amount of information increases with the increase in value of the trace level. These levels are set through the Network Manager, or by hand-editing the **sqlnet.ora** file. It is important to turn your tracing off when you are finished debugging as the trace files continue to grow, take up space, and affect performance.

**NOTE**
*Although you can currently set the trace level to 16, the keyword SUPPORT is not available at this time*

## Interpreting SQL*Net Trace Information

As we mentioned earlier, interpreting SQL*Net trace information is a non-trivial task. We will provide some information here that should help in understanding some of the trace information. Our goal is to provide users with an aid that might allow them to identify errors that are installation- and configuration-related.

### SQL*Net Trace File Header

The information in the header of a SQL*Net trace file will indicate the source of the network configuration information in your environment. We provide a sample extract below of header information in a SQL*Net trace file:

```
New trace stream is "/private/oracle/2.3.3/network/trace/cli.trc"
New trace level is 16
--- TRACE CONFIGURATION INFORMATION ENDS ---
--- PARAMETER SOURCE INFORMATION FOLLOWS ---
Attempted load of system pfile source /private/oracle/net-work/
admin/client/sqlnet.ora
Parameter source loaded successfully
```

In the above sample, the location of the **sqlnet.ora** being used can be determined.

## Packet Information

As described earlier, SQL*Net performs its duties by sending and receiving packets. If you have an interest in determining which packets have gone out over the network, set a trace level of 16. You will be able to look at the packet dumps. We must caution again that this information is not useful to the average user. We provide an extract of packet information from a SQL*Net trace below:

```
nscon: entry
nscon: doing connect handshake...
nscon: sending NSPTCN packet
nspsend: entry
nspsend: plen=187, type=1
nspsend: 187 bytes to transport
nspsend:packet dump
nspsend:00 BB 00 00 01 00 00 00 |........|
nspsend:01 33 01 2C 0C 01 08 00 |.3.,....|
nspsend:7F FF 7F 08 00 00 00 01 |........|
nspsend:00 99 00 22 00 00 08 00 |..."....|
nspsend:01 01 28 44 45 53 43 52 |..(DESCR|
nspsend:49 50 54 49 4F 4E 3D 28 |IPTION=(|
nspsend:43 4F 4E 4E 45 43 54 5F |CONNECT_|
```

There are several types of SQL*Net packets. Table 8-1 is a partial listing of some of the packet types that you might see in a SQL*Net trace file:

| Packet Name | Packet Description |
|---|---|
| NSPTCN | Connect Packet |
| NSPTAC | Accept Packet |
| NSPTRF | Refuse Packet |
| NSPTRS | Resend Packet |
| NSPTDA | Data Packet |

**TABLE 8-1.** *Partial Listing of SQL\*Net Packets*

## Error Output

If an error occurs, the trace file would contain information on the errors. The trace level setting has no impact on the error information generated. We provide below an extract of the error output as a sample:

```
nspsend: entry
nspsend: plen=244, type=6
ntpwr: entry
ntpwr: exit
-<ERROR>- nspsend: transport write error
nspsend: error exit
nserror: entry
-<ERROR>- nserror: nsres: id=0, op=65, ns=12541, ns2=12560;
    nt[0]=511, nt[1]=61,nt[2]=0
-<ERROR>- nsopen: unable to open transport
nricdt: Call failed...
nricdt: exit
```

Again, most of the information in the SQL\*Net trace files is useful to Oracle developers and support staff. Our goal here is to expose you to the kind of information that is contained in a SQL\*Net trace file.

## An Overview of ODBC

Open Database Connectivity (ODBC) is a standard application programming interface (API) for accessing data in relational and non-relational database management systems. The ODBC driver is a piece of software that allows applications that have an ODBC interface to make a connection to a DBMS. The ODBC driver processes function calls, SQL requests to the DBMS, and also returns data and errors to applications.

The Oracle7 ODBC driver allows ODBC-compliant applications to communicate with the Oracle7 RDBMS. The Oracle7 RDBMS can be on the same computer or on a remote computer. If it is on a remote computer, then SQL*Net allows communication between the ODBC application and the Oracle7 server.

# Installation

We will review the installation of Oracle7 ODBC driver on Windows 95 to illustrate ODBC installation, configuration, and troubleshooting.

Run the Oracle Installer on Windows 95 and choose to install the Oracle7 ODBC Driver. In some cases, you might have a self-extracting file that contains the Oracle7 ODBC driver. In such a case, there should be an install program called **SETUP.EXE** that you can use for the installation.

**NOTE**
*The Oracle Developer/2000 product is bundled with ODBC software called the Oracle Client Adapter. This piece of software allows Oracle tools to connect to non-Oracle databases and must not be confused with the Oracle7 ODBC driver that allows non-Oracle tools to connect to Oracle7 RDBMS.*

## Configuration of ODBC on Windows 95

Use the 32-bit ODBC icon in the Control Panel to configure the ODBC driver. You should see something similar to Figure 8-7. We will illustrate the configuration of two database definitions, one for a local Personal Oracle7 RDBMS and one for a remote Oracle7 Server defined by the SQL*Net alias *mydb*.

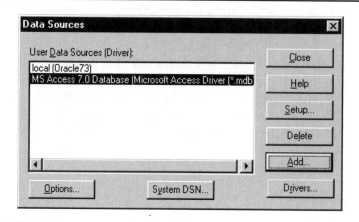

**FIGURE 8-7.** *32-bit ODBC data sources*

Click on the button labeled Drivers to get a listing of available ODBC drivers. You should see something similar to this:

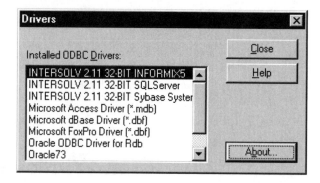

Select the Oracle7 ODBC driver (Oracle73 on this screen) and click on About. Now a dialog box similar to this should appear:

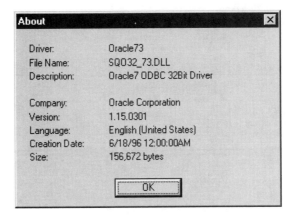

Return to the Data Sources dialog box (Figure 8-17) and click the System DSN button to see something similar to this:

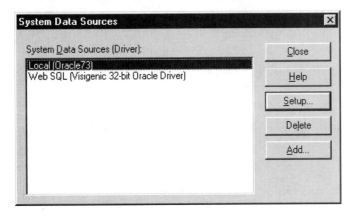

Click on the Add button to add an ODBC database definition. Select the Oracle7 ODBC driver from the listing and click on OK. You can now define the ODBC database. Specify a descriptive name for the data source in the dialog box shown below. We will choose *local* for the local database and *remote* for the remote database. You can put any text in the Description field. Specify **2:** as the SQL*Net Connect String for the local Personal Oracle7 database. Repeat the process and specify **mydb** as the SQL*Net connect string for the remote database, as shown next.

**Oracle7 ODBC Setup**

Data Source **N**ame:

**D**escription:

SQL*Net
Connect **S**tring:

OK

Cancel

**H**elp

**O**ptions>>

Close all screens and return to the Control Panel. You can verify that the database definitions are available by looking at the listing of available ODBC data sources using the 32-bit ODBC administrator utility.

## Test the ODBC driver

Oracle Corporation provides a sample program called 32-bit ODBC Test under the Oracle for Windows 95 group. If you execute this, you should see something similar to Figure 8-8.

Connect to the Oracle7 RDBMS using the data source *local* or *mydb* and execute a sample query to return something similar to Figure 8-9.

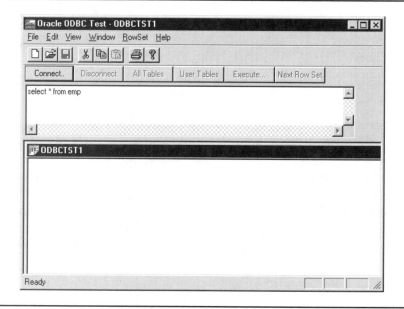

**FIGURE 8-8.** *Sample ODBC program*

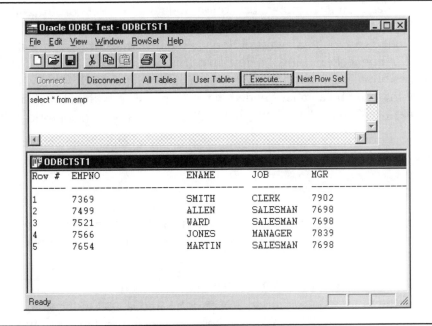

**FIGURE 8-9.** *Results of sample query*

# Frequently Asked Questions (FAQ)

**Q.** What is this parameter AUTOMATIC_IPC? How does SQL*Net use it?
**A.** Most operating systems allow for some form of communication between processes. This form of communication is called Interprocess Communication (IPC). IPC is implemented in different ways by the various operating systems. For example, UNIX could use domain sockets and Windows NT could use threads. In any case, when an Oracle client application is connecting to an Oracle7 server on the same machine, it is termed a *local* connection. IPC is the mechanism used for such a connection.

When a connection is attempted using an alias, if a **tnsnames.ora** (or other naming adapters) is not available, SQL*Net automatically assumes that this alias is an IPC connect descriptor. In fact, SQL*Net constructs its own descriptor using a standard format.

So, in the case of a name resolution via the **tnsnames.ora** file, if a client attempts a connection using the descriptor *myipc,* SQL*Net searches for a **tnsnames.ora** file. If a **tnsnames.ora** file is available, then SQL*Net will assume *myipc* to be an alias defined in the **tnsnames.ora** file. However, if a **tnsnames.ora** file is not available then SQL*Net creates a descriptor of the format:

```
(DESCRIPTION=
(ADDRESS=(PROTOCOL=IPC)(KEY=myipc))
(CONNECT_DATA=(SID=mydb))
```

If AUTOMATIC_IPC is set to ON, a connection using the IPC mechanism is automatically attempted whenever a **tnsnames.ora** file is not available.

**Q.** I have SQL*Net V1 and V2. Which one should I use?
**A.** Oracle has fully de-supported SQL*Net V1 and is attempting to migrate all its customers to SQL*Net V2. We therefore recommend that you use SQL*Net V2 in all cases.

**Q.** I have many network protocols defined. How does my application know which adapter to use?
**A.** The connect descriptor (alias) used during the connection defines the protocol used for that session. A corresponding SQL*Net adapter will be used. It is perfectly acceptable to have multiple protocols configured on your client and the server and use them for different connections.

**Q.** If I have more than one protocol installed, is it better to use one over the other? How would I choose?
**A.** Even though there are a lot of parameters that you have to take into consideration, we suggest that you use the *native* network protocol on your operating system. For example, use TCP/IP on UNIX, DECNET on VAX/VMS, and Named Pipes on Windows NT. Of course, if your site has many operating systems, choose a protocol that is common to all these operating systems. TCP/IP usually works well in such scenarios.

**Q.** I have configured a dedicated server and it works fine. Do I have to use MTS?

**A.**  We definitely recommend that you take the extra time to configure MTS. It is definitely better to share server processes among clients. This will help you conserve resources on your server. Remember that even when your client is idle, there is a process on the server if you are using a dedicated connection. This dedicated server process will use resources, no matter what it does.

**Q.**  I can't connect to Oracle using the ODBC driver on the Developer/2000 CD-ROM. What is the problem?
**A.**  The Developer/2000 CD-ROM has ODBC drivers for databases such as RDB, Informix, and SQL Server. It does not have the Oracle ODBC driver and therefore cannot be used to connect to Oracle. The drivers on this medium facilitate the connection of Developer/2000 products to non-Oracle databases. Developer/2000 does not need an ODBC layer to connect to Oracle.

**Q.**  But what is this Oracle Client Adapter on the Developer/2000 media?
**A.**  The Oracle Client Adapter (OCA) provides an ODBC interface for Oracle client tools to connect to non-Oracle DBMS. For example, you can connect Oracle Forms to a Microsoft Access database using the OCA.

**Q.**  What do I put in the SQL*Net connect string or the connect property when creating an ODBC data source for an Oracle RDBMS?
**A.**  You must put the SQL*Net V2 alias in this field if you are attempting to use a remote Oracle7 RDBMS. If you are using a local database such as Personal Oracle7, you must put **2:** as the connect string.

**Q.**  I have installed the Oracle7 ODBC driver and I want to use it with my third-party application written in Visual Basic. I am getting an error. How do I know if the ODBC driver is installed properly?
**A.**  Oracle supplies a sample ODBC program called ODBC Test. The executable is called **ODBCTST.EXE** or **ODBCT32.EXE.** You can try connecting to Oracle using this program. If you are successful, then the ODBC driver is installed properly.

**Q.**  I get errors such as *Driver not Capable* and *ODBC call failed* with the Oracle7 ODBC driver. What are these errors?
**A.**  It is most likely that you are making an invalid ODBC call. You can refer to Oracle's White Paper on ODBC for information on this at *http://www.oracle.com/support/bulletin/html/odbc.pdf.*

**Q.** What is SQLPASSTHROUGH?
**A.** The required SQL statement is passed to an ODBC database for processing without any changes at the driver level. The resulting dynaset cannot be updated.

**Q.** What is meant by Level 1 ODBC compliant and Level 2 ODBC compliant? How does that affect my application?
**A.** There are several differences between the two levels. You can get detailed information in the ODBC White Paper at *http://www.oracle.com/support/bulletin/html/odbc.pdf* or by referring to the *ODBC Programmers Reference* or *ODBC Software Developer's Kit* from Microsoft Corporation.

**Q.** Can I use the Oracle7 ODBC driver 7.0 or 7.1 with an Oracle7 7.2 or 7.3 Server?
**A.** Certainly! Later releases of Oracle are always backward compatible. However, you must not use an ODBC driver that is newer than the Oracle RDBMS. For example, do not use an ODBC driver version 7.2 with Oracle 7.1. While this might work, it will lead to unpredictable behavior and is definitely not a supported configuration.

**Q.** I have a third-party ODBC-compliant application. What do I need to get from Oracle Corporation to use this application with an Oracle7 RDBMS?
**A.** You need to get the Oracle7 ODBC driver and Required Support Files for your operating system in order to use this ODBC application. In addition, you will need proper SQL*Net software if you are connecting to a remote Oracle7 RDBMS.

**Q.** I get an error that says *Specified Driver could not be loaded*. What is causing this?
**A.** This error is mostly caused when the directory or folder containing ODBC software is not specified in the PATH variable. For example, if you have installed Oracle products in the folder C:\ORAWIN95 on Windows 95, ensure that C:\ORAWIN95\BIN is in your DOS path. In general, on all operating systems, it is recommended that you have ORACLE_HOME\BIN in your path.

**Q.** I want to execute a stored procedure in Oracle using ODBC. How do I do that?

**A.** Many methods of accomplishing this are documented in the ODBC White Paper. You might try using the CALL statement to accomplish this task. Use something like:

```
executesql((call procedure name (parm1, parm2 ...)))
```

**Q.** SQL*Net has so many configuration files. What is the purpose of all these files?

**A.** SQL*Net can prove to be quite complex in some situations. Most installations of SQL*Net use a **listener.ora**, **sqlnet.ora**, and **tnsnames.ora**. However, there are other possibilities like Multi-Protocol Interchanges (MPI) and Oracle Names. Table 8-2 provides a summary of the configuration files.

**Q.** Which platforms provide Oracle Network Manager?

**A.** ONM is provided mostly on Windows 3.1 with SQL*Net 2.1 and later. On some older releases of SQL*Net, Oracle did provide this utility for

| Name of File | Purpose |
|---|---|
| tnsnames.ora | Contains addresses of all Oracle network resources. This is not necessary if Oracle Names is enabled. |
| sqlnet.ora | Contains optional diagnostic parameters, client information about Oracle Names, and optional security parameters (encryption and checksumming). |
| listener.ora | Information about all listeners. |
| tnsnav.ora | Navigation information and MPI information for clients are provided here. |
| intchg.ora | Startup parameters for MPI are defined in this file. |
| tnsnet.ora | A map of comparative costs of sending data across different protocols. This is relevant for MPI only. |
| protocol.ora | This file contains addressing information for nodes for protocols like ASYNC and X.25. ONM cannot create this file. |
| names.ora | Startup parameters for Oracle Names. |

**TABLE 8-2.** *Configuration Files for SQL*Net*

Motif. If you have SQL*Net V2, you can obtain ONM for Windows 3.1 free of cost from Oracle.

**Q.** Does ONM also configure my network protocols? Does this mean I do not need other tools like HP OpenView and SunNet Manager?
**A.** ONM only allows you to configure SQL*Net. You will still have to depend on other tools to configure your network layer.

**Q.** I want to change the buffer size used by the network. How do I do that?
**A.** You can use the SDU parameter in **tnsnames.ora** to set the buffer size. This is an undocumented parameter. You can set values between 512 and 2048. Here is a sample descriptor that uses SDU:

```
myoracle =
     (DESCRIPTION=
     (ADDRESS=
          (PROTOCOL=TCP)
          (PORT=1521)
          (HOST=ourhost)
     )
     (CONNECT_DATA=(SID=mydb))
     (SDU=1024)
)
```

**Q.** On my Windows 3.1 machine, when I execute a long query, I cannot work with my other Windows 3.1 applications while I wait for the query to execute. Is there something that I can do?
**A.** The problem here is that Windows 3.1 is not a true multi-tasking system. You can alleviate the problem somewhat by using SQL*Net 2.1.4 or higher on Windows 3.1. These versions of SQL*Net allow Windows 3.1 to switch tasks. In addition, your query may continue to run if you are using a non-blocking client application. If you are using an application that uses Oracle client libraries Version 7.1 or higher, this should be a non-blocking application. The one exception to this is an Oracle Call Interface (OCI) application. These will be non-blocking from Oracle client libraries Version 7.2.

You must also use SQL*Net 2.1.4 or higher on Windows 3.1 if you want to interrupt long queries with CTRL-C.

**Q.** In what order does SQL*Net resolve an alias specified in a connect request from a client?

**A.** SQL*Net first searches a local **tnsnames.ora** file specified for the user (in the home directory). Next it searches the global **tnsnames.ora** file. Finally it reads the Oracle Names Server address from the **sqlnet.ora** and uses the Oracle Names server as a source to resolve the SQL*Net alias in question. If the alias is not resolved, an ORA-12154 is reported.

**Q.** Which protocols are supported by Oracle Names?
**A.** Oracle Names supports all protocols that are supported by SQL*Net V2. A single instance of Oracle Names can support name resolution requests over many protocols.

# CHAPTER
## 9

## Problem Solving
## Developer/2000

racle's Developer/2000 is an integrated suite of database tools supporting multiple operating systems, user interfaces and data sources. Oracle Developer/2000 applications are able to run on multiple operating systems because a common Oracle Toolkit is used by each tool. Developer/2000 applications also maintain native look and feel. For example, Developer/2000 on Windows 95 includes the standard features of a Windows 95 application, such as drag-and-drop.

In this chapter, we will present some tips and techniques on installation, porting, and upgrade issues related to Developer/2000, along with common errors and FAQ. All the concepts in this chapter can be extended to Developer/2000 in any environment.

# Installation

Developer/2000 can be installed in either a client-server configuration or a server-based configuration.

**NOTE**
*The next version of Developer/2000 applications can be deployed on the World Wide Web. A third layer, called the Application Server, has been added between the client and the database server in this architecture. We have not included any information on this release as it was not available when this book went to print.*

In a client-server configuration, the Developer/2000 tools reside on a machine that does not contain an Oracle7 RDBMS. With Developer/2000 on a separate machine from the Oracle7 RDBMS, you access the database using SQL*Net (see Chapter 8 on connectivity for more information on this type of installation). The database objects required by the Developer/2000 tools also reside on a remote Oracle7 RDBMS.

We recommend a client-server installation because of two advantages: First, you can enhance your performance by distributing the workload between clients and servers. Second, you do not need to upgrade your Developer/2000 tools and applications every time you upgrade the Oracle7 server or vice-versa. In fact, we recommend you install Developer/2000 and the Oracle7 server in two separate directory structures (two different ORACLE_HOMEs) even when you are using only one machine. In this manner, you can always benefit from the second advantage.

The second type of installation is a server-based installation. Here, Developer/2000 and the Oracle7 server are installed in the same directory structure (the same ORACLE_HOME). You do not need SQL*Net to connect to the RDBMS; you can use IPC for such default connections. Please refer to Chapter 8 on connectivity for a description of such connections.

There is one advantage to the server-based installation: Since Oracle tools and RDBMS share a substantial portion of code (shared libraries or DLLs), you will save disk space because the tools and RDBMS can share files.

Now that we have discussed the pros and cons of the two types of installations, you should be in a position to judge which works best for your site. Once you have made your choice, you should be able to install the Developer/2000 tools per the instructions in the installation guide. Since we have already covered installation issues in the previous chapters, we will restrict ourselves to other issues, such as environment variables, tips on porting, and upgrade techniques related to Developer/2000. We will also look at common issues like printing and some common errors encountered with Developer/2000 tools.

# Environment Variables

From our experience, about 20 percent of the calls to Oracle Worldwide Customer Support are resolved by setting the proper environment variables for the Developer/2000 tools. We will present the minimum set of variables for Developer/2000 Forms in Tables 9-1, 9-2, and 9-3. In Tables 9-4, 9-5, and 9-6 we look at similar variables for Developer/2000 Reports. Tables 9-7, 9-8, and 9-9 provide information on Developer/2000 Graphics. In these tables we cover the Windows, UNIX, and OpenVMS operating systems. In addition to the information in these tables, several more settings are documented in the installation guide for your operating system.

| Environment Variable | Purpose |
|---|---|
| FORMS45_PATH | This specifies the path where Developer/2000 Forms 4.5 will look for **.FMX**, **.MMX**, **.PLL**, and image files. You can specify as many directories as you wish in this list.<br>**Example:**<br>FORMS45_PATH=C:\FORMS;C:\MYAPPS;C:\TEMP |
| FORMS45_EDITOR | This defines the editor invoked when editing multi-line items in a form.<br>**Example:**<br>FORMS45_EDITOR=C:\WINDOWS\**NOTEPAD.EXE** |
| FORMS45_DEFAULTFONT | The font used for boilerplate text in a form is defined using this setting.<br>**Example:**<br>FORMS45_DEFAULTFONT= "Courier New"..Plain.Medium.Normal |
| TK23_ICON | This setting provides the location for icon files (**.ICO** files) used in your forms.<br>**Example:**<br>TK23_ICON=C:\FORMS\ICONS |

**TABLE 9-1.** *Environment Variables for Developer/2000 Forms 4.5 on Windows*

**NOTE**
*The TK2x_ICON parameter corresponds to the version of the Oracle Toolkit being used by the tool. You can find the version of the Oracle Toolkit being used by selecting the menu option Help/About in the designer. So for example, if you are using Oracle Toolkit Version 2.1, you must use TK21_ICON. Under normal circumstances, the Oracle Installer should have made the necessary changes on Windows platforms.*
*Also note that the TK2x_ICON parameter affects all Developer/2000 tools on your system. All tools supplied with one release of Developer/2000 will use the same version of the Oracle Toolkit.*

| Environment Variable | Purpose |
| --- | --- |
| FORMS45_PATH<br>or<br>ORACLE_PATH | This specifies the path where Developer/2000 Forms 4.5 will look for **.fmx**, **.mmx**, **.pll**, and image files. You can specify as many directories as you wish in this list.<br>**Example:**<br>FORMS45_PATH=/usr/apps:/home1/apps |
| FORMS45_EDITOR | This defines the editor invoked when editing multi-line items in a form.<br>**Example:**<br>FORMS45_EDITOR=**vi** |
| ORACLE_TERM | This defines the terminal settings for character-mode forms.<br>**Example:**<br>ORACLE_TERM=xsun5 |
| TK23_ICON | This setting provides the location for icon files (**.ico** files) used in your forms.<br>**Example:**<br>TK23_ICON=/usr/apps/icons |

**TABLE 9-2.**   *Environment Variables for Developer/2000 Forms 4.5 on UNIX Platforms*

The information in Table 9-1 applies to Windows 3.1, Windows 95, and Windows NT, and provides the important environment variables for Developer/2000 Forms 4.5 on UNIX.

Table 9-3 provides information on Developer/2000 Forms for OpenVMS.

We will now present important environment variables for Developer/2000 Reports. Table 9-4 documents settings for Windows-based systems. Tables 9-5 and 9-6 document settings for UNIX- and OpenVMS-based systems, respectively. Again, several more settings are documented in your installation guide.

Again, information in Table 9-4 applies to Windows 3.1, Windows 95, and Windows NT, while Table 9-5 provides the important environment variables for Developer/2000 Reports on UNIX.

We present similar information for Developer/2000 Reports on OpenVMS in Table 9-6.

| Logical | Purpose |
|---|---|
| FORMS45_PATH | This logical is used to locate forms, menus, and library applications. By default, this logical is undefined. You can specify as many directories as you wish while setting the logical as follows: |
| | $ define FORMS45_PATH *dir1* [, *dir2, dir3..*] |
| FORMS45_TERMINAL | This logical is used to locate terminal definitions used in character-mode forms. By default, this logical is undefined. To set this logical, use the following syntax: |
| | $ define FORMS45_TERMINAL *dir1* [, *dir2, dir3..*] |
| ORACLE_PATH | To set this logical, use the following syntax: |
| | $ define ORACLE_PATH *dir1* [, *dir2, dir3..*] |
| ORAPLSQLLOADPATH | This logical points to the directory or list of directories where the attached libraries reside. To set this logical, use the following syntax: |
| | $ define ORAPLSQLLOADPATH *dir1* [, *dir2, dir3..*] |
| ORACLE_TERM | This logical defines the terminal settings for character-mode forms. To set the logical, use the following syntax: |
| | $ define ORACLE_TERM vt100 |
| TK21_ICON | This logical points to the directory or list of directories where the icon buttons for the Oracle Toolkit reside. To set this logical, use the following syntax: |
| | $ define TK21_ICON *dir1* [, *dir2, dir3..*] |

**TABLE 9-3.** *Logicals for Developer/2000 Forms 4.5 on OpenVMS*

Next we present important environment variables for Developer/2000 Graphics. Table 9-7 documents settings for Windows based systems, and Tables 9-8 and 9-9 document settings for UNIX- and OpenVMS-based systems. Again, several more settings are documented in your installation guide.

Information in Table 9-7 applies to Windows 3.1, Windows 95, and Windows NT.

| Environment Variable | Purpose |
|---|---|
| REPORTS25_PATH | This specifies the path where Developer/2000 Reports 2.5 will look for external queries, boilerplates, and reports. You can specify as many directories as you wish in this list.<br>**Example:**<br>REPORTS25_PATH=C:\REPORTS;C:\MYAPPS;C:\TEMP |
| TK23_ICON | This setting provides the location for icon files (**.ICO** files) used in your reports.<br>**Example:**<br>TK23_ICON=C:\REPORTS\ICONS |
| REPORTS25_TMP | The designated directory is used for the creation of temporary files.<br>**Example:**<br>REPORTS25_TMP=C:\TEMP |

**TABLE 9-4.**   *Environment Variables for Developer/2000 Reports 2.5 on Windows*

| Environment Variable | Purpose |
|---|---|
| REPORTS25_PATH<br>or<br>ORACLE_PATH | This specifies the path where Developer/2000 Reports 2.5 will look for external queries, boilerplates, and reports. You can specify as many directories as you wish in this list.<br>**Example:**<br>REPORTS25_PATH=/usr/apps:/home1/apps |
| REPORTS25_TMP | The designated directory is used for the creation of temporary files.<br>**Example:**<br>REPORTS25_TMP=/tmp |
| TK23_ICON | This setting provides the location for icon files (**.ico** files) used in your reports.<br>**Example:**<br>TK23_ICON=/usr/icons |

**TABLE 9-5.**   *Environment Variables for Developer/2000 Reports 2.5 on UNIX Platforms*

| Logical | Purpose |
|---------|---------|
| REPORTS25_PATH | This logical is used to locate external objects that you use in your reports. By default, this logical is undefined. You can specify as many directories as you wish while setting the logical as follows:<br><br>$ define REPORTS25_PATH *dir1* [, *dir2, dir3*..] |
| REPORTS25_TERMINAL | This logical is used to locate terminal definitions used in character-mode forms. By default, this logical is undefined. To set this logical, use the following syntax:<br><br>$ define REPORTS25_TERMINAL *dir1* [, *dir2, dir3*..] |
| REPORTS25_TMP | This logical determines the location where Developer/2000 Reports creates temporary files. By default, this logical is set to point to SYS$SCRATCH. To define this logical, use the following syntax:<br><br>$ define REPORTS25_TMP *dir* |
| ORACLE_PATH | To set this logical, use the following syntax:<br><br>$ define ORACLE_PATH *dir1* [, *dir2, dir3*..] |
| ORACLE_TERM | This logical defines the terminal settings for character-mode reports. To set the logical, use the following syntax:<br><br>$ define ORACLE_TERM vt100 |

**TABLE 9-6.** *Logicals for Developer/2000 Reports 2.5 on OpenVMS*

| Environment Variable | Purpose |
|----------------------|---------|
| GRAPHICS25_PATH | This specifies the path where Developer/2000 Graphics 2.5 will look for external queries and files. You can specify as many directories as you wish in this list.<br>**Example:**<br>GRAPHICS25_PATH=C:\REPORTS;C:\MYAPPS;C:\TEMP |

**TABLE 9-7.** *Environment Variables for Developer/2000 Graphics 2.5 on Windows*

| Environment Variable | Purpose |
|---|---|
| GRAPHICS25_PATH or ORACLE_PATH | This specifies the path where Developer/2000 Graphics 2.5 will look for external files. You can specify as many directories as you wish in this list.<br><br>GRAPHICS25_PATH=/usr/apps:/home1/apps |

**TABLE 9-8.** *Environment Variables for Developer/2000 Graphics 2.5 on UNIX Platforms*

# Setting Environment Variables

Now that we have looked at some environment variables that are necessary to run Developer/2000 tools, we will take a quick look, for the benefit of less-experienced users, at how these variables are set. All settings on DOS- and Windows-based machines are case-insensitive, but settings on UNIX are case sensitive.

On Windows 3.1, you can provide environment settings in the **ORACLE.INI** file. This file is typically located in the C:\WINDOWS

| Logical | Purpose |
|---|---|
| GRAPHICS25_PATH | This logical is used to locate external objects that you use in your graphics. By default, this logical is undefined. You can specify as many directories as you wish while setting the logical as follows:<br><br>$ define GRAPHICS25_PATH *dir1* [, *dir2, dir3..*] |

**TABLE 9-9.** *Logicals for Developer/2000 Graphics 2.5 on OpenVMS*

directory. You can confirm the location of the **ORACLE.INI** file by looking at your **WIN.INI** file. You should have an entry similar to:

```
[Oracle]
ORA_CONFIG=C:\WINDOWS\ORACLE.INI
```

On Windows 95 and Windows NT, you can add or modify environment settings using the Windows registry. Run **regedit** and expand the key, HKEY_LOCAL_MACHINE|Software|ORACLE. You can use the Edit|Modify option to modify an existing setting or add a new one using the Edit|New|Key option.

All settings for UNIX are made in the environment. If you are using **csh** you can use **setenv,** and if you are using **sh** or **ksh** you can use **export.** The % prompt represents **csh** and the $ prompt represents **sh** or **ksh.**

```
$ csh
% setenv  ORACLE_PATH /usr/apps
% exit
$ ORACLE_PATH=/usr/apps
$ TMPDIR=/tmp
$ export ORACLE_PATH TMPDIR
```

Note that an equal sign is not provided in **csh**, but is necessary in **sh** or **ksh**. Any environment settings made on the command line remain for the duration of the session. We recommend that you modify your **.login** or **.profile** file if you are using **csh** and **.profile** for **sh** and **ksh** in order to provide your environment variable settings. You can use the **env** or the **echo** command to determine your environment settings:

```
% env | more
% echo $ORACLE_HOME
```

On OpenVMS, you can use the **define** command to set symbols or logicals.

```
$ define ORACLE_TERM vt100
```

## Temporary Files

In addition to the above settings, Developer/2000 tools need to create temporary files at times. We recommend that you designate the directory in which these temporary files are created by setting additional variables in the environment.

On Windows 3.1, you can provide these in the **AUTOEXEC.BAT** and on Windows 95 and Windows NT, you can set these in the registry.

```
SET TEMP=c:\temp
SET TMP=c:\temp
```

Ensure that the directory (C:\TEMP in this example) is available and that you have the required permissions to write to this directory. Also note that there are no spaces around the equal signs. You can use the **SET** command to look at your DOS environment settings.

```
C:> SET
```

For UNIX based systems, set the variable TMPDIR for temporary files.

```
% setenv TMPDIR /tmp
```

## Porting Considerations

One of the major advantages with Oracle's Developer/2000 tools is that applications can be ported to different environments with minimal effort. While porting is relatively simple, there are some issues that need to be addressed. We present a few ideas on porting Developer/2000 applications in this section. We also refer you to the chapter titled "Designing for Portability" in the *Developer/2000 Forms Advanced Techniques* manual. While we mostly refer to ideas that apply to Developer/2000 Forms in this discussion, you can apply them equally well to the other Developer/2000 tools.

Most users understand the term *porting* to mean the procedure of moving applications from one operating system to another. While this is true to a large extent, it is also useful to remember porting issues with reference to different devices (terminals) and user interfaces (GUI or character mode) on the same operating system. Oracle Developer/2000 applications can be ported readily to any GUI operating system by simply *regenerating* the application files (files like **.FMX and .MMX**) from the same source files (**.FMB and .MMB**). Aesthetic changes might be required on the target platform even though the Developer/2000 tools will migrate the application using native widgets.

Porting issues are a lot easier to resolve if you plan for them during the design stages of your application. You need to consider the various environments in which your users might need to run an application. For example, your sales team might use an application on portable notebook computers with very small screens running Windows 3.1, while your finance team might use the same application on character-mode VT terminals. It is a lot easier to take into account the limitations of these two environments during the design stage, and also to ensure that you do not use any operating-system-specific feature in your application.

We recommend that you define standards for the coding techniques and for the look and feel of applications at your site. You can even create template forms that can be used as a starting point to develop an application.

We present a few guidelines here that you can use to create portable applications:

■ Limit the use of operating system functionality such as OLE and ActiveX. If you must use them, create libraries for these functions. You can choose to include or exclude these libraries as needed.

■ Avoid using the *HOST*( ) built-in. Always use the *RUN_PRODUCT* built-in to invoke other Oracle Developer/2000 tools.

■ Select a font that is available commonly on operating systems. You can investigate the availability of fonts like MS Sans Serif, Courier, or Geneva/Chicago, and then choose a font that is available on all your platforms. If you cannot find any common font, you can use the *font aliasing* features of Developer/2000 tools to work around this issue. Information on font aliasing is available in the installation guide. There are also some examples in the default **UIFONT.ALI** file. This is a plain ASCII text file that you can read and edit in an editor of your choice.

■ Always use local visual attributes, if possible.

■ Avoid using external files like icon files (**.ICO**). Such files are not portable between operating systems. Icon files with an extension of **.ICO** need to be converted to **.xpm** for Motif. We also suggest that you save sound files to the database in Oracle format to avoid platform issues.

■ Avoid user exits whenever possible. User exits need to be recreated on each operating system. If you must use user exits, use the pre-processor directives **#ifdef**, **#endif**, **#define**, and **#elsif** in your code. This will allow you to maintain one copy of your source code.

```
# ifdef WINDOWSAPP
<some code here>
# elsif MOTIFAPP
<some other code>
# endif
```

■ Design your screens for the lowest common denominator of display monitors. Use the monitor with the lowest resolution and smallest size when designing your screens. If you are planning for users on a laptop, you need to design your applications such that they fit on these small screens.

■ Do not refer to explicit keys in your application. For example, a PF4 key is not available on a PC and a reference to this key in an application will not make it portable.

■ Do not hard code paths to external files. Use environment settings like FORMS45_PATH and ORACLE_PATH in your applications. This rather simple technique can avoid problems caused by the differences in file systems used by various operating systems. For example, UNIX uses "/" and Windows 95 uses "\". Also remember that some operating systems, like UNIX, are case sensitive.

■ Choose your colors carefully. Remember that when you use an application designed in color on a monochrome monitor, the colors will convert to shades of gray. If your application uses a dark foreground and a dark background, contrast will be lost when you view it on a monochrome monitor. It is best to choose a color palette consisting of black, white, light gray, and dark blue if you are planning to deploy the same application on a system with a monochrome monitor.

■ We suggest that you use the *Real Coordinate System*. This ensures that your screen objects in a GUI environment are based on size and not on physical dots. Screen resolution can drastically affect the look of applications based on the Character Coordinate System.

■ You will need to adjust the size of your windows and the positions on canvases for different GUIs. This is especially true when you are porting an application developed on Windows to Motif. Windows uses the concept of an MDI window which is not present on Motif. The number of lines visible on the screen could change during such a migration. We suggest that you identify the operating system on startup using the *GET_APPLICATION_PROPERTY* built-in and then write some code in the *When-New-Form-Instance* trigger using *SET_WINDOW_PROPERTY* to set window sizes and canvas positions as defined in Table 9-10.

■ Character-mode applications can be created using Developer/2000 tools on Motif and Windows. Most sites create a character-mode application by converting a GUI-based application. You can run an application (**.FMX** file) created in the Developer/2000 Forms Designer in character mode *Forms Runtime* with no changes as long as you pay special attention to resolve issues with fonts and functionality.

# Upgrading to Developer/2000

Oracle is regularly providing new and improved releases of its software; Developer/2000 is no exception. It might be necessary to upgrade applications written in one version of software to a newer version. Oracle Developer/2000 provides utilities that allow users to upgrade applications developed in earlier releases of Developer/2000 (or even Oracle Version 6 tools such as SQL*Forms 3.0). Before you consider the technical issues, you need to decide whether to:

■ Continue using your character-mode application in a character-mode environment.

■ Run your character-mode application in a bitmapped environment.

■ Move your character-mode application to a bitmapped (GUI) environment.

As each application is unique in its own way, we will first consider some of the issues involved in an upgrade process. Later on, we will provide some tips and techniques that should ease the process considerably.

| Platform | Window | Window | | Canvas | |
|---|---|---|---|---|---|
| | | **Height** | **Width** | **Xpos** | **Ypos** |
| Windows | Window1 | 10.00 | 3.00 | 2.00 | 2.00 |
| Motif | Window1 | 11.00 | 3.00 | 1.00 | 1.00 |

**TABLE 9-10.** *Window Sizes and Canvas Positions on Windows and Motif*

# The GUI Difference

Character-mode and bitmapped environments differ in two significant ways: how the application is displayed and how the user interacts with the application. We will highlight the common issues related to such differences.

In a character-mode environment, an application typically consists of screens with text fields and some simulated check boxes for entering and displaying data. The bitmapped environment provides graphical widgets that allow the user many ways of entering values and displaying data. Some examples are check boxes, radio buttons, list boxes, icons, scroll bars, and dialog boxes. It is important to choose the proper widgets for your application as some widgets are better suited than others for some types of data entry. Screen design and graphics are more important for GUI environments. It is very easy to get carried away with graphics, to the point of losing performance and productivity.

In a character-mode environment, all user interactions are tightly controlled by the application. You can control how users navigate within the application and the actions that are permitted rather easily by using key triggers and menu options. In a GUI environment you cannot control the manner in which users navigate, nor can you control the mouse actions. Key triggers are not helpful in this situation.

# Overview of the Upgrade Process

Developer/2000 is part of the Version 7 family of Oracle tools. If you are upgrading an application built with a tool from an older generation (Version 6 or even Version 5), then you will need to use a converter utility called *Developer/2000 Generator* to upgrade the application to

Developer/2000. SQL*Forms 3.0, SQL*Menu 5.0, and SQL*Reportwriter 1.1 are examples of such older generation tools. If you need to upgrade a SQL*Forms 3.0 application to Developer/2000 Forms 4.5 you will need to use the *Forms Generator* utility (the name of the executable varies with the operating system).

If you are upgrading an application built with a tool in the Oracle Version 7 family of tools, such as CDE or an earlier version of Developer/2000, it is sufficient to *regenerate* the application. Developer/2000 Forms 4.0 and Developer/2000 Reports 2.0 are examples of Oracle Version 7 tools that can be upgraded to Developer/2000 by regenerating the modules in Developer/2000. We strongly encourage you to make a back up before you attempt to regenerate or save a module in the newer version. There is no way to revert to the older version. For example, if you have a file called **MYFORM.FMB** that you built in Developer/2000 Forms 4.0 and you open it in the Developer/2000 Forms 4.5 Designer, regenerate it, and save it, the new **MYFORM.FMX** and **MYFORM.FMB** cannot be used with Developer/2000 Forms 4.0 any longer.

The simple rule is that if your application was built in a version of the tool that has a different *first digit* in its version number, you will need to use a converter utility. If the first digit in the version number is the same, you can simply regenerate your modules using the menu option File|Administration|Generate in the designer utility.

In any case, details are documented in the *Developer/2000 Forms Reference Manual,* but users often tend to ignore the requirements for upgradation mentioned in the installation guide. We suggest that you spend some time with both sets of documentation before you attempt any upgrades.

You should have a fairly good idea of the process required to upgrade your application by this time. We will now look at specific Developer/2000 product-related upgrade issues. We will first present issues related to Developer/2000 Forms, and then issues related to Reports and Graphics.

## Developer/2000 Forms Upgrade Options

If you already have an Oracle Forms 4.0 GUI application, you can easily move your application to Developer/2000 Forms by regenerating the application in the Forms Designer. However, if you have a character-mode application you have some choices to make. The option you select will determine the time and effort required to upgrade your application. You can:

■ Upgrade your application and continue to run in character mode.

■ Upgrade your application to run in a bitmapped environment. You can choose to disable the mouse for Forms navigation with a layer of code around your application to perform the navigation.

■ Redesign your application's visual layout and flow to run in a bitmapped environment, reusing only the validation, logic and transactional code.

**UPGRADING FROM ORACLE FORMS 4.0 (GUI) TO DEVELOPER/2000 FORMS 4.5**    There is really no upgrade if you already have an Oracle Forms 4.0 bitmapped application. You only need to regenerate your forms, menus, and libraries in Developer/2000 Forms 4.5. This produces the run-time version of your application. Before you do this, you should make a backup of your existing modules, because the Oracle Forms 4.0 Designer cannot read any module saved in Forms 4.5 format. Your applications will be functional immediately after regeneration. However, you should still test the application to verify that it works in the same way as before the upgrade.

**UPGRADING CHARACTER-MODE APPLICATIONS TO RUN IN A CHARACTER-MODE ENVIRONMENT**    We will now look at the steps required to upgrade your character-mode application to the latest version of Developer/2000 to run in a character-mode environment. The process of upgrading SQL*Forms 2.0, 2.3, or 3.0 character-mode applications to run in a character-mode environment is fairly straightforward. The following command is used to upgrade your forms:

```
f45gen <module-name> <username>/<password> upgrade=yes
    version=<version-number>
```

You have to replace **f45gen** with the appropriate *generate* executable for your platform. When upgrading version 2.0 or 2.3 forms, you also have to include the version parameter with a value of *20* or *23*. Table 9-11 provides the file formats and extensions in Developer/2000 Forms 4.5.

Form, menu, and library modules are now in a binary format by default from the designer. These binary files are portable across platforms. The executable is the runtime version of the module and is not portable.

| Type | Designer (Binary) | Runtime (Binary) | Text |
|------|-------------------|------------------|------|
| Forms | .fmb | .fmx | .fmt |
| Menu | .mmb | .mmx | .mmt |
| Library | .pll | .pll | .pld |

**TABLE 9-11.**   *Developer/2000 Forms 4.5 File Formats and Extensions*

Before you upgrade your Forms applications, we suggest that you also take the following precautions.

If you have references in your forms or menus, you have to upgrade the referenced modules before the referencing modules. Ensure that the old database tables (SQL*Forms 3.0, Oracle Forms 4.0, or SQL*Menu 5.0 tables) and 4.5 tables are available in the database. The referenced module definition must be present in the old and the new tables. After the conversion, you can delete the old tables as you only need the 4.5 tables.

You should check the built-ins and reserved words in the reference manual and resolve any conflicts in your application after the upgrade using the new global search and replace feature. Developer/2000 has more built-ins and reserved words than earlier versions.

**UPGRADING CHARACTER-MODE APPLICATIONS TO RUN IN A BITMAPPED ENVIRONMENT**    In a bitmapped environment, users navigate using the mouse instead of function keys. Hence, any code for validation or block co-ordination that is based on key triggers will not be executed. However, most applications that run in character-mode environments make use of key triggers extensively. You can handle such situations by either disabling mouse usage in the form or disabling default navigation.

The first step is to upgrade the application using the instructions in the previous section, "Upgrading Character-mode Applications to Run in a Character-mode Environment". Because of the beveling used to produce a three-dimensional effect in a bitmapped environment, the text items may be one character shorter than your item length. We suggest that you choose to use a smaller font for your text items or use the *widen_fields=yes* option of the **f45gen** command to avoid this problem. This will, however, lessen the space that you currently have between text items by one character cell and might cause the text items to overlap if they are currently flushed against each other.

If you want to ensure that your key triggers continue to work, you can limit mouse navigation within a form by using the property *Mouse Navigation Limit.* You can set this property at any level desired (*Form, Block, Record, or Item*) in your application. The mouse can still be used to select menu items.

Another approach is to disable the *Default Navigation* feature of Forms. This approach allows your users to run the application in a bitmapped environment using the mouse both for navigation and menu selection.

There are essentially eight key-triggers that cause navigation in Forms (KEY-UP, KEY-DOWN, KEY-NXTBLK, KEY-PRVBLK, KEY-NXTREC, KEY-PRVREC, KEY-NXTFLD, KEY-PRVFLD). These triggers are used in fairly standard ways in applications. We suggest some code changes for such scenarios to help you get started with your upgrade.

**NAVIGATING INTO AN ITEM THAT WOULD NOT NORMALLY BE AVAILABLE**    Some items in your application could be protected from entry by key triggers. For example, the KEY-NXTFLD and KEY-PRVFLD triggers can be coded to skip certain items in the same block in your application. However, the user can use the mouse to click in that item. If that item is *display-only*, you might have to change properties such as *Insert Allowed* to *false* in the designer. Alternativey, you can use either of the following built-ins to dynamically disable items you do not want users to update:

```
set_item_property ('item-name', ENABLED, PROPERTY_FALSE);
set_item_property ('item-name', INSERT_ALLOWED, PROPERTY_FALSE);
```

If the item is in a different block, you should put those items in a separate canvas-view, and use the *show_view* and *hide_view* built-ins to display only the relevant blocks and items.

**NAVIGATING INTO ANY ITEM IN A MULTI-ROW BLOCK**    Your application may not be prepared for the fact that the user can now click in any item in any row of a multi-row block. You should examine your code and decide how you can best transfer it to the new Developer/2000 Forms 4.5 triggers. You need to replace *KEY-NXTFLD, KEY-PRVFLD,*

*KEY-NXTBLK,* and *KEY-PRVBLK* with *WHEN-NEW-BLOCK-INSTANCE,*
*WHEN-NEW-RECORD-INSTANCE, WHEN-NEW-ITEM-INSTANCE,* and
*WHEN-VALIDATE-ITEM* triggers.

### CONVERTING POP-UP WINDOWS TO STACKED CANVAS-VIEWS

Pop-up pages are converted to content canvas-views in new windows in
Developer/2000 Forms 4.5. You may have positioned pop-up pages to
overlay certain parts of the screen in your character-mode application.
Now these windows can be moved around or even iconized with the
mouse, which may destroy the effect you want. You can still achieve the
same effect by converting these pop-up windows to stacked canvas-views.
A content canvas-view is the "base" view and occupies the entire window
in which it is displayed. A stacked canvas-view can be displayed in the
same window as a content canvas-view and any number of stacked
canvas-views. A stacked canvas-view can be anywhere in a window and
usually hides certain portions of the window. The salient steps are
described below:

1.  Open the upgraded form module in the designer.

2.  For each window that you want to convert to a stacked
    canvas-view, click on the canvas-view in the navigator to change its
    properties in the property palette.

3.  Change the Canvas-view Type property to Stacked.

4.  Change the Window property to the window in which you want to
    display the stacked canvas-view.

5.  Change the Display X Position and Display Y Position properties to
    put your stacked canvas-view in the correct position after the
    upgrade.

6.  Remove any extraneous windows.

## Upgrading Menu Applications to Developer/2000

The task of upgrading forms to Developer/2000 is relatively simple.
However, many users seem to have trouble with Menu applications. We
will highlight the major steps and checks for upgrading Menu applications.
   Like SQL*Forms 3.0, you can upgrade from SQL*Menu 5.0 to
Developer/2000 Forms 4.5 using the Developer/2000 Generator. Unlike

SQL*Forms 3.0, which has **.INP** files, SQL*Menu 5.0 does not have any files that can upgraded. SQL*Menu modules are stored in the database. It is therefore necessary to upgrade Menu modules using the database itself. This requires that the system tables or base tables for SQL*Menu 5.0 and Developer/2000 Forms be installed in the same database. In fact, you will need the system tables for Developer/2000 Forms 4.0 and 4.5 for this process. You can look at the section titled "Upgrading SQL*Menu 5.0 Apps Directly to 4.5" in the Developer/2000 Forms *Release Notes* for details on this topic. A copy of these *Release Notes* should be available in the FORMS45\DOC directory of your installation media. We will provide some minimal tests to check for the availability of system tables for SQL*Menu 5.0, and Developer/2000 Forms 4.0 and 4.5. You can run the SQL commands shown below using SQL*DBA or SQL*Plus. The objects being described here must exist. If they do not, you need to create these tables by following the instructions in the installation guide.

```
SQL> DESCRIBE MENU_B_APPL
SQL> DESCRIBE FRM40_APP
SQL> DESCRIBE FRM45_OBJECT
```

After verifying the existence of the base tables, you can use the *Forms Generator* utility **f40gen** to upgrade from SQL*Menu 5.0 to Developer/2000 Forms 4.0.

```
F40GEN MODULE=<name> USERID=<un>/<pw> MODULE_TYPE=MENU
       MODULE_ACCESS=DATABASE UPGRADE=YES
```

If you want to upgrade your SQL*Menu 5.0 roles, you need to use the *UPGRADE_ROLES=YES* option for **f40gen.** You will now have a Developer/2000 Forms 4.0 module for your SQL*Menu 5.0 application. In order to upgrade from Developer/2000 Forms 4.0 to 4.5, you can use **f45gen**.

```
F45GEN MODULE=<name> USERID=<un>/<pw> MODULE_TYPE=MENU
```

We would also like to point out that there is no facility to upgrade your SQL*Menu 4.0 applications to Developer/2000 Forms 4.5. You will have to upgrade the SQL*Menu 4.0 applications to SQL*Menu 5.0 before upgrading them to Developer/2000 Forms 4.5.

## Developer/2000 Reports Upgrade Options

We have looked at the upgrade options for Developer/2000 Forms and Menu so far. We will now present some tips and techniques to upgrade Reports applications.

If you already have an Oracle Reports 2.0 GUI application, you can upgrade your reports by regenerating your application using the Developer/2000 Reports Designer. If you have any SQL*Reportwriter 1.1 reports or customized Printer Definition files, you can upgrade them using the Reports Converter. As with Forms, you have some options with upgrading reports. You can:

- Continue to run in character-mode.

- Modify your upgraded report to run in a bitmapped environment.

- Redesign your report's visual layout and flow to run in a bitmapped environment.

**UPGRADING FROM ORACLE REPORTS 2.0 (GUI) TO DEVELOPER/2000 REPORTS 2.5**    There is really no upgrade if you already have an Oracle Reports 2.0 bitmapped application. You only need to regenerate your reports and libraries in Developer/2000 Reports 2.5. This produces the run-time version of your application. Before you do this, you should make a backup of your existing modules because the Oracle Reports 2.0 Designer cannot read any module saved in Reports 2.5 format. Your applications will be functional immediately after regeneration. However, you should still test the application to verify that it works in the same way as before the upgrade.

**UPGRADING CHARACTER-MODE APPLICATIONS TO RUN IN A CHARACTER-MODE ENVIRONMENT**    The *Reports Converter* utility converts all existing SQL*ReportWriter 1.1 reports and any customized printer definition files to Reports 2.5. The name of the executable varies with the operating system (for example, on Windows 95, it is called **R25CON32.EXE**). You can refer to your Reports documentation for details. You can generate run-time reports using the Reports Designer and run them with no changes. You can use the command-line option **MODE=CHARACTER** at run time.

**UPGRADING CHARACTER-MODE APPLICATIONS TO RUN IN A
BITMAPPED ENVIRONMENT**     You can again use the *Reports
Converter* utility to convert existing SQL*Reportwriter 1.1 reports.
Developer/2000 Reports 2.5, however, supports a wide spectrum of report
types that did not exist in SQL*ReportWriter 1.1. The tool has also been
greatly enhanced to better handle report types that were difficult to create
with SQL*ReportWriter 1.1. Below we present some features that you can
use to your advantage after the upgrade.

**&SQL**     SQL*ReportWriter 1.1 allows the application developer access to
dynamic SQL in the report using the &SQL function. Typically &SQL is
used for computations based on fields from different groups in the group
tree or to issue DML statements against the database (e.g. updating a history
table). Developer/2000 Reports 2.5 supports PL/SQL on the client side,
which, in most cases, will eliminate the need for database access.

In the cases where database access is needed (e.g. DML operations), the
Reports local PL/SQL engine guarantees that parsing and execution of the
SQL is done in an optimal way. The local PL/SQL is then compiled and
saved with the report definition.

Using PL/SQL to replace &SQL will not only speed up most operations
(e.g. calculations), but it will also make the report definition easier to read.

**TRIGGERS**     SQL*ReportWriter 1.1 has no explicit support for
report-level triggers. The application developer had to obtain the implicit
behavior of a trigger by creating a hidden field with a source group of
"Report", and assign an &SQL statement as the source of the field.

Reports 2.5 has several explicit trigger points that fire at well-defined
places (Before Parameter Form, After Parameter Form, Before Report,
Between Page, and After Report). Along with the five report-level triggers,
each layout object can have a format trigger associated with it. Also, the
PL/SQL statement can be a function, a procedure, or even a call to a stored
procedure. Again, the use of triggers rather than hidden fields will greatly
enhance the readability and maintainability of the report.

Reports 2.5 also allows the application developer to control how and
when database actions are committed or rolled back. Two new
command-line parameters (*ON_SUCCESS*, and  *ON_FAILURE*) allow full
control over which action to take ("*NONE*", "*ROLLBACK*", or "*COMMIT*")
depending upon the report status (success or failure).

**MATRIX REPORTING**    SQL*ReportWriter 1.1 allowed the application developer to create matrix reports but required the application developer to use three queries: one for the columns, one for the rows, and one for the cells of the matrix. Developer/2000 Reports 2.5 provides greater flexibility with respect to matrix reporting since it allows the application developer to choose between using one query instead of three, which in most cases will provide better performance.

**CONDITIONAL FORMATTING**    Conditionally formatting objects can only be accomplished in SQL*ReportWriter 1.1 through the use of *dummy queries*. Dummy queries made it possible to leave out sections of the report, thereby giving the impression of conditional formatting. Reports 2.5 allows the application developer to apply a *format trigger* to any object on the layout. The format trigger contains the logic to conditionally print or suppress the object from printing.

Other features, such as conditional highlighting and relative positioning, are also available with Developer/2000 Reports 2.5.

**PRINTER CODES**    SQL*ReportWriter 1.1 required that printer codes be used for any formatting attributes included in a report. With Reports 2.5, if the report is not run as a character-mode report, these are no longer needed. In this case, you should remove all printer code references from the report and specify appropriate attributes.

## Developer/2000 Graphics Upgrade Options

If you have Graphics modules built with an earlier release, you can automatically upgrade these modules by loading them in Graphics Designer. We want to bring some additional issues to your attention.

**MODULE REGENERATION**    Any Graphics modules created with a prior release must be loaded, recompiled and saved before use with the current release. Graphics will prompt automatically for recompilation if your module was saved with a prior release.

**DEFAULT COLOR PALETTE**    Modules created with previous versions of Graphics will contain a color palette that differs from the default color palette supplied with this release. This issue is significant when building Forms applications since the same default color palette is being used in the latest release of Forms. Keeping a consistent color palette between Graphics and Forms is vital for maintaining optimal performance in any integrated application. Upgrade your old Graphics modules with the new default color palette. You can find this new color palette in a file called **DEFAULT.PAL** (the location of this file varies with the operating system. On Windows 95, it resides in the ORAWIN95\TOOLS\COMMON folder). Please refer to the Graphics documentation for instructions on importing color palettes.

We have looked at a variety of issues concerning the upgrade of Developer/2000 applications. These are by no means exhaustive, but we hope that we have pointed you in the proper direction. In the remainder of this chapter, we will present issues related to printing of reports and some common errors reported to Oracle Worldwide Customer Support.

## Developer/2000 Reports and Printing

There are scores of printers and printer drivers available in the market today. Oracle Worldwide Customer Support sees many calls from customers who are having trouble with printing from Developer/2000 Reports. We present some details and common issues involved in printing from Developer/2000 Reports on UNIX and Windows.

## Printing on UNIX

You first need to choose an appropriate Postscript Printer Definition (PPD) file for your printer. PPD files are used by the Oracle Toolkit (which in turn is used by Developer/2000 Reports) to obtain information on the postscript printer. PPD files are necessary since the Oracle Toolkit cannot communicate directly with the printer. Oracle currently supports PPD files from Adobe Systems.

**NOTE**
*From Developer/2000 Release 1.3.2, which includes Developer/2000 Reports 2.5.5, Oracle also supports Printer Command Language (PCL) output.*

PPD files provide information on the paper sizes, available fonts, resolution, etc. to the Oracle Toolkit. They are located in the

$ORACLE_HOME/guicommon/tk21/admin/PPD directory. Corresponding Adobe Font Metrics (AFM) files for all the postscript fonts defined in the PPD file must be available in the $ORACLE_HOME/guicommon/tk21/admin/AFM directory. An AFM file is necessary to get font attributes such as style, weight, width, and character set. Oracle provides PPD and AFM files for common printers. If you cannot find the PPD or an AFM file you need, you can contact your printer manufacturer or Adobe Systems. Most of the files you need should be available on the World Wide Web if you have access.

Apart from the PPD and AFM files, you need to provide a listing of available printers in the **uiprint.txt** file located in the $ORACLE_HOME/guicommon/tk21/admin directory. The format for an entry in this file is:

```
printer: printer driver: Toolkit driver : printer description:
    PPD file
```

where *printer* is the name of the printer as used by **lp** or **lpr**, *printer driver* is the type of the print driver, valid values are PostScript and ASCII, and *Toolkit driver* specifies the version of the printer driver. Current values are *1* for ASCII or Level 1 PostScript printers and *2* for Level 2 PostScript printers. *printer description* is a free-format text definition of the printer.

We illustrate with an example that defines a printer called "ourprinter" that uses the **default.ppd** file.

```
ourprinter:PostScript:1:Our Network Printer on the
    floor:default.ppd:
```

**NOTE**
*The trailing colon in definition is important.*

Once the PPD file is defined, you then need to specify the printer to be used by Developer/2000 Reports. The printer is determined on Motif by looking at the values for the environment variables in the order shown below:

1. TK21_PRINTER

2. ORACLE_PRINTER

**3.** PRINTER

**4.** The first entry in the **uiprint.txt** file

**NOTE**
*The TK2x_PRINTER variable will depend on the version of the Oracle Toolkit. For example, your version of Developer/2000 may use Oracle Toolkit Version 2.3, and therefore your variable might be TK23_PRINTER.*

Be sure to test the setup for the printer by selecting the File|Choose Printer menu option. You should get a listing of available printers from the **uiprint.txt** file. You could alternatively choose the name of a printer available to you. In this case, Developer/2000 Reports will use the **default.ppd** file.

## Printing on Windows

We will now look at troubleshooting techniques for printing issues on Windows-based platforms. Many issues with printing on Windows can be resolved with a little care and testing.

On Windows, you must first configure printers that you want to use with your applications. In Windows 3.1, you can do this using the icon labeled Printers in the Windows Control Panel. In Windows 95 and Windows NT, you can use the Add Printers icon when you select Start|Settings|Printers.

You can view the status of print jobs on Windows 3.1 using the Print Manager. On Windows 95 and Windows NT, you can select Start|Settings|Printers and double-click on the printer in question.

Once you have defined a printer, we suggest that you first ensure that you can print to this printer using Notepad or Wordpad. Next, you need to ensure that you can run the report to the Screen. This will help eliminate any errors in the report itself. Next, you can choose to run the report to Preview or File to ensure that Developer/2000 is using the printer driver properly.

If you have an issue with printing, try to determine whether the issue is with all reports or just a few. Try to print the same report to a different printer, if you have that option. This should help you determine whether there is a problem with a particular printer, a font, or a report. In some cases, the fonts may be getting replaced when reports are sent to the printer.

If you are still having trouble, ensure that Developer/2000 Reports is able to write temporary files. Verify that the REPORTS25_TMP variable is set to a valid directory and that you have at least 20 MB of disk space available for temporary files. It might also be useful to run a utility like Microsoft ScanDisk to repair any disk problems.

If you are having trouble with the format of the printed report, try using a TrueType font. These fonts are marked TT in the font listing on Windows. TrueType fonts guarantee that the output on the screen and the printer match.

# Common Errors in Developer/2000 Tools

Almost all the errors obtained when you start up a tool are caused by errant settings for required environment variables. Every Oracle Developer/2000 tool requires a set of files (message files and resource files) that are in the product directory. For example, Developer/2000 Forms 4.5 has a FORMS45 directory and Developer/2000 Reports 2.5 has a directory called REPORTS25. If you change the setting for these variables, or delete them, you will get errors on startup. We will take a look at some common error messages from the Developer/2000 tools.

**FRM-10221: Cannot read file <filename>**    A module or library that is being called does not exist or you do not have proper permissions to read the file associated with it. The module or library being called could also be corrupt. This is a fairly common error with attached Menus. Developer/2000 Forms is unable to locate the specified **.MMX** file.

**FRM-10256: User is not authorized to run Developer/2000 Forms Menu**    Ensure that the Oracle user has access to the Developer/2000 Forms system tables (also called Database Tables in some Oracle manuals). You need to run the *Forms Grant* script as the Oracle user SYSTEM. Refer to your installation guide for help on creating these system tables.

Even if you are accessing the Menu module from the file system and not the database, Developer/2000 Forms will try to read the access information from the system tables.

**FRM-10260: No active items in selected menu**    If you get this error, it means that you do not have access rights to any item in a menu. You can obtain rights to the menu items or the application developer can choose to hide menu items for which you do not have access.

**FRM-91111: Internal Error: window system startup failure**    This error is mostly caused on Motif due to an invalid setting for the DISPLAY environment variable. Ensure that you have set the DISPLAY environment properly by issuing the **echo** command:

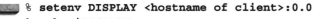

```
% setenv DISPLAY <hostname of client>:0.0
% echo $DISPLAY
```

If the DISPLAY is set properly and you still get this error, ensure that you have permitted the server to open a window on the client. You can use the **xhost** command to accomplish this.

```
% xhost + <hostname of server>
```

**FRM-40028: Error opening message file <filename>.MSB**    This error is obtained while attempting to start Developer/2000 Forms. It is caused by missing or bad FORMS45 and/or LANGUAGE (NLS_LANG) setting. If your setting is proper, ensure that you have some files with the extension **.MSB** in the directory specified by FORMS45.

**REP-001: Unable to initialize message subsystem**    This error is obtained while attempting to start Developer/2000 Reports. It is caused by missing or bad REPORTS25 and/or LANGUAGE (NLS_LANG) setting. If your setting is proper, ensure that you have some files with the extension **.MSB** in the directory specified by REPORTS25.

**REP-0118: Unable to create a temporary file**    Developer/2000 Reports is unable to create temporary files. Check the REPORTS25_TMP setting. Ensure that it points to a directory that exists and that you have write permissions to this directory. If you are using your operating system environment setting, ensure that you have the variables TMP and TEMP set on the Windows platforms and TMPDIR set on UNIX platforms.

# Frequently Asked Questions (FAQ)

**Q.** When I print small reports using Developer/2000 Forms, it seems to take a really long time. Why is it slower for me to print a report from Developer/2000 Forms?

**A.** You can avoid some overhead and improve your performance by using a program called *Reports Server*. The Reports Server, once started, stays resident in memory and you should see a considerable improvement in performance.

**Q.** I have these PostScript output files that I got from Developer/2000 Reports. Is there any way I can view them before I print them?

**A.** You can use a utility called *Ghostview* to view PostScript files. There is a lot of information available on the WWW.

**Q.** I looked at the output of a report using the SCREEN as well as the PREVIEW setting in the Developer/2000 Reports Parameter form. They look the same. Is there any difference?

**A.** If you format a report using the screen font, it will look good in the previewer. However, if you print the same report using screen fonts, it will probably look different from the way it looked on the screen. If you use PREVIEW, then it will look good when printed since Developer/2000 Reports will use the printer (instead of screen) metrics to format the report. In some cases, the output may not look good on the SCREEN, since the printer fonts will be re-mapped to screen fonts.

**Q.** Does Developer/2000 Reports always print PostScript? How do I get an ASCII text output on a PC?

**A.** If you are using Developer/2000 Reports 2.5, you can print ASCII reports by setting MODE=Character. In this case, Developer/2000 Reports will bypass the printer driver and send the ASCII output directly to the printer.

**Q.** When I am writing PL/SQL code in Developer/2000 Forms triggers, when do I need to enclose PL/SQL blocks in a BEGIN ... END?

**A.** Triggers in Developer/2000 Forms are written as *Anonymous Blocks*. Developer/2000 Forms automatically adds BEGIN ... END to all anonymous blocks. If you are defining a procedure, a function, a package body, or a package specification, then you need to use BEGIN ... END in your PL/SQL blocks.

**Q.** How do I reference procedures or functions in a library? What about packages?
**A.** Developer/2000 tools first search for a procedure, a function, or a package in the calling module. If the required call is not found, then a search is made in attached libraries. In fact, Developer/2000 searches attached libraries in the order they show up in the attachment listing. The first definition in the attachment listing will be used.

You can reference a procedure or a function by simply invoking the name, but you need to prefix the package name if the procedure is defined in a package. For example, let us assume that a procedure definition A and a function definition B are available along with another procedure C in a package D. You can reference A or B in a PL/SQL block using

```
A (arguments here);
returnval = B (arguments);
```

If you want to reference C, you must prefix the package name D.

```
D.C (arguments);
```

**Q.** Can I provide multiple definitions for the same procedure in different attached libraries?
**A.** While this is a highly dangerous practice, Developer/2000 does allow you to have a procedure definition in separate attached libraries. The definition that is used is from the library that shows up earlier in the attached library listing.

**Q.** I upgraded my SQL*Menu 5.0 application to Developer/2000 Forms 4.5 and I now get an FRM-10242 error *Cannot call linked-in Developer/2000 Forms from Developer/2000 Forms* when I try to run this application. What is wrong?
**A.** It is likely that you used a *Type 4* command in a SQL*Menu 5.0 application to invoke SQL*Forms 3.0. The *Type 4* command forces Developer/2000 Forms 4.5 to call the Forms code again internally, which leads to this error. Modify all the *runform* or *runform30* commands in SQL*Menu 5.0 application to *CALL_FORM.*

**Q.** I upgraded my SQL*Menu 5.0 application to Developer/2000 Forms 4.5 and I cannot access SQL*Plus. What do I do?

**A.** On some operating systems, like Windows 3.1 and Windows 95, the SQL*Plus executable name has been changed to either **plus31**, **plus32**, or **plus33** depending on the version of SQL*Plus being used. Replace the *sqlplus* call in your SQL*Menu 5.0 application with the appropriate SQL*Plus executable.

**Q.** How do I avoid logging on to Oracle in order to run a Developer/2000 application during run time? I always get the Connect dialog box when I start my application.

**A.** You can avoid the Connect dialog box by trapping the log on feature. For example, in Developer/2000 Forms, create a Form-level ON_LOGON trigger and put dummy code for this trigger. The following code is sufficient to disable the Connect dialog box.

```
BEGIN
    NULL;
END;
```

**Q.** The Developer/2000 Forms generator allows me to upgrade a SQL*Forms 2.3 and 3.0 application. I can also upgrade SQL*Menu 5.0. What about SQL*Menu 4.0?

**A.** You must first convert SQL*Menu 4.0 applications to 5.0 and then use the Forms generator to convert these applications to Developer/2000.

# CHAPTER
## 10

Problem Solving Oracle
Precompilers

racle precompilers allow 3GL programs to embed SQL statements in their source. This allows 3GL programs to access an Oracle database in a standard manner. A precompiler translates the embedded SQL to standard Oracle runtime library calls. Oracle makes precompilers for all the popular 3GLs including C, Pascal, FORTRAN, and COBOL. Some precompilers might not be available on certain operating systems. Refer to your installation guide or your product media to get a listing of the available precompilers on your operating system. On some operating systems, you might even have to obtain a separate product set, such as Oracle's *Programmer/2000,* to get access to a precompiler.

In this chapter, we present information on Oracle precompilers that covers various aspects of program development. We present sections on a variety of topics that contain useful tips, and which will allow you to avoid common pitfalls.

# Developing Programs Using Precompilers

Except for an additional step called *precompilation,* the process of creating a program does not change. You can embed SQL statements into your source code using an editor of your choice. This source code is then used as input for the precompiler, which in turn translates all the embedded SQL statements into native code. Finally, you can compile and link this code to create an executable after including some Oracle libraries that are necessary to resolve the Oracle calls. Figure 10-1 shows the major steps that are involved in this process. We would like to emphasize that the Oracle precompiler for the most part simply replaces the *text* of the embedded SQL. You can optionally run some checks for proper SQL syntax during this stage.

# Treatment of *float* and *double*

In programming languages such as C, data types like *float* and *double* are used to hold real numbers using a binary representation. Both of these data

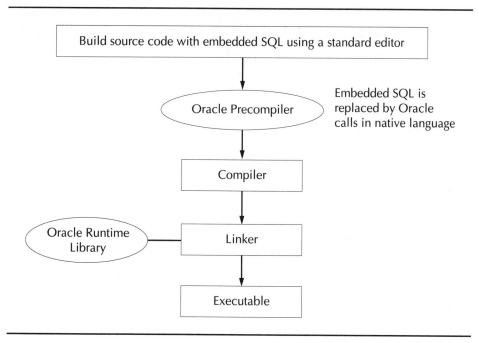

**FIGURE 10-1.** *Program development using precompilers*

types store the given number as an approximation of the real value. The level of accuracy is usually defined at the operating system level (the **float.h** file on UNIX). On the other hand, all numbers are stored in Oracle using a special decimal representation. When you use floats and doubles in your program, Oracle converts between the binary representation of float and double and its own decimal representation. In performing the conversion, Oracle reads all the binary digits of the float or double (which is really an approximated value), and then stores this value in its own format using all the available digits. This could lead to problems, as the value stored in Oracle could now differ from what you require. In order to avoid this, we suggest that you always use the SQL function *ROUND* when accepting input from host variables that are defined as float or double before inserting these values into the database. If you do not use the ROUND function, then the value that is stored will differ slightly from what you expect; when you attempt to retrieve that data, you could see an *ORA-1403 - No data found* error. In fact, it is best to completely avoid using a float in a *WHERE* clause.

# Treatment of *CHAR* and *VARCHAR*

Users often complain about unexpected behavior with *CHAR* and *VARCHAR* data types. We will provide some tips that should help you avoid pitfalls with *CHAR* and *VARCHAR*.

We will first look at an example of using the *WHERE* clause against data stored in an Oracle RDBMS (CHAR or *VARCHAR2*).

Assume that the following columns are defined and the string 'XYZ' has been stored in them:

```
COL1    CHAR(5)
COL2    VARCHAR2(5)
```

In Oracle7, COL1 will contain the string 'XYZ' and will be padded with two blanks. COL2 will contain the string 'XYZ' with no padded blanks.

Assume that you now have the following definition in your C program:

```
char    mydata(5);
```

Table 10-1 provides a summary of the *SQLCODE* that you can expect if you use the host variable *mydata* in the *WHERE* clause of a SQL statement.

It is clear from Table 10-1 that with Pro*C 1.5 and 1.6 with mode=oracle, you must have blanks padded. With Pro*C 1.5 and 1.6 with mode=ansi, you must have a null terminator at the end of the data. Null terminated data works fine with Pro*C 2.0 also.

**NOTE**
*-1480 is normally returned when there is a truncation and 1403 is returned when there are no matching data sets. A SQLCODE of 0 means successful completion. You could also use the setting dbms=v6_char to force Oracle to use the Version 6 semantics, if you want Version 6 character handling. Please refer to the* Programmers Guide to the Oracle Precompiler *for complete documentation on the DBMS and MODE options.*

| Pro*C Version with Mode | mydata = "XYZ " (blank padded) | mydata = "XYZ\0" (null terminated) | mydata="XYZ \0" (blank padded and null terminated) |
|---|---|---|---|
| Version 1.5 mode=oracle | 0 | 1403 | 1403 |
| Version 1.5 mode=ansi | -1480 | 0 | 100 |
| Version 1.6 mode=oracle and (dbms=native) | 0 | 1403 | 1403 |
| Version 1.6 mode=ansi and (dbms=native) | -1480 | 0 | 100 |
| Version 2.0 mode=oracle and dbms=native | -1480 | 0 | 1403 |
| Version 2.0 mode=ansi and dbms=native | -1480 | 0 | 100 |

**TABLE 10-1.**   *SQLCODE Set in Various Situations with WHERE Clause*

We will now look at another example where we examine the data returned by a *SELECT* statement using the *INTO* clause against data stored in an Oracle RDBMS (*VARCHAR2*).

Assume that the following column is defined. We have stored the string 'XYZ' into this column. Note that there are no trailing blanks stored in a VARCHAR2 column.

```
COL1    VARCHAR2(5)
```

Assume that you now have the following definition in your C program:

```
char    mydata(5);
```

Table 10-2 provides a summary of the behavior that you can expect if you use the host variable *mydata* in the *INTO* clause of a SQL statement.

| Pro*C Version with Mode | Data Returned from SELECT Statement | Length of Returned Data | Description |
|---|---|---|---|
| Version 1.5 mode=oracle | "XYZ " | 5 | Blank padded at the end of data. |
| Version 1.5 mode=ansi | "XYZ \0" | 4 | Null terminated. Blanks are placed at the end of the data as required. |
| Version 1.6 mode=oracle and (dbms=native) | "XYZ " | 5 | Blank padded at the end of data. |
| Version 1.6 mode=ansi and (dbms=native) | "XYZ \0" | 4 | Null terminated. Blanks are placed at the end of the data as required. |
| Version 2.0 mode=oracle and dbms=native | "XYZ \0" | 4 | Null terminated. Blanks are placed at the end of the data as required. |
| Version 2.0 mode=ansi and dbms=native | "XYZ \0" | 4 | Null terminated. Blanks are placed at the end of the data as required. |

**TABLE 10-2.** *Data in Various Situations with INTO* Clause

# LONG RAW Data

Programmers often find it difficult to deal with situations where they have to store or retrieve raw chunks of data into Oracle7. There might be a need to read a file, say an image, and store it into a *long raw* column in the database, or there might even be a need to do the opposite. The trick is to operate on 64 K chunks of data in a loop until the entire data transfer operation is completed. We present some sample code on UNIX to insert data into an Oracle *long raw* column. This code can be modified suitably to read from an Oracle column and store in a file.

```
/* This module reads data from the given file in 64K chunks and inserts it
into a long raw column in separate records */
#include <stdio.h>
#include <string.h>
```

```
#include <sys/types.h>
#include <sys/stat.h>
typedef char asciz[40];
typedef struct blob_struct
      {
        long len;              /* to hold actual length of data */
        char arr[65536];       /* a buffer for the data */
      } document;
EXEC SQL BEGIN DECLARE SECTION;
EXEC SQL TYPE asciz IS STRING(40) REFERENCE;
EXEC SQL TYPE document IS LONG VARRAW(65536);
asciz       userpwd, keyfield;
int         seqno, filesize, SQLCODE;
document     document_store;
EXEC SQL END DECLARE SECTION;
EXEC SQL INCLUDE sqlca;
FILE *fp;
long readdoc();     /* Read chunks from file into the array */
void sqlerror();    /* error handling      */
void main(argc, argv)
int argc;
char *argv[];
{
  char docname[60];
  struct stat buf;
  if ((argc !=2) && (argc !=3) && (argc !=4))
  {
    printf("\n Arguments are: username/password (docname) (keyfield)\n");
    exit(1);
  }
  strcpy(userpwd, argv[1]);
  EXEC SQL WHENEVER SQLERROR DO sqlerror();
  /* Login to Oracle */
  EXEC SQL CONNECT :userpwd;
  printf("Connected\n");
  if (argc>=3)
  {
    /* Document filename was specified on command line */
    strcpy(docname, argv[2]);
  }
  else
  {
    /* Document filename was not specified on command line */
    printf("Enter Filename:");
    gets(docname);
```

```
    }
    if (argc==4)
    {
      /* Document keyfield was specified on command line */
      strcpy(keyfield, argv[3]);
    }
    else
    {
      /* Document keyfield was not specified on command line */
      printf("Enter Keyfield (MUST be unique):");
      gets(keyfield);
    }
    if ((stat(docname, &buf))==-1)
    {
     printf("\nUnable to get file information\n");
     exit(1);
    }
    if ((fp = fopen(docname,"r"))==NULL)
    {
     printf("\nUnable to read file %s\n",docname);
     exit(1);
    }
    filesize=buf.st_size;
    printf("filesize is %d\n", filesize);
    seqno =1;
    while (filesize > 65536)
    {
      document_store.len = readdoc(document_store.arr, 65536);
      EXEC SQL INSERT INTO SOURCE_DOCS (KEYFIELD, SEQNO, DOC, FSIZE)
               VALUES (upper(:keyfield), :seqno, :document_store, 65536);
      filesize -= 65536;
      seqno++;
      printf("64K Inserted\n");
    }
    document_store.len = readdoc(document_store.arr, filesize);
    EXEC SQL INSERT INTO SOURCE_DOCS (KEYFIELD, SEQNO, DOC, FSIZE)
             VALUES (upper(:keyfield), :seqno, :document_store, :filesize);
    printf("%d bytes Inserted\n",filesize);
    EXEC SQL COMMIT WORK RELEASE;
    fclose(fp);
}   /* ends main */
long readdoc (doc_ptr, sizeofdoc)
char    *doc_ptr;
int     sizeofdoc;
{
```

```
    int someint;
    someint=fread(doc_ptr, sizeofdoc, 1, fp);
    printf("fread returned %d\n",someint);
    return sizeofdoc;
}
void sqlerror()
{
  EXEC SQL WHENEVER SQLERROR CONTINUE;
  printf("\n Unexpected Oracle error \n");
  printf("\n% .70s \n", sqlca.sqlerrm.sqlerrmc);
  EXEC SQL ROLLBACK WORK RELEASE;
  exit(1);
}
```

# C++ Compilers

Oracle does support C++ compilers with the newer versions of Pro*C. You can refer to the *Programmer's Guide to the Oracle Pro*C/C++ Precompiler* to obtain information on using C++ as your compiler.

Pro*C uses a system configuration file that can be used to specify all the command line options. You can specify options such as *code, sys_include,* and *parse* in this configuration file. For the location of the configuration file on your platform, type the **proc** command at the command prompt. For example, on our Sun Solaris 2.5 server we got the following output:

```
Pro*C/C++: Release 2.2.2.0.0 - Production on Fri Apr 25 10:17:51 1997
Copyright (c) Oracle Corporation 1979, 1994.  All rights reserved.
System default option values taken from:
/home3/oradata/app/oracle/product/7.3.2/precomp/admin/pcscfg.h
Option Name    Current Value  Description
-------------------------------------------------------------------------
asacc          no             use ASA carriage control formatting
auto_connect   no             allow automatic connection to ops$ account
code           kr_c           the type of code to be generated
comp_charset   multi_byte     the character set type the C compiler supports
config         default        override system configuration file with another
cpp_suffix     *none*         override the default C++ filename suffix
dbms           native         v6/v7 compatibility mode
def_sqlcode    no             generate '#define SQLCODE sqlca.sqlcode' macro
define         *none*         define a preprocessor symbol
errors         yes            the destination for error messages
```

```
fips              none      FIPS flagging of ANSI noncompliant usage
hold_cursor       no        control holding of cursors in the cursor cache
iname             *none*    the name of the input file
include           *none*    a directory path for included files
ireclen           80        the record length of the input file
lines             no        add #line directives to the generated code
lname             *none*    override default list file name
lreclen           132       the record length of the list file
ltype             none      the amount of data generated in the list file
maxliteral        1024      maximum length of a generated string literal
maxopencursors    10        maximum number of cached open cursors
mode              oracle    code conformance to Oracle or ANSI rules
nls_char          *none*    specify National Language character variables
nls_local         no        control how NLS character semantics are done
oname             *none*    the name of the output file
oraca             no        control the use of the ORACA
oreclen           80        the record length of the output file
pagelen           80        the page length of the list file
parse             full      control which non-SQL code is parsed
release_cursor    no        control release of cursors from cursor cache
select_error      yes       control flagging of select errors
sqlcheck          syntax    amount of compile-time SQL checking
sys_include       *none*    directory where system header files are found
test              no        reserved for internal use
threads           no        indicates a multi-threaded application
unsafe_null       no        Allow a NULL fetch without indicator variable
userid            *none*    a username/password [@dbname] connect string
varchar           no        allow the use of implicit varchar structures
xref              yes       include a cross-reference in the list file
```

Note the line immediately after the Oracle banner that indicates the name and location of the system configuration file.

As an alternative, you could also make some changes to the makefile provided by Oracle. We suggest that you make the following changes to a copy of the **proc.mk** file and not modify the original copy supplied by Oracle.

Add the following necessary precompiler options:

- CODE should be set to CPP:

  ```
  code=cpp
  ```

- SYS_INCLUDE needs to be set to the directory for the C++ *include* files. For example, on Sun SPARC Solaris 2.x you can use:

  ```
  sys_include=/opt/SUNWspro/SC4.0/include/CC
  ```

- PARSE should be set to PARTIAL or NONE:

  ```
  parse=none
  ```

- Finally, you must ensure that you edit the **proc.mk** file to provide the full path to your **cc** file:

  ```
  CC=<the path to your C++ compiler>
  ```

(e.g. CC=/u1/lang/CC --- Note the use of CC for compilation of C++ programs.)

Most operating systems also allow you to set an environment variable called *CC* that points to your compiler. You could alternatively use this environment variable if you do not wish to edit your **proc.mk** file.

For more information, see the *Programmer's Guide to the Oracle Pro*C/C++ Precompiler Release 2.1.*

# Supported Compilers

After pre-compilation, you will still need to use a standard compiler (and linker) on your operating system to create an executable. Oracle precompilers are supported with specific versions of compilers on each operating system. Be sure to refer to your installation guide for these requirements. These requirements do change quite frequently. In Tables 10-3 through 10-11, we present information that we have compiled for some common operating systems.

| Oracle Precompiler | Supported Compiler |
| --- | --- |
| Pro*C 1.6.x | VAX C 3.2-05 |
| Pro*C 2.x | VAX C 3.1+ |
| Pro*C 2.1.x | VAX C 3.2-05 |
| Pro*COBOL 1.6.x | VAX COBOL 5.1-10 |
| Pro*FORTRAN 1.6.x | FORTRAN 6.0-1 |
| Pro*Ada 1.6.x | VAX ADA 2.3-2 |
| Pro*Pascal 1.6.x | VAX Pascal 4.4-89 |
| Pro*PL/1 1.6.x | VAX PL/1 3.5-124 |

**TABLE 10-3.**   *Supported Compilers on DEC VAX/VMS*

| Oracle Precompiler | Supported Compiler |
| --- | --- |
| Pro*C 1.6.x | DEC C 4.0-000 |
| Pro*C 2.x | DEC C 4.0-000 |
| Pro*C 2.1.x | DEC C 4.0-000 |
| Pro*C 2.2.x | DEC C 5.3 |
| Pro*COBOL 1.6.x | DEC COBOL 2.0-271 |
| Pro*COBOL 1.8.x | DEC COBOL 2.3 |
| Pro*FORTRAN 1.6.x | DEC FORTRAN 6.2 |
| Pro*Ada 1.6.x | DEC ADA 3.0A-7 |
| Pro*Pascal 1.6.x | DEC Pascal 5.2-19-274F |
| Pro*PL/1 1.6.x | DEC PL/I 4.0-5 |

**TABLE 10-4.** *Supported Compilers on DEC Alpha VMS*

| Oracle Precompiler | Supported Compiler |
| --- | --- |
| Pro*C 1.6.x | Sun C Compiler |
| Pro*C 2.x | Sun C Compiler |
| Pro*C 2.1.x | Sun C Compiler |
| Pro*C 2.2.x | Sun C Compiler |
| Pro*COBOL 1.6.x and 1.8.x | Micro Focus COBOL/2 1.2 and COBOL/3 3.0 |
| Pro*FORTRAN 1.6.x - 1.8.x | FORTRAN77 Compiler 1.0 FORTRAN77 Compiler 1.4 |
| Pro*Ada 1.6.x - 1.8.x | Sun Ada Compiler 1.1 |
| Pro*Pascal and Pro*PL/1 are not available | |

**TABLE 10-5.** *Supported Compilers on Sun SPARC SunOS 4.1.x*

| Oracle Precompiler | Supported Compiler |
|---|---|
| Pro*C 1.6.4 | SPARCworks C Compiler 2.0.1 and 3.0 |
| Pro*C 1.6.5 - 1.6.9 | SPARCworks C Compiler 3.0.1 |
| Pro*C 2.0.x | SPARCworks C Compiler 3.0.1 and 4.0 |
| Pro*C 2.1.x | SPARCworks C++ Compiler 4.0.1 and 4.1 |
| Pro*COBOL 1.6.5 - 1.8.x | Micro Focus COBOL/3 V3.2 and Sun Nihongo COBOL 1.0.1 |
| Pro*FORTRAN 1.6.x | FORTRAN77 Compiler 3.0 |
| Pro*FORTRAN 1.7.x - 1.8.x | FORTRAN77 Compiler 3.0.1 |
| Pro*Ada 1.6.x - 1.8.x | Sun Ada Compiler 2.1 |
| Pro*Pascal and Pro*PL/1 are not available | |

**TABLE 10-6.**   *Supported Compilers on Sun SPARC Solaris 2.x*

| Oracle Precompiler | Supported Compiler |
|---|---|
| Pro*C 1.6.7 | XL C 1.3 AIX 3.2.5<br>C Set++ 3.1 AIX 4.1.2 |
| Pro*C 2.0.x | XL C 1.3 AIX 3.2.5<br>C Set++ 3.1 AIX 4.1.2 |
| Pro*C 2.1.x - 2.2.x | XL C 1.3 AIX 3.2.5<br>C Set++ 3.1 AIX 4.1.2 |
| Pro*COBOL 1.6 - 1.7 | Micro Focus COBOL 3.2 |
| Pro*COBOL 1.8 | Micro Focus COBOL 4.0 |
| Pro*FORTRAN 1.6 - 1.8 | XL FORTRAN |
| Pro*Ada 1.6.7 - 1.8.x | Verdix Ada 6.2 |
| Pro*Pascal and Pro*PL/1 are not available | |

**TABLE 10-7.**   *Supported Compilers on IBM AIX*

| Oracle Precompiler | Supported Compiler |
|---|---|
| Pro*C 1.6.4 | HP C 9.34 |
| Pro*C 1.6.5 - 1.6.7 | HP C 9.69 |
| | HP C 10.0 |
| Pro*C 1.6.8 - 1.6.9 | HP C 09.76 |
| Pro*C 2.0.x | HP C 9.69, 10.0x |
| Pro*C 2.1.x | HP C 09.76 and 10.10 |
| Pro*C 2.2.x | HP C 10.13 |
| Pro*COBOL 1.6.5 - 1.6.6 | HP COBOL/UX B.07.50 |
| | HP COBOL/UX B.09.x |
| Pro*COBOL 1.7.x | HP COBOL/UX B.08.15 |
| Pro*COBOL 1.6.7 | HP COBOL/UX B.09.15 |
| Pro*FORTRAN 1.6.x | HP FORTRAN77 9.0 |
| Pro*FORTRAN 1.7.x - 1.8.x | HP FORTRAN77 10.0 |
| Pro*Ada 1.6.x - 1.7.x | Alsys Ada 5.5.1 |
| Pro*Ada 1.8.x | Alsys AdaWorld 5.5.5 |
| Pro*Pascal 1.6.x - 1.8.x | HP Pascal 9.12 |
| | HP Pascal 10.0x |
| Pro*PL/1 is not available | |

**TABLE 10-8.**  *Supported Compilers on HP-UX*

| Oracle Precompiler | Supported Compiler |
|---|---|
| Pro*C 1.4.x - 1.5.x | Microsoft Visual C++ 1.0 and 1.5 |
| | Borland 4.0 |
| Pro*C 2.0.x | Microsoft Visual C++ 1.5 |
| Pro*COBOL 1.6.5 | Micro Focus COBOL 3.2.20 |
| Pro*FORTRAN, Pro*Pascal, Pro*Ada, and Pro*PL/1 are not available | |

**TABLE 10-9.**  *Supported Compilers on Windows 3.1*

| Oracle Precompiler | Supported Compiler |
|---|---|
| Pro*C 2.1.x | Microsoft Visual C++ 2.2 and 4.0 |
| Pro*C 2.2.x | Microsoft Visual C++ 4.0 / 4.1 and Borland |
| Pro*COBOL 1.7.x | Micro Focus COBOL 3.3 and 4.0 |
| Pro*COBOL 1.8.x | Micro Focus COBOL 4.0 |
| Pro*FORTRAN, Pro*Pascal, Pro*Ada, and Pro*PL/1 are not available | |

**TABLE 10-10.** *Supported Compilers on Windows 95*

| Oracle Precompiler | Supported Compiler |
|---|---|
| Pro*C 2.1.x | Microsoft Visual C++ 2.2 |
| Pro*C 2.2.1.x | Microsoft Visual C++ 4.0 and 4.1 |
| Pro*C 2.2.2.x | Microsoft Visual C++ 4.2 and Borland 5.0 |
| Pro*COBOL 1.7.x | Micro Focus COBOL 3.3 and 4.0 |
| Pro*COBOL 1.8.x | Micro Focus COBOL 4.0 |
| Pro*FORTRAN, Pro*Pascal, Pro*Ada, and Pro*PL/1 are not available | |

**TABLE 10-11.** *Supported Compilers on Windows NT*

# Frequently Asked Questions (FAQ)

**Q.** How do I embed a PL/SQL block in the source code?

**A.** A PL/SQL block can be treated as one SQL statement. You can enclose an entire PL/SQL block into one embedded *EXEC SQL* statement as shown below:

```
EXEC SQL EXECUTE

    <your PL/SQL block>

END-EXEC
```

You need to include the statement terminator for your language after END-EXEC.

**Q.** What kind of data types can I use in my programs?

**A.** You can use both *internal* and *external* data types. Internal data types are Oracle data types as used in the definition of columns (*VARCHAR*, *NUMBER*, etc.). External data types are those that can be defined in your host language (such as *int* and *float* in the C language).

**Q.** What is SQLCA? Is it always necessary?

**A.** *SQLCA* (SQL Communication Area) is a structure that is included to trap errors and warnings from your programs. Information such as status codes, warning flags, error messages, the count of rows processed is available in the SQLCA. You can include SQLCA in your programs by using the syntax:

```
EXEC SQL INCLUDE SQLCA;
```

You could also use the native language *include* statement:

```
#include <sqlca.h>
```

You could use *SQLCODE* or *SQLSTATE* instead of SQLCA, but you must use SQLCA if you want to obtain the error message as well as the error number.

**Q.**   Often times, I get warnings during the compile stage when I try to assign to a VARCHAR pointer. I have also seen other warnings when I use string functions like *strcpy( )*. I know these are warnings, but how do I get rid of these?

**A.**   These types of warnings are harmless, but if you really want to get rid of them, then you can do so with a little work. We will illustrate a fix that should work with an example for Pro*C. Assume that you have the following declaration in a Pro*C program:

```
varchar *empname;
varchar ename[15];
```

After precompilation, you should see these declarations converted to:

```
struct {unsigned short len; unsigned char arr[1];} *empname;
struct {unsigned short len; unsigned char arr[15];} ename;
```

You will get a warning if you attempt the following assignment:

```
empname = &ename;
```

Declare a structure, say *x*, as shown below.

```
struct {unsigned short len; unsigned char * arr;} x;
```

You can now use the following assignment:

```
(struct x *) empname = (struct x *) &ename;
```

Other common warnings seen are in situations where functions like *strcpy( )* and *strlen( )* are used. Both strcpy( ) and strlen( ) expect an argument of type *char *  * and not *unsigned char *  *. You can provide explicit type casting to get around such warnings. We provide an example below to illustrate this:

```
strcpy(ename.arr, "John Doe");
```

can be rewritten as

```
strcpy((char *)ename.arr, "John Doe");
```

**Q.**   I get an error *ld: fatal: Symbol referencing errors* while linking my program. How do I find out where the missing symbols are defined?

**A.** It is fairly common to run into errors that are caused by the linker's failure to resolve an external reference. You will see an error similar to:

```
Undefined symbol          first referenced  in file
sqlcex                    sample.o
sqlglm                    sample.o
ld: fatal: Symbol referencing errors. No output written to sample.
```

The solution for such errors is to find the library that contains the definition of the missing symbols and make sure that the linker can find these libraries. On UNIX, you can use the **nm** utility to find libraries containing missing symbols.

```
% cd $ORACLE_HOME/lib
% nm * | grep sqlcex
```

It is useful to remember that symbols that start with *sql* (such as those above) will always mean that *sqllib* (*libsql.a* on UNIX) was missing from the link list. This is the most common omission from our experience.

On some platforms, Oracle provides a utility called **symfind** that will allow you to track down missing symbols. Look in the $ORACLE_HOME/bin directory for this utility.

**Q.** My executable is too big. Is there something I can do about the size of the executable?
**A.** This is a problem that is reported by many users. The Oracle libraries contain a lot of comments that can be stripped in order to reduce the size of the executable. You must refer to the documentation of your linker to find the command or utility available to strip comments. On some UNIX platforms, you can use the command **mcs** as shown below:

```
% mcs -d myprog.exe
```

**Q.** I want to use shared libraries. Can I link with shared libraries?
**A.** On some platforms, Oracle does allow you to link using the shared library **libclntsh.so**. This facility is available starting with Oracle Version 7.3. You can consult your *UNIX Administrators Guide* to get complete information on this facility. A makefile called **clntsh.mk** is provided to create the shared library. An environment variable called ORA_CLIENT_LIB is required to link shared libraries.

**Q.**   Does Oracle provide sample programs that I can use to build my program?
**A.**   Oracle does provide sample programs and makefiles that you can use to create your own programs. In Oracle Versions 7.2 or earlier, a separate directory was created for each precompiler that contained sample programs and makefiles. Programmers had to create a copy of the makefile provided for each precompiler, and edit it. In Version 7.3, Oracle has created a precomp directory that contains a sub-directory called demo for sample programs. There are also two makefiles provided. A makefile called **env_precomp.mk** is provided in the $ORACLE_HOME/precomp directory. This file is intended to be included in any makefiles written by programmers. A second makefile specific to the precompiler is provided in the $ORACLE_HOME/precomp/demo/pro<lang> directory. For example a file called **proc.mk** is available in the $ORACLE_HOME/precomp/demo/proc directory.

In Version 7.3, there is no need to edit the **env_precomp.mk** file. You can override any settings by using flags in your copy of the **pro<lang>.mk** makefile.

**Q.**   I get an error, *ora-01002: fetch out of sequence*, in my program. How do I solve this?
**A.**   This error is reported when you attempt to fetch from a cursor when the cursor is no longer valid. A common cause for this is that you have attempted to fetch data beyond the point where data is available. If you are using a loop to fetch data, you must always check to see if the fetch returned any data. If it did not, you must terminate the loop.

Another common cause for this error is when you have issued a SELECT FOR UPDATE and you are attempting a fetch across commits. The following code illustrates this situation:

```
DECLARE
        EMP_NAME EMP.ENAME%TYPE;
        CURSOR C1 IS SELECT ENAME FROM EMP FOR UPDATE OF SAL;
    BEGIN
        OPEN C1;
        LOOP
            FETCH C1 INTO EMP_NAME;
            UPDATE EMP SET SAL = 50;
            COMMIT;
        END LOOP;
```

```
        CLOSE C1;
     END;
```

In this example, the program obtains locks on the records to be updated when the cursor is opened. When you issue the COMMIT (or a ROLLBACK) inside the loop, the locks are released and the cursor becomes invalid. A FETCH issued after this point in time will result in an ORA-1002. To resolve this problem, move the COMMIT outside the loop.

**Q.** What is Programmer/2000? Do I need this to create my programs?
**A.** Programmer/2000 is a product bundle that contains all 3GL Programmatic Interfaces available on a particular platform. The contents of the Programmer/2000 depends on the platform. However, on most platforms it will contain the Oracle Call Interface (OCI), Oracle Precompilers, and SQL*Module. On some desktop operating systems like Windows 3.1, it also contains other software like the Oracle ODBC Driver. If you want to use Oracle precompilers or OCI, you might need to purchase Programmer/2000 for your platform. Sometimes, the precompiler of your choice or OCI might be available with the Oracle7 Server media. However, you might still be required to purchase an additional license to use these products.

# CHAPTER
## 11

Interacting with
Oracle Worldwide
Customer Support

Throughout this book, we have looked at some practical troubleshooting techniques to help you get started with Oracle products on a variety of operating systems. While we hope that the information in this book helps you solve a good portion of the problems, we realize that we have definitely not solved all of them. In this chapter we provide information and tips that should help you interact effectively with Oracle Worldwide Customer Support. We have summarized this information from our combined 12 years of experience with the Oracle Worldwide Customer Support organization.

# About Oracle Worldwide Customer Support

Oracle Worldwide Customer Support (WWCS) provides total support for Oracle products and your business around the world through a network of 93 local support centers and four supercenters. A variety of services are available to an Oracle customer 24 hours a day, seven days a week. These services include telephone assistance, product updates and patches, electronic services, subscription to the *Oracle SupportNotes* and alerts, just to name a few.

There are several programs available, and each program allows you access to a set of services. Be sure to sign up for a program that suits your business needs. A brief description of the different levels of support offered by WWCS is given below. Please refer to the World-wide Web site *http://www.oracle.com/support/html/services.html* for details.

## Oraclemetals

Oracle knows that no two organizations or applications environments are exactly alike and has therefore designed Oraclemetals with the flexibility to meet individual customer requirements. All Oraclemetals support services have been designed with the same set of core components. So whether BRONZE, SILVER, or the highest level, GOLD, is chosen, customers can be assured their investment in Oracle software is maintained with online information services, as well as problem fixes, maintenance releases, and a comprehensive upgrade service.

## Oraclefoundation

Incorporating a highly configurable set of options, the Oraclefoundation support program has been specifically designed to address customer support requirements for installation assistance, infrequent telephone support needs, and electronic support for around-the-clock service.

# Oracle Product Information

Keep the complete version information of the Oracle product(s) that you have installed. It is always best to provide WWCS with the RDBMS version, client-tool version, and SQL*Net version. You can obtain this information readily by looking at the Oracle registration file on your computer. The name of the file varies with the operating system. On Desktop and UNIX systems, the extension of this file is always **.rgs** and it resides in the **orainst** subdirectory of your Oracle Home. In OpenVMS, the file has a **.TXT** extension and resides in the UTIL subdirectory under your Oracle root directory. Table 11-1 provides the location of the registration file on major operating systems.

The registration file is always a text file and therefore it can be printed readily. In addition to the registration file, there can be some configuration files used by your Oracle product that you should be familiar with. For example, SQL*Net uses files such as **LISTENER.ORA, SQLNET.ORA** and **TNSNAMES.ORA.**

If you have not completed your installation, then locate the files with an extension **.PRD** on your installation media. These files will contain version

| Operating System | Location |
| --- | --- |
| Windows 3.1 | C:\ORAWIN\ORAINST\**WINDOWS.RGS** |
| Windows 95 | C:\ORAWIN95\ORAINST\**WIN95.RGS** |
| Windows NT | C:\ORANT\ORAINST\**NT.RGS** |
| UNIX | $ORACLE_HOME\orainst\**unix.rgs** |
| VAX/VMS | ORA_ROOT:[UTIL]**PRODUCTS.TXT** |

**TABLE 11-1.**   *Location of Oracle Product Registration File on Major Operating Systems*

information on the products available on that media. These files should be located in a directory called **INSTALL** or **ORAINST** on your media. These files are named according to operating system; **WINDOWS.PRD** on Windows 3.1, **WIN95.PRD** on Windows 95, **unix.prd** on UNIX, and so on.

# Operating System Information

In addition to information on your Oracle installation, it is important to have configuration information on your Operating System and Hardware itself. We provide a listing of the information on a range of operating systems to give you an idea of what type of information is useful to Oracle WWCS.

## General Information for Personal Computers

There is a wide variety of PCs and peripherals available in the market today. It is helpful to provide some information on your hardware. Do not spend too much time collecting hardware information as some of it might be rather difficult to obtain. Try to do the best you can to find the following:

- Manufacturer/vendor of machine
- Manufacturer of motherboard
- CPU (make, type, and clock speed)
- Amount of physical RAM
- Motherboard bus types (ISA, EISA, PCI, ...)
- Disk controller type (SCSI, IDE, EIDE, ...)
- Disk controller manufacturer (Adaptec, Buslogic, ...)
- Disk controller model (AHA154x, BT742A, ...)
- Disk drive information (for all drives):
  - Manufacturer(s)
  - Model(s)
  - Capacity

- Make and model of network card

- Make and model of video card

- Display driver

- Screen resolution

- Colors displayed

- Printer and printer driver

- Mouse and mouse driver

- Other peripherals (sound card, joysticks, etc.)

In addition to the above hardware information, we will now list some specific information for some of the PC-based operating systems.

## Windows 3.1

We will assume that C:\ is the *root* directory on your PC, that Windows 3.1 is installed in C:\WINDOWS, and that Oracle products for Windows 3.1 are installed in C:\ORAWIN. Here is a listing of files that are useful to Oracle WWCS:

| | |
|---|---|
| C:\**CONFIG.SYS** | C:\WINDOWS\**ORACLE.INI** |
| C:\**AUTOEXEC.BAT** | C:\WINDOWS\**ODBC.INI** |
| C:\WINDOWS\**WIN.INI** | C:\WINDOWS\**VSL.INI** |
| C:\WINDOWS\**SYSTEM.INI** | C:\ORAWIN\ORAINST\**WINDOWS.RGS** |

If you are calling other batch files (files with an extension of **.BAT**) from the **AUTOEXEC.BAT**, be sure to include a listing of those files. Some of the files above might not be available, depending on the products that you have installed. In any case, if any of the above files are not available on your PC do make a mention of it.

In addition to the above files, some information on the environment is useful. You can collect this information easily into files as shown below (the **MAP** command is for Novell Netware clients only):

```
C:\ SET > ENV.TXT
C:\ MEM/C > MORE.TXT
C:\ MAP > MAP.TXT
```

It is also useful to provide information on some related software. Below is listed some common software and related information:

- Make and version of DOS
- Windows 3.1 or Windows for Workgroups 3.11
- Windows shell (Program Manager, Norton Desktop, Dashboard, etc.)
- Network software vendor (FTP, Novell, Microsoft, etc.)
- Network file server (Novell, Windows NT, etc.)

You can get useful information about your PC by running C:\WINDOWS\**MSD.EXE** or C:\WINDOWS\**SETUP.EXE**.

## Windows 95

We will assume that C:\ is the root directory on your PC, that Windows 95 is installed in C:\WINDOWS, and that Oracle products for Windows 95 are installed in C:\ORAWIN95. Here is a listing of files that are useful to Oracle WWCS:

C:\**CONFIG.SYS**               C:\WINDOWS\**SYSTEM.INI**
C:\**AUTOEXEC.BAT**             C:\ORAWIN95\ORAINST\**WIN95.RGS**
C:\WINDOWS\**WIN.INI**

If you are calling other batch files (files with an extension of **.BAT**) from the **AUTOEXEC.BAT**, be sure to include a listing of those files.

In addition to the above files, some information on the environment is useful. You can collect this information easily into files as shown below (the **MAP** command is for Novell Netware clients only):

```
C:\ SET > ENV.TXT
C:\ MEM/C > MORE.TXT
C:\ MAP > MAP.TXT
C:\ VER > VER.TXT
```

You can also include an export file of your Windows registry. Run **regedit** and expand HKEY_LOCAL_MACHINES|SOFTWARE|ORACLE. Now select File|Export Registry File and provide that file to WWCS.

It is also useful to provide information on any software that you are using for your networking.

## Windows NT

Most of the information for Windows 95 applies to Windows NT. We will assume that C:\ is the root directory on your PC and that Windows NT is installed in C:\WINNT and Oracle products for Windows NT are installed in C:\ORANT. Here is a listing of files that are useful to Oracle WWCS:

C:\**CONFIG.SYS**             C:\WINNT\**SYSTEM.INI**

C:\**AUTOEXEC.BAT**          C:\ORANT\ORAINST\**NT.RGS**

C:\WINNT\**WIN.INI**

If you are calling other batch files (files with an extension of **.BAT**) from the **AUTOEXEC.BAT**, be sure to include a listing of those files.

In addition to the above files, some information on the environment is useful. You can collect this information easily into files as shown below (the **MAP** command is for Novell Netware clients only):

```
C:\ SET > ENV.TXT
C:\ MEM/C > MORE.TXT
C:\ MAP > MAP.TXT
C:\ VER > VER.TXT
```

You can also include an export file of your Windows registry. Run **regedit** and expand HKEY_LOCAL_MACHINES|SOFTWARE|ORACLE. Now select File|Export Registry File and provide that file to WWCS. If you are getting some errors in the event log, you can provide such information by using the Windows NT event viewer.

It is also useful to provide information on any software that you are using for your networking.

# General Information for UNIX-Based Computers

The most important information on UNIX relates to the environment. You should always be aware of the environment in which you run an Oracle product. We have seen many calls come in to Oracle WWCS that are simply solved by adding or changing the setting of an environment variable. Get a listing of your environment in a file by executing

```
% env > env.txt
```

Pay special attention to the environment variable ORACLE_HOME. It is of paramount importance and is used by almost all Oracle products.

A lot of other issues on UNIX relate to permissions for files. Always be aware of the user information (Oracle owner), the group information (dba group), and permissions for files under ORACLE_HOME.

You should keep a record of the operating system version information and the patches applied to your operating system. On Sun SPARC Solaris 2.x, you can use the **pkginfo** or **showrev** commands to get this kind of information.

A lot of database performance issues are related to the load on your machine. Be aware of performance trends on your machine. You can use commands like **vmstat** and **sar** to get a detailed report on memory and swap usage on your machine. Obviously, the Oracle parameter file, **init.ora**, plays a large role in the performance of your database. Keep a hard copy of this for reference.

# General Information for VAX or ALPHA OpenVMS Systems

There are two .COM files that you are supposed to run which will set up your environment on OpenVMS. All the necessary logicals are defined in these files. These files are **ORAUSER_*SID*.COM** and **ORA_DB_*SID*.COM.** The first file sets your Oracle home directory and Oracle SID logicals. The logical ORA_ROOT sets your Oracle home and the logical ORA_SID sets your SID. Make sure these logicals are always defined. At the OpenVMS prompt, you can verify this by using the following command:

```
$ show logical ora_root
```

The second file, **ORA_DB_*SID*.COM,** sets some important logicals such as ORA_DB, ORA_PARAMS and ORA_CONTROL*. These logicals point to the database directory, the **INIT.ORA** file and the control files respectively.

If you want to monitor a specific process, you can use the following commands:

Do remember that it is better to provide an overkill of information rather than inadequate information. At the same time, you have to strike a balance in the amount of time you spend trying to collect this information.

## Tip 5: Ensure that Relevant Individuals Are Available

When you contact Oracle WWCS, ensure that all relevant site administrators are available. Many times, especially on larger systems, it might be necessary to have the Oracle Database Administrator, the UNIX System Administrator, the Network Administrator, the Application developer, and even management available. It is best to provide all information required by WWCS in one call. You can waste a lot of time playing phone-tag with Oracle WWCS if you are unable to provide all assistance to the WWCS analyst when you have him or her on the line.

## Tip 6: Provide Accurate Error Messages and Symptoms

It is amazing how many times customers call Oracle WWCS and are unable to provide an accurate description of the symptoms and error messages. An accurate description of the issue can go a long way toward getting an accurate answer from WWCS. Statements such as "*I was running Oracle and I got some error message*", or "*Oracle is not working*" are not very useful in such situations. Remember, by providing accurate error numbers and error messages, you are helping WWCS diagnose the problem promptly and accurately.

## Tip 7: Provide Test Cases

Many a time, it is very difficult to describe the problem that you are having over a telephone or through FAX. In such situations, a *test case* is extremely useful. A test case is simply a collection of files, modules, steps, or trace files that describe your problem. Oracle WWCS has many tools available that allow its analysts to diagnose the problem quickly and accurately for most customers. Below we present some guidelines for test cases that will help Oracle WWCS provide you with better service.

You should first try to reproduce the problem using a standard Oracle schema such as *SCOTT* with one of the standard demo tables such as *EMP* and *DEPT*. If you can create a reproducible test case with standard Oracle objects, there is no need for you to send your own application to Oracle.

If you do have to send your own application, provide a minimal reproducible test case. Do not send a large application as a test case if you can avoid it. An Oracle WWCS analyst will take more time to understand large test cases. Remember that the Oracle analyst knows very little about your application compared to you. It would be ideal if you could localize the problem to a specific action or transaction, if possible. Of course, in some cases, the size of the application (number of inserts or updates, etc.) does make a difference in reproducing the problem.

Ensure that external dependencies are met. If you are invoking another module or program from your application, be sure to include that in your test case. You might need to provide an export file of some database objects used by your application.

Provide a **README** file with your test case that includes explicit step-by-step instructions on your test case. Include information on your application environment (operating system information, RDBMS version, SQL*Net versions, etc.). It is best to assume that the Oracle WWCS analyst knows nothing about your application and provide superfluous information rather than leave out some important details.

Be sure to include your contact information and also a *Technical Assistance Request* (TAR) number along with your test case and address it to the right group or contact at Oracle WWCS.

## Tip 8: Track Your Problem

Oracle WWCS assigns a TAR number (some countries use a PMS number) to every problem reported to them. Be sure to keep this TAR number with you and reference it every time you contact WWCS with the same issue. If you have many issues, Oracle WWCS will create different TARs for each of these issues; this allows for better tracking from both sides.

# Frequently Asked Questions (FAQ)

**Q.**  I get a TAR number every time I call Oracle WWCS. What is this TAR number?

**A.**  Oracle WWCS maintains a customer support database to track all issues reported by customers. When you call in with a new problem, a new record is created in this database. Each record, or *Technical Assistance Request* (TAR), is identified by a unique number. A status code is assigned to every TAR at various stages and when the issue is resolved the TAR is considered *closed.*

**Q.**  How is the CSI number different from a TAR number?

**A.**  A *Customer Support Identification* (CSI) number is assigned to every Oracle customer who has purchased a customer support contract. Oracle WWCS tracks the level of support, customer information and the products supported using the CSI number. When you call WWCS with a new issue, you will be asked for the CSI number. A new TAR is created for you after this CSI number is validated by the system.

**Q.**  How about bugs? What do I do if I encounter a bug?

**A.**  If you believe that you are encountering a bug in Oracle software, it is important that you report it to Oracle irrespective of the impact on your business. Oracle Corporation is continually attempting to improve the quality of its software. Bugs reported by customers are helpful in identifying problems with the software. Remember, no bug is too small or trivial to fix.

**Q.**  How do I report bugs?

**A.**  Your local Oracle Support Center is your link to Oracle Development. A support analyst will take the details regarding your problem. If the bug is causing you loss of functionality, the analyst will attempt to offer a suggestion or workaround to circumvent the issue, and convey the details of the bug to the concerned Oracle product development team.

**Q.**  What should I do before reporting a bug?

**A.**  Some good questions to ask yourself before calling Oracle Worldwide Customer Support to file a bug are listed here.

- Is the problem reproducible?

- Has the errant behavior occurred consistently in your application?

- If not, what has changed since the time that it worked?

- Does the situation change if you remove or comment out this newly added functionality?

- Do you still have a copy of the previously working version to compare with the current one?

- Did this work in a previous release of the product?

**Q.** What happens after a bug is reported?
**A.** All software bugs, documentation bugs, and enhancement requests are tracked in the Oracle Bug Database. If the support analyst is able to reproduce the problem you report with the information you provide, and that problem has not been previously reported, a record of the problem will be logged in the system and it will be assigned a tracking number (bug number). You will be notified automatically when the bug is resolved or a suitable workaround has been established. In fact, if you have access to the Oracle Bug Database, you can monitor the progress of your bug yourself.

**Q.** Why does Oracle WWCS have such a complicated phone system? I get completely lost in the maze of options.
**A.** Oracle WWCS has many groups that consist of analysts with expertise in specific areas. The groups are organized by product area and also by operating system. In order to cover the large *variety* of problems that are reported to WWCS, it is necessary to program the telephone system such that you are routed to the group that can help you the best. Spend a few minutes to identify the problem area before calling Oracle WWCS. This will help you reach the correct group the first time and you will not be transferred to other groups. This will also maximize your chances of getting a correct response the very first time.

**Q.** What are my options to get help from Oracle support? Is online support available?
**A.** Oracle WWCS has many services tailored for a variety of needs. A wide variety of electronic services are available. You should have information on the services available to you with your support contract. If you are not sure of the options available to you, you should talk to the

Oracle marketing representative. You can also visit the Oracle Worldwide Customer Support web pages using the URL *http://www.oracle.com* for complete information.

You can visit *http://support.oracle.com* for an example of online support available.

**Q.**   Is there any way for me to look at my TARs and bugs?

**A.**   While Oracle WWCS maintains great deal of confidentiality with customer data, it allows you to access their system to see only those TARs that were filed by you. You can monitor the progress and also edit the TAR information. The Oracle Bug Database is also available to customers under some support schemes. You should contact Oracle WWCS Marketing for detailed information on the options available in your country.

# INDEX

**D**

# P

# X

# Get Your **FREE** Subscription to Oracle Magazine

Stay informed and increase your productivity with every issue of *Oracle Magazine*. Inside each FREE, bimonthly issue, you'll get:

- Up-to-date information on the Oracle RDBMS and software tools

- Third-party software and hardware products

- Technical articles on Oracle platforms and operating environments

- Software tuning tips

- Oracle client application stories

## Three easy ways to subscribe:

**1** **MAIL:** Cut out this page, complete the questionnaire on the back, and mail to: *Oracle Magazine,* 500 Oracle Parkway, Box 659952, Redwood Shores, CA 94065.

**2** **FAX:** Cut out this page, complete the questionnaire on the back, and and fax the questionnaire to **+ 415.633.2424.**

**3** **WEB:** Visit our Web site at **www.oramag.com.** You'll find a subscription form there, plus much more!

If there are other Oracle users at your location who would like to receive their own copy of *Oracle Magazine,* please photocopy the form on the back, and pass it along.

# ☐ YES! Please send me a FREE subscription to Oracle Magazine.    ☐ NO, I am not interested at this time.

If you wish to receive your free bimonthly subscription to *Oracle Magazine,* you must fill out the entire form, sign it, and date it (incomplete forms cannot be processed or acknowledged). You can also subscribe at our Web Site at **http://www.oramag.com/html/subform.html** or fax your application to *Oracle Magazine* at **+415.633.2424.**

**SIGNATURE (REQUIRED)** ✓ _____    **DATE** _____

NAME _____    TITLE _____

COMPANY _____

STREET/P.O. BOX _____

CITY/STATE/ZIP _____

COUNTRY _____    TELEPHONE _____

# You must answer all eight of the questions below.

**1 What is the primary business activity of your firm at this location?** *(circle only one)*
- 01. Agriculture, Mining, Natural Resources
- 02. Communications Services, Utilities
- 03. Computer Consulting, Training
- 04. Computer, Data Processing Service
- 05. Computer Hardware, Software, Systems
- 06. Education—Primary, Secondary, College, University
- 07. Engineering, Architecture, Construction
- 08. Financial, Banking, Real Estate, Insurance
- 09. Government—Federal/Military
- 10. Government—Federal/Nonmilitary
- 11. Government—Local, State, Other
- 12. Health Services, Health Institutions
- 13. Manufacturing—Aerospace, Defense
- 14. Manufacturing—Noncomputer Products, Goods
- 15. Public Utilities (Electric, Gas, Sanitation)
- 16. Pure and Applied Research & Development
- 17. Retailing, Wholesaling, Distribution
- 18. Systems Integrator, VAR, VAD, OEM
- 19. Transportation
- 20. Other Business and Services ____

**2 Which of the following best describes your job function?** *(circle only one)*
**CORPORATE MANAGEMENT/STAFF**
- 01. Executive Management (President, Chair, CEO, CFO, Owner, Partner, Principal, Managing Director)
- 02. Finance/Administrative Management (VP/Director/Manager/Controller of Finance, Purchasing, Administration)
- 03. Other Finance/Administration Staff
- 04. Sales/Marketing Management (VP/Director/Manager of Sales/Marketing)
- 05. Other Sales/Marketing Staff

**TECHNICAL MANAGEMENT/STAFF**
- 06. Computer/Communications Systems Development/Programming Management
- 07. Computer/Communications Systems Development/Programming Staff
- 08. Computer Systems/Operations Management (CIO/VP/Director/Manager MIS, Operations, etc.)
- 09. Consulting
- 10. DBA/Systems Administrator
- 11. Education/Training
- 12. Engineering/R&D/Science Management
- 13. Engineering/R&D/Science Staff
- 14. Technical Support Director/Manager
- 15. Other Technical Management/Staff

_____

**3 What is your current primary operating system environment?** *(circle all that apply)*

| | |
|---|---|
| 01. AIX | 12. Solaris/Sun OS |
| 02. HP-UX | 13. SVR4 |
| 03. Macintosh OS | 14. Ultrix |
| 04. MPE-ix | 15. UnixWare |
| 05. MS-DOS | 16. Other UNIX |
| 06. MVS | 17. VAX VMS |
| 07. NetWare | 18. VM |
| 08. OpenVMS | 19. Windows |
| 09. OS/2 | 20. Windows NT |
| 10. OS/400 | 21. Other _____ |
| 11. SCO | _____ |

**4 What is your current primary hardware environment?** *(circle all that apply)*
- 01. Macintosh
- 02. Mainframe
- 03. Massively Parallel Processing
- 04. Minicomputer
- 05. PC (IBM-Compatible)
- 06. Supercomputer
- 07. Symmetric Multiprocessing
- 08. Workstation
- 09. Other _____

**5 In your job, do you use or plan to purchase any of the following products or services** *(check all that apply)*

**SOFTWARE**

| | Use | Plan to buy |
|---|---|---|
| 01. Accounting/Finance | ☐ | ☐ |
| 02. Business Graphics | ☐ | ☐ |
| 03. CAD/CAE/CAM | ☐ | ☐ |
| 04. CASE | ☐ | ☐ |
| 05. CIM | ☐ | ☐ |
| 06. Communications/Networking | ☐ | ☐ |
| 07. Database Management | ☐ | ☐ |
| 08. Education | ☐ | ☐ |
| 09. File Management | ☐ | ☐ |
| 10. GIS | ☐ | ☐ |
| 11. Image Processing | ☐ | ☐ |
| 12. Laboratory Control | ☐ | ☐ |
| 13. Materials Resource Planning (MRP, MRP II) | ☐ | ☐ |
| 14. Multimedia Authoring Tools | ☐ | ☐ |
| 15. Office Automation | ☐ | ☐ |
| 16. Order Entry/Inventory Control | ☐ | ☐ |
| 17. Programming/Systems Development | ☐ | ☐ |
| 18. Project Management | ☐ | ☐ |
| 19. Scientific and Engineering | ☐ | ☐ |
| 20. Spreadsheets/Financial Planning | ☐ | ☐ |
| 21. Systems Management Products | ☐ | ☐ |
| 22. Workflow | ☐ | ☐ |

**HARDWARE**

| | Use | Plan to buy |
|---|---|---|
| 23. Macintosh | ☐ | ☐ |
| 24. Mainframe | ☐ | ☐ |
| 25. Massively Parallel Processing | ☐ | ☐ |
| 26. Minicomputer | ☐ | ☐ |
| 27. PC (IBM-Compatible) | ☐ | ☐ |
| 28. Supercomputer | ☐ | ☐ |
| 29. Symmetric Multiprocessing | ☐ | ☐ |
| 30. Workstation | ☐ | ☐ |

**PERIPHERALS**

| | Use | Plan to buy |
|---|---|---|
| 31. Bridges/Routers/Hubs/Gateways | ☐ | ☐ |
| 32. CD-ROM Drives | ☐ | ☐ |
| 33. Disk Drives/Subsystems | ☐ | ☐ |
| 34. Tape Drives/Subsystems | ☐ | ☐ |
| 35. Video Boards/Other Multimedia Peripherals | ☐ | ☐ |

**NETWORK/COMMUNICATIONS**

| | Use | Plan to buy |
|---|---|---|
| 36. Communications Controllers | ☐ | ☐ |
| 37. Local Area Networks | ☐ | ☐ |
| 38. Modems | ☐ | ☐ |
| 39. Wide Area Networks | ☐ | ☐ |

**SERVICES**

| | Use | Plan to buy |
|---|---|---|
| 40. Computer-Based Training | ☐ | ☐ |
| 41. Education/Training | ☐ | ☐ |
| 42. Maintenance | ☐ | ☐ |
| 43. Online DatabaseServices | ☐ | ☐ |
| 44. Support | ☐ | ☐ |
| 45. **None of the above** | ☐ | ☐ |

**6 What Oracle products are in use at your site?** *(circle all that apply)*
**SERVERS**
- 01. Oracle7
- 02. Oracle Media Server
- 03. Oracle7 Workgroup Server
- 04. Personal Oracle7
- 05. Oracle Rdb

**TOOLS**
- 06. Designer/2000 (CASE)
- 07. Developer/2000 (CDE, Forms, Reports, Graphics)
- 08. Oracle Media Objects
- 09. Oracle Power Objects

**APPLICATIONS**
- 10. Oracle Financials
- 11. Oracle Human Resources
- 12. Oracle Manufacturing
- 13. Other _____
- 14. **None of the above**

**7 What other database products are in use at your site?** *(circle all that apply)*

| | |
|---|---|
| 01. CA-Ingres | 11. Progress |
| 02. DB2 | 12. Sybase System 10 |
| 03. DB2/2 | 13. Sybase System 11 |
| 04. DB2/6000 | 14. Sybase SQL Server |
| 05. dbase | 15. VSAM |
| 06. Gupta | 16. Other _____ |
| 07. IMS | 17. SAP |
| 08. Informix | 18. Peoplesoft |
| 09. Microsoft Access | 19. BAAN |
| 10. Microsoft SQL Server | 20. **None of the above** |

**8 During the next 12 months, how much do you anticipate your organization will spend on computer hardware, software, peripherals, and services for your location?** *(circle only one)*
- 01. Less than $10,000
- 02. $10,000 to $49,999
- 03. $50,000 to $99,999
- 04. $100,000 to $499,999
- 05. $500,000 to $999,999
- 06. $1,000,000 and over

**OMG**

## About the CD

This CD-ROM includes over 400 technical documents and bulletins published by Oracle Worldwide Customer Support. These documents contain useful technical information, alerts, sample scripts, and other sample files. We have organized the documents to correspond to the chapters listed in this book (shown below). After you've finished reading a particular chapter, you should visit the CD-ROM to access even more helpful information. Although some of the documents here might seem outdated, we have included them because we believe that each one of them presents useful concepts that should benefit all levels of Oracle users.

## How to Use this CD

The documents and bulletins on the CD are stored as standard HTML documents, and can be viewed using a standard browser. Simply put the CD in your CD drive and load your browser. Now go to File on the menu bar, select the Open File option, then your CD drive, and finally the file called index.htm. This will load up the *Oracle Troubleshooting* CD with the Table of Contents (listed below). Simply click on the information you wish and the hot-links will take you to it.

### NOTE

*To use the files on this CD, you need to have a browser on your computer. These files will work with any standard browser including Internet Explorer and Netscape Navigator.*

As mentioned above, we have downloaded these documents from various sources at Oracle Worldwide Customer Support and attempted to organize them by chapters corresponding to the book, as shown here:

Chapter 1   Preventive Maintenance on Microsoft Windows 3.1
Chapter 2   Preventive Maintenance on Microsoft Windows 95
Chapter 3   Preventive Maintenance on Microsoft Windows NT
Chapter 4   Preventive Maintenance on Solaris 2.x
Chapter 5   Preventive Maintenance on UNIX
Chapter 6   Preventive Maintenance on OpenVMS
Chapter 7   Problem Solving Oracle RDBMS
Chapter 8   Problem Solving Connectivity Issues
Chapter 9   Problem Solving Developer/2000
Chapter 10   Problem Solving Oracle Precompilers
Chapter 11   Interacting with Oracle Worldwide Customer Support

We wish to acknowledge the efforts of the several hundreds of employees of Oracle Worldwide Customer Support around the world. In particular, we would like to thank the individual authors of the documents on this CD-ROM. We have retained the names of the original authors of the documents to the best of our ability.

## System Requirements

The documents and bulletins on the CD are stored as standard HTML documents, and can be viewed using a standard browser. To use the files on this CD, you need to have a browser on your computer. These files work with any standard browser including Explorer and Netscape Navigator.

## Copyright Statement

This software is protected by both United States copyright law and international copyright treaty provision. Except as noted in the contents of the CD-ROM, you must treat this software just like a book. However, you may copy it into a computer to be used and you may make archival copies of the software for the sole purpose of backing up the software and protecting your investment from loss. By saying, "just like a book," Osborne/McGraw-Hill means, for example, that this software may be used by any number of people and may be freely moved from one computer location to another, so long as there is no possibility of its being used at one location or on one computer while it is being used at another. Just as a book cannot be read by two different people in two different places at the same time, neither can the software be used by two different people in two different places at the same time.

WARNING: BEFORE OPENING THE DISC PACKAGE, CAREFULLY READ THE TERMS AND CONDITIONS OF THE FOLLOWING LIMITED CD-ROM WARRANTY.

## Limited Warranty

Osborne/McGraw-Hill warrants the physical compact disc enclosed herein to be free of defects in materials and workmanship for a period of sixty days from the purchase date. If the CD included in your book has defects in materials or workmanship, please call McGraw-Hill at 1-800-217-0059, 9am to 5pm, Monday through Friday, Eastern Standard Time, and McGraw-Hill will replace the defective disc.

The entire and exclusive liability and remedy for breach of this Limited Warranty shall be limited to replacement of the defective disc, and shall not include or extend to any claim for or right to cover any other damages, including but not limited to, loss of profit, data, or use of the software, or special incidental, or consequential damages or other similar claims, even if Osborne/McGraw-Hill has been specifically advised of the possibility of such damages. In no event will Osborne/McGraw-Hill's liability for any damages to you or any other person ever exceed the lower of the suggested list price or actual price paid for the license to use the software, regardless of any form of the claim.

OSBORNE, A DIVISION OF THE McGRAW-HILL COMPANIES, INC., SPECIFICALLY DISCLAIMS ALL OTHER WARRANTIES, EXPRESS OR IMPLIED, INCLUDING BUT NOT LIMITED TO, ANY IMPLIED WARRANTY OF MERCHANTABILITY OR FITNESS FOR A PARTICULAR PURPOSE. Specifically, Osborne/McGraw-Hill makes no representation or warranty that the software is fit for any particular purpose, and any implied warranty of merchantability is limited to the sixty-day duration of the Limited Warranty covering the physical disc only (and not the software), and is otherwise expressly and specifically disclaimed.

This limited warranty gives you specific legal rights; you may have others which may vary from state to state. Some states do not allow the exclusion of incidental or consequential damages, or the limitation on how long an implied warranty lasts, so some of the above may not apply to you.

This agreement constitutes the entire agreement between the parties relating to use of the Product. The terms of any purchase order shall have no effect on the terms of this Agreement. Failure of Osborne/McGraw-Hill to insist at any time on strict compliance with this Agreement shall not constitute a waiver of any rights under this Agreement. This Agreement shall be construed and governed in accordance with the laws of New York. If any provision of this Agreement is held to be contrary to law, that provision will be enforced to the maximum extent permissible, and the remaining provisions will remain in force and effect.

NOTE:  NO TECHNICAL SUPPORT IS PROVIDED WITH THIS CD-ROM.